Fine WoodWorking TECHNIQUES 6

Selected by the Editors
of Fine Woodworking magazine

 The Taunton Press
Newtown, Connecticut

Typeface: Garamond and Univers
Paper: Warrenflo, 65 lb., Neutral pH

The Taunton Press, Inc.
52 Church Hill Road
Box 355
Newtown, Connecticut 06470

A FINE WOODWORKING Book

FINE WOODWORKING® is a trademark of The Taunton Press,
Inc., registered in the U.S. Patent and Trademark Office.

International Standard Book Number 0-918804-22-1
Library of Congress Catalog Card Number 78-58221
Printed in the United States of America.

CONTENTS

Continued...

v

INTRODUCTION

Welcome to *Fine Woodworking Techniques* 6. This series of reprints brings together the technical information from back issues of *Fine Woodworking* magazine and preserves it in durable, easy-to-use volumes. *Techniques* 6, the latest in the series, is based upon the technical articles from 1982, issues No. 32 through 37. As in past *Techniques* volumes, the main articles are paced by selections from the magazine's reader-written *Methods of Work* department.

Each article and method in *Techniques* 6 is reprinted in its entirety. Changes have been made only where corrections or cross-references were needed. The articles are arranged according to subject matter for easy reading, and indexed for ready reference.

Whether you work wood as a hobby, a trade or a profession, we trust you will find this book a handy and useful tool.

WOOD

Woodlot Management
Thinning and pruning for more valuable trees

by Irwin and Diane Post

Growing trees is, in many ways, akin to raising vegetables in a backyard plot. Just as a rich harvest rewards the gardener's weeding and watering efforts, so too can labor in the woodlot produce dramatic, if slower, results. And woodlot management holds a special value for the woodworker—the pleasure of working wood he or she has helped to grow.

Forest management need not be complex nor does it have to be practiced on boundless tracts of land. The techniques we've outlined in this article can be used by anyone, on woodlots as small as an acre or less. Most management work consists of cutting and pruning trees following a thoughtful evaluation of the woodlot. From some woodlot work, you will have to wait for results, but other benefits come quickly. We've begun to manage only a small portion of our 50-acre woodlot in Vermont and we already have 3,000 board feet of hardwood plus 50 cords of firewood to show for our work.

Our management plans are aimed at meeting our future needs for lumber and firewood for ourselves and for sale, and at growing a healthy forest. You can shape your plan to suit your needs, and the climate, soil and type of trees that grow best in your area. You can design your own management plan, or seek help and advice from county, state or consulting foresters in your area.

Where is the woodlot? How big is it?—It's amazing how many people don't know their property boundaries. The first step in woodlot management is to find and mark the boundaries. The penalties for cutting someone else's trees are high in terms of good, neighborly relations, and even higher in possible legal costs and damages. Sometimes the boundaries are marked with stone walls, fences or blazes left by a neighbor or previous owner. Other times it will be necessary to hire a surveyor. In any event, be certain of the boundary before marking it—few things are more troublesome than a boundary mark that's in the wrong place.

It's also important to know the real size of your woodlot. The size determines the value of the land and the property tax on it, and it is the basis for estimating your wood harvest. Until the advent of electronic calculators, finding the area of an irregular parcel was tedious and fraught with error. As a result many parcels were guesstimated and recorded as, say, 25± acres, with no limits on the plus or minus. We recently helped a neighbor resurvey a parcel that was recorded as 150± acres; it turned out to be only 120 acres. If you are buying a woodlot, we suggest requiring the seller to have a survey map prepared as a condition of sale.

The traditional way to mark forest boundaries is with painted blazes on unmarketable trees on, or nearly on, the boundary line. A blaze is made by chopping several square inches of bark off the tree at about chest height, then paint-

Irwin and Diane Post are forest engineers living in Barnard, Vt.

ing the wound a bright color. If you wait a few weeks before painting the wound, the paint will stick better. The blazed trees should never be harvested and they should be close enough together for the boundary to be easily followed. Repaint the blazes every few years.

A blaze is a wound, and a potential doorway for disease. If you want to avoid this risk, you can nail colored plastic to the trunk at eye level. Use brass or copper nails to avoid damage to sawblades if the tree is ever harvested, and plan to replace the plastic every couple of years.

Evaluating the woodlot—Once the boundaries are established, you can begin learning the characteristics of your land and of its trees. A forester "cruises" the woodlot by recording observations on a map and making field notes while walking through the woods.

A site index is a shorthand method of indicating the quality of the land and its ability to grow trees. The site index is a number indicating the average height of a tree species at a given age, usually 50 years. Thus a site index of 80 for white pine means that a 50-year-old white pine tree can be expected to be 80 feet tall. The site index reflects soil quality, topography, water availability and drainage. It does not depend on the number, health or size of the trees currently growing. A woodlot with a site index of 80 for white pine will still have a site index of 80 even after it has been clearcut.

You can figure site index by determining the ages and heights of representative trees of each species on your woodlot. These figures are then matched with a published table to find the index numbers. You can get site-index tables, comparative indexes, and help in evaluating your data from a state, county, or consulting forester.

The age of your trees can be found with an increment borer, an auger-like tool that removes a small core of wood from the tree trunk. Counting the annual growth rings from the pith to the bark gives the age of the tree, although you should add several years to account for the time it took the tree to reach the height of the bore. If you don't have an increment borer, you will have to figure age by felling trees and counting the annual rings. Cutting only a few trees will give enough data for figuring the site index.

Tree height can be measured with a variety of instruments including relascopes, clinometers and optical altimeters. But the simplest and cheapest instrument is a log and tree scale stick. This tool, resembling a truncated yardstick, is available from forestry supply houses and has a scale for determining tree height based on a simple sighting method.

Other qualities of the stand that should be noted during the cruise include tree diameters, rate of diameter growth, basal area, tree quality and species composition.

Tree diameter is usually measured at 4½ ft. above ground and is given as "DBH" or "diameter at breast height." Diam-

Short of felling trees and counting the annual rings, an increment borer, left, is the best way to tell the age of trees. The tool removes a small, fragile cylinder of wood, right. The rings aren't as easy to see as in a cut tree, and must be counted carefully.

eter growth rates can be gauged from the increment core: widely spaced annual rings indicate vigorous growth while close rings show slow growth. Slow-growing stands usually need thinning.

Basal area is a relative measure of how dense a stand is and it helps you decide if thinning is needed. To understand basal area, imagine one acre of your woodlot with all the trees cut at breast height. Measure the cross-sectional area in square feet of all the stumps and add them up to arrive at basal area in square feet per acre. The more crowded the stand, the higher the basal area. Management plans often specify thinning to a certain basal area, taking into account site index and management objectives. In New England, for example, we generally recommend that hardwood stands be thinned to 50 to 70 square feet per acre and softwood stands to 70 to 80 square feet. Foresters measure basal area by "point sampling"

with a prism or tools such as a Cruz-All or Cruise-Angle. The forester stands at a randomly selected point in each forest type and makes a 360° sweep while looking through the instrument's sight. Each instrument comes with instructions on which trees should be counted for determining basal area.

Tree quality, unlike the measurements described thus far, is almost entirely subjective. It includes such factors as straightness of the trunk, limbiness, evidence of rot, and size and health of the crown. Tree quality is a predictor of log quality, so we want to remove trees of low quality, thereby "releasing" nearby high-quality trees from competition.

Ground conditions should also be noted during the cruise because they will affect access to the timber at harvest. Steepness of slope, stoniness and location of bogs and watercourses should all be recorded on the woodlot map.

Woodlots, no matter how small, are seldom uniform. There are usually differences in species, tree size and site index from place to place. Homogeneous areas are known as forest types. The management plan treats each forest type separately, with specific recommendations for each type.

The management plan—The management plan consists of a statement of the overall management objective, the forest-type map, the description of each forest type and the management recommendations for each forest type. Most woodlot owners want several benefits, so conflicting objectives have to be weighed. It's important to have a good picture of how different management strategies will change the appearance of the woodlot and it is useful to examine managed woodlots nearby and to talk with their owners. As you set your goals, remember that your needs may not align with those of the commercial lumber producer. Burls or spalted lumber, for example, are highly valued by some craftsmen but are virtually useless to a professional logger.

There are two general management strategies: even-age and uneven-age. In even-age management all the trees on a given parcel are the same age and they will mature and be cut at the same time. After the harvest, a new stand will be established through planting or natural regeneration. Uneven-age management is not so orderly. There are trees of every age from seedlings to sawlogs and the stand will be harvested and

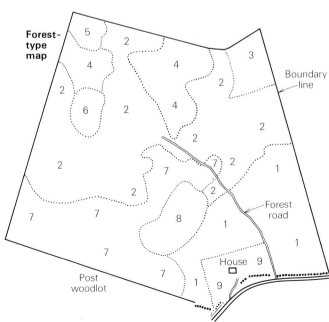

The completed forest management plan should include a detailed map of the woodlot. The numbers represent forest types. Area 2, for example, is a 19-acre tract with sugar maple, ash and beech as the predominant species. Each forest type on the map has a specific management objective and a list of recommendations to reach the objective.

3

thinned every 10 to 15 years. The best management for your woodlot depends on what trees you already have and their ages, the species you hope to regenerate, and aesthetics. For example, some species, such as the birches and oaks, require nearly full sunlight to the forest floor for good regeneration, while other species like sugar maple and beech regenerate well under the shade of standing trees.

Management recommendations also tell what products can be expected in the near term such as firewood, pulpwood or sawlogs and what equipment is necessary for harvest. The duration of a management plan is usually ten to twenty years, after which it should be updated.

The management plan prescribes the harvesting, thinning or pruning for each forest type in the woodlot. How do you decide which trees to cut and which to leave? Generally, the higher-value species that grow well on the site should be favored over short-lived species that don't reach sawlog size, species that don't do well on the site, diseased or poorly-formed trees and weed species. For example, on our woodlot, sugar maple, white ash, yellow birch and white birch do very well. Black cherry does less well but we favor the healthy cherries because we prize their wood for cabinetwork. Gray birch is a short-lived species that rarely attains sawlog size, so we cut it for firewood. We cut our beech trees also, because they have contracted scale disease. Striped maple is a weed species that can blanket the forest and prevent regeneration of the species we want. We cut all the striped maple we find.

A management plan can also benefit wildlife. We have a small deer yard on our land, an area of dense coniferous growth where deer find shelter in winter. From a wood production viewpoint this deer yard should be thinned, but we prefer to leave this stand uncut for the deer.

If you plan to do the management work yourself or if you have a large woodlot, it may not be possible to do all the work in one year. You should set work priorities, thinning first the areas with good site indexes and with forest types that will benefit most from attention. Schedule the work carefully. If you plan to sell your wood, your timetable should be flexible enough to suit market fluctuations. For instance, it has not been possible to sell pulpwood in our area for the past year, so we aren't cutting it now.

It's easy to underestimate how much work managing a woodlot is—particularly during the first treatment of previously unmanaged forest. It can be very discouraging to fall far short of your goals, and it's no fun when every spare moment must be spent in the woodlot. Most people would find a goal of treating about one acre a year of previously unmanaged woodlot about right. A first thinning in a typical New England forest would mean coping with between 5 and 15 cords of wood per acre.

Picking trees to cut—In an old field that grows up naturally into forest, many thousands of seedlings may sprout, but as they compete for sunlight, water and nutrients, most will die. By the time they reach 18-in. DBH, perhaps only 75 trees per acre will survive. Nature, however, does not always select the same trees that we would select. We want straight, clear, sound logs of the species we value. By judiciously lowering the competition among pole-size trees with good prospects of becoming quality sawlog trees, we can improve the quality of our future harvests.

The total amount of wood grown on an acre of land will be the same whether we manage it or not. Thus, by reducing the competition among the best stems through careful cutting, we don't reduce total growth but concentrate it in the best stems. These trees increase in diameter faster and attain sawlog size sooner than if we let nature run its course. Vigorous, fast growing trees are also healthier than slow growing trees, and are less susceptible to disease and insect damage.

Given the object of producing high quality sawlogs, we can readily decide which trees to cut and which to leave for future growth. For illustrative purposes, think of an uneven-age hardwood stand with everything from seedlings to sawlog trees. Large trees that are obviously hollow or very poorly formed should be cut, unless you wish to leave a few as den trees for wildlife. These trees may not yield a single sawlog despite their large diameter. Sawlog trees that have a lot of dead branches in the crown should also be harvested. Such trees are overmature and growing very slowly. Certain other mature trees may have taken over more of the forest than they deserve, with too many branches and too large a crown. These "wolf trees" cut off sunlight from large areas of the forest floor, distressing and weakening surrounding trees. Healthy sawlog trees should be cut only if you need the wood or if they are overcrowded. The pole-size trees, 4-in. to 10-in. DBH, will dramatically respond to thinning by increasing their rate of diameter growth. Trees of good form of the desired species should be favored by releasing them from competition on at least two sides. Trees with a strong lean should be cut because they usually contain large amounts of reaction wood, a source of trouble for the woodworker. Pole-size trees cut during a thinning make good firewood and rarely need splitting. It is generally not worth thinning saplings and seedlings because tight young stands encourage these trees to grow straight and to self-prune their lower branches.

Picking which trees to thin and which to save is easier to do from an armchair than in the woodlot, but it can be learned with practice. We mark the trees we want to cut, but you can just as easily mark the crop trees you want to save. *Two cardinal rules of marking a stand are to look up and to look at all sides of a tree before deciding to favor it.* Many straight trunks are topped by dead or nearly dead crowns. A trunk that looks sound on one side may be hollow or cracked when viewed from another angle. Special marking paints can be used, but any bright-colored paint will work. We walk in parallel strips 50 feet wide looking for high quality trees of the species we want to keep. Diseased or low quality trees are marked for removal. We then look closely at the remaining trees (see the box on p. 86) and decide which should be cut to give space on at least two sides of a good tree's crown. We next examine trees of desired species but of only intermediate quality, and those of high quality but of less desirable species. We cut any of these trees whose removal will give space on two sides of the favored trees' crowns.

Ideally, our crop trees will be evenly spaced. However, we don't hesitate to leave two good trees closely spaced if there are poor trees around them that will be cut. In hardwood stands where there are no potential sawlogs, poor quality trees may be left standing. These trees provide future firewood and shade that favors regeneration of desired trees. Removal of all shade encourages brambles and short-lived pioneer species. We leave an occasional (one to four per acre) old but healthy tree with a good crown. These trees have little lumber value but offer food for wildlife, and nest sites in hollow branches.

Pruning is an often overlooked route to producing high quality logs. Post uses a standard 17-ft. saw to prune a white pine stem.

Pruning future sawlogs—Pruning is one of the most overlooked ways of improving sawlog quality and it's the route to the clear boards we so prize in our woodworking. Pruning is simply cutting off the lower branches of trees very close to the trunk with a polesaw. The tool is available from forestry supply houses for about $25. Trees are usually pruned to a height of 17 ft., producing one "standard" 16-ft. sawlog with an ample allowance for stump waste. Pruning any higher with a polesaw is difficult and is generally not done.

To reduce the risk of infection, the cut should be made immediately outside the branch collar—where the trunk swells at the branch's base. Vigorously growing trees soon heal over the wound and grow clear wood. All of the dead branches and a few of the lower live branches can be pruned without hurting the tree. Don't leave stubs when you prune—the tree can't heal over them. As a stub rots, it provides entry for moisture, fungi and insects into the heart of the tree.

The branches of pole-size trees are small, and pruning wounds heal quickly. However, large diameter trees have thicker branches that heal over slowly, making it likely that they will be harvested before pruning does them much good.

Since there are many more pole-size trees to the acre than there are future sawlog trees, only the trees with the best potential should be pruned. Since there is little point in pruning firewood, it is sensible for pruning to follow thinning.

Harvesting and regeneration—Harvesting your own timber can be very satisfying. Through harvesting, you change the character and appearance of your woodlot, as well as obtain valuable wood. With patience and care, you can leave your woodlot in better condition than most loggers would.

On the other hand, it takes heavy and expensive equipment as well as a lot of time and skill to harvest sawlogs. And it is dangerous work. Many woodlot owners find that they are better off selling the stumpage rights to a logger. We strongly recommend that every such timber sale be supervised by a consulting forester. In most cases, the forester marks the trees that will be harvested (and those the logger should remove as culls), prepares a notice of the timber sale, shows the woodlot to loggers, takes bids and helps the landowner decide which bid to accept. The forester draws a contract, oversees the harvest and holds a damage deposit from the logger to pay for any damages. The forester has the authority to shut down the logging operation in adverse weather, when heavy equipment might damage the forest floor, or if excessive damage is done by the logger. The forester's fee is more than made up by the advantages of competitive bidding and of having a third party decide questions of safety and damage. Many states have regulations that the logger must satisfy before he finishes, such as cutting evergreen slash (the tops and other debris) to a low height to reduce the risk of fire, and taking steps to reduce erosion. If you have special concern for the condition the roads are left in, possible erosion problems, or trees you don't want cut, the forester will specifically include these in your contract.

When the harvest is over, attention must be given to growing new trees in the woodlot. Planting seedlings or spreading seed is sometimes necessary, but usually natural regeneration will do the job.

Artificial regeneration is usually limited to conifers in woodlots that have been clearcut or to new plantations on former agricultural land. Hardwoods, with the exception of prized species like walnut, are rarely planted for future sawlogs. Whenever trees are planted or seeded, it is important that they be suitable for the local soil, climate and water conditions. It is wise to plant species that are in reasonable demand. Thousands of acres of red pine were planted in the past, but there is currently so little demand that nobody knows what to do with them now. If you plan to start a tree plantation, remember that plantations need thinning just as often as natural stands.

Trees regenerate naturally in two ways: by germinating from seeds and by sprouting from stumps. Most hardwood species send up stump sprouts after a tree is cut. Some species are more prolific sprouters than others, and small-diameter stumps sprout more than do stumps of large diameter. Stump sprouts start life with a large root system and they often grow more than 5 ft. the first year. The problem with such sprouts is that there are often too many of them, and a stump may sprout double, triple and quadruple-stemmed trees. Cutting all but the best sprout from each stump may solve this.

In a given location, trees of a given species tend to have years of good seed production and years of poor seed production. It is often possible to affect the species composition of naturally regenerated forest stands by timing harvesting to follow an abundant seed crop of the species you wish to favor.

Although our efforts at harvesting and regeneration parallel those of the gardener, we do not have the gardener's ability to change crops from year to year. Our actions in the woodlot shape the forest for generations to come and that alone should give us pause to think twice about which trees we cut and which we encourage to grow. Few of us will live long enough to harvest sawlogs from seedlings we plant, but our children and grandchildren will benefit from our foresight if we decide wisely. □

For more information...

State, county and consulting foresters have lots of information on basic woodlot management, and much of it is free. Government foresters are often able to visit woodlots and offer advice, also free of charge. Some government foresters offer services at a nominal charge or they may charge for work that requires more than one day to complete. Check the white pages of your phone directory under the county and state listings to find the local government forester. If none are listed, ask the county agricultural extension agency for advice.

Consulting foresters are independent professionals, who must be licensed in some states. They can be contacted through the yellow pages, but it's better to check with the local government forester. Consultation fees vary, so discuss price before hiring a forester. Local foresters should also have information about tax advantages offered by some states to encourage woodlot management. Vermont's program, for example, reduces by 80% the taxes on our woodlot.

The tools described in this article, if unavailable locally, can be ordered from the following suppliers: Forestry Suppliers Inc., 205 Rankin St., P.O. Box 8397, Jackson, Miss. 39204; Ben Meadows Co., 3589 Broad St., Atlanta, Ga. 30366, and T.S.I., P.O. Box 151, 25 Ironia Rd., Flanders, N.J. 07836.

The American Forestry Association (1319 18th St. N.W., Washington, D.C. 20036) publishes a monthly magazine called *American Forests*. Useful books include: *Essentials of Forestry Practice* by Charles H. Stoddard, Ronald Press Co., New York, N.Y. and *Handbook for Eastern Timber Harvesting* (stock number 001-001-00443-0) by Fred C. Simmons, from the U.S. Government Printing Office, Washington, D.C. 20402. A booklet, *Woodlot Management*, is available from Garden Way Publishing, Charlotte, Vt. 05445.

Tree quality: the good, the bad and the firewood

It doesn't take a trained eye to spot a perfect sawlog: it rises arrow-straight and branchless for 15 ft. or 20 ft., large enough to yield clear boards and showing no signs of wounds, fungus or insect damage. Deciding which of the many less than ideal trees in the woodlot will yield good quality lumber and which to consign to the cordwood pile is more difficult. Here are a few tips to help you make these decisions as you thin and harvest your woodlot.

Crooks: An abrupt zig-zag in the trunk caused by the tree's changing growth direction as it seeks better light. Small crooks can be sawed but larger ones make handling the log difficult.

Curves and bows: Sweeping form in the trunk common in trees growing on hills. Curves occur, like crooks, because the tree wants better light. Trunks with curves usually contain reaction wood, difficult to saw, dry and use (see "Abnormal Wood," *FWW* #26).

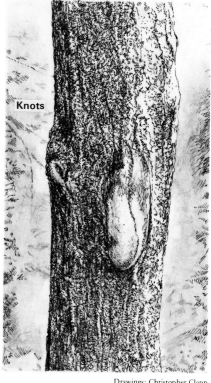

Drawings: Christopher Clapp

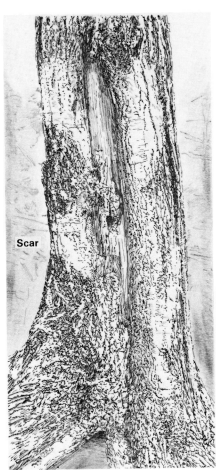

Bird damage

Overmature tree

Stem fork

Scar

Knots: A common feature in nearly all logs, knots occur where branches grow out of the trunk. If the branch is alive when the tree is cut, the knot will probably be sound. If the branch is dead, particularly if it is large, the knot in the finished lumber may be loose.

Stem forks: Two stems on one trunk occur when the "leader" stem dies or stops growing. A second stem then forms and becomes the new leader. Stems that occur very low on the trunk reduce the lumber value of the logs.

Major dead branches: These occur when a tree is under stress and near death. If there are no good reasons to leave the tree standing, it should be removed for lumber or firewood.

Scars: Called "catfaces," scars are the signs of damage caused by fire or by previous logging operations. The wounds go through the bark to bare wood. If the tree survives, the wood above and below the scars may be sound.

Dead crowns: A healthy crown tops a healthy tree and those with dead or skeletal crowns are usually under stress. When the leaves have fallen check the crown's major branches for smaller branches; if these are numerous, the crown is probably healthy.

Cracks: Vertical cracks or seams caused by extremely cold weather or lightning can be several feet long and ¼ in. or so wide. The cracks heal over on the surface, but they can ruin a good log.

Insect and bird damage: Worm holes and loose bark can indicate significant insect damage. Bird damage is more apparent and sometimes the two are related because some birds feed on insects infesting trees.

Epicormic branching: Previously shaded trunks exposed to sunlight can grow small branches which cause minute blemishes in lumber cut from the logs. Care should be taken when thinning to keep trunks of potential sawlog trees at least partially shaded.

Overmature trees: Old trees with large, short trunks and heavy upper branches are often survivors from when the forest was an open field. Their lumber value is low but they do serve as wildlife shelters and are sometimes left standing for that reason alone.

Wind or ring shakes: Shakes are rarely detectable by reading a tree's bark but they will turn up as a defect in the lumber. They are caused by wind-created mechanical stresses that separate the tree's annual rings. —I.P., D.P.

Wind shakes in a maple log.

7

Chainsaw Lumbermaking
Good-bye to vibration and fumes

by Will Malloff

Anyone can make lumber. All you need is a chainsaw attached to a mill, a straight board, a hammer and three nails. The board, positioned and nailed to a log, is a guide for the mill, which is adjusted to the depth of cut plus board thickness. The mill is pushed along the board and the sawbar pivoted out of the log at the end of the cut. That's all there is to it. But for efficient lumbermaking and the best results, there are a number of other considerations. Over the years I've developed and refined milling equipment and techniques, and now I feel I have the most effective, simplest system for ecological lumber production. To my surprise, a lot of people agree with me.

With a chainsaw, the logger decides what to harvest—trees that are mature, damaged or crowding other trees. A tree is felled and milled where it falls. Only usable lumber is removed, leaving the by-products to feed the land. Once you

EDITOR'S NOTE: This article is adapted from Will Malloff's *Chainsaw Lumbermaking,* The Taunton Press Inc., Newtown, Conn. (Hardcover, 224 pp., $23.00.) Malloff, of Alert Bay, B.C., is a professional logger and lumbermaker. Besides describing and illustrating the milling process in great detail, Malloff's book explains how to choose and modify ripping chains and mills, and how to make milling gear for timber joinery, natural boat knees, and more.

start to make your own lumber, you begin to notice usable wood everywhere you go. You're not restricted to milling only standing trees and you're not limited to working with the sizes and species available at the lumberyard.

Ripping chain—The most important factor in successful lumbermaking is properly prepared and maintained saw chain. Although you can use standard crosscutting chain, this will result in inefficient milling. You really need ripping chain, which you can make by modifying crosscut chain, using either a grinder or a hand file (figure 1). It's better to modify regular chain than skip-tooth chain or safety chain. I use a Stihl 090 saw for most of my milling, and I usually start with Oregon square-edge chisel chain (model 52L) made by Omark (Oregon Saw Chain Division, 9701 S.E. Mc-Loughlin Blvd., Portland, Ore. 97222).

You'll find that a good disc-wheel chain grinder will soon pay for itself by its accuracy and speed in modifying and sharpening ripping chain. And one properly shaped grinding stone will do the work of several dozen hand files.

Chain modification—I grind my ripping chain cutters straight across the fronts with the round-edged grinding stone

Minimum milling: a chainsaw mill, a plank to guide the first cut, and a few nails to hold the plank on the log. Malloff, a chainsaw logger by profession, has improved every aspect of this setup, developing the rig shown on the following pages.

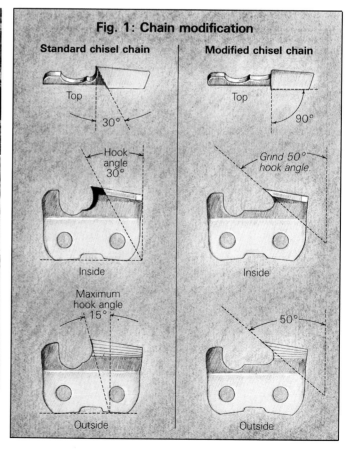

Fig. 1: Chain modification

Standard chisel chain

Top

30°

Hook angle 30°

Inside

Maximum hook angle 15°

Outside

Modified chisel chain

Top

90°

Grind 50° hook angle.

Inside

50°

Outside

Photos: Beth Erickson; drawings: Lee Hov

The winch ropes, fig. 2, pass through the cheek blocks on the yoke, fig. 3. One rope hooks to the nosebar end of the mill, the other to a short bridle rope, attached between the saw itself and the surgical tubing on the throttle attachment, fig. 4. As the winch ropes tighten, the attachment pivots, and the ¼-in. bolt on the end of the lever depresses the chainsaw's trigger switch to bring the saw to full throttle before forward pull is applied to the mill. A quick turn back on the winch returns the saw to idle.

Fig. 2: Winch

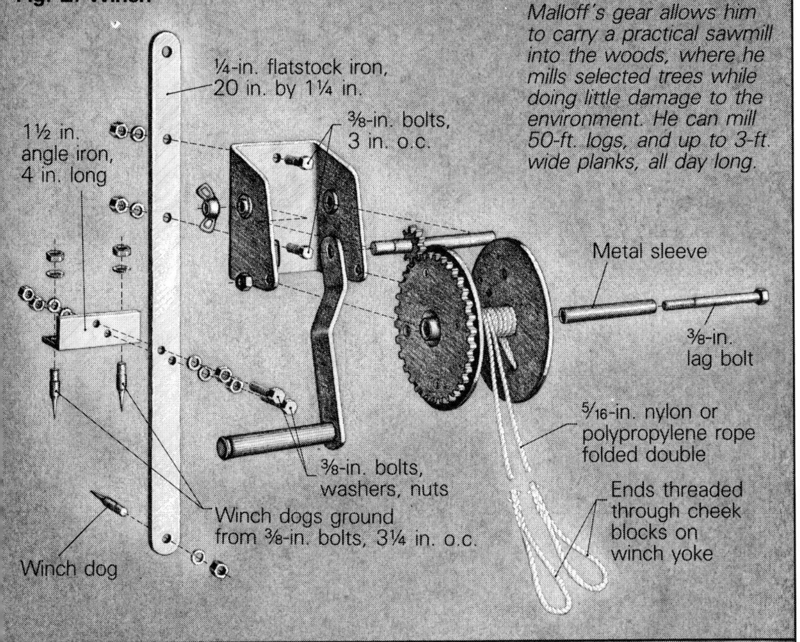

¼-in. flatstock iron, 20 in. by 1¼ in.
1½ in. angle iron, 4 in. long
⅜-in. bolts, 3 in. o.c.
Metal sleeve
⅜-in. lag bolt
5⁄16-in. nylon or polypropylene rope folded double
⅜-in. bolts, washers, nuts
Ends threaded through cheek blocks on winch yoke
Winch dogs ground from ⅜-in. bolts, 3¼ in. o.c.
Winch dog

Malloff's gear allows him to carry a practical sawmill into the woods, where he mills selected trees while doing little damage to the environment. He can mill 50-ft. logs, and up to 3-ft. wide planks, all day long.

Fig. 3: Winch yoke

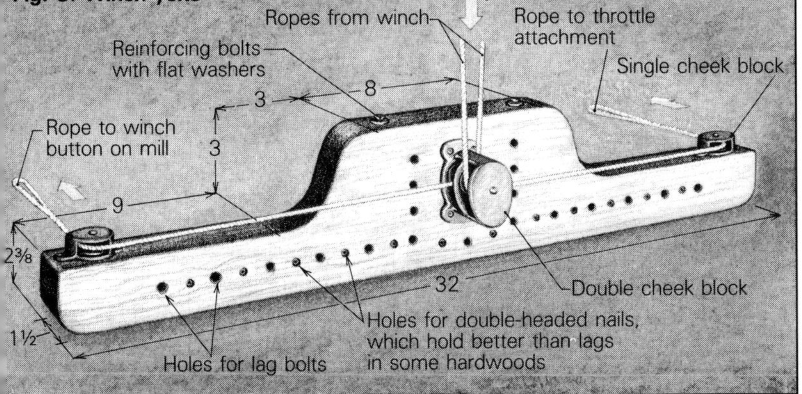

Ropes from winch
Rope to throttle attachment
Reinforcing bolts with flat washers
Single cheek block
8
3
Rope to winch button on mill
3
9
2⅜
32
Double cheek block
1½
Holes for double-headed nails, which hold better than lags in some hardwoods
Holes for lag bolts

Fig. 4: Throttle attachment

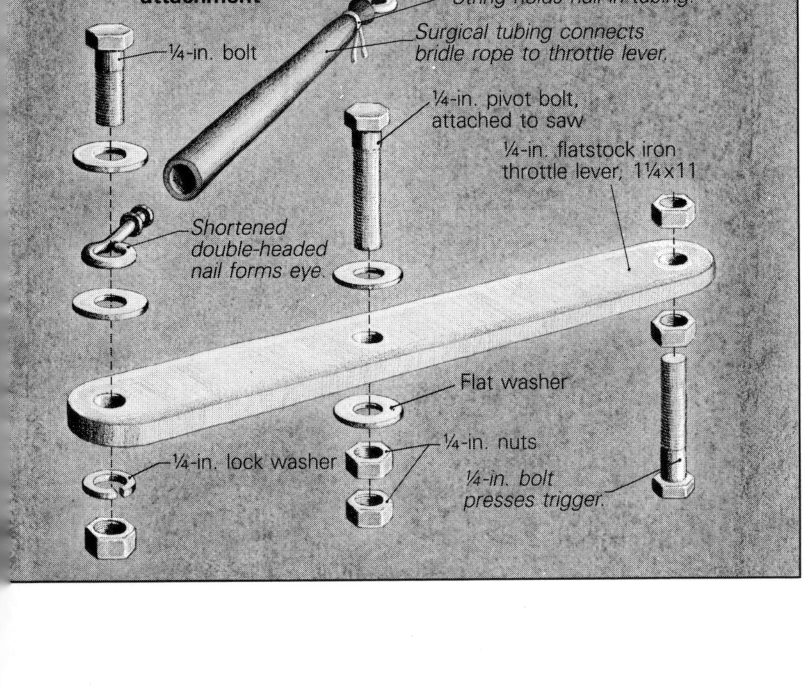

String holds nail in tubing.
Surgical tubing connects bridle rope to throttle lever.
¼-in. bolt
¼-in. pivot bolt, attached to saw
¼-in. flatstock iron throttle lever, 1¼x11
Shortened double-headed nail forms eye.
Flat washer
¼-in. nuts
¼-in. lock washer
¼-in. bolt presses trigger.

adjusted 50° from vertical (40° from horizontal). Commercial sawmills grind their blades for circular saws, gangsaws and bandsaws this way for a smooth, fast cut. Adjust the grinder so the stone is 90° to the chain, then tilt the stone to a 50° hook angle. Mount your chain in the chain track and adjust the stone to grind off the entire angled edge of the cutter—no more and no less. It is critical that the teeth be the same length and that the depth gauges be filed evenly.

Hand-filing—Chain modification with a file guide and round file is essentially the same as with a grinder; but file a 45° hook angle on each cutter instead of a 50° hook. The round file leaves a hollow-ground edge; if the hook were filed to 50°, the cutting edge would be weakened. Because guides are normally set by the factory to cut a 5° hook angle, you have to shim the file under both clamps to lower it so it will make the 45° hook. Start off with the file diameter recommended for your chain, but switch to the next smaller size (1⁄32 in. less) when the chain's cutters are about half-worn.

Keep filing until the hook angle on the side of the cutter is 45° and the top plate is 90° across. The bottom of the cutter gullet should be just above the top of the drive link. At least two files will usually be necessary to modify one chain.

The winch and yoke—In lumbermaking, you normally have to push the mill and roaring chainsaw through a cut, breathing exhaust fumes and spitting out sawdust all the while. But with my setup (photo, next page), you can stand back from the noise and vibration, and move the saw through the cut with minimum labor—all you have to do is crank a winch handle. Besides the winch, you'll need a remote throttle attachment for your saw, winch buttons to hold the ropes, and a winch yoke to pull the mill straight. The yoke also helps keep the guide rails of the mill level on the top plank.

I use a small boat-trailer winch as the base mechanism (figure 2). Make winch dogs (spikes that attach the winch unit to the log) by tapering ⅜-in. bolts. Hold each bolt in the chuck of an electric hand drill and, with the drill switched on, grind the taper on a bench grinder.

Assemble the winch and mount the winch rope. Cut a length of ¼-in. or 5⁄16-in. nylon or polypropylene rope a little longer than double the length of the log you'll be milling, then splice or tie an eye to each end. Fold the rope in half and attach the fold to the winch drum. Later you'll thread the rope ends through the cheek blocks on the winch yoke (figure 3).

Throttle attachment—Because the operator is at one end of the log and the saw at the other when milling with my system, you need to build a remote throttle attachment to work the saw trigger (figure 4). This one is designed for a Stihl 090, so if you're using a different engine, you might have to adapt a little. The surgical tubing should be long enough (about 6 in. to 8 in.) to provide proper tension in both the open-throttle and closed-throttle positions. Through the saw handle, drill and tap a ¼-in. thread and mount the attachment by screwing the bolt into the hole and locking it with a nut and washer. I'll explain how to use this remote throttle attachment when we get to setting up.

Saw bridle button—I use a modified Granberg Mark III mill, but any mill should work. The winching rope is attached at one end to the mill and at the other end to the

Careful layout is the route to precision milling. Above, Malloff checks the height of the lag bolts that will support the guide plank. The end boards have been carefully aligned with vertical and horizontal layout lines drawn on both ends of the log. In this case, he's milling directly through the heart center of the log. If the heart were off center, he might mill to the average center instead.

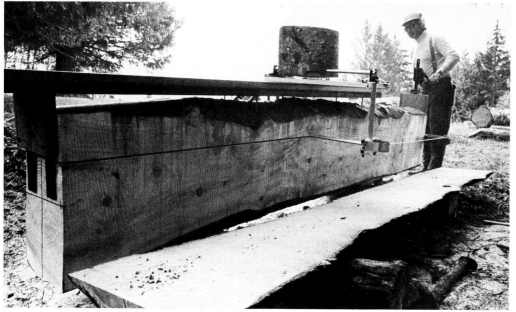

A yoke, fastened just below the line of cut, keeps the cut straight as Malloff cranks the winch, above. One rope is attached to the modified Granberg mill; the other rope is connected, by means of an adjustable bridle rope, to the saw itself and to a lever that controls its throttle. The mill, with its log-section counterweight, will be pulled to the end of the guide plank. Then the plank will be slid forward on the supporting lag bolts until it rests on the end board. The winch is attached to the plank itself, and the cut continues. Subsequent cuts don't require the plank and lags because the mill can ride directly on the flat-cut surface of the log. At left, with steel end dogs in place to control twisting, milling is well under way.

middle of a length of rope I call the bridle rope. One end of the bridle rope goes to the remote throttle attachment; the other end must attach to the saw. But since there's no place on the saw to accept a rope, you have to make a holding button. I call this the bridle button. On the Stihl 090, I substitute a 5/16-in. by 1½-in. bolt for the original shorter metric bolt in the handle to make this bridle button. This is the logical place for it, as the bolt is in a strong position on the saw and in the line of pull when winching through a cut.

End dogs—The inner tensions that have grown into a tree often make boards twist or bend while they're being sawn. This distortion can throw off a properly aligned milling system. So I've designed end dogs to help keep boards straight until the cut is complete—the dogs tack the board and log together, so the board can't deform during the cut (bottom photo, facing page).

The best end dogs can be forged from short pieces of automobile leaf spring, though other hardened steel would probably do as well. To make them, first round the ends of the spring stock. Then heat and bend the ends so that they are at right angles to the flat stock. Reheat the dog to a dull red, and allow it to cool slowly in the air. Grind the upturned ends from the outside to a sharp edge and then grind the edge straight across so that it is about 1/32 in. to 1/16 in. wide. End dogs with edges that are too sharp eventually deform and become difficult to drive.

I insert wooden kerf wedges every few feet in the cut. The wedges support the piece being milled and keep the kerf open, allowing the bar to travel freely. I also insert wedges behind the saw just before the end of the cut. This allows the mill to exit easily and eliminates end run-off. Six or eight wedges are enough for most jobs.

Setting up—Before you can begin to mill any lumber, you must establish a level surface on each log to guide the first cut. My system consists of a straight guide plank resting on end boards and pairs of leveled lag bolts placed along the length of the log. The wider the plank, the more support for the mill. The plank should also be thick enough to support the weight of the mill with minimum help from the lag bolts. The guide plank needn't be as long as the log, because you can mill in stages by sliding the plank off the end board and along the lag bolts as you go.

To stiffen the plank and help keep it straight, and to allow the plank to slide along the lag bolts without damage, attach two 3/16-in., 1½-in. by 1½-in. angle irons to the plank edges, using countersunk screws about every 12 in.

The guide plank is supported at both ends of the log by end boards nailed or lag-bolted into the log end. The top edges of the end boards must be the same distance above horizontal index lines, reference points drawn on the ends of the logs, from which you calculate your milling patterns (upper left photo, facing page). I usually make pairs of end boards from common, 2-in. thick, dressed lumber. Heights of 4 in., 6 in., 8 in. and 10 in., cut to the width of the guide plank being used, cover most milling situations.

Measure and mark the log for the supporting lag bolts. When using a 10-ft. guide plank, I usually place a pair of lags every 4 ft. Remember to make sure the lags don't go so deep that they're in the path of the cut.

Position the guide plank, looking under it to make sure the angle irons rest securely on the lags and end boards. You'll need an overhang of at least 12 in. to support the mill as it begins the cut, so pull the plank out that far.

If you're milling with a winch, you'll need a weight to counterbalance the saw engine and to hold the guide rails of the mill flat on the plank. Make this from a block of log that is slightly larger in diameter than the space between the mill guide rails. Notch the log to fit over the mill handle.

The first cut—Determine how high to set the mill for the first cut by measuring on a vertical index line drawn on the end of the log. Mount the mill on the guide plank. Keep the thrust skid against the log and begin the cut with the nose end of the sawbar. Come to full throttle and cut until the back guide rail of the mill just passes the end board. Pause, and drive in both end dogs, spacing them as far apart as possible without splitting the slab.

Now position the winch yoke. Center it on the butt end of the log so that the outside pulleys are 1 in. or 2 in. below the mark on the vertical index line, and thread the winch ropes through the cheek blocks. Now slip one end of the bridle rope over the bridle button on the saw engine, and hook the other end of the bridle rope to the eye on the remote throttle attachment's surgical tubing. Gently take up the slack in the winch rope, and thread it through the bridle rope so that it will pull the throttle wide open before it begins to pull the mill forward.

When the winch is set up, start the saw engine and position the counterweight. As you start cranking the winch, the engine should open up to full throttle. To stop milling, or if the saw sticks in the cut, quickly crank the winch handle several turns backward. This will stop the pull and allow the engine to return to idle. Keep an eye on the guide rails of the mill to be sure they remain flat on the guide plank, and mill up to the last set of lag bolts. Crank the winch backward quickly to stop milling, allow the engine to idle and then turn the engine off. Leave the mill in the cut.

Pull the guide plank forward to the next cutting position. In the last position, the plank will just cover the end board. So set the winch dogs into the end of the guide plank and continue milling, adding kerf wedges as necessary. When the mill comes close to the end of the cut, remove the counterweight, winch ropes and yoke. Pull the guide plank forward so it projects beyond the end board to support the mill as it finishes the cut. Complete the cut by hand, keeping a firm downward as well as forward pressure on the mill.

You can mill a board or two off the top slab if you invert it in place on top of the log. Estimate the center of weight of the slab and drive a wedge on either side to provide a pivot. Absolute balance is not necessary, but the closer you guess, the easier it will be to move the slab. Swing the slab with a peavey, so that it crosses the log. Use a peavey or jack to flip the slab over. Swing the slab back into place, then lift it to near level and block it with wedges.

I don't normally use the winch yoke on shallow cuts. I attach the winch rope to the bridle rope at the engine end as when using the yoke, but attach the nose-end rope by slipping the loop over the mill's riser post. Once the counterweight is in position, you can start milling. The winch system is more complicated than hand-milling, but certainly less tedious. I often hand-mill short and narrow cuts, but find a day's work much easier with a winch. □

Air-Drying Lumber

Usable stock comes from a carefully stickered stack

by Paul Bertorelli

Air-drying your own lumber can be a cheap alternative to expensive and sometimes unavailable kiln-dried wood. If you live near a sawmill or have your own woodlot, green wood can be had for a fraction the cost of commercially dried stuff. But once you've got the wood, the real challenge is converting it into a material you can use in the shop. Conventional wisdom recommends air-drying green stock for one year per inch of thickness. That seems easy enough, but having seen more than a few piles of stained and checked boards, I suspected there was more to it. I visited Paul Fuge to find out.

Fuge, of Shelton, Conn., has made a business of buying sawmill-green lumber and air-drying it himself. After air-drying, he runs it through his small kiln before selling it. He got into drying his own for the same reason most of us do: he couldn't find decent wood at a price he could afford. Six years and several hundred thousand board feet later, he has learned that there's a bit more to lumber seasoning than neat piles.

Fuge dries thousands of board feet at once, but his techniques can be successfully applied in seasoning any amount of wood. Here's how he does it.

Sites and foundations—The worst checking, staining and warping is liable to happen very soon after the lumber is cut from the log. Therefore, Fuge picks drying sites before he buys lumber, allowing him to quickly stack, sticker and, if conditions warrant, cover his wood. He avoids swampy, damp, low-lying spots, and sites where high winds will dry the wood too quickly. Fuge's stacks are on south-facing slopes where nearby trees and shrubs moderate the winds. He places gravel or tarpaper under the stacks to control ground moisture.

Lumber piles should be oriented with the wood's final use in mind. Some checking is acceptable in siding and structural lumber, for instance, so such stacks can be placed to achieve a high drying rate. That means exposing their sides to the prevailing winds, on a site with plenty of sun. Furniture lumber, on the other hand, should dry more slowly, so pick a more sheltered area and aim the ends of the stack into the wind, so the stickers will prevent it from blowing through the pile.

Fuge builds sturdy foundations for his stacks, and he is careful to keep the boards in parallel planes as the stack is built. The foundation should be high enough to keep the bottom layer of wood 1 ft. off the ground. For a foundation 10 ft. long, Fuge places two rows of three concrete blocks on their sides, each on relatively level ground. The rows are 30 in. apart and the blocks in each row are 36 in. apart. Atop the blocks, Fuge sets a pair of 10-ft. 4x6 timbers called mudsills. He sights along both mudsills to make certain they lie in the same plane, and shims under each concrete block to ensure uniform support. Next, six 4x4 bolsters go across the mudsills on 24-in. centers. With all the bolsters in place, Fuge uses a long, straight board to check them for alignment, and shims any that are not in line. If everything is in the same plane but still isn't level, Fuge is pleased. A pitched stack will shed any water that finds its way inside.

Stacking and stickering—Fuge keeps a large supply of carefully dimensioned stickers on hand. "I like white oak but if I have sassafras or locust, I'll use them too because they're lighter," he says. A 4-ft. long sticker, 1-in. square in section, seems the ideal size. Smaller stickers slow air movement and larger ones waste lumber and add weight. Don't use stickers with sapwood because it harbors the fungi that cause blue or sticker stain, a major source of lumber degrade. Stickers with bark are also rejected, says Fuge, because they deform under the pile's weight. Stickers can be grooved or coved along their length to reduce contact and moisture build-up on the lumber that can also cause stains.

With a sticker on each bolster, Fuge begins his pile with a layer of low-grade lumber that will act as a shield against ground moisture. If he is mixing lumber of various thicknesses, the heavier stock goes in the lower third of the pile where slower drying rates make it less likely to check. Fuge takes great pains to align each sticker vertically with the one below it, and to keep all the stickers over the bolsters' 24-in. centers. If the stickers creep out of line, the boards won't be supported evenly and those at the bottom will kink.

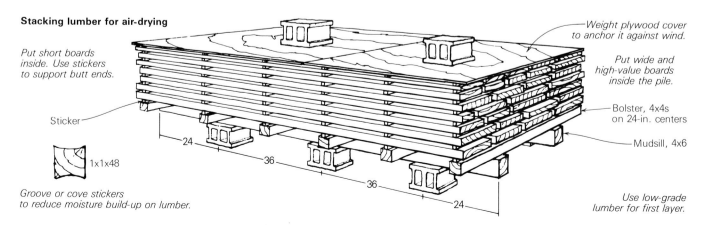

Stacking lumber for air-drying

Put short boards inside. Use stickers to support butt ends.

Sticker

1x1x48

Groove or cove stickers to reduce moisture build-up on lumber.

24

36

36

24

Weight plywood cover to anchor it against wind.

Put wide and high-value boards inside the pile.

Bolster, 4x4s on 24-in. centers

Mudsill, 4x6

Use low-grade lumber for first layer.

Drawing: Claudia Westerbeke Chapman

As he stacks, Fuge also sorts boards by length and width. The longer stock goes to the outside of the pile, the shorter stock to the inside. High quality and extra-wide boards also go on the inside where slower drying makes degrade less likely. Extra stickers can be placed at odd locations inside the pile where the butt ends of short pieces meet between the fixed 24-in. centers. Bowed boards should be stacked with the bows facing each other, allowing the weight of the pile to straighten them. Cupped boards are stacked with cups down, permitting water that seeps into the stack to drain.

As the pile rises, Fuge sometimes finds that the sawmill has given him lumber tapered or wedge-shaped in thickness. To keep everything in the right plane, he keeps some odd-sized stickers around so he can shim out the variations. If the stack is building neatly, Fuge isn't afraid to make it plenty high—those in his yard go 10 ft. and better. "I figure if I'm going to go to the trouble to build a good foundation, there's no point in starting another pile unless I have to," he says. Mixing species is okay too, but you must remember that different woods have different drying rates. If the stack will be taken down all at once, it should be air-dried long enough to suit the slowest-drying wood.

When the stack is complete, Fuge tops it out with a layer of low-grade lumber followed by a roof of sawmill slabwood, plywood or other materials, canted to shed water, and anchored against the wind. Fuge advises against using plastic for roofs because it slows ventilation in the top layer and quickly decomposes and starts falling apart in sunlight. "Besides," he adds, "it looks like hell."

Moisture control and maintenance—With the lumber stacked and roofed, Fuge turns his attention to controlling the drying rates and minimizing degrade. If he has built his pile during the peak drying months—April to October in the Northeast—he coats the butt ends of wide and heavy boards with glue or latex paint. This slows end-grain moisture loss and thereby reduces checking. "But if you don't coat them in the first two or three days, forget it, because the damage will be done already," Fuge warns. If a stack goes up in late fall or winter, little need be done until warmer weather approaches. And when spring does arrive, Fuge is ready. He shields his lumber against severe drying rates of hot, dry days by covering the pile with burlap or old blankets. The fabric is porous enough to slow (but not stop) moisture loss from the wood. As the weather moderates, Fuge uncovers the piles. If a stack end faces into the sun, it should be shielded with fabric or plywood throughout the drying cycle.

Fuge likes to leave 4/4 and 5/4 stock air-drying for a full season, that is, April to October. So a stack that goes up in the middle of the summer isn't considered dry until the middle of the following summer. Stock 6/4 and thicker may need two but certainly no more than three full drying seasons.

"After it's been out that long, it isn't going to get any drier and you might as well move it inside," Fuge says. He monitors moisture content with an electric moisture meter but an ordinary household oven and an accurate scale or balance will work just as well. Find moisture content by cutting a 1-in. cube about 2 ft. in from the end of a sample board. Weigh the cube and cook it in the oven at 212° to 221° until it no longer loses weight. Calculate moisture content by subtracting the oven-dry weight from the sample's wet weight. Then divide that figure by the oven-dry weight and multiply by

Paul Fuge makes sturdy foundations for his lumber stacks. He checks alignment of bolsters with a long, straight board fresh from the sawmill. To build a foundation with lighter stock, shore up with more concrete blocks or make a smaller pile.

100. If he is in a hurry, Fuge checks the stack's moisture content every two weeks. When it reaches the 18% to 22% range, it's ready for the kiln even if it hasn't been out for a full season. The one year per inch guide is hardly written in stone. Vagaries in climate and species moisture content and drying characteristics make monitoring the lumber a must.

If you don't have a kiln, bring your air-dried lumber indoors to dry for final use. Fuge recommends stacking and stickering it in a heated, dry room for an entire winter. A small fan to circulate air through the stack will speed things along and by spring the lumber should be ready. "If you're willing to live with your wood in the house and treat it like you treat yourself, there's no reason you can't dry it entirely without a kiln," Fuge says. If domestic considerations make indoor drying impossible, Fuge suggests a dry garage, attic or shed. Any space in fact, will work except the basement—even the driest of basements is probably too moist for further wood seasoning. Once wood is dried down to about 12% it will pick up moisture in a damp basement.

With air and inside drying complete, stack your lumber tightly without stickers in a dry place. Further air movement through the pile will only restore part of the moisture you've worked so hard to remove. □

Paul Bertorelli is assistant editor of this magazine. For more on drying lumber see these FWW *back issues: R. Bruce Hoadley's* Water and Wood *in #4,* Drying Wood *in #6, and* Wood has to breathe, doesn't it? *in #14; William W. Rice's* Dry Kiln *in #6; Paul J. Bois'* Solar Kiln *in #7; Dale Nish's* Harvesting Green Wood *in #16; and Sam Talarico's* A Barn For Air-Drying Lumber *in #22.*

FROM CRATEWOOD TO CRADLE

BY RICK LIFTIG

I had a hard time believing the wood was free. "You made that from cratewood?" I asked as I admired Sam's new pistol case. "Yep, and all the bikes come packed in it. This stuff is just like mahogany."

The Honda Motorcycle Company has graciously decided to crate its goodies in Asia's most available wood, which happens to be lauan from the Philippines. This is rough-cut cratewood, but some of it is very dense hardwood. The local Honda shop was glad to see the wood being used rather than being trucked to the dump.

Though the wood intrigued me, a use for it evaded me for a while. I was still in school and had no room for a shop, let alone time to think about woodworking. One year later, with school behind me, I realized that I owed a folk-singing friend a wedding present. I'd built dulcimers in the past using only hand tools, and figured that making him one would be the perfect gift. I started thinking about it. . . .

Procastination, however, has a subtle way of altering plans. One year later I still owed the wedding present, but the dulcimer idea had to be scrapped in favor of a cradle. Eagerly, I started tearing apart Honda crate after Honda crate, giving no thought to what I would use for a shop, tools or bench. When I finally thought of those three items, I realized that this could become a very expensive belated gift.

I got together the various trade bibles and chose every tool that I could ever need. I checked prices on power tools, combination tools, and every other tool. When the pipe dreams cleared, I once again realized I wasn't wealthy—that was the reason I was using cratewood in the first place.

In one area I didn't spare the cash: that was with books. I read voraciously about cabinetmaking, tools and design before I finally started cutting. This turned out to be the best investment I could have made. A book on joinery really got me going. It looked so simple that at first the cradle was going to be all mitered dovetail (hah!). After practicing a few through-dovetails with hand tools I thought that I'd better buy a router instead. The shop then consisted of a 7-ft. x 15-ft. porch, a Black and Decker workmate, a set of chisels, an old plane in need of a chipbreaker, a few clamps and a backsaw. The router was my only major tool purchase for the project.

It took me about an hour to disassemble each crate and remove the nails and hardware. Only about one quarter of the wood was usable. There was also the problem of arriving at the Honda shop ten minutes after the weekly dump run had been made, but through perseverence I garnered a respectable pile of lauan, mostly ⅜ in. to ½ in. in thickness and 3 in. to 4 in. wide. All smoothing and jointing had to be done with my plane, but after much frustration, I found an inexpensive scrub plane that cut my work in half. Finally the boards had been planed, squared, jointed, glued and planed again to thickness. I began to appreciate the invention of electrically powered jointers and thickness planers. Each board though, taught me something new about the properties of wood and the hand tools that I was using. I could never have gotten the same experience using machines. I was all set for my new router to dovetail the whole thing together in a matter of minutes, but the commercial dovetail jig did not enjoy ⅜-in. stock. Out of desperation, I started practicing hand dovetails again and found that each joint was getting better. At the first properly made practice joint, I let out a whoop and started a joint on the cradle. I learned how to hide many mistakes that night.

After a four-month gestation, oblivious to its humble beginnings as a Honda crate, a handsome cradle stared back at me. It had its faults, but in no way could those little mistakes reduce my grin. I applied a tung-oil finish, delivered the cradle, and then faced the final test. . . the baby was rocked asleep in moments.

By completing an ambitious project with few power tools I learned a lot about woodworking. I realize now which power tools will be useful to me and that most of the hand tools I originally drooled over would have been little use if I couldn't use the basic ones well. The books were my life preserver and teacher. Read, read, read, make your mistakes, get discouraged and then learn. Jump in and swim. Even if you ruin some of your stock on the way, remember, it's only cratewood. □

Rick Liftig is a dentist living in Northfield, Conn. He's built himself a sturdy workbench and is just about to buy either a tablesaw or a car. Photos by the author.

Powderpost Beetles
Controlling the bugs that dine on your wood

by Tom Parker

For practically every kind of wood that we have come to use, there is an insect that likes to make a meal of it. Termites are undeniably the most destructive wood-eating bugs, but powderpost beetles run a close second. Once established, powderpost beetles can do enormous damage despite their small size. They display a tenacious talent for survival—one species can even gnaw its way through lead-sheathed telephone cables to get at the paper insulation inside. It's worth the small amount of time and effort to inspect your lumber piles and structures for powderpost. If you catch an infestation early on, it can be eliminated before the beetles riddle your wood to the point of collapse.

Though there are dozens of species of wood-boring insects, American woodworkers are likely to encounter only two types of powderpost: anobiids and lyctids. A third family, bostrichids, is rarely seen. All are less than ¼ in. long, the anobiids being slightly larger than the lyctids. Anobiids are found in both hard and softwoods, but they do not infest living trees. The beetle life cycle runs about a year. The adult lays its eggs in checks or cracks in lumber having a moisture content between 8% and 30%. Each egg hatches into a larva which eats its way through the wood, forming circuitous galleries. As the cycle nears its end, the larva pupates into an adult beetle and emerges from the wood leaving a tell-tale round exit or flight hole. The lyctid life cycle is similar, but it infests only large-pored hardwoods, laying its eggs inside the open pores. Emerging adults may lay up to 50 eggs in the same board or they may fly off to a new source of food nearby.

I've seen insect infestations in all parts of the country in a wide range of woods. Powerpost are particularly fond of freshly cut and stacked lumber, but they'll gladly eat wood in old furniture, particularly if the piece doesn't have a hard surface finish like shellac or lacquer. Ash, oak, elm, walnut, cherry, poplar and a host of softwoods are susceptible to powderpost attack. The beetles eat only the sapwood, feasting on the starch stored in the parenchyma cells. They may occasionally wander into heartwood, but the lack of nutrients and the extractives in heartwood make it unattractive.

Wood suspected of infestation should be inspected closely. On horizontal surfaces, small, crater-shaped piles of powdery sawdust surrounding small round holes strongly indicate active powderpost beetles. Vertical surfaces may show drift lines where the powder has fallen away from the hole and collected on the nearest horizontal surface. Anobiids bore an exit hole ¹⁄₁₆ in. to ⅛ in. in diameter; lyctids leave a hole ¹⁄₁₆ in. or smaller. A better way to identify the beetle is to rub a bit of the powder or "frass" between your fingers. If it feels distinctly granular, anobiids are responsible. Lyctid frass is as fine as talcum powder and virtually disintegrates at the touch.

Holes in the wood but no signs of frass may indicate an infestation or damage done by some other type of insect before the tree was cut. Inspect the exit holes closely. If they appear dark or weathered or if holes in old furniture have drops of finishing materials in them, the infestation is probably over. Bore-holes that pass entirely through the wood are likely to have occurred before the wood was sawn, since no sensible wood-eating insect chews its way in one side and out the other. Similarly, wood surfaces that show exposed grooves or galleries were probably sawn after the infestation, and the insects have long since gone. The best way to handle the pow-

Pencil shows lyctid powderpost damage and exit holes in bamboo. Galleries at right have made the piece extremely fragile.

U.S. Forest Service

This infestation, caused by a boring beetle, is over. Holes that pass entirely through a board, or exposed galleries (across center of photo), indicate the wood was sawn after infestation.

Frass piles around this lumber are a sure sign of powderpost infestation. The powdery nature of the frass indicates that lyctids are at work. Beetles can completely destroy the wood if left unchecked.

derpost problem is, of course, to avoid it in the first place. Look for beetle frass and exit holes in any lumber you are buying while it's still in the stack. If you are air-drying lumber outside, store it up off the ground and cover it with plastic or canvas once it no longer needs exposure for drying. In new home construction, particularly where wooden structure is exposed above a dirt crawl space, I always tell contractors to install a layer of heavy plastic on the ground under the beams to keep the wood from absorbing ground moisture. Vents in crawl spaces and foundations will keep moisture below levels attractive to powderpost beetles. During construction, don't throw wood cutoffs and waste into the crawl space and don't bury it near the house either since that invites other kinds of wood-eating insects. If you're putting in new vents and sealing off the soil beneath an existing crawl space with polyethylene sheeting, do only half of it at a time, or the wood will dry out too quickly.

You can rid infested wood or furniture of beetles in several ways. Rough lumber can be kilned so that all parts of the wood are heated to 150° for three hours. That should kill powderpost beetles at all stages of their development. Interestingly, high kiln temperatures may make the wood more attractive to powderpost infestation later on. Above 113°, parenchyma cells are killed quickly and their starch content is fixed. Kilning below 113° depletes the starch and lessens the food available to the insects. Even this wood, however, may retain enough starch to support an infestation.

If you cut away badly riddled portions of once-infested sapwood, you can use the rest of the wood. Be sure to burn the sapwood cutoffs. A coat or two of a hard surface finish such as varnish or lacquer should prevent any remaining adult beetles from laying their eggs.

I've found one of the easiest and most effective weapons against powderpost beetles is the pesticide lindane. Following the instructions furnished with the product, mix a 1% emulsion of lindane, and spray or paint it on infested wood or on lumber that you want to protect. The emulsion will crystallize in the wood and kill the beetles as they emerge to lay eggs. It will also kill newly hatched larvae as they tunnel into the wood. Lindane can be used on in-place structural timbers, log cabins, barns, wagons and other outdoor objects. On old furniture, it might be wise to apply the emulsion on an unseen part of the furniture to see if it stains or discolors the finish. After it has dried lindane is considered safe for use around children and pets, but I wouldn't put it on lumber that will eventually come into contact with food.

When massive infestations in old houses or furniture can't be treated with lindane, there is an expensive last resort. Fumigation with highly toxic gases such as methyl bromide or Vikane is a sure-fire way to end powderpost problems. To fumigate a building, the entire structure is covered with a huge tarp and carefully sealed. The gas is pumped in under controlled conditions, and special monitors and fans ensure a uniformly deadly mixture. After 24 hours the building is thoroughly ventilated, and sensitive instruments sample the air for safety. Furniture and lumber can be similarly treated in air-tight chambers or temporary tents. But I suggest turning to fumigation only after all else has failed. The gases are extremely dangerous and are so penetrating that they can seep through a concrete-block wall in minutes. These gases are sold only to licensed users, so you must hire a professional to do the actual fumigation. The bill is likely to be large—I recently fumigated a museum in Pennsylvania, for example, and the job cost $15,000 and took a week. That particular building had other kinds of insect infestations, and fumigation was the only choice. Woodworkers who inspect their lumber carefully and use common-sense storage techniques will invite the powderpost beetle to have his next meal elsewhere. □

Tom Parker is an entomologist who specializes in the control of insects that infest museums, historic houses and libraries. He conducts seminars throughout the country.

Wood Identification at FPL

Sharp eyes and lots of experience get it right

by Paul Bertorelli

As a material, wood has a lot of things going for it—not the least being its enormous variety. There are more than 20,000 different kinds of trees growing in the forests of the world. So many of these woods are favored by man for his shelter, furniture and objects that just telling them apart is nearly a full-time job for a handful of laboratories in the U.S. and abroad.

One of these places is the U.S. Department of Agriculture's Forest Products Laboratory, located in Madison, Wis. There, a staff of three wood scientists divide their time studying wood anatomy and identifying thousands of samples sent in each year. To aid their research and to compare knowns with unknowns, the FPL scientists have the world's largest wood research collection—some 100,000 cigarette-pack-size blocks stored in banks of indexed drawers. The collection grows by 200 to 300 specimens each year.

About half of the lab's identification work is done for the wood industry. The rest of the samples to be tested come from the general public or various government agencies and museums, and more than a few bar bets have been settled by the lab, according to Regis Miller, who supervises it. Miller says the lab likes to guarantee satisfaction but can promise only to identify a particular wood's family and genus—picking the species is usually not possible.

Miller begins the task of identifying a strange wood by slicing a small chunk off the specimen's end grain. Next he wets the cut surface so the wood's characteristics can be scrutinized through a 14-power hand lens. If the wood happens to be a distinctive domestic species, Miller can usually identify it just by looking through the lens. At this stage, he can sometimes use color, odor and density for a quick identification.

More frequently, though, he must take thin slices off the sample, making sure to get radial and tangential sections. These match-head-size shavings are then placed on a glass slide with a solution of half glycerine and half alcohol, and boiled on a hotplate. This process drives out air bubbles that can obscure the wood's inner structure.

Peering through a lighted microscope at the thin slices, Miller begins what can be a complicated mental juggling act by asking himself if he has seen this cellular pattern before. "There's no substitute for experience . . . you've got to know what you're looking for, and the only way to know is to have seen it before," he says. With more of the wood's inner structure revealed, Miller can sometimes call up the proper mental image to identify the wood, or he can at least get close enough to root out a sample with which to compare it.

If the wood's identity still isn't apparent, the real work begins. Miller falls back on his knowledge of wood anatomy to pick out the sample's dozens of individual characteristics. He then pages through hefty books called dichotomous keys, which list thousands of wood samples by anatomical detail, an arrangement that permits a methodical narrowing of possibilities. Notes kept on index cards help Miller supplement information printed in the keys. Eventually, this process of elimination points to a small number of wood families.

Woods from temperate climates, particularly North America, are the easiest to identify because they are few in kind, and Miller has seen many of them before. There are, however, thousands of tropical species, some of which have never been identified at all. And tropical woods have a way of passing in and out of commercial importance, a fact that diverts a fairly steady stream of tough-to-pick unknowns into the lab. Computers can make wood identification faster, and FPL researchers are designing computer-assisted identification systems for domestic and tropical species.

Miller estimates that only 1% of all the samples examined can't be identified, either because they don't appear in the keys or his notes, or because he can't find a sample in the collection with which to compare them. "You get to a point where you've worked on a sample for two or three days and you've gotten nowhere. We have other work and we just have to move on," Miller says.

Because of limited time and staff, the lab requests that samples be sent only by people with a clear need for identification, and in limited numbers. Samples should be at least 1 in. by 3 in. by 6 in., though smaller pieces can also be identified. Place of origin and local popular name, if they are known, will help. Specimens should be sent to the Center for Wood Anatomy Research, U.S. Forest Products Laboratory, PO Box 5130, Madison, Wis. 53705. There is no charge for the identification service. □

Wood anatomists at the U.S. Forest Products Laboratory in Madison, Wis., have nearly 100,000 specimens of wood for research and identification. Here, Regis Miller, the lab's supervisor, searches for a sample.

Paul Bertorelli visited FPL this past spring. For more information on the world's huge variety of woods, contact the International Wood Collectors Society, c/o Bruce Forness, Drawer B, Main St., Chaumont, N.Y. 13622. The IWCS, formed in 1947, is dedicated to the advancement of knowledge about wood. The Society sponsors wood identification workshops, regional and national conventions and an annual wood auction, and it publishes a monthly newsletter. Its members frequently swap wood samples. IWCS membership costs $10.50 in the U.S. and $12.50 in Canada.

TOOLS

Workbench
An island with dogs and drawers

by Dwayne J. Intveld

I've accumulated quite a selection of tools over the years, but when I was setting up the basement workshop in my new home recently, I found my tools to be poorly organized and my bench—a knock-up affair of plywood and 2x4s—in dire need of replacement. I decided a bench should be my first project, so I set out to design one to suit my needs.

I've always admired European-style benches for their solidity, clamping flexibility, and beauty. But since my shop is small, my new bench would have to function as both work surface and storage cabinet. I needed a large surface for assembly, and I also wanted to be able to work on all four sides. The design I settled on is an island-type bench which has the bench dogs that make European benches so versatile.

Construction of the bench is straightforward. The base carcase consists of a framework of 2½-in.-sq. maple rails and stiles mortised and tenoned together. I used ¼-in. maple plywood for panels in the base, letting them into grooves in the various frame members. I installed three ¾-in. fir plywood dividers inside the carcase—this breaks it into four compartments. I used three of these compartments for drawer banks, and installed a door on the fourth to provide storage for tools too bulky to fit in drawers.

I dovetailed the drawers together, using maple for the fronts, pine for the sides and backs, and hardboard for the bottoms. I chose the size and number of drawers to suit what

would be stored in them. Before the drawers were assembled, I cut a series of vertical dadoes ¼ in. wide by ¼ in. deep so I could adjust the dividers in the drawers later. I used metal drawer slides for all the drawers except the top ones, which are too shallow; these ride on wooden slides.

The fourth compartment, accessible through a door at the end of the bench, has a shelf set on adjustable metal standards let into the frame legs and divider panel. On the opposite end of the bench, I installed a pegboard that's useful for hanging miscellaneous tools.

The bench top overhangs the base on the vise side so that dust and chips will fall through the two rows of bench-dog slots to the floor instead of into the drawers. I made the top of 1¾-in. hard maple ripped into strips 2½ in. wide and glued up, but a commercially-made maple block top could also be used, if you can find one the right size. To avoid a lot of tedious clean-up work, I glued up the top in three pieces, ran the sections through a surface planer and then glued them together, leaving only two glue lines to clean by hand. For bench-dog holes, I dadoed slots in two 3½-in. wide pieces of maple and glued these (edge up, and with a narrow section of bench top in between) to one long edge of the bench top. With the top glued up and trimmed to length, I routed grooves into the ends of the bench top and attached end caps with bolts.

My Sears vise isn't equipped with bench dogs, so I made an adapter block that screws to the vise jaw and accepts two dogs. Two inches of lost vise opening seemed like a small price to pay for the greater clamping range of the dogs. A sprayed lacquer finish protects the bench from moisture, dirt and spills. □

Dwayne J. Intveld, of Hazel Green, Wis., is a design engineer for a construction equipment manufacturer. Photos by the author.

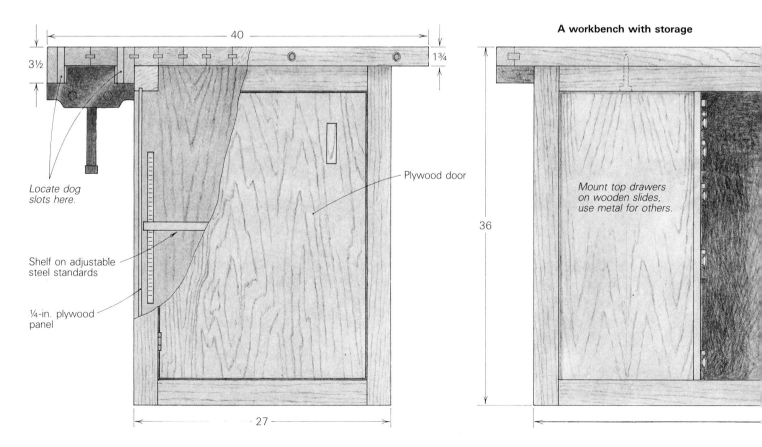

Locate dog slots here.

Shelf on adjustable steel standards

¼-in. plywood panel

Plywood door

A workbench with storage

Mount top drawers on wooden slides, use metal for others.

40

3½

1¾

36

27

Workers with limited shopspace need to make use of every nook and cranny, and Intveld's island-style bench does just that. A large, maple-block work surface is mounted over a frame-and-panel cabinet that has 18 drawers—plenty of storage for tools and supplies. Carcase frame is made of 2½-in.-sq. members mortised together and paneled with ¼-in. plywood. Intveld modified his Sears vise, shown at lower left, by attaching a maple block that will mount two European-style steel bench dogs. Dog slots in the bench stop should be spaced no farther apart than the maximum throw of the vise. And they should be located beyond the edge of the bench so debris will fall to the floor instead of into the cabinet. The bench's end compartment, below, has a plywood door and adjustable steel standards for a shelf, but it could be fitted with drawers instead. A rack on the door stores easy-to-lose items like arbor wrenches, saw throats and other small tools.

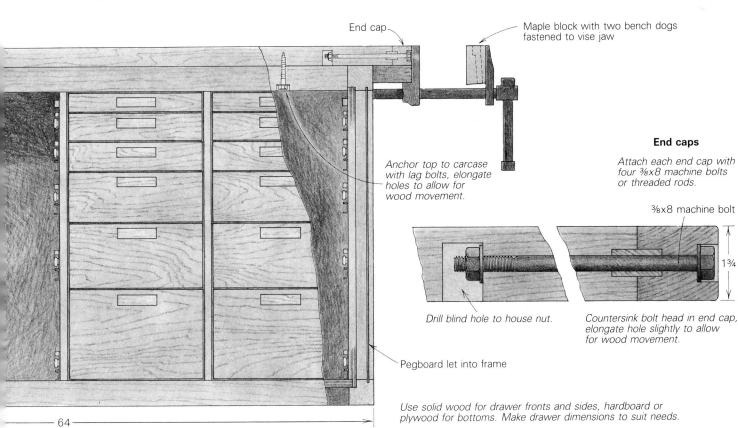

End cap

Maple block with two bench dogs fastened to vise jaw

Anchor top to carcase with lag bolts, elongate holes to allow for wood movement.

End caps

Attach each end cap with four ⅜x8 machine bolts or threaded rods.

⅜x8 machine bolt

1¾

Drill blind hole to house nut.

Countersink bolt head in end cap, elongate hole slightly to allow for wood movement.

Pegboard let into frame

Use solid wood for drawer fronts and sides, hardboard or plywood for bottoms. Make drawer dimensions to suit needs.

64

The Set-Up Table
An old door makes an adaptable, low work surface

by Henry T. Kramer

Someone starting out to equip a home workshop must be made of stern stuff if, after totaling the cost of all the needed tools, he doesn't give it up and turn to ocean racing or something else closer to his budget. The set-up table—which is nothing more than a well-placed, plainly dressed work surface—won't replace expensive power tools, but it can ease the pain by allowing you better use of hand tools.

The set-up table is a triple threat. It serves as an ordinary worktable, it's an aid to setting up and assembling, and it makes working with hand tools a positive joy. (It also offers a safe retreat for the dog when he comes to visit.) It's not intended to replace the typical workbench, but after you've used both for a while, don't be surprised if you favor the set-up table for its simplicity and ease of use.

The top of my present set-up table is a 1¾-in. solid-core door, 36 in. by 80 in., which was given to me by a friend. I finished it with a synthetic varnish (awful stuff, but tough as the back of a shooting gallery) and then waxed it. One can't avoid dropping glue on the table occasionally, but the surface is so smooth that a fingernail will get the glue right off.

I made a base of rough 4x4s and pine lumber. I doweled the base together, even though I know that some good and true men are on record against dowels—in this table, they're strong enough and quick to make. The top rests on the tops of the legs and is fastened to the rails with blocks and screws.

I made my table 28½ in. high, but you can build yours to suit you. For best leverage when using hand tools, the set-up table should be lower than the typical workbench. Height ought to be a function of your height, specifically, about ¾ in. less than the height of your fingertips with your arms at your sides—give or take a fingernail. This is very close to the ideal sawhorse height, making the table suitable for handsawing, boring with a brace and bit, and use with other hand tools.

Depending on the size of your shop, a set-up table may be as long as you want, but 80 in. is enough for me. When deciding on width, remember that you'll often want to be able to reach comfortably beyond the midpoint. Thirty-six inches is right for me. If you've got arms like an ape, make it wider. The most important feature of the set-up table is that the top overhangs the base on all sides by at least 5 in. This overhang gives you plenty of room to clamp work and tools to the table—without the vises, bolt heads or drawers of the typical workbench getting in the way.

The set-up table ought to be located as centrally in the shop as possible, and you should be able to get around all four sides of it. Because the table is lower than the work surface of most major machine tools, it shouldn't interfere with long boards passed through them. Put the table on the off-feed side of the tablesaw and you can clamp a roller table to it when you're cutting long stock.

As a jack-of-all-trades work surface, the set-up table is hard to beat. You can clamp portable tools such as vises,

A set-up table, a universal shop work surface, could hardly be simpler. Here, Kramer uses a brace and bit with his work clamped to the table with a hand screw. Size can vary, but the height ought to be less than that of a conventional workbench.

grinders and miter boxes to the table, and then stow them away on a shelf underneath when they aren't needed. For assembling large jobs such as big frames and cases, the set-up table offers plenty of space for clamps, tools and glue bottles—all the stuff that always gets knocked off small benches during the heat of glue-up.

But the nicest thing about the table, I find, is that it's just plain easier to use hand tools with the work clamped to the table. Everything doesn't have to be done on a big power tool just because it's there and it cost so much. Besides, it's more pleasant to see what you are doing and to do it right, because once you start a cut with a power tool, you are committed to finishing it whether it works out well or not.

It's surprising how many words it takes to describe how useful such a simple thing can be in the home workshop. It is this very simplicity and universality that appeals to the person who works wood for fun and doesn't take himself or his work too seriously. If you plan and build a set-up table, you'll be amazed at how it will change your work habits. □

Henry T. Kramer is a retired reinsurance specialist and an amateur woodworker in Sommerville, N.J.

Homemade bench vise

Unless you're lucky enough to own a European workbench with well-designed, sturdy vises, you are likely relying on inadequate ways of holding your work. Trouble is, most of the commercially available wood vises are just too small. And it is awkward to hold workpieces vertically because the center screw is in the way.

My alternative to the commercial vises is shown in the sketch below. It is a simple, inexpensive, effective means of keeping

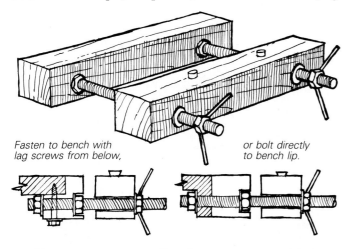

Fasten to bench with lag screws from below,

or bolt directly to bench lip.

work where I want it. At first the two wing-nut vise screws might appear to be inconvenient, but in most cases you can hold narrow stock by tightening only one screw. In fact, because of the independent movement allowed by two screws, it is routine to secure work with non-parallel sides.

The feature that has been most useful is the ability to hold panels up to 17 in. wide in a vertical position right down to the floor. This feature is invaluable for planing end grain and cutting dovetails and tenons.

I made my vise from two 24-in. lengths of 4x4 scrap hardwood, salvaged from a freight skid, and two 19-in. long sections of 1-in. threaded rod with matching nuts and washers. A friend spot-welded the wing handles on two of the nuts. You could epoxy the nuts into wooden wings instead. Be sure to angle the handles away from the jaw.

Drill 1-in. holes in the rear jaw, but drill 1³⁄₁₆-in. holes in the front jaws to allow for free jaw movement. Be sure to align the holes properly. I clamped both jaws together and drilled through one jaw, allowing the tip of my drill bit to register the hole in the other jaw.

—*Joe Loverti, Miamisburg, Ohio*

Homemade scraper plane

The cabinet scraper sets the standard of excellence for smoothing wood, but it has some drawbacks: tired, blistered fingers (these things get hot!) and uneven surfaces. Scraper planes are available, but the most common one (which resembles a large iron spokeshave) has such a short sole that it is difficult to control and often chatters.

With these thoughts in mind I decided to make a simple wooden scraper plane. It went together in only a couple of hours and proved to be quite successful.

The body of the plane is laminated from three pieces of wood as shown in the illustration. The block against which the blade bears must be dished slightly to spring the blade into a curve. The back of the wedge must be correspondingly convex. This curve should be roughly ¹⁄₃₂ in. across a 2½-in. wide throat. The wedge must fit accurately and should extend through the body nearly to the sole. The support provided by the wedge, the curve of the blade and the length of the plane

work together to prevent chattering.

A scraper plane is useless unless the blade is properly sharpened. To sharpen, joint the edge with a file, then bevel the edge on a stone to a 45° angle. Hone the edge just as you would a plane iron. Then with a burnisher or hard steel rod, rub back and forth. At first hold the burnisher parallel to the bevel, then gradually tilt it until it is perpendicular to the blade. This technique produces a razor-sharp curl every time.

—*Bradley C. Blake, Redwood, Miss.*

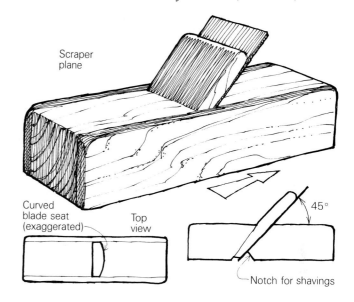

Scraper plane

Curved blade seat (exaggerated)

Top view

45°

Notch for shavings

Auxiliary shop-vac tank

For sawdust collection I use a couple of Sear shop-vacs that I connect to my tools through normal methods. But by using auxiliary dust-collection tanks, I'm able to stretch the filter-cleaning cycle considerably. To make the tank, start with a

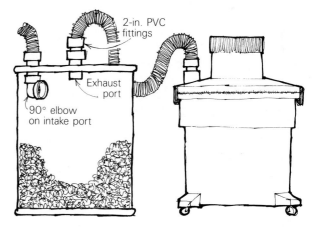

2-in. PVC fittings

Exhaust port

90° elbow on intake port

55-gal. drum or a fiber barrel (the kind with the removable clamp-on lid works well), and install 2-in. PVC pipe intake and exhaust ports as shown in the sketch. The 90° elbow on the intake port sets up a cyclone action that drops dust and chips at the perimeter and bottom of the tank. You can fill the auxiliary tank to the elbow and still have the vacuum filter open and breathing.

—*D.J. Greenwald, Hudson, Wis.*

Veneering with sandbags

The easiest way to apply even pressure on veneer being glued to a curved surface such as a serpentine drawer front is to use several pillow sacks filled with sand. Store the sandbags near the stove. Their warmth will shorten the glue curing time.

—*Granton James, El Paso, Tex.*

Using Bench Planes
These basic tools still do what machines can't

by Ian J. Kirby

In woodworking, there is no sound quite as delightful as the clear hiss of a sharp plane taking off a thin shaving. Nor can any other tool so precisely remove a modicum of wood tissue while leaving a perfectly flat and smooth surface. Of the three basic woodworking tools—saw, plane and chisel—the plane alone projects such a false sense of complexity that much modern woodworking is done without it. To be sure, many of its operations can now be done faster by machine. Where the cabinetmaker once had bench, plow and molding planes, he now has power jointer, router and spindle shaper.

For those woodworkers intent on a more developed level of workmanship, however, the hand plane still has an assured place in the shop. No machine, no matter how cleverly contrived, can match the plane's virtuosity in fitting drawers and doors, aligning twisted frame assemblies or leveling surfaces. The plane is unique in its ability to deliver a smooth, clear surface unattainable in any other manner.

Woodworkers of yesterday had dozens of planes to pick from. Though many are still available today, you need to own only one or two to perform most planing work.

In this article, I'll explain the various types and parts of modern metal planes, how to select and adjust them and, most important, how to use them. These principles apply to wooden planes also.

Why planes?—The woodworker's plane has been around for centuries. Unearthed tomb paintings depict Egyptian carpenters using planes to square up timbers. This remarkable history stems from the plane's basic usefulness; except for the adze and drawknife, no other primitive tool can prepare cleft or roughsawn wood to final dimensions. In its basic function and form, the plane has changed little: all planes consist of a blade or iron firmly mounted on a bed in the body of the tool. The blade must be adjustable and easily removable for sharpening. The bottom, or sole, of the plane must be kept flat and out of winding. The whole assembly, blade and body, must accommodate the hands or have handles so the operator can control the tool.

These requirements can be met with different designs and materials. Japanese planes, for example, are made of wood and are pulled. Western bench planes, whether metal or wood, are pushed. The result is the same: a smooth, accurate surface. Often the question is asked, which is better, metal or wood, and one can only reply that the answer lies with personal preference. Wooden planes are more difficult for the beginner to adjust and sharpen. A metal plane also delivers a clearer tactile sensation of the shaving being removed than does a wooden plane. Wooden planes can be made in the shop, and their soles can be flattened with another plane rather than with a grinding machine. A century ago, wooden planes evolved in such great variety because they suited the manufacturing technology then available. Each tradesman—

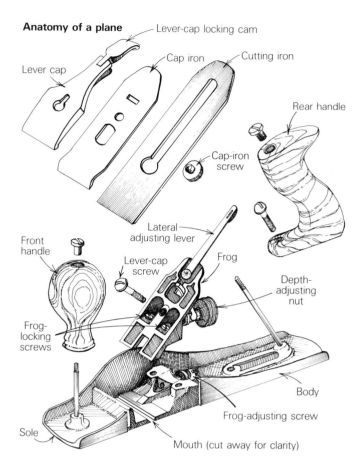

Anatomy of a plane — Lever-cap locking cam · Lever cap · Cap iron · Cutting iron · Rear handle · Cap-iron screw · Lateral adjusting lever · Front handle · Lever-cap screw · Frog · Depth-adjusting nut · Frog-locking screws · Body · Frog-adjusting screw · Sole · Mouth (cut away for clarity)

joiner, cabinetmaker, cooper, coachmaker, and so on—had his own array of planes suited to his own particular work. Some, an ogee molding plane for example, were designed for a single job and were thus used only occasionally. But the bench plane, because it could do many jobs well, was used constantly. The working specialty planes have vanished along with the trades to which they belonged, or else their functions are now better done with machines. The electric router, for instance, makes grooves much better and more quickly than plow planes can. Woodworkers today still need the utilitarian planing tools that the early tradesmen found so indispensable, and thus the bench plane has survived in very much its original configuration.

Three types of bench planes are commonly sold today, and these are distinguished by their lengths. The longest, about 22 in., is called a jointer. Of the lot, it is the most versatile; its length is designed for spanning and accurately flattening irregularities when making finished boards from roughsawn lumber. The smoothing plane is the shortest and has a body about 9 in. long. Its short sole cannot bridge irregularities in a board, so it's not the tool for making an accurately flat surface or edge. The smoothing plane is best for producing finished surfaces of high quality, when flatness is not impor-

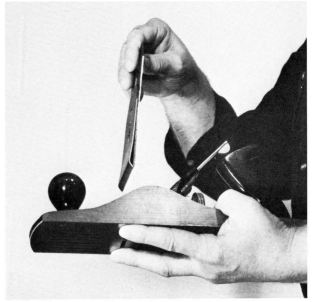

Kirby uses the lever cap's tapered end as a screwdriver to disassemble and assemble the cutting iron. If you use a screwdriver, make sure it is large enough to avoid damaging the screw. When reassembling, the cutting and cap irons should initially be put together at right angles, above left. The screw is then finger-tightened and the cap iron is rotated into place. The cap iron should be placed about $\frac{1}{16}$ in. from the back or non-beveled edge of the cutting iron, as shown below. For best performance, this distance is critical; if too small, shavings will jam and if too large, the iron may chatter. To put the cutting iron back in the plane, grasp the tool as shown in the photo, above right. Then, holding the cutting-iron assembly between the thumb and forefinger, drop it into the plane and make certain it seats against the bed and engages the depth-adjusting mechanism. At right, the frog-locking screws are loosened to move the frog forward and backward. Use your forefinger to feel how far the lower edge of the frog projects into the mouth.

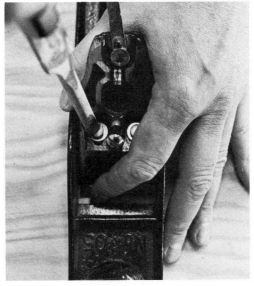

tant. In the middle, at about 14 in. long, is the jack plane, supposedly named because its medium length makes it a "jack-of-all-trades." I've always found this plane to be of limited use—it has neither the jointer's accuracy nor the smoothing plane's handiness. If I were to buy but one plane, I would get the jointer. It will do its job as a preparation plane and can also be used for truing subassemblies and for finishing and smoothing work. I find little use for the jack except in instances where the jointer is uncomfortably heavy.

Adjusting the plane—Before it can be used, the plane must be tuned up or "fettled" (see box, p. 27), its cutting iron must be sharpened and its various parts must be put in proper adjustment. Begin by removing the cutter and cap iron. With the plane on the bench, place your forefinger firmly on the lever cap and, using your thumb and middle finger, release the locking cam. Bear down with your forefinger to keep the lever cap from bouncing about. After you have removed the cutting-iron assembly, disassemble the cap iron from the cutting iron and sharpen the cutting iron (sharpening is discussed in *FWW* #29, p. 66). Holding the cutting iron in the palm of your hand, loosen the screw just enough to slide the cap iron free.

After sharpening the iron, reassemble the cap and cutting iron, making sure the cap iron doesn't slide across or bump the sharpened edge. Tighten the screw and slide the cap iron to within $\frac{1}{16}$ in. of the cutting iron's edge. This setting is critical and getting it right may take some trying—too small, and shavings will jam; too large, and the iron will chatter.

To put the iron assembly back into the plane, grasp the body in the palm of your hand with fore and middle fingers at opposite ends of the mouth. Hold the assembly between your thumb and forefinger, and lower it into place onto your fingers. As the iron seats itself, you will feel it slide through the mouth to contact your fingers evenly on each side. Sight alongside the iron to make sure that it has firmly seated on the frog—the cast-iron assembly that beds the cutting iron in the plane body—and that the depth-adjusting mechanism has engaged the window in the cap iron. Place the lever cap over its screw and lock it down with the locking cam.

Adjusting the frog varies the space between the cutting edge and the front of the plane's mouth. This space should be made about $\frac{1}{32}$ in. if delicate shavings are to be made, although for hogging off roughsawn stock it might be $\frac{1}{16}$ in. or wider. The frog is held in place by recessed screws, and to get at them you'll have to remove the cutting-iron assembly

Grip the plane with your index finger extended (above). This triangulates the grip and gives you more control than wrapping all four fingers around the handle. When edge-planing, curl the fingers of your other hand up under the sole so your fingernails ride against the face of the board. Stand close enough to the work so that your shoulder is aligned with the cut (right). Standing too far away will cause you to tilt the plane, producing an out-of-square cut. Start the edge-planing cut with the toe held against the work (below left). Stand with one foot well below the work and the other spread about a walking pace back. The back leg should be straight, the front leg slightly bent (below center). Remember, this is a lower body action, not an arm movement. As you make the cut, uncurl your body and crouch into the work. Follow through by leaning well over the board (below right), extending your arms if you start to become unbalanced.

again. With the locking screws loose, a screw under the adjusting nut moves the frog forward and backward.

Unfortunately, the frog does not ride on a track; it can slew from side to side as it is moved. Its alignment can be gauged only with the cutter assembly in place, so the adjustment is a matter of trial and error. A likely starting place is with the leading edge of the frog just overlapping the mouth. Lock the cutting iron back in place, then turn the plane over. With the lateral adjusting lever centered, you want the cutting edge to be only $\frac{1}{32}$ in. from the front of the mouth. The edge should be parallel to the mouth opening. Adjust the frog to make it so, and recheck the adjustment with the cutting iron in place. When you've got it right, tighten the locking screws. Then apply a light film of machine oil to the frog, the cutting iron and the cap iron, and put the cutting-iron assembly back in place.

To adjust the cutting iron, back off the depth-adjusting nut until the cutting edge is inside the mouth. Then turn the plane over and sight down the sole. Turn the depth-adjusting nut clockwise until the edge of the iron appears as a black hairline projecting from the mouth. The edge of the iron should be parallel to the surface of the sole; if it isn't, adjust it with the lateral adjusting lever. When setting the depth of cut, never adjust the plane to take a thick shaving with the intention of backing the iron off for a thinner cut. Start from zero and make small adjustments downward to get the shaving you want. Once you've got it, back the adjuster off in the counterclockwise direction until it just stops turning freely—this will take up the slack in the mechanism and keep the cutter from creeping downward and taking too large a cut. Smear paraffin or candle wax on the sole for lubrication, and you're ready to make a test shaving.

Select a board with an already planed edge, preferably not one done on a machine jointer. With the plane set for a fine cut, make a single pass and inspect the shaving. If it is uniformly thick and curls neatly against the cap iron, the plane is set correctly. If only crumbs appear in the mouth, advance the depth adjustment until a shaving can be made.

Using the plane—As with any tool, grip and stance are vital when using the plane. Other than working with a dull cutting iron, I find that ignoring these two points is the most common planing fault. Begin by learning to grip the plane: grasp the rear handle with three fingers and your thumb, and place the forefinger on the frog casting, almost touching the depth-adjusting nut. Resist the impulse to cram your forefinger around the handle. It will be uncomfortable and you will lose the triangulation afforded by the proper grip. For edge-planing, grasp the toe of the plane in your other hand, with your fingers curled up under the sole so your fingernails can ride lightly against the face of the board as a fence. If you are surface-planing, grip the plane's front knob in whatever manner seems most comfortable.

In learning stance, it's helpful to remember that planing is a push from the lower body, not an arm movement. Stand close enough to the work so that the shoulder pushing against the back handle of the plane is directly over the direction of the cut. Stand with your front foot well under the work and your leg bent; your rear foot should be spread about a walking pace back, and your leg should be kept straight or flexed slightly. As you push the plane over the wood, uncurl your body and crouch into the action.

Start the cut by placing the plane's toe firmly on the board. Maintain an even downward pressure on both handles as you follow through. Skewing the plane in relation to the direction of the cut will ease the work, but keep the entire length of the sole on the work. Boards to be edge-planed can be held on the bench in a vise, with dogs or against a bench stop. I prefer the stop because there is no chance of the work becoming distorted by undue holding pressure, and it forces you to learn to keep the plane flat against the edge. If you are

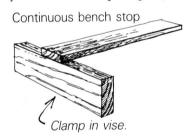

Continuous bench stop

Clamp in vise.

doing it wrong, the board will just flop over. Boards to be surface-planed can be held against the stop, or else the continuous bench stop shown at left can be made up of hardwood and clamped in the vise for wider support.

Contrary to the opinion that a block plane is the tool for planing end grain, I find that full-size bench planes are better for squaring and smoothing the ends of a board. All you need do is knife a line around the board to be squared and then plane down to the line, taking as light a cut as possible. To avoid tear-out, plane in from each edge toward the center, clamp blocks on the edge of the board, or plane a small chamfer on the edges.

All of the skills I've described in this article can be mastered with a perseverance that can be enjoyable. The plane is the ideal tool for many woodworking operations that are frequently done with power tools and sanders. Once you've tuned up and learned to control this tool, you will wonder how you ever got along without it. □

Ian J. Kirby teaches design and woodworking at Kirby Studios in North Bennington, Vt. For more information on choosing planes, see FWW #3, p. 28. Tuning up planes can be read about in #1, p. 22; #2; and #14, p. 52. Japanese planes are discussed in #19, p. 91; #20, p. 60; and #29, p. 71. Another article on using planes appears in #13, p. 52. A book, Planecraft, *published by C. and J. Hampton Ltd., is available from Woodcraft Supply Corp., 313 Montvale Ave., Woburn, Mass. 01802.*

How to tune up a plane

As a production item, the metal plane emerges from the factory as a nearly perfect tool. All the necessary parts are there, and made of materials suited to the job at hand. But if the plane is to be used to its maximum potential, it must be tuned up or "fettled." This means taking up where the factory left off by cleaning and adjusting the various parts. For a really superb job, enlist a machine shop to grind the plane's sole perfectly flat. Even planes with years of use behind them can benefit from this attention.

I begin fettling a plane by filing the cam that locks the lever cap and iron assembly to the frog. The cam works against a spring, and on new planes it is sometimes a bit rough and burred from casting. As a result it binds against the lever cap spring. Use a fine-cut file to dress the cam until it operates smoothly.

Next, true the end of the cap iron where it will bear against the cutting iron. It must rest perfectly flat against the cutting iron, or else shavings can jam up and break off in the mouth of the plane instead of curling smoothly away. You can do this on a bench stone. Keep the ground edge of the cap iron at right angles to its sides, so it will be parallel to the cutting iron's edge.

Use a straightedge to inspect the cutting iron for flatness in length and width. If the iron is bent along its length, straighten it by placing it over a block of softwood and bending it in the proper direction. Put the convex side up, and strike the iron sharply one or two times with a steel hammer. Final flatness is achieved by backing off on the sharpening stone. Next, tend to the brass adjusting nut. This nut should travel smoothly throughout. Usually, brass running on steel needs no lubrication. If you find, however, that a few drops of light machine oil won't correct a stiff nut on a new plane, send it back for replacement.

The most important, and difficult, part of fettling is getting the sole perfectly flat. I've tried several hand methods, with only marginal results. Now I send planes to a machine shop. The machinist makes up a cradle to hold the plane, so that a few passes of a precision grinder will flatten the sole. Leave the frog in place during grinding, or else the sole will be distorted when you torque the screws to reinstall it.

Planes come from the factory supposedly ground to tolerances of about 0.003 in., which seems quite fine by woodworking standards. Yet I've seen as much as $\frac{1}{32}$ in. of metal removed to achieve flatness. Grinding the sole is expensive and you have to decide whether it's worth the money. I find the difference quite noticeable; a well-fettled plane can take consistently finer cuts than one that has not been tuned. Before grinding, the edges at the heel and toe of the sole should be chamfered slightly with a file, to prevent burrs from forming if the tool is inadvertently struck against a hard surface. Lightly file off any burrs or paint on the inside of the mouth opening and on the working surfaces of the frog. Either of the handles can be shaped to improve comfort and grip: scoop out the rear handle near its base to fit your own hand. —*I.J.K.*

How to Make a Molding Plane
Sticking with an 18th-century tool

by Norman Vandal

You still can spot old molding planes in antique shops or junk shops, but they aren't as common as they used to be. Prices can be as low as $8 to $15, so people snap them up to use as decorations. I can see displaying these old tools because they are aesthetically pleasing, but it's really a shame not to fix them up and use them. They were fine tools once and can work just as well again.

I make a lot of period furniture, and I can't get along without my set of old planes. When I needed a reverse ogee molding with cove for a cornice on a cabinet, I decided to make a plane to do the job, designed around an old iron I'd found that had become separated from its original block.

I'll describe how to make such a plane from scratch, so that if you come across an old molding plane or iron you will be able to get it working again, regardless of its condition. Whether you are starting with an old plane block or an old iron, or from scratch, this is the general scheme: First you must know the molding profile, which will determine the width of the iron. Next you must shape the sole of the plane to the reverse profile of the molding. Then you can true the iron to the sole and start making molding.

If you come across a plane with a poorly shaped iron, don't change the shape of the sole to conform. The contour of the sole represents the molding the plane was designed to make. A poorly matched iron is usually the result of inept sharpen-

ing or grinding. Recondition a damaged iron by annealing it (softening it by heating), filing it to fit the sole and then re-tempering it.

The style of plane I've chosen is based on the finer 18th-century examples, and all the standard dimensions discussed are characteristic of this period. You may, of course, alter the design, but this pattern is a good starting point.

Molding shapes—Planes with an average length of 9 in. to 10 in., a height of 3 in., a thickness of from 1 in. to 2½ in. and no handle have erroneously been accepted as "molding planes." Many of these planes are for rabbeting, tongue-and-grooving, dadoing and other purposes that have nothing to do with making moldings. Molding planes produce moldings on the edges of frame members called sticks, hence the process is called sticking. Figure 1 shows some standard moldings, and the bibliography at the end of this article includes books that contain full-size drawings.

Simple moldings (composed of segments of circles or ellipses) are beads, quarter rounds, hollows and rounds, coves or scotias, and astragal beads. Planes for making these profiles are called simple molding planes. Complex moldings, often broken up or set off by flats or fillets, are ogees, reverse ogees, ovolos or compositions of various curves. Planes to stick these shapes are called complex molding planes. There is another

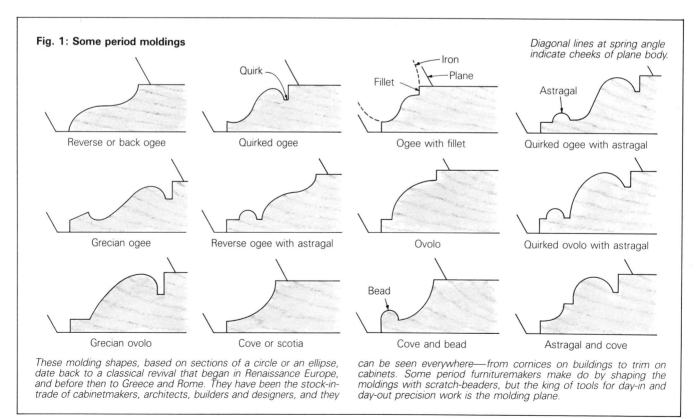

Fig. 1: Some period moldings

Diagonal lines at spring angle indicate cheeks of plane body.

Quirk

Iron — Plane
Fillet

Astragal

Reverse or back ogee · Quirked ogee · Ogee with fillet · Quirked ogee with astragal

Grecian ogee · Reverse ogee with astragal · Ovolo · Quirked ovolo with astragal

Bead

Grecian ovolo · Cove or scotia · Cove and bead · Astragal and cove

These molding shapes, based on sections of a circle or an ellipse, date back to a classical revival that began in Renaissance Europe, and before then to Greece and Rome. They have been the stock-in-trade of cabinetmakers, architects, builders and designers, and they can be seen everywhere—from cornices on buildings to trim on cabinets. Some period furnituremakers make do by shaping the moldings with scratch-beaders, but the king of tools for day-in and day-out precision work is the molding plane.

Drawings: David Dann

The plane shown above began with an old iron. Vandal annealed and reshaped the iron, then made a yellow-birch block to suit. In the photo sequence below, the plane is tilted, or sprung, so the fence will be pressed against the work. A series of passes then takes progressively wider shavings, until the depth stop contacts the work, and the plane ceases to cut.

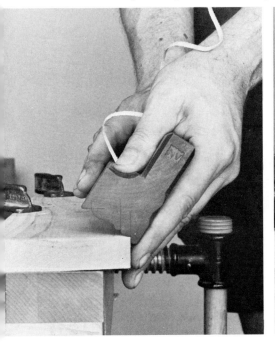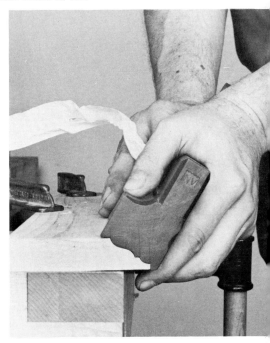

class of planes generally used to cut wider moldings. These planes are from 12 in. to 14 in. long, and have a throat, wedge system and handle similar to common bench planes. They have been dubbed "crown molding planes," though this type of plane cuts many sorts of moldings other than crowns or cornices.

The design—The first step in making any molding plane is choosing the molding. Draw its section full-size, and refine the drawing before beginning the plane. Simple planes can make moldings up to about 2½ in. wide. Wider moldings will have to be made with more than one plane, or with a crown molding plane.

Use the molding section to construct a full-size drawing of the heel, or rear, of the plane, as this will settle the size of the

block needed. The sole of any molding plane is the reverse profile of the molding it cuts, plus the integral fence and the depth stop. Looking at my plane from the rear, the fence is on the left and the depth stop on the right (figure 2, top of next page).

In use, the stock is fastened horizontally to the bench and the plane is tilted, or "sprung," so that the fence is vertical and the depth stop horizontal, as shown in the photos above. An unsprung plane can wander, but a sprung plane gives greater control because the guide fence is pressed against the stock. The plane, even though tilted, cuts straight down the side of the work, gradually taking a wider and wider shaving until the full profile has been stuck. When the depth stop contacts the top of the work, the iron stops cutting. Not only is a sprung plane easier to use, but its geometry will also

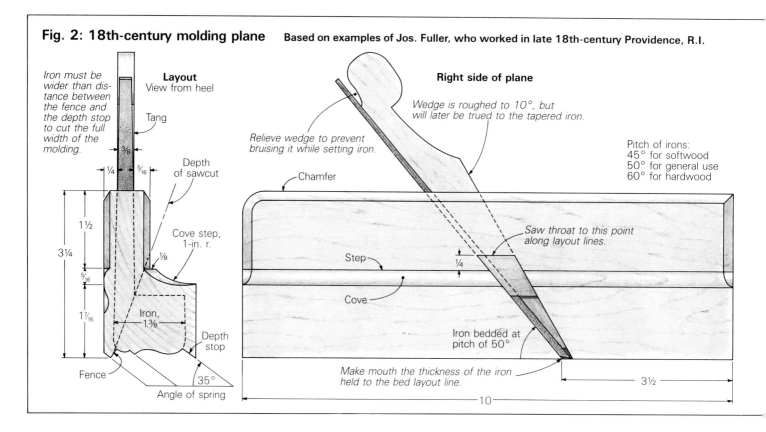

Fig. 2: 18th-century molding plane Based on examples of Jos. Fuller, who worked in late 18th-century Providence, R.I.

Iron must be wider than distance between the fence and the depth stop to cut the full width of the molding.

Layout
View from heel

Tang

Depth of sawcut

Cove step, 1-in. r.

Iron, 1⅜

Depth stop

Fence

35°

Angle of spring

Relieve wedge to prevent bruising it while setting iron.

Chamfer

Step

Cove

Right side of plane

Wedge is roughed to 10°, but will later be trued to the tapered iron.

Pitch of irons:
45° for softwood
50° for general use
60° for hardwood

Saw throat to this point along layout lines.

Iron bedded at pitch of 50°

Make mouth the thickness of the iron held to the bed layout line.

allow its mouth to be more uniform in width (figure 3, top of facing page). Not all 18th-century molders were sprung, however, and a sprung plane won't cut some molding shapes.

Draw the molding with the appropriate spring, which can vary—good working angles are shown in figure 1. Then add the fence and depth stop to the molding profile. I allow ¼ in. on the fence side, and ⁵⁄₁₆ in. on the depth-stop side. Your drawing now shows the total width of the plane.

The top of a molding plane is stepped down in thickness. The width of the stepped portion will be the width of the iron's tang plus ¼ in. at the left and ⁵⁄₁₆ in. at the right. The extra width makes up for the wood that will be cut from the throat. You can judge from figure 2 the height of a typical step.

The stock—Yellow birch was used by 18th-century plane-makers, but by the turn of the 19th century beech had become the wood of choice. I prefer quartersawn yellow birch, but beech, maple or cherry will work as well. Select as fine a block of wood as you can—straight-grained and consistent throughout. Avoid figured wood, or you'll have problems shaping the sole.

My rough block length for a 10-in. long plane is 12 in., which gives me an inch at each end to experiment with when shaping the sole profile, and also allows for cutting off bruises inflicted during shaping. The finished height of most blocks is about 3¼ in. Standard dimensions meant planes could be stored and transported in fitted boxes without rattling around.

The iron—Since I figure that I'll use any molding shape sooner or later, I frequently buy old irons that have lost their blocks, then make new blocks to fit. I've had some good luck, but looking for a usable iron that's also a shape you need can be futile, so I recommend that you make your own.

The easiest way to make an iron is to start with a piece of dead-soft sheet tool steel, work it with a file and hacksaw,

and then temper it after shaping. Alternatively, you can have a blacksmith forge an iron out of spring steel, which can be annealed and shaped, then tempered as a last step. Hayrake tines and old buggy springs forge into excellent irons.

Iron thickness can be from ⅛ in. to ³⁄₁₆ in. The thicker irons will chatter less, but will be more difficult to shape. Old plane irons were tapered in thickness. A light tap on the end of the tang would loosen a tapered iron slightly while driving it deeper into the block. Then a sharp tap on the wedge could secure the iron without altering the set. The tapered iron, while nice to have, is not a necessity. And a uniformly thick iron is much simpler to make. Keep in mind that the iron must be wider than the cutting portion of the sole—if the profile ends at the side of the iron, you won't be able to set the iron deep enough to cut the full width of the molding.

Layout—When your block is planed and trued square, lay out the cuts and mortises. Start by making a full-size template of the sole profile, directly from the full-size drawing of the molding. To make the template, I use aluminum flashing. It is easy to work, and the edges of the template remain crisp during tracing. Position the template in the same place on each end of the block and trace the sole profile.

Next, lay out the throat, mouth and wedge slot using the dimensions given in figure 2. I suggest a 50° pitch for the iron—a compromise for cutting either hard or soft woods. The wood which the iron rests against is called the bed. The opposite side of the mortise will be cut at an angle 10° greater, to allow for the wedge taper. Carry the layout lines all around the body of the plane to define the mouth opening and the tang mortise on top of the block. Lay out the mortise width according to the width of the tang.

Last, use a marking gauge to scribe the step. The step makes the plane easier to handle, helps the shaving out of the throat, and makes cutting the mortise for the wedge and iron

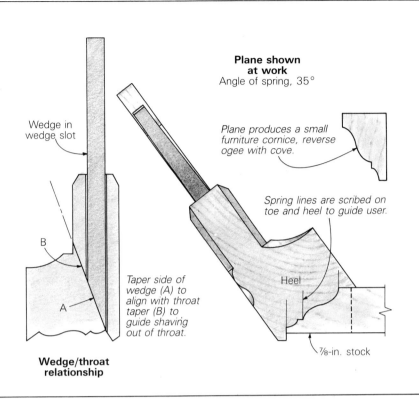

Wedge in
wedge slot

B

A

**Wedge/throat
relationship**

Taper side of
wedge (A) to
align with throat
taper (B) to
guide shaving
out of throat.

**Plane shown
at work**
Angle of spring, 35°

Plane produces a small
furniture cornice, reverse
ogee with cove.

Spring lines are scribed on
toe and heel to guide user.

Heel

⅞-in. stock

Fig. 3: Spring allows uniform mouth

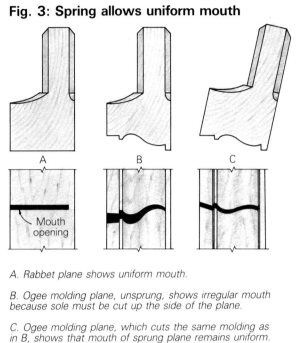

A   B   C

Mouth
opening

A. Rabbet plane shows uniform mouth.

B. Ogee molding plane, unsprung, shows irregular mouth
because sole must be cut up the side of the plane.

C. Ogee molding plane, which cuts the same molding as
in B, shows that mouth of sprung plane remains uniform.
This plane must be a bit wider than plane B to cut the
same contour.

*An intricate sole can be shaped by a series of cove and straight
cuts on the tablesaw, and then sanded with shaped blocks.*

Boxing the sole

Slivers of Turkish boxwood can be let into the sole of a
plane to reinforce it at points where use would wear it
down. Boxwood—the familiar yellow wood used in old
Stanley folding rules—is dense, tight-grained and extremely
wear-resistant.

Planemakers plowed narrow grooves into the sole of the
plane, inserted thin slips of boxwood, then trued up the
sole. In order to make the slips even more wear-resistant,
makers set the grain of the boxwood nearly at right angles
to that of the plane body, so that the tougher end grain was
exposed to take the abuses.

Boxing was not common in 18th-century planes, but it
caught on fast—it is found in almost all molding planes
produced after the turn of the 19th century.   —*N.V.*

easier, as we shall see. The edge of the step can be decorated
in a number of ways—molded with ogee or quarter-round
profiles, chamfered, or simply beveled off. I decorate my steps
by cutting a cove the full length of the plane. Lay out the
decoration now, too.

Shaping the sole and step—Period planemakers duplicated
many profile molders. Instead of shaping each sole with files
and gouges, they devised a "mother plane," made in reverse
profile, to stick each profile. The mother plane saved time,
and it ensured that all the planes for a specific molding would
be the same, at least those from any one workshop. I've never
bothered to make a mother plane, though, because I've never
needed more than one plane of each shape.

Cut the sole and the step decoration prior to sawing out
the mouth and throat—these gaps would interfere with the
shaping. It's vital that the sole be uniform from end to end,
or you won't be able to set the iron properly. Various tools
and techniques can be used to shape the sole. For the fence
and depth stop, or any other flat portions of the profile, I use
the tablesaw to make cuts the full length of the sole.

The concave areas can be gouged and filed, or cut on a
router table using various cove or fluting bits. By making a
number of repeated cuts, not quite to the layout line, you can
remove most of the material. The sole can then be scraped or
sanded smooth, with the sandpaper wrapped around a dowel.
For shaping convex areas I generally use hollow planes, but
other methods work too. Again you can remove most of the
material using router or tablesaw, then clean up with chisels,
scrapers and a shaped sanding block.

Check the sole with a straightedge, and then true any hollows or high spots.

The steps on period planes were probably cut with a large
rabbet or fillister plane—chatter marks from the iron are often
visible. I cut the step on the tablesaw and scrape the surfaces

smooth, saving the waste to make the wedge. At this point you can cut the decoration on the step.

Sawing out the mouth—Surprisingly, a good deal of the mouth and wedge slot can be made by simply sawing out the area between the layout lines. Mark out how far up the body of the plane you wish to saw. This cut is a compromise between leaving enough wood above the step for strength and providing a gentle angle to guide the shaving out of the throat. I usually stop the sawcuts ¼ in. above the step.

Figure 2 shows how deep to cut across the sole. I use a miter box to start the cuts at the proper angles for the blade and the wedge—the miter box also ensures that the throat will begin straight across the sole. I use the backsaw freehand to finish the cuts.

The wood between the kerfs can now be chiseled out, and pared as smooth as possible. You will find that a ⅛-in. chisel is a great help in clearing out the mouth.

Mortising the wedge slot—The angled mortises in period planes were, I believe, chopped out without pre-boring—production planemakers of yesteryear had plenty of practice. I find it a lot safer to pre-bore the wedge slot with a bit slightly smaller than the width of the mortise, using a guideblock bored at the correct angle. A drill press could be used, or any number of jigs worked out. It's important to bore accurately, without cutting into either the bed or wedge ends of the mortise. Bore all the way through to the throat.

Now pare the sides and ends down to the layout lines. Some chopping is required, but don't rush it—many a plane has been spoiled at this point. You have to chisel the wedge end of the mortise into end grain at a 40° angle. Patience and an absolutely sharp chisel will prevail.

After my wedge-slot mortise has been cut, I use a set of planemaker's floats (*FWW* #30, p. 63) to true up the bed and the mortise. Floats are single-cut files of various shapes and sizes with widely spaced teeth, each of which functions like a tiny chisel. Original floats are extremely scarce, and command high prices. I have a set that a friend made me on his milling machine, and I value them highly. Although they make truing up a lot easier, floats aren't strictly necessary—careful paring with a chisel can produce as good a result.

The width of the mortise isn't crucial, just make sure there is adequate clearance for the iron without removing too much wood. The bed, however, must be perfectly flat—or the iron will chatter. For the final fitting, use your iron to check out the bed surface, the mortise width and the mouth. But check the iron itself for flatness first. The wedge end of the mortise must also be flat, and square to the plane's sides.

Much of the angled mortise can be started with a backsaw and then pared away, but the inside should be drilled and chopped.

The plane's wedge is made from the scrap left over when the step was cut. Its lower end will be tapered to guide the shaving out.

Making the wedge—Take the cutoff you saved when you made the step, and thickness it to the width of the tang. Taper it to 10° so it will fit the mortise. I make the angled cut with a fine-tooth handsaw and plane it true and smooth with a block plane. Now set the iron in the plane and insert the wedge against it with the grain of the wood parallel to the iron. The wedge must fit tight to hold the iron firmly against the bed, and to prevent shavings from catching between the wedge and iron, jamming up the mouth and throat. Carefully pare away wood from the mortise until you get a perfect fit.

Shaping the iron—The blank has to be annealed, so that it can be worked to shape, then rehardened. To anneal the iron, you can use a propane torch, or better yet a hotter MAPP gas torch, heating the iron to a dull red glow, then letting it cool slowly for an hour or two. If the steel is properly annealed you should be able to cut it with a file or hacksaw.

Once you've shaped the tang so the iron fits neatly in the plane, the cutting edge can be laid out to the shape of the sole. This must be done while the iron is set flat on the bed. I make a full-size template of the iron out of aluminum flashing. Place the template in the plane as a substitute iron, holding it tightly in place with the wedge and making sure that its full width protrudes slightly beyond the sole. Using a sharp marking awl, scribe the contour of the sole on the underside of the template. Remove the template and cut out the traced profile with a tin snips or knife. The line of the cutting edge must pass into the body of the plane at the fence and depth stop—carry this line out to the sides of the template. This will not give you an entirely exact profile for the cutting edge, but it's as close as you can come at this point.

Next, paint the bottom inch of the wedge side of the iron with either machinists' blue layout dye or flat black paint. When this is dry, lay the aluminum template on it and, using the awl, scribe the cutting edge's contour. You can use a grinder for roughing out, but a file will give you the greatest accuracy for the final cuts to the scribed line. Place the iron in a vise, paint side toward you, and go at it. Don't worry about the bevel of the iron yet, just file square to the contour.

Now turn the underside of the iron toward you to file the

bevel: all but the cutting edge itself must clear the sole. Thus the bevel angle is dependent upon the angle at which the iron is bedded, the pitch. For a plane with 50° pitch I give the iron at least a 55° bevel (a 5° clearance angle), which usually proves sufficient. Set a bevel square to the bevel angle and file up to the cutting edge.

When the edge is formed, position the iron with the wedge in the plane, so that the iron protrudes about 1/32 in. Check for clearance, and sight down the sole of the plane from toe to heel to see that the iron protrudes uniformly. Remove the iron and touch it up with a file where necessary.

When everything is right, remove all traces of the paint or layout dye. File all parts of the bevel as smooth as you can, because once the iron is tempered, a file will not easily cut the steel. Next, polish the iron. I use a muslin wheel charged with gray compound (tripoli). The shiny, buffed surface will allow you to see the colors of the steel—your clue to the correct temperatures—while you temper the iron.

Tempering—I confess I have little scientific knowledge of tempering. I learned from a local blacksmith who was even less scientific than myself. I don't have my own forge, but a MAPP gas torch works quite well on small pieces such as plane irons. Heat the iron until it glows dark cherry red in dim light. This is about 1550°F to 1600°F. Don't direct the flame at the cutting edge—the edge reaches a hotter temperature anyhow, and there's no sense in burning it. When the color is right, plunge the iron vertically into a pail of cool, salted water. When cool, the iron will be in the hard state. Buff it until it shines again, and test it with a file.

Next, temper the iron by heating it until the polished surface turns a light straw color. This will be about 500°F to 600°F—nowhere near as hot as when heating to harden. When the color is right, plunge the iron into the water. Then check it for hardness with a file, which should be barely able to cut. If it isn't hard enough, start over.

Buff the tempered iron clean, and use a set of Arkansas slip stones to hone the tricky spots. Use plenty of lubricating oil until the entire bevel gleams.

Finishing the wedge—With the rough wedge against the iron in the plane, mark the wedge's decorative profile. Then shape the wedge on the bandsaw or scroll saw, and sand the edges smooth. The wedge in figure 2 is typical of a prolific 18th-century planemaker, Joseph Fuller, of Providence, R.I.

Taper the tip of the wedge to allow the shaving to escape the mouth and be directed up and out of the throat. The tip will sometimes have to be cut back a little. Taper from the end up to the bottom of the angled mortise—if the taper extends into the mortise you will trap shavings.

After chamfering and carving some decoration on the block, I stain the yellow birch and apply three coats of Minwax antique oil as a sealer and final finish. The plane is now about ready to go to work.

Setting the iron—Place the iron in the plane and insert the wedge loosely. Sighting down the sole from the rear of the plane, set the iron so the cutting edge is just shy of the mouth, and drive the wedge, but not as tight as it will be during use. It helps to have a light positioned behind you, to reflect off the bevel as it protrudes. Get the final set by tapping the end of the iron, then drive the wedge tight. Use a mallet on the wedge and a ball peen or other small hammer on the iron. To loosen the wedge, hold the plane in your left hand and give the heel a sharp blow with the mallet. Be careful the iron doesn't fall out of the mouth of the plane.

Lubricate the sole to minimize friction and to prevent pitch buildup. Cabinetmakers used to use tallow, kept in cups fastened beneath their benches. I use paste wax, and sometimes mineral oil, though mineral oil tends to darken the sole.

Depending on the wood and the amount of set, it might take twenty to forty passes to stick your molding. Start with the plane sprung so the fence is flat against the edge of the board. Keep pressure against the fence with each pass, and be sure to keep the spring lines vertical, otherwise the molding may end up with a tilt.

Making wooden planes in the old manner is an all-but-forgotten trade. I hope you will be inspired to give it a try—to experience the immense pleasure of using a tool you have restored or, better still, designed and built on your own. □

A molding plane can yield a crisp, traditional molding, free of machine-tool marks and needing no sanding.

Further reading

Wooden Planes in 19th-Century America, Kenneth Roberts, Kenneth Roberts Publishing Co., Fitzwilliam, N.H., volume one. Note: Volume two, available soon, features the most comprehensive material ever published on making wooden planes.
Dictionary of Tools Used in the Woodworking and Allied Trades, R.A. Salaman, Charles Scribner's Sons, New York, 1975. Includes planemakers' tools and the processes involved.
Alex Mathieson & Sons, 1899 Woodworking Tools, a catalog reprint, Kenneth Roberts, Kenneth Roberts Publishing Co., Fitzwilliam, N.H. Many full-size drawings of period moldings.
Chapin-Stephens Catalog No. 114, 1901, a catalog reprint, Kenneth Roberts, Kenneth Roberts Publishing Co., Fitzwilliam, N.H. Molding planes in sticking positions; useful for designing.
Explanation or Key, to the Various Manufactories of Sheffield, Joseph Smith, 1816, a reprint by Early American Industries Assn., South Burlington, Vt., 1975. Historical information.
Woodworking Planes, a Descriptive Register of Wooden Planes, Alvin Sellens, Augusta, Kans., 1978. A valuable compilation.

Norman Vandal, of Roxbury, Vt., makes period architectural components in the summertime and period furniture during the winter. He wrote about panel planes in FWW #18. For more on tempering, see FWW #4, pp. 50-52.

Curved Moldings on the Radial-Arm Saw
Shaper setup can cut a swan-neck

by Wallace M. Kunkel

My particular interest is copying 18th-century furniture, and nothing delights me more than bonnet-tops for highboys and tall clocks. Many woodworkers are capable of all the necessary joinery for such pieces yet are stymied by the swan-neck or sweeping ogee moldings. I make many joints by hand, but my moldings are a product of my DeWalt 10-in. radial-arm saw.

The swan-neck molding is a series of parallel profiles describing an ogee curve. On clocks and highboys, it is returned with a straight molding of the same profile along the sides of the case. This type of shaping is often done on the spindle shaper, but the radial-arm saw can make the series of cuts with a molding head, guided by a template screwed to the board being molded.

I usually make all four pieces of the molding—the right-hand swan-neck and the mirror-image left-hand swan-neck, each with its accompanying straight sec-

tion—at the same time, on opposite edges of a single board. You can also use two shorter boards, as in figure 1. If you do, just flip the template for the mirror-image molding. Start by laying out the innermost curve of the molding on one edge of each board. You can enlarge the curve from figure 1, which is taken from Lester Margon's *Construction of Early American Furniture Treasures,* or you can design your own profile. For the molding shown here, I started with a straight-grained cherry board 26 in. long, 8 in. wide, and 1⅛ in. thick. The molding stock should be screwed, down the center, to a piece of ¾-in. particleboard that is the same width as the molding stock but 6 in. longer on each end. The particleboard will serve as a template and it will elevate the molding stock to give the arbor nut room under the molding head. The particleboard's extra length makes entering and exiting the shaping operation

safer. With the molding stock attached to the particleboard template, transfer the curve to this assembly and bandsaw the shape. Hand-sand or use a drum sander to smooth the curve, particularly on the template since it determines the smoothness of the final cut.

I use a Rockwell 4-in. molding head with interchangeable knives. This 3-knife head describes a 5½-in. diameter circle with knives in place. If you are making moldings requiring a tighter inside radius, Rockwell sells a smaller head that works inside a 2¾-in. diameter, using the same knives.

To set up, make a new back table for your saw. Since you won't be using the fence for this operation, make the new table ¾ in. wider than the old one. Use a flat piece of particleboard or plywood, and make sure the joint between the front and back table surfaces is flush. With the new back table temporarily locked in place, remove the sawblade,

Swan-neck moldings are a dramatic element of 18th-century furniture that can readily be made on the radial-arm saw. The sweeping ogees and returns of this clock were made with a molding head and guide jigs. Rosettes were laid in after shaping.

Drawings: Christopher Clapp

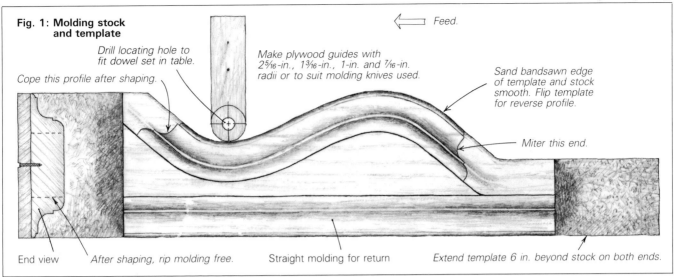

Fig. 1: Molding stock and template

Drill locating hole to fit dowel set in table.

Cope this profile after shaping.

⟸ Feed.

Make plywood guides with 2⁵⁄₁₆-in., 1³⁄₁₆-in., 1-in. and ⁷⁄₁₆-in. radii or to suit molding knives used.

Sand bandsawn edge of template and stock smooth. Flip template for reverse profile.

Miter this end.

End view

After shaping, rip molding free.

Straight molding for return

Extend template 6 in. beyond stock on both ends.

collar and guard, and swing the arbor to the vertical position. Then move the arbor about 3 in. behind the table joint and mark the arbor center on the back table. Remove the back table and drill an arbor-size blind hole (usually ⅝ in.) in the tabletop, almost but not quite through the thickness of the table. Put the back table in position, and move it and the motor until the arbor drops into the hole as you lower the arm. Lock the back table in this position. Then lock the roller head in the arm and leave it locked throughout the entire shaping operation. To add extra rigidity, I next adjust the roller-head bearings so they bind in their track—that way the roller head won't wobble. Keeping the motor rigid is important, otherwise the cutter may chatter during shaping. Elevate the arbor out of the hole. The arbor-size hole you drilled will be filled with a dowel that sticks ¼ in. above the table surface. This dowel serves as a positioner for the guides.

Next make the guides—various-size ¼-in. plywood jigs tacked to the saw table that control the distance the template is held from the center of the arbor, and hence the depth of the cut. Making them is no problem if you understand the relationship between molding head diameters and the cuts they make. The Rockwell cutterhead with knives installed describes a 2¾-in. radius at the outermost portion of the knife. The simplest profile, that made by the Rockwell #104 straight knives, will have a radius of 2¾ in. at all points. If the knife describes a 2¾-in. radius and you wish to make a cut 1 in. into the material, for example, you need to make a guide that has a radius of 1¾ in.

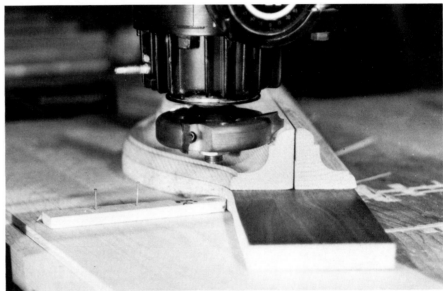

A radial-arm saw won't cut all the moldings that a spindle shaper will, but it works well for swan-necks. The stock to be molded, here ripped into two pieces for clarity, is screwed to a particleboard template. The saw's fence is then removed and replaced by a radiused-end plywood guide that bears against the template as the stock is fed into the cutter. Make the template 6 in. longer on each end so you'll have a bearing surface to start and finish the cut.

Any kind of molding head can be used, but make sure you check its radius before making the guides.

The sizes I use are shown in figure 1, but you can vary them to suit the radius of your molding head and knives. The length of the guide should be at least 6 in. The locating hole in the guide must be the same diameter as the dowel pin set in the table. Touch up the edges of the radius with sandpaper.

For my molding head, four guides are needed—from ⁷⁄₁₆-in. to 2⁵⁄₁₆-in. radius, as shown in figure 2 on the next page. Each guide is placed over the dowel, squared with the table and secured with two brads at the back. Changing knives and guides can be tricky. Without unlocking the motor in the arm, you can raise the arm and pivot

the motor to the crosscut position to make it easier. Also, you can swing the arm to the side to give yourself room to hammer brads to attach guides.

On deep cuts, the nut on the bottom of the arbor might rub against the wood, marring it. To prevent this, the first cut is made with the straight knives and it removes enough wood to allow the second cut to be made without the arbor nut rubbing. This "relief" cut won't be part of the finished profile, but it must follow the edge of the template.

With the setting up done, the actual shaping is a matter of feel. Running the first or relief cut is good practice since the results are not critical. With the 2⁵⁄₁₆-in. guide, make the relief cut with the straight cutters ¼ in. into the stock and to a depth of 1¼ in. To start the

35

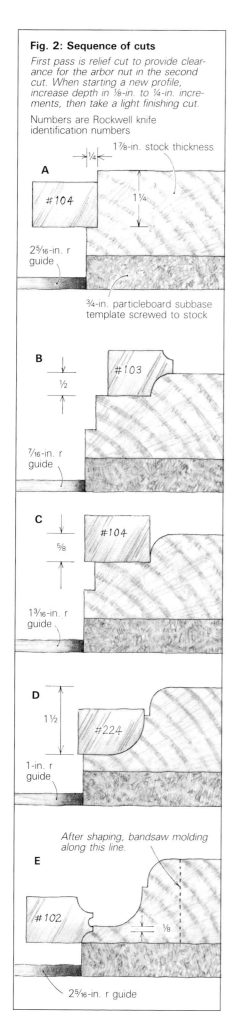

Fig. 2: Sequence of cuts

First pass is relief cut to provide clearance for the arbor nut in the second cut. When starting a new profile, increase depth in 1/8-in. to 1/4-in. increments, then take a light finishing cut.

Numbers are Rockwell knife identification numbers

A #104

1 7/8-in. stock thickness
1/4
1 1/4
2 5/16-in. r guide

3/4-in. particleboard subbase template screwed to stock

B #103
1/2
7/16-in. r guide

C #104
5/8
1 3/16-in. r guide

D #224
1 1/2
1-in. r guide

After shaping, bandsaw molding along this line.

E #102
1/8
2 5/16-in. r guide

cut, lower the cutters with the motor off until they touch the top of your material. Move the stock away from the cutters and lower the arm exactly three turns—3/8 in. Turn the motor on, and with the extended portion of the particleboard template held against the guide, feed the stock slowly into the cutters. Despite the curves, feed the work as nearly parallel to the fence line as possible. The subbase template will guide you into and out of the cut easily, and the stock sort of wraps around the molding head as the radius of the curve nears the radius of the head. Continue with the first cut in increments of two or three turns of depth until you reach the full depth of 1 1/4 in. Continue shaping using incremental depth settings and the sequence of knives shown in figure 2.

As you begin each new profile, you can take cuts as deep as 1/4 in. But after that, stay with 1/8 in. until you get the feel of the cut. Total depth measurements are shown for each profile, but you can vary them to suit your own needs. Remember that each turn of your elevating handle equals 1/8 in. in depth. Each pass must be made on both edges of your stock—the curved edge and the straight edge. Be patient, and as you approach the final depth of each profile, leave a quarter turn of the handle for a clean-up cut. Fine sandpaper will smooth any remaining irregularities.

For a clean, safe cut the molding knives require hand-honing. Work the flat face (bevel up) on a fine slip stone until the entire profile shows the result of the honing. The bottom edge of the knives is relieved (slightly beveled), so you also hone that bevel because most of these cuts reach deep into the material, and the bottom of the knives must do some planing. The knives described here are among the most useful. Whether you purchase them specifically for this molding or not, you'll need them sooner or later if you plan to do much shaping. They cost about $15 per profile plus $40 for the head. After you have made this molding, one of the most difficult, you'll be able to apply the same method to other radial-arm shaping jobs with ease. The key is understanding how the guides work and getting the feel of moving the stock into the cutters. □

Wallace M. Kunkel operates the Mr. Sawdust School of Professional Woodworking in Chester, N.J. Photos by Jeff Kunkel.

Clock tops and planing on the radial-arm saw

by Raymond H. Haserodt

I often hear people insist that a radial-arm saw is just too inaccurate to do really fine work, but I've found that with patience and a little thought, I'm able to use it to perform all the operations I need to do in my shop—from planing rough boards to shaping fancy, radiused moldings. A radial-arm saw's settings need more attention than a tablesaw's, but the reward is greater versatility. I've improved the performance of my saw—a Sears 10-in.—with these jigs, which you can make or have made inexpensively by a machine shop.

Locking the roller head: Getting the roller head to stay put is always a chore on a radial-arm saw, particularly when you want to nudge the saw this way or that to make fine adjustments for ripping. I made a pair of aluminum clamps that fit in the arm track, bearing firmly against both sides of the roller head (figure 1, at top of facing page). Adjusting screws allow me to move the roller head in increments of as little as a few

This is the radiused molding on one of the twelve clocks Haserodt made for his grandchildren. The molding is returned along the sides of the case.

Christopher Clapp

Fig. 1: Clamp

Steel dowel

This dimension fits saw track

Steel dowels, screwed to clamp, seat in saw track

Adjusting screw

1-in. minimum

Locking screw

Alignment screw

To set up his radial-arm saw for planing, below, Haserodt rotates it to the rip position with the blade closest to the extra-high fence. With the aluminum blade-stiffening disc installed (visible behind blade), he feeds the stock on edge between the blade and fence. A spring attachment, right, is clamped to the table to hold the stock against the fence on the out-feed side. Note the aluminum clamps (figure 1, left) holding the roller head in place. The clamp's adjusting screws must bear firmly on the roller-head frame.

thousandths of an inch—that's certainly more than accurate enough for woodworking applications.

The dimensions aren't critical, but the throat opening of the clamps must match the track of the saw on which the clamps will be used. On my radial-arm saw, the roller head rides in a cove-shaped track, so I screwed small steel dowels to the clamp. The dowels fit tightly into the cove, so the clamps seat snugly when tightened down.

Radial-arm planing: Since I don't have a planer, I've developed a method that lets me do the job on my saw. I rotate the roller head to the rip position, as in the photo at right, and run the stock vertically against the fence. I turned an aluminum disc (figure 2) which stiffens a 12-tooth raker blade I use for planing. The surface produced is surprisingly smooth and accurate. I've found that finer blades don't produce a better surface and do take more power to turn. Since I can't plane boards wider than 4 in., I rip boards in the rough, plane them and glue them up to the width I need.

Curved moldings: I use a molding head and the jig shown (photo, bottom right) for making radiused moldings for the clocks I build. I don't have a bandsaw, so I glue up the stock in bricklay fashion in roughly the shape of the radius. Then I attach it to the jig from below with screws and mount the assembly on the saw table. Jig and molding stock pivot on a dowel located so that the molding-head cutter arc passes through the stock at the proper point. I cut the inside radius first, then I move the roller head and cut the outside radius. You can use any combination of knives to get the profile you want. □

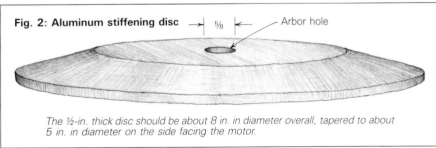

Fig. 2: Aluminum stiffening disc → 5/8 ← Arbor hole

The ½-in. thick disc should be about 8 in. in diameter overall, tapered to about 5 in. in diameter on the side facing the motor.

Raymond H. Haserodt is a retired tool-and-die maker. He lives in Lynd-hurst, Ohio.

Haserodt cuts radiused moldings for his clocks by attaching the stock to this jig with screws. The jig itself pivots on a dowel screwed into the saw table, at right. An arm is attached to the jig to swivel it. Several passes, moving both roller head and depth controls, produce the desired profile.

Cutting Gauge
The right tool for cross-grain layout

by John Lively

Nothing quite beats the cutting gauge for scoring across the grain. For striking dovetail baselines and shoulder lines for tenons, dadoes and rabbets, it's an especially accurate and handy tool. It can also be used to eliminate splintering when crosscutting by scoring the wood prior to sawing, though this requires an initial crosscut to within an inch or so of the final length to give the gauge an edge to ride against.

Unlike the ordinary marking gauge whose steel scribing pin is designed to mark along the grain, the cutting gauge is equipped with a cutting spur, which when properly ground and honed, severs cross-grain fibers cleanly. Used across the grain, the marking gauge can tear the wood and produce a ragged line, but the cutting gauge incises a neat, clearly visible cut, just the right thing to accept the edge of a sharp chisel when paring away the last bit of end-grain tissue.

The only commercially available cutting gauge on the American market is made by Marples (England) and is sold by most mail-order tool suppliers for about $14. Usually made from beech, the fence has two brass wear strips let into its face, and is bored and tapped to receive a plastic thumbscrew which tightens against the stock and locks the fence in place at any distance from the spur. The Marples cutting spur is ground to a spear point and beveled on both skewed faces and is flat on the back. The spur is held firmly in the stock by a brass wedge. If you buy one of these or already have one, you'll get it to work better by regrinding the spur to a round-nose profile as described below.

Instead of buying a cutting gauge you might want to make one. Start by selecting and dimensioning the material for the fence and stock. A stable, relatively dense hardwood like maple or cherry will do. Though the pieces themselves are small, it's best to cut the blanks large enough to machine them. The fence blank should be planed to a finished thickness of 1 1/16 in., ripped to a final width of 2 3/16 in., but leave the block about 14 in. long for now. Thickness the blank for the stock (bar) to 3/4 in. square, cut it to its finished length of 7 1/2 in. or 8 in. and put it aside.

Now pencil the outline of the fence in the middle of the blank. The fence is about 2 3/4 in. long (its length really depends on what size most comfortably fits your hand), and it is radiused top and bottom. Orient the layout so the grain runs vertically, from one rounded end to the other. To mortise the fence to receive the stock, locate the center of the fence and construct a 3/4-in. square about it, knifing-in the lines on both faces so that you have two squares directly opposite one another. Next bore a 5/8-in. hole through the block, centering the bit in the square. Enlarge and square up the hole, finally paring from knife line to knife line on all four sides of the mortise. The stock should slide freely through the mortise, but with no wobble side to side or up and down.

Fence and stock are locked together by a wedge, which requires tapering the top of the mortise at about 10°. Find the angle with a sliding bevel, and knife a line on the inside of the fence the proper distance above the top of the mortise. The tapered slot for the wedge is 5/8 in. wide; this will leave a 1/16-in. wide untapered shoulder on either side of the mortise. These keep the stock from flopping up and down when the wedge is removed. Pare down the end grain with a 5/8-in. chisel to form the slot, taking care to stop the taper just short of breaking through at the other end. Cut the wedge to fit the angle of the slot, but make it about 1/16 in. narrower than the slot is wide. The lateral play here, along with the prominent hump on the rear of the wedge, lets you wiggle the wedge side to side when you want to remove it.

Cut a 1/2-in. wide by 1/8-in. deep rabbet down both sides of the block on the face side (opposite the wedge side). These receive wear strips which you can make from a dense tropical wood like lignum vitae, ebony or rosewood. Finally, bandsaw the fence from the blank and epoxy the wear strips in place. When the glue has cured, sand the strips flush with the face, and smooth the rounded top and bottom edges.

Grind the cutting spur from a length of old hacksaw blade. It is 5/16 in. wide and 1 1/2 in. long. You ought not break it off until you've ground and honed the edge. The business end is first rounded and then beveled to a sharpening angle of about 20°. The rounded edge keeps the tool from digging in and dragging. Back off the unbeveled side on a stone, hone the bevel, then back it off again. Soften the upper edge with a file after snapping it off.

Cut the mortise for the spur and its retaining wedge about ½ in. from the end of the stock. Proceed as you did when mortising the fence, only taper the outside wall the full width of the mortise; lastly, fashion the wedge from the same tropical wood you used for the wear strips.

Traditionally used, the cutting gauge (and the marking gauge for that matter) is pushed into the work rather than pulled. This requires adopting a special grip to get consistent, accurate results. As shown in the photo at right, the index finger wraps around the top of the fence, while the thumb, positioned against the stock directly above the cutter, powers the tool. If you try to push the tool by its fence, it's liable to get slightly askew and bind against the wood. Trying to cut the full depth in the first pass can also cause the cutter to bind, drag and even wander; so first make a light pass. Having easily cut a shallow groove straight and true, you can make a second pass to final depth without risk of binding or wandering, because the scoring spur cannot deviate from the groove it cut first, and half the work is already done.

The orientation of the cutter is important, and can be different, depending on whether you are left or right-handed. If the toe of the spur is inclined toward the fence even slightly, you'll have a hard time getting a straight cut because the spur will want to push the fence away from the edge as you move the tool along. If the heel of the spur is angled toward the fence, it will wedge the fence against the edge during the cut, tight enough to cause binding if the angle is too great. Ideally the cutter should heel-in toward the fence one degree or less; this combines ease of operation with a slight wedging action, which means that you don't have to jam the fence against the edge of the board with barbaric force. Shave small amounts of end-grain tissue off the rear wall of the mortise in the stock until you get the right degree of skew.

For most woodworking operations, the bevel of the spur

Used across the grain, a cutting gauge will score wood cleanly. A marking gauge has torn the wood fibers and left a ragged mark.

should face the fence, a condition that means that the beveled side of the scored groove is in the waste and that the groove wall on the other side is perfectly vertical to the face of the board. This vertical wall is plainly visible (the end-grain has been burnished by the spur), and it makes the task of end-grain paring *(FWW #27, March '81, p. 72)* considerably easier. You've already got a ledge about ⅟₃₂ in. wide on either side of the board to position the edge of your chisel for the final, leveling shave.

The cutting gauge is more than a marking tool. Its spur actually cuts the visible shoulder line of the joint it's laying out. The careful chiseling you do between the scored lines, the nice end-grain surface you leave behind, gets covered up when the joint goes together. But the clean, straight line you scored with the cutting gauge is what you see and feel once the shoulder is pulled up tight. In laying out a joint with a cutting gauge, you make the final cut first. □

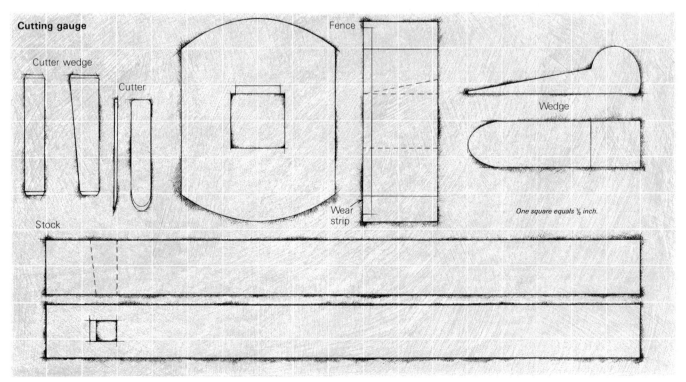

Cutting gauge

Cutter wedge

Cutter

Fence

Wedge

Stock

Wear strip

One square equals ½ inch.

Illustrations: E. Marino III

Wooden Bar Clamps
How to make these essential tools

by Tom Gerson

For edge-joining boards and gluing up frame or leg/rail assemblies, sturdy and stable bar clamps are indispensible. The trouble is that a really good bar clamp can cost upwards of $40, depending on its length, and to equip a shop with a couple dozen of these could mean a thousand-dollar investment. Many woodworkers try to get by with pipe clamps, but though these are comparatively inexpensive, they are cumbersome and the pipes bend easily, their jaws wobble, and they never seem to want to lie flat and steady on your glue-up table. Give one a nudge and it will fall over.

The solution is to make your own bar clamps. Shown here are some very practical and inexpensive homemade bar clamps that have been in use for nearly ten years and are still going strong. Their bars are flat and stable, their jaws stay consistently perpendicular to the bars, they sit flat on a table and they will not easily flop over. These clamps consist of a rectangular-section hardwood bar, a headstock which houses a nut for a threaded rod, a movable front jaw powered by the rod and an adjustable rear jaw whose bit and bridle allow it to be secured at 1-in. intervals along the bar.

The bar—Material for the bar can be any strong, close-grained wood. The clamps shown here are of cherry and maple. You can use the same wood to make the other parts of the clamp. The stock must be dimensioned 1¼ in. thick, 2 in. wide and as long as you choose, though you should increase the sectional dimensions for clamps longer than 24 in. The half-holes along the bottom of the bar are bored by clamping two bars together, bottom to bottom. Using a ⅜-in. machine spur bit in the drill press, bore exactly through the line of juncture between the two beams. Spaced 1 in. apart, the half-holes will provide plenty of rear-jaw adjustment.

The headstock end of each bar must be grooved on both sides. Plow these grooves ¼ in. wide and ⅛ in. deep so that the top of the groove is about ¼ in. below the top edge of the bar. The grooves should be at least 8 in. long, which gives the movable jaw about a 4-in. lateral run after the headstock side plates are attached. Within reasonable limits, the dimensions of the grooves can vary, depending on the diameter of the pins that will ride in the grooves; but I wouldn't make them any deeper than ¼ in., nor any wider than ⁵⁄₁₆ in.

The headstock—The headstock is just a small block of wood 1¼ in. thick by 1½ in. wide by 2½ in. long. Its job is critical, and you must take care to do precise work when making it. It's bored along its length to house the tightening screw for the movable jaw, and mortised across its width to capture the nut for the screw, which can be made from Allthread or from a ⅜-in. by 8-in. hex bolt, or square-head bolt. An ordinary ⅜-in. hex nut or square nut can be fitted into the mortise, but you will get greater thread length, and therefore less wear and longer life for the threads, by using threaded connectors. The connectors come in 2-in. lengths, and can be cut in half to yield two nuts. Acme (square) threaded rod and nuts can be used in place of Allthread.

Drill a ⅜-in. pilot hole through the length of the headstock to accommodate the screw. Accuracy in boring this hole is important, as any deviation from the true axis is going to be magnified when the screw is fully extended. Skewing can cause the movable jaw to bind on the bar. The hole must be centered in the thickness of the block and ⅝ in. above the bottom edge where it joins the bar. The ⅝-in. measurement is about right for gluing up panels and frames up to 1¼ in. thick, assuming that it's best for the screw to be centered in

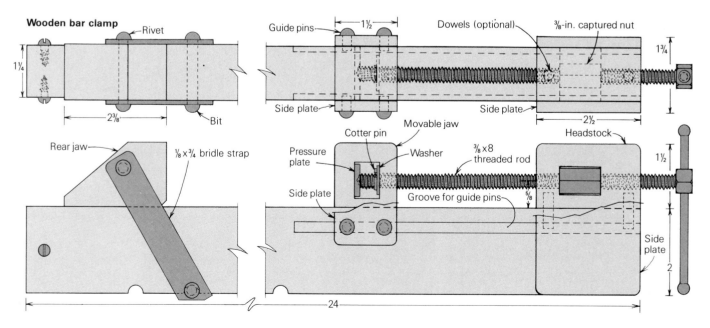

Wooden bar clamp

Rivet · 1¼ · 2⅜ · Bit

Guide pins · 1½ · Dowels (optional) · ⅜-in. captured nut · 1¾ · Side plate · Side plate · 2½ · Headstock

Rear jaw · ⅛ x ¾ bridle strap

Cotter pin · Movable jaw · Pressure plate · Washer · ⅜ x 8 threaded rod · 1½ · Side plate · Groove for guide pins · ⅝ · Side plate · 2 · 24

the thickness of the stock being joined. For clamping thicker stock, you might want to make several clamps whose tightening screws are ¾ in. to 1 in. above the bar.

Next cut the mortise for the captured nut. It's easier to cut the mortise all the way through the block, making it square top and bottom and centered on the axis of the bore. It should be just wide enough for the nut to fit snugly, and tall enough to house the nut and prevent it from turning. If you use a threaded connector you can secure it in the mortise by filling around it with epoxy putty (but not at this point in the process). The mortise should be positioned somewhat forward of the middle of the headstock since clamping pressure will be exerted toward the rear, and more wood is needed there to support the nut or connector. Mortising complete, ream the hole using a ²⁵⁄₆₄-in. twist drill; this will keep the screw from dragging when you use the clamp.

Now glue the headstock to the bar. You can reinforce the joint with a couple of short ⅜-in. dowels if you want, but they are not really needed. Make sure that the sides of the headstock are flush with the sides of the bar. The side plates are now glued in place and will tie the headstock to the bar, strengthening the entire structure. When these are glued on, the nut is forever sealed up, so be certain to have the screw in place before gluing on these plates.

The movable jaw—First dimension a block 1½ in. square by 1⁵⁄₁₆ in. wide (¹⁄₁₆ in. wider than the bar, for clearance). Like the headstock block, the movable jaw is bored and mortised, but in this case the hole stops in the mortise. The mortise accommodates a pressure plate against which the screw bears as the clamp is tightened. Made from a piece of hacksawn and filed ⅛-in. thick steel strap, the pressure plate is counterbored slightly with a ½-in. twist drill. The lead end of the screw is rounded, either by filing or turning in a metal lathe, to nest neatly in the counterbore. Epoxy the pressure plate against the rear wall of the mortise.

A thin washer, slipped over the screw on the inside of the mortise and retained by a cotter pin, prevents the screw from backing out of the jaw on retraction. Having fitted the hardware, shave off the bottom of the jaw about ¹⁄₃₂ in. so it will be free to slide along the bar.

Make a pair of side plates 1½ in. wide by 2¼ in. long by ¼ in. thick and temporarily clamp them to the sides of the jaw so that they are flush at the top and overhang at the sides ¾ in. Now mark the centers for two bores on the bottom edge of each plate so that the holes will line up precisely with the grooves. Remove the plates, bore them, and glue them in place, inserting wax paper under the jaw to keep glue off the bar. The guide pins can be made from rivets or from carriage bolts sawn to the proper length and dressed lightly with a file for a sliding fit in the grooves; the jaws should not wobble. Fitting done, epoxy the guide pins in the holes.

Provide for fitting a crank handle to the tail end of the screw by sweat-soldering a hex nut onto the threads, and drilling a hole through both the nut and the rod. You can make the handle from a 30d common nail or any other mild-steel bar stock. I turned the knobs on the ends of the handle from brass, but aluminum or wood would do as well. An acceptable alternative would be to thread the ends of the handle a few turns and screw a small hex nut on either end.

The rear jaw—This part can be made in any shape that suits the builder's eye, but it must be ¹⁄₁₆ in. wider than the bar. The two bridle pieces are made from ⅛-in. by ¾-in. steel or aluminum strap, and are riveted to the jaw at such an angle to allow it to be tilted forward and moved along the bar. If the angle of the bridle is too steep, you can't tilt the jaw, and if it's too shallow the metal straps will cut across the front face of the jaw and bite into the workpiece.

The rivets shown here are made from ¼-in. steel rod. To prevent the straps from marring the bar when I peened the rivets, I turned a small shoulder on the rods to hold the metal clear of the wood, and bored the holes in the bridle the size of this minor diameter. If you don't have access to a metal lathe, you can attach the bridle to the jaw with a stove bolt or carriage bolt. The bit (the rod engaged by the half-holes) can also be a carriage bolt.

A couple of coats of lacquer will finish the project, and keep glue squeeze-out from adhering to the jaws and bar. Besides saving money, these clamps are lighter than pipe clamps or metal bar clamps, and I find them handier to use. □

Tom Gerson is a retired accountant who makes furniture, taxidermy panels, and bootjacks in Stillwater, Minn.

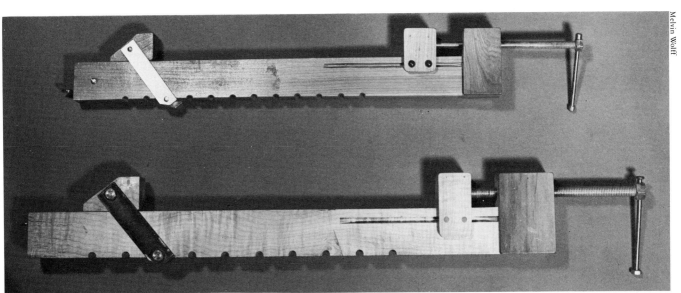

Made from ordinary hardware and clear hardwood, these bar clamps are easy to build and serve well in place of expensive metal bar clamps.

Horizontal Boring Machine
A translating mechanism with many uses

by Michael G. Rekoff, Jr.

A horizontal boring machine is really nothing more than a drill press on its side. But unlike the drill press, the boring machine can bore into the edges of boards of any length and width while the work is supported on its widest dimension. This makes the boring machine a good tool for fast, accurate doweling. The horizontal borer is often considered standard equipment only in high-volume shops, but the one I designed can be shop-built cheaply by anyone with moderate metalworking skills.

My boring machine uses a simple horizontal translating mechanism that smoothly moves the bit, spindle and motor, to bore work clamped to an adjustable table. This mechanism can be adapted to other uses: a router mounted horizontally or vertically, for example, could become a slot mortiser.

The translating mechanism consists of a mandrel mounted on a carriage that slides back and forth on a pair of steel rods. A steel cable connected to a foot pedal delivers the force to pull the bit into the work. I made a sleeve for attaching the bit to the mandrel, but a chuck could be substituted. Although most of the parts are readily available, some could be

This shop-made horizontal boring machine can simplify doweling and other drilling operations. It can be made from readily available materials with simple tools. You may need the services of a machine shop, however, to make some of the parts.

made by a machine shop. Since my machine isn't in constant use, I designed the motor mount so the motor can be easily removed for use on other machines. The dimensions given can be altered to suit your needs, and I suggest that you round up all the parts—particularly the mandrel—before you start.

Making the base—Begin construction with the base, on which the spindle/motor carriage slides back and forth. It's made of two pieces of angle iron connected by two ¾-in. separator rods and spanned by two ⅝-in. guide rods, on which the channel-iron carriage slides. Make sure the holes in the base ends line up, or these rods won't be parallel and the carriage won't slide smoothly (detail A). After you've bored the holes, assemble the base on a flat surface, and test-fit the guide rods. Incidentally, separator rods can also be made with ⅜-in. ID gas pipe sleeves over a threaded rod.

Making the carriage—The guide-rod holes in the carriage will be fitted with Oilite bearings—oil-impregnated brass sleeves in which the guide rods run. Drill them to final size, and drill and tap holes for the tension bolts that connect the carriage flanges (detail B). These bolts keep the channel iron from distorting when the mandrel is snugged. I had to fiddle with their tightness to get the carriage to move smoothly.

Any mandrel should work, although it should have a collar to prevent longitudinal shaft motion in the bearings. Use a straight output shaft if you plan to use a sleeve to hold the drill, or a threaded shaft for a chuck. Make sure the mandrel axis is perpendicular to the edges of the carriage.

Next install the Oilite bearings, and assemble the carriage and base. Put a light coat of oil on the rods and, holding the bearings in place with your fingers, slide the carriage back and forth. It should move smoothly and freely through its entire travel. If it doesn't, you may have to ream out the bearing holes a little or dress the rods with emery cloth. This will relieve any binding in the guide rods and allow the bearings to self-align for the smoothest operation. Then fix the bearings in place with a slow-drying epoxy.

A ½-HP 1,750-RPM motor is adequate. I made up a motor-mounting system that pivots the motor so the drive belt can be installed and tensioned. The support brackets suit the motor I had on hand; you'll have to modify the dimensions to fit your motor. Before screwing the brackets to the carriage, make sure that the position you select will result in good alignment between the motor drive pulley and the mandrel pulley. Put an adjustable collar on one guide rod between the carriage and the front end of the base, to serve as a depth stop when boring. The belt tightener is a block of steel screwed to the carriage, with a bolt threaded into it so the head bears against a plate attached to the motor. Unscrewing the bolt tightens the belt.

To complete the spindle, make the sleeve by boring

Horizontal boring mechanism

In the photo and drawing, the motor is swung back to show the spindle. Motor and spindle ride on a pair of steel guide rods, and the steel cable threaded through the pulley feeds the carriage for boring. The large spring returns the mechanism.

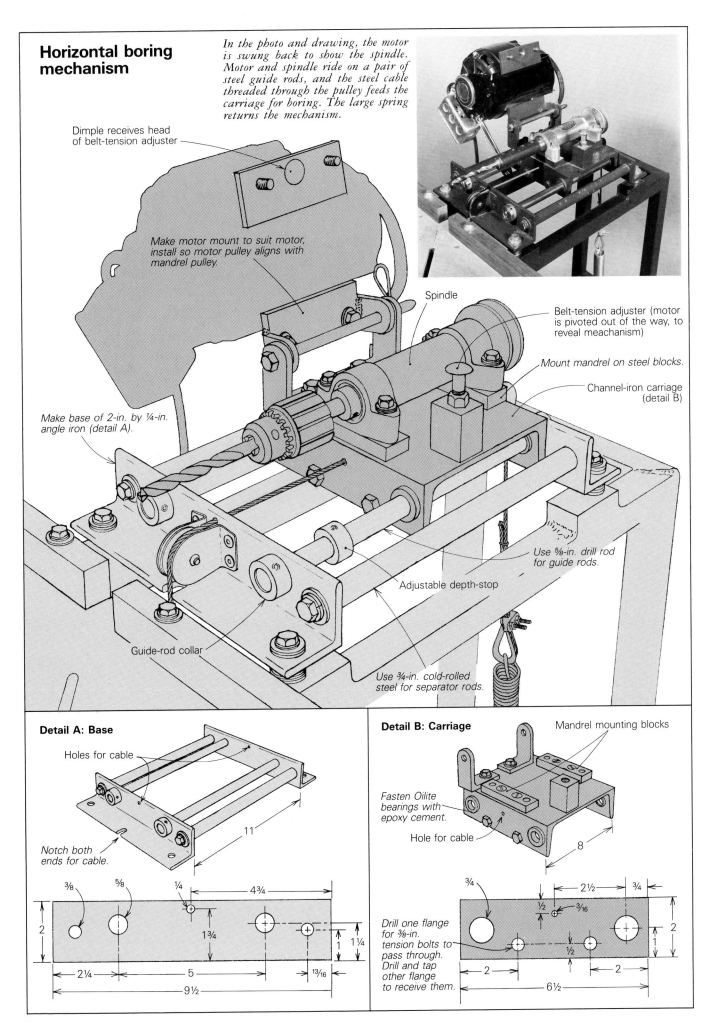

Dimple receives head of belt-tension adjuster

Make motor mount to suit motor, install so motor pulley aligns with mandrel pulley.

Spindle

Belt-tension adjuster (motor is pivoted out of the way, to reveal meachanism)

Mount mandrel on steel blocks.

Channel-iron carriage (detail B)

Make base of 2-in. by ¼-in. angle iron (detail A).

Use ⅝-in. drill rod for guide rods.

Adjustable depth-stop

Guide-rod collar

Use ¾-in. cold-rolled steel for separator rods.

Detail A: Base

Holes for cable

Notch both ends for cable.

11

3/8   5/8   1/4   4¾

2   1¾   1   1¼

2¼   5   13/16

9½

Detail B: Carriage

Mandrel mounting blocks

Fasten Oilite bearings with epoxy cement.

Hole for cable

8

3/4   2½   3/4

1/2   3/16   2   1/2   1

Drill one flange for ⅜-in. tension bolts to pass through. Drill and tap other flange to receive them.

2   2

6½

Stand

Make stand of welded steel tubing or of plywood.

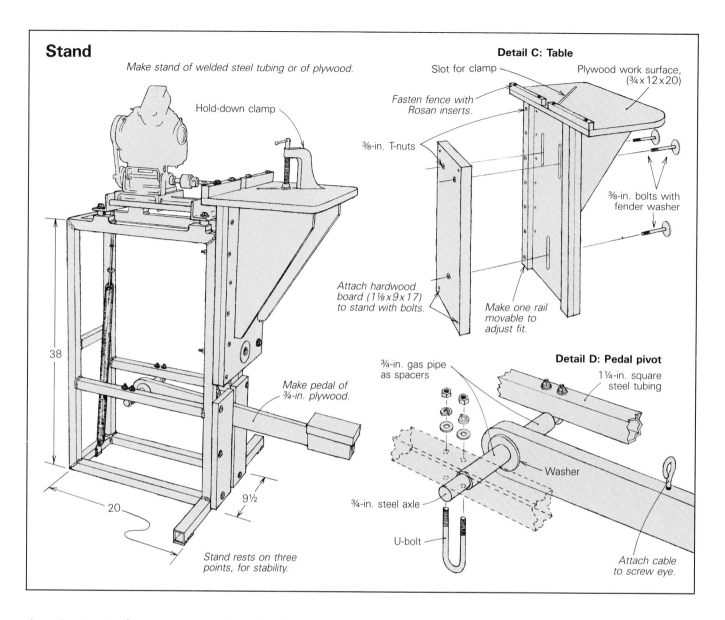

Hold-down clamp

38

Make pedal of ¾-in. plywood.

20

9½

Stand rests on three points, for stability.

Detail C: Table

Slot for clamp

Plywood work surface, (¾ x 12 x 20)

Fasten fence with Rosan inserts.

⅜-in. T-nuts

⅜-in. bolts with fender washer

Attach hardwood board (1⅛ x 9 x 17) to stand with bolts.

Make one rail movable to adjust fit.

Detail D: Pedal pivot

¾-in. gas pipe as spacers

1¼-in. square steel tubing

Washer

¾-in. steel axle

U-bolt

Attach cable to screw eye.

through a length of 1-in. rod stock and tapping for setscrews, or have it made by a machine shop. If you are using a chuck, thread it onto the mandrel.

Making the stand—I made my stand in two pieces—a frame and a platform—using square steel tubing welded together. The platform has three-point contact with the floor, making it easier to level the machine. The machine can be mounted on a bench top, in which case a feed lever could replace the pedal. The actual dimensions of the stand depend upon your particular needs. I made the machine's adjustable table and fence out of plywood, as in detail C. It slides up and down on the front uprights, aligned by a pair of hardwood rails, one of which is adjustable. I milled slots in the table and fitted them with bolts and T-nuts to lock the table in position. A clamp that also rides in a slot holds the stock down.

The critical requirement of the table is that it must hold the work parallel and at right angles to the travel of the drill bit, and this alignment must be adjustable. The table's maximum upward travel should go no higher than the lower edge of the drill bit, and its downward travel shouldn't be lower than the feed pedal in its released position.

Make and fit the feed pedal, install the steel feed cable and use a heavy-duty door spring to return the carriage. I ran the cable through thimbles before attaching it with cable clamps

to the spring and the pedal eyebolt. Another cable clamp inside the carriage flange transfers cable movement to the carriage. Experiment with cable length and spring tension to achieve full carriage travel and comfortable pedal movement.

Aligning the machine—You'll need a dial indicator with clamping fixtures for this job. With the machine on a flat, level surface and drill rod in the chuck, clamp the indicator to one of the guide rods. Check vertical alignment first by placing the sensing tip on the top edge of the drill rod. Move the carriage back and forth to check runout, and correct it by putting shims under the mandrel mounting blocks. Then check horizontal alignment by putting the sensing tip against the side of the rod. Correct runout here by loosening the mandrel mounting bolts and repositioning the mandrel slightly. This is a trial-and-error process that should be continued until no runout is indicated. Mount the table and clamp the indicator to the drill rod to test the table for vertical alignment. Finally, install the fence so it's at right angles to the spindle's horizontal travel. □

Michael Rekoff is a professor of electrical engineering at the University of Tennessee at Chattanooga. He wrote about building a stroke sander in FWW #3, p. 46. Photos by the author.

Using the Tablesaw
Some basic rules for safe, accurate results

by Ian J. Kirby

Ripping is the tablesaw's forte, but it's a versatile machine, used for dimensioning wood as well as for cutting joints. The tablesaw is so simple and universal that it is frequently used without the operator's ever having taken the time to learn its common-sense fundamentals. In most small shops the tablesaw usually has improper guards and an inadequate rip fence. In the interest of keeping fingers attached to hands, a review of tablesaw basics may be of value.

The ordinary tablesaw is nothing more than a steel table with a circular blade projecting through its surface. The blade projection is adjustable for cutting wood of varying thicknesses. The blade can be fixed perpendicular to the table, or it can be tilted for cutting wood at an angle.

For safety's sake, tablesaws need a blade guard, though even the best guard can't keep fingers out of the blade. A guard should serve as a visual reference to the blade's location, warning the sawyer of the danger zone—any point within 9 in. of the blade. The best guard is mounted on an arm suspended above the blade. The guard should not be attached to the riving knife or splitter, and it should be adjustable, set as close as possible over the stock being sawn. There are several variations of this mounting method and any guard is better than no guard.

The machine's electrical power switch should be easy to reach, mounted on the saw cabinet just under the table or on a nearby wall or post. When switching on, place one finger on the start button and a second on the stop button. This allows for a quick shutoff if something goes wrong. A foot-activated switch allows the sawyer to control the wood with both hands while operating the switch. Many saws have mechanical or electrical brakes that stop the blade quickly when the switch is turned off. In the absence of a brake, use two push sticks—one rubbing each side of the blade—to stop its coasting. When changing rip-fence settings never stick a tape or rule between a moving blade and the fence. Wait until the blade has completely stopped. The saw depth of cut should be set so the blade protrudes about ½ in. out of the workpiece. Carbide-tipped blades should be adjusted so the entire tooth projects above the wood during the cut. A 10-in. saw should be operated at 3,000 to 3,500 RPM at the arbor, or at a speed that runs the blade's periphery at 10,000 feet per minute.

Noise can be a major barrier to safe machine operation. The racket muddles thought and can force the operator to adopt timid and unsafe working practices. So ear protection—as well as goggles—should always be worn when using the saw. To concentrate without the distraction, the novice woodworker can develop safe habits by practicing moving wood past the blade with the machine switched off.

Ian J. Kirby is a consulting editor to this magazine. He teaches woodworking and design in North Bennington, Vt. Drawings by the author.

Fig. 1: Stance

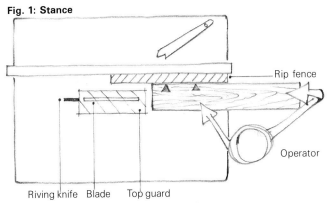

Rip fence

Operator

Riving knife   Blade   Top guard

Stand to one side of the blade when ripping. Hold the work against the fence with the left hand, feed with the right.

Fig. 2: Guard, knife and fence

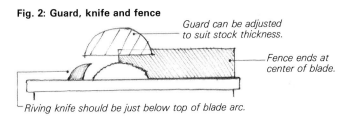

Guard can be adjusted to suit stock thickness.

Fence ends at center of blade.

Riving knife should be just below top of blade arc.

Proper stance is also important to safe tablesaw operation. When ripping or crosscutting, the operator should stand with his weight equally distributed on both feet. Stand to one side of the sawblade to stay out of harm's way and to have a better view of the cut. Figure 1 shows a good position—during ripping, kickbacks can be hurled from the saw like spears and you could be skewered.

Because the tablesaw is at its best when used for ripping, the rip fence is its most vital attachment. The fence should be mounted parallel to the blade. Whether it's used on the right or left side of the blade is the preference of the operator. Virtually all of the tablesaws sold in the United States have rip fences extending the full length of the saw table. This fence forces the wood to remain in contact with the back of the blade during the rip, thus inviting binding, burning and kickbacks, particularly when cutting refractory wood. The fence should end at the front of the blade, just where the cut is completed. This allows both pieces to move clear of the blade for safer, cleaner results. The quickest fix for tablesaws equipped with a full length fence is to fit them with a board ending at the center of the blade, as in figure 2. Actually, it's good practice to mount a board on the steel fence of any machine. This will prevent damage if the blade accidentally touches the fence.

To keep the kerf from closing up and pinching the blade during ripping, tablesaws should have a riving knife or splitter mounted in line with and just beyond the back of the blade. The knife is a fin-shaped piece of steel, tapered in sec-

Fig. 3: Ripping

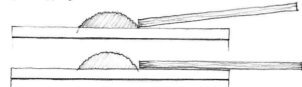

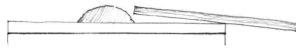

Feed the stock angled to the rear or flat against the table, above.

Never start the cut with the front of the board elevated, below.

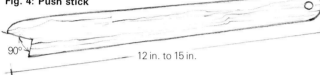

Fig. 4: Push stick

90°

12 in. to 15 in.

Make push stick of solid wood or plywood, ⅜ in. to ½ in. thick.

Fig. 5: Crosscutting

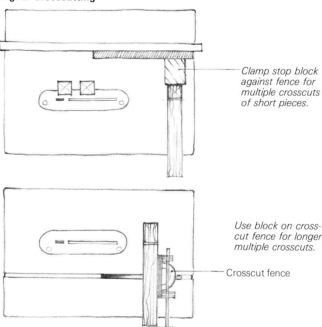

Clamp stop block against fence for multiple crosscuts of short pieces.

Use block on crosscut fence for longer multiple crosscuts.

Crosscut fence

Fig. 6: Miters

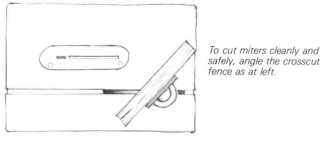

To cut miters cleanly and safely, angle the crosscut fence as at left.

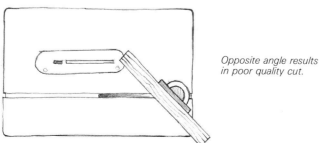

Opposite angle results in poor quality cut.

tion and as thick at its back edge as the kerf is wide. It should be permanently mounted at a height just below the top of the blade's arc, as in figure 2. The knife should maintain this relationship to the blade for every cutting depth. Some saws, particularly the cheaper variety, have no riving knife at all, but the payback in safety and improved cutting makes it worth the effort to install one.

When ripping, the wood should be offered to the blade very gently at first, especially when using carbide-tipped sawblades, whose teeth are brittle and can break under heavy impacts. Feed the board into the saw flat against the sawtable or angled as in figure 3. Never touch the board to the blade with its front end tilted above the table, or the blade will grab the stock and slam it to the table. Make sure a push stick is handy before starting any cut; keep one on the sawtable on the opposite side of the fence. Figure 4 shows a simple push stick design. Keep plenty of sticks around—their absence is no excuse for a missing finger. With the cut started, hold the wood against the fence with your left hand (if the fence is to the right of the blade), while feeding the stock into the blade with your right hand. As the rip progresses, make sure you hold the board firmly against the fence. Keep your eye on the contact point between board and fence—some wood may tend to run away from the fence during the cut. Feed into the saw at an even rate. If fed too slowly, the blade will burn in the kerf, while too quick a feed will stall the saw. Never move your left hand beyond the leading edge of the blade. This is unsafe and merely pushes the waste to the blade, not the stock to the fence. As the cut nears its end, remove your left hand from the wood and use a push stick to complete the rip.

If the saw stalls during a rip, withdraw the wood quickly, or turn off the saw immediately—a good reason to have a foot-operated switch. It isn't advisable to rip warped or twisted boards, but when you must, crosscut the stock into the shortest lengths possible, and then rip with the concave side of the board up, so the wood is level with the table as it meets the blade. Rip a cupped board as close to its center as possible and exert even pressure, to minimize rocking during the cut. Long boards or large panels should be cut with the help of a second person, or use a table or roller on the saw's off-feed side for support. The sawyer's helper should clearly understand that his job is only to support the stock (keeping it level with the table and parallel to the blade) as it comes off the saw and not to pull it through—he could pull the sawyer's hands into the blade. When the cut is complete, the takeoff man then takes control of both pieces.

Wood is crosscut on the tablesaw with the miter gauge or crosscut fence. This angle-adjustable attachment usually runs in grooves milled in the table surface parallel to the blade. The fence must slide smoothly in the grooves. A board about 12 in. in length can be attached to the crosscut fence to offer more support to the stock. Crosscut fences are sometimes equipped with clamps to stop the work from slewing as it is fed through the blade.

Crosscutting should be done from the same stance as ripping. To test 90° crosscuts, cut a test piece and check it with a square rather than attempting to square the blade directly to the crosscut fence. With the crosscut fence set, hold the stock firmly against it while advancing the wood evenly into the blade. Only practice will reveal the best way to grip the stock against the fence. When the cut is complete, move the crosscut fence beyond the back edge of the blade or back to the starting point. To avoid binding the stock against the blade, slide the wood slightly away from the blade as the crosscut fence is returned. Small stock may have to be clamped to the crosscut fence to be crosscut safely. To crosscut many parts to the same length, clamp a stopping block to the rip fence ahead of the blade as in figure 5, or attach a stop block to the crosscut fence. Never bring the rip fence over to stop the

length of a crosscut, as the cut piece is liable to lodge between the fence and the blade, and bind or kick back.

For 45° miters make a test cut to set the crosscut fence accurately. Grip the stock firmly and feed it into the saw as shown in figure 6, the blade shearing with the grain. Because of the fibrous nature of wood, mitering it from the opposite direction results in a cut of lesser quality. □

Choosing a blade

Which blade for which cut? That's the first problem the woodworker faces when using the tablesaw. You want to rip and crosscut, leaving smooth, tear-out-free edges on solid wood or plywood. No blade does everything well. Many types of blades are available but you need only a few to start out.

There are two categories of readily available sawblades: those made of carbon steel alloyed with nickel and chrome and those of steel with tungsten-carbide tips brazed on to form the teeth. New steel blades are inexpensive, and although they dull quickly, you can resharpen them yourself. For information on sharpening, see *FWW* #10, p. 80. Carbide blades cost more and cut smoother, but you must send them out for sharpening. You have to weigh cost against use—carbide blades are preferred for repeated high-quality cuts.

Alloy steel blades—There are three basic types of steel blade: rip, crosscut and combination. These blades can have spring-set or hollow-ground teeth. Teeth on most steel blades are ground in the same way—with the tops of the teeth alternately beveled, and the fronts left flat or beveled. Set—the alternate and uniform bending of teeth to the right and left—creates clearance for the blade during cutting. This keeps the blade cool and prevents binding and burning. For ripping heavy wood to rough dimensions use a hefty alloy steel rip blade (figure 1) with a lot of set and 20 to 40 teeth. The thicker the wood, the fewer the teeth. This blade will produce a quick but fairly rough cut with little binding or burning. Rough crosscutting can be done with a steel crosscut blade with 40 to 60 teeth (figure 2), but a combination blade (figure 3) will do the job just as well. Combination blades, designed to rip and crosscut, are a good value for the money. They have four alternating front-beveled teeth followed by a flat or raker tooth with a deep gullet to clear sawdust quickly and prevent overheating. Properly sharpened and set, a combination blade will work well for most general purpose work.

The hollow-ground combination blade (figure 4) tends to be a smoother cutting blade than the spring-set. This blade has about the same number of teeth as the combination, but its teeth have no set. The body of the blade below the gullets is ground thinner than the teeth so the saw won't bind. Tolerances for a hollow-ground blade are small—it must be accurately cut and sharpened to work well, otherwise it will bind and burn.

Tungsten-carbide blades—Plywood, particleboard and solid wood impose different loads on a sawblade. Carbide blades are better for plywood and particleboard. For a given type of blade, sharp carbide almost always produces a smoother cut than sharp steel, and because it is harder, carbide stays sharper longer than steel does. Carbide blades don't have set, and usually the tops rather than the fronts of the teeth are ground. A good general purpose carbide combination blade for solid wood and man-made boards (figure 5) should have between 40 and 60 teeth ground in a series of four alternately top-beveled teeth, followed by a flat or raker tooth. If you can afford only one carbide blade, this is the type to buy.

For ripping only, a 24-tooth carbide blade with flat-ground teeth (figure 6) is excellent. If you need to cut plastic sheets or laminates, choose a 50 to 70-tooth carbide blade that has alternating triple-beveled teeth with a raker tooth in between (figure 7). Properly sharpened and maintained, all carbide blades leave a smooth, almost finished surface. For more information on saws and blades see *FWW* #23, pp. 72-75 and #24. pp. 48 and 49. —*I.J.K.*

Alloy steel blades

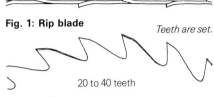

Fig. 1: Rip blade

Teeth are set.

20 to 40 teeth

File teeth faces perpendicular to blade.

Fig. 2: Crosscut blade

40 to 60 teeth

File teeth faces with alternating bevels.

Fig. 3: Combination blade

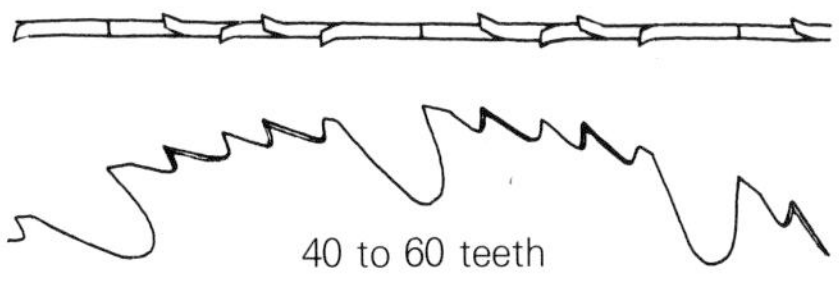

40 to 60 teeth

Raker tooth, with deep gullet, clears chips.

Fig. 4: Hollow-ground combination

Blade body below teeth is ground thinner (here exaggerated). Teeth have no set.

Carbide-tipped blades

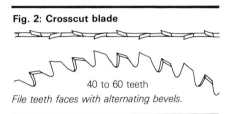

Fig. 5: Carbide combination

40 to 60 teeth

Four alternating top-beveled teeth are preceded by flat-ground, raker tooth.

Fig. 6: Carbide rip

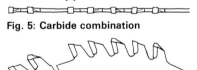

24 flat or raker teeth

Fig. 7: Carbide triple-chip

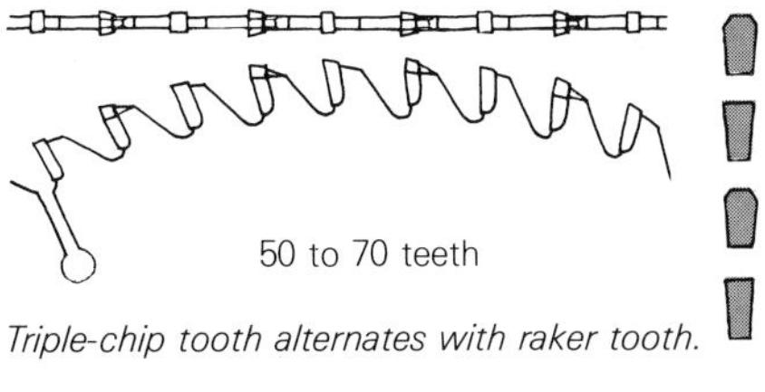

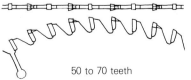

50 to 70 teeth

Triple-chip tooth alternates with raker tooth.

Shop-Built Panel Saw
Cutting plywood sheets down to size

by William F. Nelson

The counterbalanced saw carriage rides on steel-tube guide bars. U-bolts sheathed with short lengths of steel tubing act as bearings.

To support my woodworking hobby I practice architecture. Last year when we decided to move our offices, I offered to build the cabinets, and my partners accepted the proposal without hesitation. After drawing the cabinets and working up the bill of materials, which called for 75 sheets of plywood, I suddenly realized that my small shop had neither the space nor the equipment to handle that volume of material. Despite awful visions of wrestling dozens of cumbersome pieces of plywood around the shop and over the table saw, I was committed to the project and had to proceed.

A couple of weeks before, I had been in a woodworking-equipment store in Houston. One of the things that had caught my attention was a panel saw, the kind with a vertical frame for holding large panels and with a circular saw mounted in a sliding carriage. I certainly couldn't afford to spend the $850 the thing cost, so I decided to make one.

I began by making a freehand sketch of the frame and the saw carriage, and was able to solve most of the construction problems on paper. The basic triangulated framework was fabricated from ordinary thin-walled electrical conduit and Unistrut steel channels, which I bought from an industrial supply store. Unistrut channels are commonly used to build warehouse shelving units and pipe racks. Because I have an acetylene welding rig, I decided to braze the metal parts of the frame together (figure 1a), but you could make it just as strong by using an assembly of wood top and bottom rails drilled to receive the vertical tubing members, fastening them together with sheet-metal screws through the back side of the wood into the tubing (figure 2). The framework must be rigid; it shouldn't rack or twist.

When the metalworking was done, I added the horizontal wooden strips and the wooden stock-support shelf at the bottom. I fastened the wood to the metal tubing with countersunk sheet-metal screws, which meant drilling pilot holes through one wall of the tubing. Be sure that the support shelf is perfectly straight and square to the frame. The saw carriage must clear the shelf and the blade must travel through it to complete the cut; the measurements given in the drawing accommodate 4x8 panels. For metric size plywood (about 5 ft. square), make the frame 1 ft. taller.

The part of the design that gave me trouble was the sliding saw carriage and guide bars. It was easy enough to make and attach the tubular guide bars to the frame, but providing for sliding bearings between the carriage and the bars was another matter. Finally I decided to use U-bolts on the carriage sides and to reduce friction and binding against the guide bars by making roller bearings from short lengths of stainless-steel tubing, whose inside diameter was the right size to fit over the U-bolts (detail A).

The guide bars are attached to the center tubular uprights at the top by means of right-angle flanges, threaded rod and nuts, as shown in detail B. The flanges can be either brazed or bolted to the uprights. Nuts on the threaded rod allow the guide bars to be adjusted so that the saw carriage will travel at a precise 90° to the base on which the workpiece rests, with no play between carriage and guide bars. At the bottom of the frame, the guide bars are fastened with a threaded rod to a ⅛-in. steel plate which is attached to the Unistrut bottom rail.

The saw carriage itself was the only part that I couldn't make in my shop. Because the design required channel-shaped flanges at each side to accommodate the U-bolts, I had to have it bent (brake-formed) in a sheet-metal shop. Two pulleys at the top of the uprights (one of them is fastened to an arm that is welded to the frame) and a counterweight complete the saw-carriage assembly. Without the counterweight, the saw is difficult to manage and will not stay at the top of the frame while you position the stock. To determine the exact weight to counterbalance the saw, I experimented with a plastic gallon jug filled with water.

My inexpensive 7¼-in. circular saw bolts to the carriage through the saw's base and is reinforced by a hose clamp and 18-ga. steel strap around the motor housing. I use a carbide-tipped blade because the glues in plywood and particleboard quickly dull standard blades. I installed a toggle switch at the top of the frame so I can pull the saw into the cut with the tubular crossmember on the carriage rather than by grasping the trigger switch in the plastic handle. I connected the saw to my dust collection system by setting a 3-in.-to-4-in. step-up PVC drain coupling astride the sawblade housing; a flexible hose fits snugly into the 4-in. part of the coupling (see photo above).

The saw is easy to use, and will produce accurate finish cuts the full width of a 4x8 plywood panel. It has been a real timesaver, too. Without rushing I was able to cut seven sheets of plywood into 62 finished pieces in 90 min. My cabinetmaking project took only 10 weeks, working evenings and weekends. During that time I also built myself a desk and credenza. I have since found the panel saw useful in ways I hadn't anticipated. Because it cuts at a perfect 90°, it's just the right tool for crosscutting long boards. With casters, the saw can be moved around the shop and then stored where it's least in the way. □

William F. Nelson lives in Beaumont, Texas. Photo and drawings by the author.

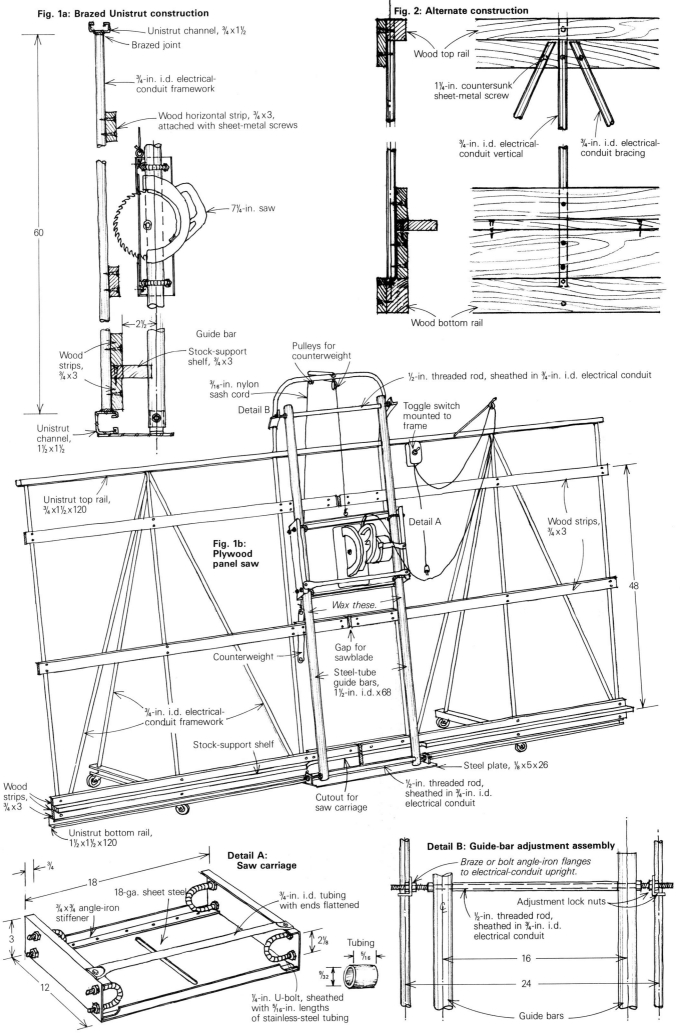

Fig. 1a: Brazed Unistrut construction

Unistrut channel, ¾ × 1½

Brazed joint

¾-in. i.d. electrical-conduit framework

Wood horizontal strip, ¾ × 3, attached with sheet-metal screws

7¼-in. saw

60

2½

Guide bar

Wood strips, ¾ × 3

Stock-support shelf, ¾ × 3

Unistrut channel, 1½ × 1½

Fig. 2: Alternate construction

Wood top rail

1¼-in. countersunk sheet-metal screw

¾-in. i.d. electrical-conduit vertical

¾-in. i.d. electrical-conduit bracing

Wood bottom rail

Pulleys for counterweight

Detail B

³⁄₁₆-in. nylon sash cord

½-in. threaded rod, sheathed in ¾-in. i.d. electrical conduit

Toggle switch mounted to frame

Detail A

Wood strips, ¾ × 3

Unistrut top rail, ¾ × 1½ × 120

Fig. 1b: Plywood panel saw

Wax these.

Gap for sawblade

Steel-tube guide bars, 1½-in. i.d. × 68

Counterweight

¾-in. i.d. electrical-conduit framework

Stock-support shelf

Cutout for saw carriage

48

Steel plate, ⅛ × 5 × 26

½-in. threaded rod, sheathed in ¾-in. i.d. electrical conduit

Wood strips, ¾ × 3

Unistrut bottom rail, 1½ × 1½ × 120

Detail A: Saw carriage

¾

18

18-ga. sheet steel

¾ × ¾ angle-iron stiffener

3

12

¾-in. i.d. tubing with ends flattened

2⅛

Tubing

⁵⁄₁₆

⁹⁄₃₂

¼-in. U-bolt, sheathed with ⁵⁄₁₆-in. lengths of stainless-steel tubing

Detail B: Guide-bar adjustment assembly

Braze or bolt angle-iron flanges to electrical-conduit upright.

Adjustment lock nuts

½-in. threaded rod, sheathed in ¾-in. i.d. electrical conduit

16

24

Guide bars

49

Woodworking Injuries
A hand surgeon looks at how accidents happen

by Dr. E. Jeff Justis

Woodworkers relish the feel of a tenon sliding into its mortise, and the smooth texture of a newly finished piece of furniture. Our fingertips are so sensitive that we can feel blemishes and flaws in our woodwork that are too slight to be perceived by the eye. Where would we be without these sophisticated sensors? Human evolution is, in part, the result of our early manipulation of our environment with our hands, and this is perhaps at the root of the creative impulses that make woodworking so satisfying.

It's no wonder, then, that people who have severely injured a hand or lost a limb often have emotional difficulty adjusting to their impairment. In fact, sometimes psychiatric care must supplement physical therapy. As a woodworker and a hand surgeon who has seen too many injuries, I am vividly aware of the risk in using power tools. I've also come to realize that virtually all injuries are preventable.

I have treated many patients with hand injuries inflicted by woodworking tools. Surprisingly, about one-third of all accident victims seen in hospital emergency rooms have an injury to the arm or hand. A 1964 study in England found that woodworking tools are responsible for most industrial injuries. Even so, research has not been done on the question of which tools are the most dangerous; hospitals don't generally obtain such information, and medical personnel don't always know the differences among various tools. A medical report may attribute an injury to a handsaw when in fact the injured patient was using a portable circular saw. I've never been injured by my tablesaw or my portable circular saw, but my own experience as a surgeon clearly suggests that circular saws account for the majority of serious hand injuries among woodworkers. I routinely discuss the mechanism of injury with patients, and I have concluded that there are three major causes of serious injuries from a power tool: inattention through repetition, an unanticipated happening, and inexperience or overconfidence. Many accidents involve some combination of the three, not to mention bad judgment brought on by fatigue (see p. 52).

Inattention through repetition—A woodworker performing a number of repetitive cuts, such as a series of crosscuts to length, may become dangerously inattentive. The whine of the machine and the repetitious physical movement can lull the worker in an almost hypnotic way. A tragic example comes to mind: A cabinetmaker with 20 years of experience in a local shop was making repetitive cuts with a radial-arm saw, using his left hand to feed the stock and his right to pull the saw through. In an instant, his right hand moved too fast for his left, and the saw passed over his hand, severing all four fingers of his left hand just above the knuckles but sparing his thumb. Although his ability was permanently im-

E. Jeff Justis is a hand surgeon in Memphis, Tenn.

paired, the man was able to resume woodworking by, as he put it, "doing the best I can under the circumstances, but I never realized how important my left hand was until this happened." Another patient, who severed his thumb just beyond the base joint in a similar accident, told me afterward that he had never been aware of how much he used his left thumb, especially when trying to hold work against the miter gauge of a tablesaw or the fence of a radial-arm saw.

Interestingly, a 1975 study of 1,071 hand-injury patients showed that although 90% of them were right-handed, their injuries were nearly evenly divided between right and left hands. In virtually every case, the fingers bore the brunt of the injury. Inattention through repetition seems most likely to occur in the production shop, but all woodworkers must avoid being complacent when working with machines. It pays to pause deliberately after every couple of repeat operations to refocus on the task and to carry on with full awareness—a habit that can be acquired.

An unanticipated happening—Power cutting tools operate at high speeds. When something goes afoul, it occurs quickly and surprisingly. Kickbacks caused by binding are a common unanticipated event that can quickly draw fingers into a blade. Putting the fingers too near the blade can result in unpleasant surprises. One patient of mine recently reached with his left hand beyond the sawblade to catch a waste strip. The strip began to slide backward, and as he attempted to catch it, he caught his thumb on the sawblade. Fortunately, the blade was set just above the level of the board and his thumb wasn't severed. But a tendon and two nerves were cut, and although he has regained motion, sensation in his thumb will never be the same. Many of us forget that the regenerative capacity of the human body is limited. Any cut into the sub-dermal layer, no matter how well healed and painless, leaves a scar that is not normal tissue. Thus, a hand that suffers a major injury cannot be fully restored. Even a small cut, on the wrist for example, can result in a nerve injury that is the functional equivalent of an amputation.

Many times an unanticipated event will occur through inexperience, poor planning or a lack of understanding of how tools and machines work. For example, it should be obvious that trying to shape a small piece without a guard or a jig can end in disaster. Jointers can mangle fingers when the operator attempts to machine a small piece. Similarly, failure to anticipate the "breaking through" of the bandsaw blade can result in an injured finger. As a youngster, I recall slicing through the pulp of my left thumb with a scroll saw when the blade passed quickly through a soft spot in the puzzle I was making. My attention was so focused on guiding the saw accurately that I failed to anticipate its moving through the wood so fast. The same can happen with hand tools, particularly sharp edge-cutting tools such as chisels and planes. A cut

A quick way to lose fingers is by passing small pieces over the jointer, above left. Don't machine stock shorter than 12 in., use a push stick and leave the cutterhead guard in place. Some tablesaw operators hold their thumbs near the blade during a rip, as in the photo above. An unanticipated kickback can pull the thumb into the spinning blade. The drill press, left, seems like a benign tool. But when haste wins out over safety, it can do considerable damage in short order. Always clamp the stock being drilled. Bandsawing small pieces is risky enough, but in the photo at right the operator will be in for a painful surprise when the blade breaks through the stock and into his finger.

from a sharp chisel is less traumatic than a severed finger, but both are painful. Yet with attention and care, both injuries can be avoided.

Inexperience or overconfidence—Some general accident studies show that the greatest incidence of injury occurs at two extremes of experience: the rank novice and the highly expert. I've seen many young patients who had summer jobs requiring the use of radial-arm saws, jointers or tablesaws. Within days of beginning work, they sustained serious hand injuries. One young man was using a tablesaw under pressure from his supervisor to keep his speed up while ripping boards. When a board jammed between fence and blade, it pulled his hand into the blade. His index finger was so mangled that it had to be amputated. Fortunately, with reconstructive surgery, he regained acceptable use of his middle finger and hand. Not surprisingly, however, his enthusiasm for woodworking and tools was forever diminished. In his case, the combination of inexperience, repetitive motion and an unanticipated event had tragic results.

At the other end of the scale, a high school shop teacher with 20 years of experience had grown so accustomed to using his tablesaw that he thought nothing of making routine passes with his thumb just millimeters away from the blade. A sudden grabbing of the wood pulled his right thumb into the blade, instantly severing the tip of that digit. Experience,

though a good teacher, can lead us to believe we know more than we do, and the subsequent risks we are willing to take can cost us dearly. Even seemingly harmless tools such as the drill press can do grievous damage if they are misused or treated with less respect than they deserve.

The experiences I've described here, no matter how grisly, can teach us important lessons about safety. You can't avoid repetitive operations when using machinery—particularly in production shops. But you can be alert to the hypnotic effect of this type of activity and you can teach yourself to be constantly vigilant. Keep fresh by breaking up a long routine of cutting or machining with another, less redundant operation. And never work around machines when you are tired or under the influence of alcohol or drugs that might make you drowsy.

By definition, the unanticipated happening can't be predicted. Using common sense and a bit of ingenuity, however, will ensure that your hands are out of the way when such events do occur. Build jigs and fixtures to keep the wood under control and your hands well away from cutters and blades. Don't alter or ignore the machinery's own built-in safety devices. And keep the workshop liberally supplied with push sticks—it's far better to have them or a project chewed up than to lose one of your fingers. Push sticks can be made by the dozens and projects can be started over, but damage to the hands may be irreparable, and lost function is an impairment to be carried forever. *(continued next page)*

"It was over in a millisecond..."

by Paul Bertorelli

What Rame Nelson remembers most vividly about losing three fingers is how quickly it happened:

"It was over in a millisecond...I was ripping the piece and the next thing I knew my fingers were gone and one of them was lying there on the tablesaw. It's kind of funny, it wasn't all that painful...just a hell of a shock at seeing my fingers gone." When I visited him in the hospital last February, just a week after his accident, Nelson had still not quelled his disbelief, and he was only beginning to understand how his accident had happened.

Nelson was working late that night, pushing himself hard to finish a chest for display in the Michigan Woodworkers Guild show set to open two days later. While plunge-ripping a maple board on the tablesaw for the chest's base, Nelson missed his mark slightly. To line it up, he inched the board backward, with the rotation of the sawblade. "I was using my right hand to push it against the fence," he told me, "and I had my left hand on top of it. The thing caught the blade and pulled my hand right into it."

The damage was extensive. The sawblade raggedly severed at the knuckle the little and ring fingers on Nelson's left hand. He lost his middle finger nearly at its base. As such injuries go, Nelson was actually lucky. His father happened to be working with him at the time, and his shop in Walled Lake, Mich., is only 40 miles from Detroit's Harper-Grace Hospital, a leading center for the treatment of hand injuries.

In his 13 years of woodworking, Nelson has considered the prospect of injury, even having gone so far as to post the names and numbers of hand surgeons by his telephone. "My first reaction was that I would bleed to death. In my panic, I didn't think to call anyone...I just wrapped my hand in a rag and we headed for the hospital." In their hasty departure, the two men collected Nelson's severed middle finger but missed his ring finger—which had landed on the jointer five feet away. His mangled little finger had been hurled into the recesses of the shop.

Three hours later, Nelson was in surgery at Harper-Grace Hospital. His surgeon, Dr. Ronald Rusko, decided that only the middle finger could be saved. The other two fingers, retrieved later by Nelson's brother-in-law, were too chewed up to work with. Peering through a microscope and using sutures small enough to pass through a human hair, Dr. Rusko painstakingly spliced the severed digital tendons, nerves and blood vessels in Nelson's hand. A steel pin was used to join the shattered bone. By the time I visited Nelson in the hospital, signs of healing were already evident. Although the reattached finger was still completely bandaged, he could feel sensation returning to it. And with the healing came the "phantom limb" effect, the eerie attempt by the nervous system to convince the brain that the missing extremities were still there.

Dr. Rusko considers the operation a success, and when I talked to Nelson in June he reported steady but slow healing. "It's weird, though," Nelson said. "I can't believe how often I reach for something and come up short." Reattachment microsurgery has been practiced only since the mid-1970s, and though much progress has been made, it cannot work miracles. "In general terms, no reattached limb is ever going to be normal. The worse the injury, the worse the outcome is going to be functionally," Dr. Rusko told me. Patients can expect stiffness, weakness and extreme sensitivity to cold in salvaged fingers. Sometimes, reattachment isn't worth the effort; surgeons frequently counsel against single-finger reattachment because the patient can often regain more use from a limber, well-formed stump than from a stiff replant. Nelson's middle finger was reattached because the doctor figured he stood a good chance of gaining rather than hindering function. Most reattachments require more surgery later, to remove scar tissue around tendons and nerves which can make the replant stiff and useless. Not surprisingly, injuries that are clean-cut offer the best prospects for success.

With his practice located amidst hundreds of auto and manufacturing plants, Dr. Rusko sees his share of the bloodiest hand injuries, and Nelson's outcome is fairly typical. Others, however, can't count on being as fortunate. Time is important in reattachment, and since not every hospital is equipped to do this type of microsurgery, the closest help may be hours away. Depending on the circumstances, severed fingers can be replanted up to 12 hours or more after the injury, but the longer the wait, the fewer the surgeon's choices. Dr. Rusko says the injured person can help himself most by keeping his wits after the injury. You aren't likely to bleed to death even after losing several fingers. Sterile dressings kept in the shop can be used to wrap the injured hand for the trip to the hospital. Apply direct pressure to the wound (tourniquets are rarely necessary) and elevate the hand higher than the heart. As gruesome as it may be, you've got to pick up the lost fingers and carry them with you to the hospital in a container or a clean towel. Don't bother with any topical treatments like iodine or ointments. Nelson's list of hand surgeons near the phone is a good idea, but it's even better to know the location of the closest hospital equipped to do microsurgery.

Even the best surgeon and a quick trip to the hospital after the injury, however, fall far short of avoiding the accident in the first place. This point is not lost on Rame Nelson. "I'm embarrassed that I could do something so stupid. I've always had a second nature about safety and I'm still surprised this could happen to me."

Sitting in Nelson's hospital room, I couldn't help thinking about all the times I've worked late or done crazy things with machines while trying to finish a job in a hurry. I've taken false comfort in my lack of injury, but now I wonder if my intact hands are due more to dumb luck than to skill and good sense. The point isn't lost on me either. Next time I feel brain-fade from exhaustion, I'll turn out the shop lights and try again the next day. □

Router jigs for making molding

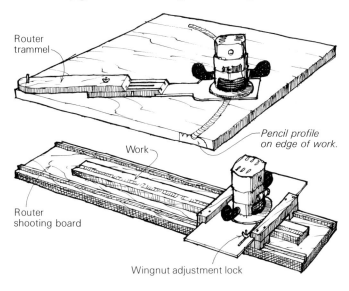

Router trammel

Pencil profile on edge of work.

Work

Router shooting board

Wingnut adjustment lock

The sketches above show two jigs which, when used with a portable router, can produce both semicircular and straight molding in patterns difficult to produce with a shaper. The first jig is an adjustable router trammel used to make curved molding. The jig's two-part base adjusts by means of a slot-and-track arrangement and locks with a bolt and wingnut. The router is screwed to a ¼-in. hardboard foot which is, in turn, screwed to the base.

The second jig consists of a sliding adjustable router holder and a "shooting board" which has two parallel tracks. The slotted hardboard in the holder allows the router to be adjusted laterally.

To use these jigs, first pencil the molding profile on the edge of the workpiece. Position the work and the jig so the router is right over the molding. Take repeated cuts adjusting the bit depth, changing bits and adjusting the router's lateral position as needed. When all the routing is complete, separate the curved molding from the waste stock with a bandsaw. Some sanding is necessary to finish the molding.

—*S. Gaines Stubbins, Birmingham, Ala.*

Producing round tabletops on the lathe

Here's how I use my lathe and a sanding disc to produce a perfectly round tabletop. First locate the center of the tabletop blank and cut it roughly to shape. Now cut a short length of

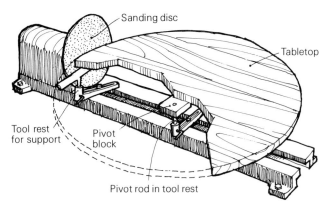

Sanding disc

Tabletop

Tool rest for support

Pivot block

Pivot rod in tool rest

metal rod that can be held in your tool-rest base. Using a bit the same size as the rod, drill part way through a piece of 2-in. scrap. Screw or clamp the scrap block to the underside of the tabletop at its center. Now mount the work on the lathe's tool rest with the block and the rod acting as a pivot. To level

and support the work near the sanding disc, mount another tool rest parallel to and about 1 in. from the disc.

Now turn on the lathe and rotate the tabletop against the disc. If the pivot turns out off-center, loosen the tool rest. Advance the work and finish the entire circumference to the shortest radius. —*Robert S. Maxwell, Washington, D.C.*

Making sectional molding

Sectional molding for cabinet doors is easy to make on the tablesaw and lathe. Cut the straight sections on the tablesaw with a molding head. To make the semicircular section at each corner, remove the cutter from the molding head and bolt it to a heavy strap-iron handle. This provides a scraping tool for shaping a circle on the lathe's faceplate. Separate the molding from the waste wood with a parting chisel. Then cut each of the four corner sections from the circle at the proper miter angle. —*Duane Waskow, Cedar Rapids, Iowa*

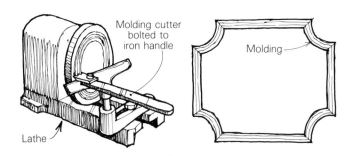

Molding cutter bolted to iron handle

Molding

Lathe

Auxiliary tailstock for boring

To bore holes through lamp bases and similar turned items, I made an auxiliary tailstock to hold the work so I could pass a long drill bit through the regular tailstock. The key feature of this special tailstock is the bearing from a bicycle crank hanger. This bearing has a 1-in. bore, so I turn a 1-in. tenon on the end of my lamps to fit it. The rest of the device consists of a ¼-in. thick aluminum-plate upright, a short section of 1-in. angle-iron base to span the lathe ways, and a wooden dog, which tightens under the ways to lock the unit in place. To keep wood chips out of the bearing, I turned a cover for the bearing that also holds the bearing in the upright.

In use, the ram from the tailstock is removed and the drill bit is passed through the tailstock into the lamp, which is supported in the auxiliary tailstock.

—*Ralph Luman, Virginia Beach, Va.*

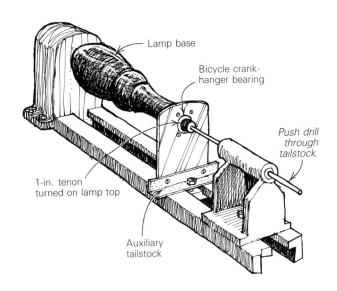

Lamp base

Bicycle crank-hanger bearing

Push drill through tailstock.

1-in. tenon turned on lamp top

Auxiliary tailstock

TURNING, CARVING

The Taming of the Skew
Subtlety, not force, wins favor

by Mike Darlow

For each piece of wood, an efficient turner employs the minimum number of tools, each, if possible, only once. This means being able to use each tool for a variety of cuts. No tool in a turner's kit has greater potential for this than the skew chisel—it planes surfaces smooth, cuts balls and beads, defines fillets and even makes coves, working all the while with a precise, responsive touch—yet the skew has a reputation for being the most unforgiving and unpredictable turning tool. It requires large, confident movements to slice its thin shavings, but a single small movement in the wrong direction can cause the tool to dig in and ruin the work. Indeed, the *Fine Woodworking Design Books* confirm, to my eye, that many turners deliberately avoid cuts requiring the skew, compromising on the preferred design in order to be able to use a gouge or scraper. If you slice with a skew instead of scraping, you will cut cleaner and produce finished work faster. We can create confidence in the skew by understanding the tool's geometry and practicing the various cuts.

Tool geometry—The skew is a long, straight-bladed chisel with its cutting edge ground at an angle to produce two very different points—an acute one called the long point, and an obtuse one called the short point (figure 1). There are two bevels, usually equal, ground on the sides of the tool to form the cutting edge. Perpendicular to the sides are two edges: one

leading to the long point, called the long edge, and one leading to the short point, called the short edge.

For consistency, it is essential that the skew's sides are truly parallel, so that the cutting edge can be parallel to both of them, and that the long and short edges are at 90° to the sides. The width of the sides defines the nominal size of the skew, and sizes vary between ¼ in. and 2 in. Most general turning is done using a ¾-in. or 1-in. skew. This is a compromise between a long cutting edge (an advantage in planing) and narrow sides (which allow work in tight places). If a constricted space dictates using a smaller tool for part of the work, a production turner must decide whether to use a small skew for the whole job, or to pick up two or more different skews. If there is a large proportion of planing in the work, the turner will probably use two. Where a skew with sides narrower than ¼ in. is required, it is preferable to grind the long edge down at the end to make a shorter cutting edge in order to preserve reasonable stiffness. The minimum thickness of a skew should be ¼ in., or else the tool will be flexible and hence dangerous.

An important advantage of the skewed cutting edge is that this skewness provides a clearance angle for making certain cuts. When the tool is correctly shaped and sharpened, you can make the finishing cut on a shoulder, for instance, without the skew digging in. Set the skew's long edge flat on the

---

Fig. 1: The geometry of a skew chisel

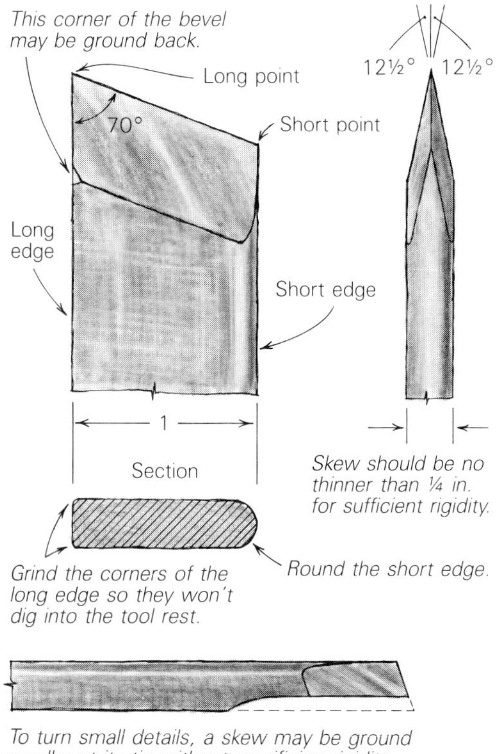

This corner of the bevel may be ground back.

Long point

70°

Short point

12½° 12½°

Long edge

Short edge

1

Section

Skew should be no thinner than ¼ in. for sufficient rigidity.

Round the short edge.

Grind the corners of the long edge so they won't dig into the tool rest.

To turn small details, a skew may be ground smaller at its tip without sacrificing rigidity.

Fig. 2: Squaring a shoulder using the long point

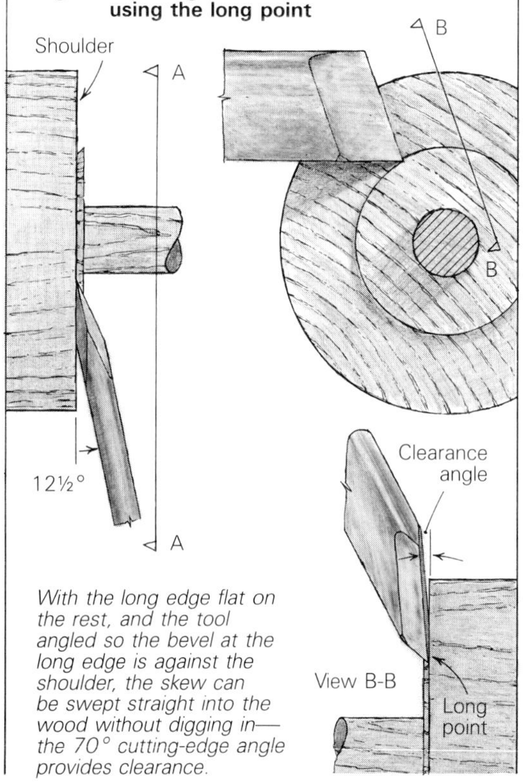

Shoulder

A

A

12½°

With the long edge flat on the rest, and the tool angled so the bevel at the long edge is against the shoulder, the skew can be swept straight into the wood without digging in— the 70° cutting-edge angle provides clearance.

View A-A

B

B

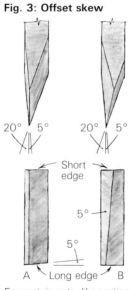

Clearance angle

View B-B

Long point

Fig. 3: Offset skew

20° 5°   20° 5°

Short edge

5°

5°

A   Long edge   B

For certain cuts, like parting off close to the headstock, an offset edge positions the tool more conveniently. Offset the edge by grinding bevels at different angles. To provide an adequate clearance angle, either grind the long edge at a 5° angle (A), or grind the cutting edge at a 5° angle to the section of the tool (B).

tool rest with the left-hand bevel at right angles to the lathe axis (figure 2), and push the skew straight in—the clearance angle makes the cut both easy and safe. Good turning is based upon confidence which is, in turn, based upon your tool's being predictable. The clearance angle is only about 5°, and hence if the tool is incorrectly shaped or sharpened the clearance angle may be larger on one side and smaller on the other, and predictability is lost.

In use, a side or an edge of the skew must always be in contact with the tool rest. To facilitate smooth movements over the rest, it helps to grind the short edge of the skew slightly convex, and to round the corners of the long edge. The tool rest and the sides of the tool should be smooth.

Sharpening—An angle of skewness of about 70° is the optimum compromise between retaining a strong long point and providing an adequate clearance angle. When grinding, hold the cutting edge parallel to the grinding wheel axis, the bevel flat on the wheel, and aim for an angle on each bevel of about 12½°, as shown in figure 1. I find that this sharpening angle works well on all woods, even our native Australian hardwoods (some of which are very hard indeed). The optimum diameter of the grindstone is 8 in. to 10 in. If smaller, excessive hollow grinding weakens the cutting edge; if larger, the bevel will be rather flat, which makes both grinding and honing more difficult. The grit and composition of the wheel depend on the type of steel. For my high-speed steel tools, I use a Norton 19A 60KVBE. Take care to keep the two bevels the same length, so that the cutting edge, when looked at head-on, is centered and parallel to the sides. Then the clearance angle will be the same on both sides.

There are two misconceptions about sharpening: that the bevel need not be hollow-ground, and that honing is not required after grinding. The bevels need to be hollow-ground so that there is a straight line of sight along the bevel. The turner can then sight along the true cutting edge, the microsharpened bevel, when making cuts with the long point. Although gouges are more easily honed by moving the stone over the tool, I pre-

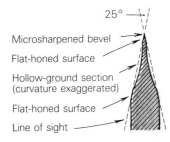

25°
Microsharpened bevel
Flat-honed surface
Hollow-ground section
(curvature exaggerated)
Flat-honed surface
Line of sight

fer to use a fixed stone for the skew. Try a shallow tray holding a fine-grade 6-in. by 2-in. oilstone immersed in kerosene, plus the slips for the gouges, mounted adjacent to the lathe and covered with a lid. Hone the skew with short to-and-fro strokes, and with both the heel and the toe of the bevel bearing on the stone. After both bevels have been honed, any burr can be stropped off.

Some turners do not hone, perhaps because the ragged edge straight from the grindstone gives an illusion of sharpness. An unhoned edge, however, scratches the wood surface and does not last. In addition, it is far quicker to rehone than to regrind, and your tools will last much longer.

A convex bevel is occasionally recommended in the belief that it polishes the cut surface. Actually, the texture of the wood contacted by the bevel is little affected by bevel shape, and the loss of the clear line of sight is a disadvantage.

Steel—Almost all ready-made turning tools are carbon tool steel, as it is easier for the manufacturers to fabricate. Here, in

A pencil gauge is used to mark a roughed-out cylinder. A shallow groove in the plywood supports the pencil point, allowing the turner to precisely transfer marks to the spinning work.

Australia, professionals usually use high-speed steel—it takes a finer edge, is more resistant to abrasion and does not lose its temper as readily as carbon tool steel does. It is especially recommended for the skew chisel with its exposed long point, which overheats easily. The amateur can change to high-speed steel by making his own long-and-strong skews. Hardened and tempered rectangular tool bits about 1 ft. long need only to have the bevels and tang ground by the turner himself. Of the vast range of tool steels available, American Iron & Steel Institute classifications T1 and M1 are best, being the least brittle of the true high-speed steels. Sears sells high-speed steel turning tools at a reasonable price, but the blades are shorter than I like.

Handles—The skew should be worked with a sensitive touch, not brute force. On spindle turning the skew will usually be used for most of the turning time, and it will go through many complex movements. For good balance and leverage, the overall length should be about 18 in., and the handle should be light and fairly short rather than long and heavy. It's less tiring and gives better balance when you use the tool one-handed. My 12-in. tool blanks allow me to make long-and-strong tools with a 9-in. blade showing and a 9-in. handle. Although a rack of tools with matched handles looks very smart, having them all different, both in shape and wood, helps you find one fast when you want it.

Laying out the cuts—Where a few identical items are to be turned, I begin each with a roughing gouge (*FWW* #12, pp. 60-64) to remove the bulk of the wood. A truly sharp one will leave the surface ready for marking out and detailed turning. Then I use a pencil gauge, as in the photo above. The gauge is ¼ in. to ½ in. thick, about 3 in. wide, and usually about 1 in. longer than the work. Draw the pattern full-size on the gauge, and project the main reference points to the edge. File short grooves where the lines meet the edge of the gauge. To mark out, rest the gauge on the tool rest with its top edge lightly touching the rotating wood, and hold a pencil point against the turning at the grooves.

A conventional turning has several features, as shown in figure 4. A bead, an approximately semicircular convex curve, frequently ends at a short fillet forming a break between the bottom of the bead and a cove. A bead turned on a long curve is called a ring. Some spindle turning requires only a roughing gouge, a skew and a detail gouge, each being used only once during the process. Here are some of the cuts that can be made with the skew, roughly in the order in which they might be used.

V-cuts—To turn a bead, there must be clearance for the skew to move into and for the shavings to escape. The V-cut, with the skew resting on its long edge, is the first clearing cut. It spears into the wood, leading with the long point. To begin cutting a bead, three V-cuts are usually necessary. For the first, hold the tool at right angles to the lathe axis, with its

Fig. 4: A typical turning

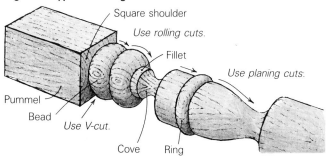

Left, the third V-cut: Move the tool laterally to the right, then swing and rotate the handle so the cutting edge points along the intended line of cut. Sweep the point down to make the cut. To leave a pummel (right), cut the shoulder before the stock is roughed out. Make a series of V-cuts to achieve enough depth, then align the bevel at the skew's long point with the shoulder. With the long edge flat on the rest, arc the skew into the work, taking a light cut. The skew's built-in clearance angle makes the cut safe and easy.

long edge on the tool rest, and position the long point above the mark for the outer edge of the bead. Raise the handle so the point sweeps down into the wood. This initial cut is admittedly crude—the skew's tip crushes the wood on each side of the bevel, resulting in considerable friction and heat. There is little metal at the long point, so heat is only slowly conducted away into the body of the blade. Too heavy and sustained a pressure will create temperatures at the tool tip that are high enough to soften carbon steel. The two succeeding V-cuts widen and, where necessary, deepen the groove. Move the skew a little to the side of the first cut. Swing and rotate the handle so that the cutting edge points at the bottom of the first cut. Then raise the handle so that the long point sweeps down in an arc until it reaches the bottom of the first cut, as shown in the photo, bottom left. The process can be repeated, deepening and widening the V until sufficient depth is reached.

To leave a square, or pummel, on a turned piece, the procedure is similar, although the V-cutting precedes roughing. Obviously, because of the greater depth of wood at the corners, more than three V-cuts are usually required. Make alternate perpendicular and sloping cuts until the shoulder is deep enough. These initial V-cuts leave a rough surface, so a final, light V-cut should be taken down the face of the square to the full finished depth. At the long point itself, the bevel facing the square should be at right angles to the lathe axis, which requires that you swing the handle slightly, as shown in the photo, bottom right. As long as the long edge is flat on the tool rest, you will come to no harm.

In cutting a bead, V-cuts define both the bead's lateral extent and, more important, its depth. After the V-cuts have angled in to clear room, the short point can make a series of rolling cuts to shape the curve. On stock of the size in the photos on the facing page, cutting each side of a bead usually requires three V-cuts followed by at least two rolling cuts.

Rolling cuts—In bead-cutting, use the very end of the cutting edge at the short point. The cut starts with the skew almost flat on its side. Hence to start a rolling cut, the handle must be rotated to tilt the cutting edge slightly so only the short point cuts. Also, the handle must be angled slightly behind the cut so that the cutting edge, not the short edge, is presented to the wood, as shown in the top photo and the bottom left photo on the facing page. Then, as shown in the middle photo, simultaneously rotate the short point to take a deeper cut, and—to keep the cutting edge in the work—move it around the side of the bead and vertically downward. It is often necessary to slide the blade along the rest. This involves quite large movements of the handle, swinging through a wide lateral arc and rising steadily, in order to keep the bevel rubbing and the short point cutting.

The underhand turning grip, visible in the photo at the top of the next page, makes control easier than conventional overhand grips. In this grip, which is widely used in Australia, the forefinger of the left hand extends under the tool rest and is used to steady the hand and power the tool. Left hand, tool and tool rest are tied together and can act as a unit. Provided that there is a gap of at least ½ in. between the work and the tool rest, the finger is safe.

To achieve a full semicircular bead at the end of the rolling cut, the skew has to cut perpendicularly to the lathe axis. Unfortunately, the clearance angle—of such assistance when

To begin a full rolling cut with the short point, start at the top of the bead with the skew almost on its side. Angle the handle slightly behind the cut to keep the cutting edge, not the short edge, in contact with the wood. When making rolling cuts, Darlow uses the Australian underhand grip, his forefinger gripping the back of the tool rest for better control.

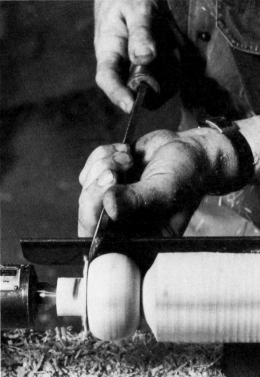

Almost flat on its side, the short point begins to cut (left). Move the skew laterally along the tool rest to continue (center), rotating the handle to keep the overhanging cutting edge clear. Keep your elbows near your body for better control, swinging your body to pivot the skew on the tool rest. Raise the handle and move the

cutting edge down into the work to keep the short point cutting. At the completion of the cut (right), the handle is rising and moving forward—Darlow has swung it far to the right with his body and rotated it so that the cutting edge, beyond the vertical, can form the side of the bead perpendicular to the work.

you are using the long point—becomes an interference angle when you are using the short point. Therefore, at the end of the cut the handle must be rotated so the blade tilts about 5° away from the cut, as shown in the photo at far right. This is why it helps to round the short edge of the skew, so that there is no sudden change in the cutting edge's relationship to the work when you transfer from one fulcrum to the other.

There are three main problems when making rolling cuts. First, if you fail to rotate the handle enough as you move around the bead, the overhanging part of the cutting edge will bite into the part of the bead you have just cut. This causes the working length of the cutting edge to increase suddenly from virtually nil to up to perhaps ¼ in. The cutting force increases almost instantaneously. Human reaction time is too slow to keep control of the tool, and it is shoved back, riding up and out of the bead. Second, if you inadvertently take too thick a shaving—by raising the handle too far, swinging it too soon around the bead or rotating it excessive-

ly—the strong shaving formed outside the short point will force the cutting tip farther into the side of the bead, ruining the shape. Third, if you persist in using a dull tool, it will not be able to penetrate the wood at the correct working angle—the tool will ride on top, compressing and glazing the surface, and making penetration even more difficult. When you try to get below the burnished surface, the tool will dig in. There is no cure except to sharpen your skew.

Rolling cuts are the main cause for the skew's notoriety. They require simultaneous lateral, vertical and rotational movements of the cutting point, plus lateral movement of the blade along the rest to make smooth curves without digging in. Needless to say, they need to be taken slowly, and they require considerable practice so that they become almost automatic. A bead of about ½-in. diameter is a good size to practice. It rolls naturally without the necessity of moving the skew laterally along the rest, although the handle still rises and swings through its broad arc, and the tool must be guid-

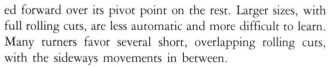

The planing cut, with the bevel rubbing the work to support the cutting edge, leaves a smooth, polished surface. Darlow guides the skew with his thumb while his left hand dampens vibration in slender stock, above. Generally, as shown at top right, neither the short point nor the long point should contact the work. The bottom right photo shows a modification: the slide cut, a planing cut that gradually leads up to using the extreme short point to cut the end of a curve without marring the side of a bead. As in all turning where most of the tool movement is horizontal, the conventional overhand grip is used.

ed forward over its pivot point on the rest. Larger sizes, with full rolling cuts, are less automatic and more difficult to learn. Many turners favor several short, overlapping rolling cuts, with the sideways movements in between.

When practicing, do not attempt too much at once and do not practice when you are tired or when things begin to go badly. Take a rest to restore your concentration. Don't use too large a square at first, 2 in. to 3 in. is about right. Use a gouge to clean up any scars on the work before proceeding or you may dig in again in the same place.

In the series of rolling cuts necessary to complete a bead, you are aiming for a constant shaving thickness. The cuts should be taken slowly and purposefully so that all the varying movements can be coordinated. There is also the problem of whether to watch the skew's cutting tip or the evolving bead profile. Obviously it is best to watch both simultaneously, but for those without Eddie Cantor's optical facility, watch the tip initially, and once the cut is started, switch to the profile. When you are comfortable making full rolling cuts with the short point, you will have few problems with the rest of the skew's repertoire. Here are some tips on the other cuts.

Long-point cuts—Most beads can be cut with either the long or the short point. The short point works better. It cuts down into the wood, thus burnishing the surface, whereas the long point lifts the ends of the wood fibers, so an inferior, almost porous surface is left. In addition, because the micro-sharpened bevel at the short point is supported by the work, there is less tendency for a jerky rolling action than when you are using the relatively unsupported long point. But do use the long point for very small beads, where the greater visibil-

ity helps. Ideally, you should execute the cut the same as you would with the short point, starting with the skew on its side and rotating the cutting edge through a full 90° until the blade rests on its long edge.

Where you cannot lay the blade on its side to start the rolling cut—as on the far side of a bead adjacent to a square section, where the corners of the square would hit the skew—you can use the long point, held more vertically, to make a series of rounded V-cuts to define the bead. Alternatively, and this means a time-consuming tool change, a very small skew or a nosed gouge could be used for a better surface.

When similar beads are adjacent, it is not possible to rotate the skew far enough to make the bead bottoms truly vertical. Cut as close to vertical as you can, until the skew begins to bind, then reach in with the long point to cut out any rags left in the cusp.

Cutting fillets—After completing the shape of the bead, and clearing some room, cut the fillet using the short point. As with the start of a rolling cut, angle the handle away slightly to present the short point of the cutting edge to the wood. It is easiest to keep the tool at one point on the tool rest, and to swing the handle so the cutting point levels the fillet. Don't contact, and hence spoil, the side of the bead above the fillet. Normally, fillets are cut parallel to the lathe's axis, although where room is constricted they are often sloped to avoid having to switch to a narrow skew.

Planing cuts—The planing cut, shown in the photos above, is a finishing cut that leaves curved and straight sections smooth and even. It consists of mostly lateral motion of the skew along the tool rest. The planing cut is made with the short point leading, the supporting bevel almost tangential to the surface, and the cut always moving level or downhill. The cutting edge usually works at about 45° to the lathe axis, giving both a cutting and a riving action. The full length of the cutting edge can be used, with the exception of the long and short points themselves. The larger the diameter of the work, the larger the skew that should be used, in order to keep the points safely away from the work. If the long point becomes buried, the shaving is cut only on its near side. The shaving thus offers more resistance, and pushes the long point down into the wood, resulting in a deep tear. If only the short point is cutting, the action becomes purely riving, and splinters, not shavings, will result.

Sensitive control, which is one of the joys of using the skew, is accomplished by slightly varying the presentation of the tool to the work. The movements, in various combinations, become so ingrained that they seem instinctive: To take a deeper cut, merely raise the handle. To increase the downhill gradient of the cut, slightly steepen the angle of the cutting edge by rotating the handle. Raising the tool rest for the planing cut is unnecessary and time-consuming. Simply lower the handle so that the tool is presented with the bevel supporting the cutting edge.

If you are planing thin work and encounter vibration that causes your skew to chatter, it is perfectly safe to support the work with your left hand as it turns. The photo at the left on the facing page shows me steadying a turning while I guide the skew along the cylinder with my thumb. Your left hand can also feel how successful the steadying is—if you've got it right, the turning will feel smooth.

The riving component of the cutting action causes tear-out on interlocked or non-axially grained wood unless the cuts happen to be fairly steeply downward. To minimize tearing out, angle the handle back behind the direction of travel so that the cutting edge is more nearly square—say, about 70°—to the lathe axis.

If you are doing work where the corner of the bevel at the long edge digs into the finished surface, you can grind the offending corner away, as shown in figure 1, or tilt the skew more steeply so the corner clears the work.

Where a long curve meets a ring or similar projection, modify the planing cut into what could be christened the slide cut. As you approach the projection with the skew planing, gradually slide the tool forward so that the short point itself cuts, as in the lower right photo on the facing page.

Planing cuts can define convex and concave profiles, as well as straight ones. Hollows with a surprisingly small radius can be cut with a skew, using a modified planing cut and firm control. The lower middle section of the cutting edge is used and the angle of the tool is somewhat steeper than the tangent at the point on the hollow being cut. With large work, control is difficult because the bevel is not supported, but with practice the technique will be found risk-free and safe. Use a small skew on work less than 1 in. in diameter. Always cut down toward the bottom of the cove from both sides—don't try to cut uphill.

Parting cuts—You can make V-cuts one-handed with the long point for parting off, which frees your other hand to steady and catch the finished turning. Slacken the tailstock a little toward the end of the cut so that the work will come

The skew can quickly remove waste. Keep the bevel rubbing, and the edge moving forward, as the diameter goes down. A firm grip is necessary.

away freely. Don't part off work too large to control or turnings with square sections at the left-hand end.

If you do much parting off from a chuck, you will want to be able to part off close to its face, which should be covered by a guard. The offset skew (figure 3) allows this, with its 5° right-hand bevel.

The skew can also set diameters and remove waste. Hold the cutting edge parallel to the lathe axis with the lower bevel rubbing, as in the photo above. The action is identical to that of the conventional parting tool—which should slice rather than scrape—except that the skew will tend to move sideways in the direction of its long point. You cannot make this cut, of course, unless there is clearance for the short edge of the tool. If holding the skew with only the right hand (the left hand holding the caliper), brace the handle beneath your forearm, extend your forefinger down the tool for firmness, and don't use a skew wider than ½ in.

Steering the skew—The right hand provides most of the power and steering. When doing a series of cuts with a particular tool, it is natural to regrip for each cut so that the right hand is comfortable during that cut. For rolling cuts, however, it is best to grip the tool so that the right hand reaches the natural, comfortable position at the completion of the cut. This makes the cut almost automatic because the right hand wants to return to an unstrained position.

Extending the forefinger, as I usually do, is a way of getting a more precise feel of the tool, as well as of adding firmness when needed. For control and balance, keep your right arm close to your side.

With any human activity, practice of the correct techniques, while perhaps not making perfect, at least makes much better. Unfortunately, new techniques tend to feel unnatural, so keep on turning and be prepared for things to get worse before they get better. □

Mike Darlow, 38, keeps four lathes busy turning lace bobbins, restorations, production work, bowls and gallery pieces in Chippendale, N.S.W., Australia. Photos by Peter Johnson, Sydney.

Methods of Work

edited and drawn by Jim Richey

Thickness-sander attachment for lathe

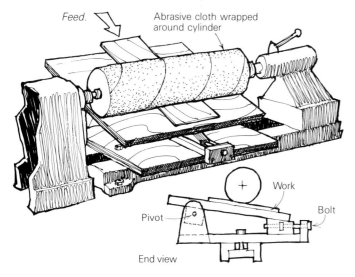

Feed.

Abrasive cloth wrapped around cylinder

Work

Pivot

Bolt

End view

The sketch above shows the thickness-sander lathe attachment I made to sand dulcimer tops and sides. The design is similar to the sanders shown in *FWW* #21, p. 50, but because the device uses the lathe's motor, spindle and bed, it is much easier to make. By using the lathe's variable-speed pulleys you can always find the perfect sanding speed. The sanding drum is simply a turned wooden cylinder spirally wrapped with abrasive cloth. The plywood and hardwood base bolts to the lathe bed and adjusts with a simple wedge mechanism.

—*Charles R. Adams, Westmoreland, N.H.*

Two methods for turning duplicates

Turning copies of a spindle on a hand lathe can be tedious work. Templates, gauges and other gadgets help but don't substantially increase speed and accuracy. In contrast, this method, which uses the bandsaw, is the best turning aid I've found yet. On one face of the square stock, mark out with a template the desired profile and make bandsaw cuts to within $\frac{1}{16}$ in. of the profile at convenient reference points. Bevel the square's corners as you usually do, mount the stock on the

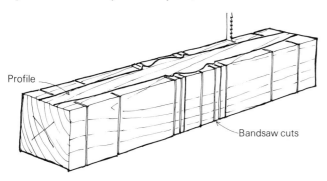

Profile

Bandsaw cuts

lathe and begin turning. The cut lines will be easy to see and will allow quick and accurate shaping without so many stops for caliper checks. The secret to this method is accurate layout and careful sawing. —*Robert M. Vaughan, Roanoke, Va.*

Lee Watkin's method for making dowels using a router and lathe (*FWW* #25, p. 22) arrived just before I put the finishing touches on the deck I was adding to my house. Here's how I adapted his method to make the deck railing a cut above the usual. Starting with the straight U-shaped fixture used to make dowels, I sawed off a curved section from each end. I screwed a V-shaped block to the bottom of the router base. This allowed the router to follow the profile of the top

of the fixture and to transfer the shape to the spinning blank below. The shape I wanted in the railing was similar to the backrest supports in a chair. The fixture helped me produce 85 identical spindles quite nicely.

—*Donald B. Sherman, Merrimack, N.H.*

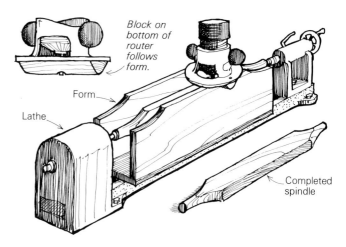

Block on bottom of router follows form.

Form

Lathe

Completed spindle

Improved spade bit

You can improve the performance of the common spade bit by regrinding it to the shape below. The reground bit will cut a smoother hole and won't tear out the grain as much when it comes out the other side. —*Ray Yohe, Altoona, Pa.*

Grind away areas indicated.

Ersatz sanding disc

A tire valve stem makes a cheap, simple and flexible mounting for sandpaper. Cut the stem from the tube, glue on sandpaper and chuck the stem in a drill press or portable drill. I use the discs to sand irregular bowls. —*Bart Brush, Cherry Valley, N.Y.*

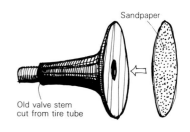

Sandpaper

Old valve stem cut from tire tube

Edge-sanding fixture

Here's a fixture that turns a belt sander into an edge sander. Simply build a wooden fixture that supports and locks your belt sander in a horizontal position. Bolt the fixture to the tablesaw's rip fence as shown, and use the saw's flat cast-iron surface for the work. —*Wayne Hausknecht, Tucson, Ariz.*

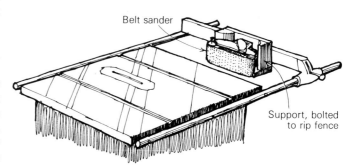

Belt sander

Support, bolted to rip fence

Turning Tips

Advice from a mill man

by R. Perry Mercurio

Are you trying to sharpen your turning tools on a bench grinder with a wheel so hard and fine that the slightest touch of steel burns a blue spot of drawn temper? You can't turn without sharp tools and you can't keep them sharp that way. Find a mill supply house (most cities have at least one in the phone book) and let them help you select a good sharpening wheel. I'd suggest a Norton #32A60-J5VBE or a Universal-Simonds #RA60-J-V8 in a size to fit your grinder. These are soft wheels and should never be used for anything except sharpening hard steels. Your good wheel will last longer if you put a harder, general-purpose wheel on the other end of the grinder, and use it for rough work.

You won't get a good edge if your tools bounce around, so it's important to keep grinding wheels round and true and free of vibration. This is easily done with a star wheel or a diamond-tipped truing tool, or even with a piece of broken grinding wheel. The star wheel will give you the best surface.

If you don't have a regular grinder, you can make one by rigging up a stand, either of wood or of angle iron, whose top is a comfortable elbow height. Mount pillow blocks on the stand, then fix the grinding stones to the shaft and power it with a separate motor and V-belt.

Honing: There are as many ways of honing as there are stars in the sky, but my 40 years of mill experience has shown that a $1.19 Crystolon pocket stone plus a couple of hard Arkansas slip stones will do a very acceptable job. The pocket stone bites off the required amount of metal, then the finer Arkansas stone smooths and polishes. For these fine stones I'd suggest a Norton #HS-3, which has a tapered cross section with round edges, and a Norton #HF-843, which is diamond-shaped in section with sharp edges. These three stones will also do nearly all of your carving tools.

To touch up gouges, make a socket of some sort for the butt end of the handle, to steady it while you hone. Hold the tool firmly between your left thumb and fingers so you can rotate the gouge easily while stoning with your right hand.

To keep stones clean and free-cutting, keep them moist at all times. Make a shallow tray from the bottom of a large tin can. Put a few layers of cloth in the bottom, saturated with a mixture of half kerosene and half motor oil. Stones can't absorb too much oil, and it makes metal particles picked up by

the stone during honing loosen and shed. Hang an old towel nearby to wipe fingers and chisel.

Some sizing tips: Duplicate turnings can be made faster by laying out their profile on a strip of masking tape along the tool rest, with parting-tool cuts indicated by double lines. Diameters for each cut can be noted right on the tape.

If you make duplicate turnings having a tenon on one or both ends and you have trouble keeping tenon size uniform, make a simple sizer. Choose a hard block of maple or hornbeam and turn a ½-in. shank on one end to hold in the lathe's chuck. Turning this block by its shank, bore a hole in the end that's a little larger than the desired tenon size, and a little deeper than the tenon is long. If you don't have a drill bit the correct size, you can grind a drill bit slightly off-center—then it will bore a slightly larger hole. Make a ⅟₃₂-in. by ⅟₃₂-in. counterbore at the front end of the bore to help start the tenon into the hole. Remove from the lathe and remove wood off one side until you break into the bore with a gap about ¼ in. wide. Using a piece of old scraper blade, plane iron or whatever, make a flat knife as shown in the sketch at the lower left and attach it to the sizer with its cutting edge just behind the center of the gap. If you rough out your tenons to within ⅟₃₂ in. of size, this tool will align and finish the job accurately. Mount the sizer in the lathe chuck, and set the lathe to about 500 RPM. Hold the work in your left hand, and advance it with the tailstock crank.

If you occasionally need a few dowels of an odd size that can be made by turning down a larger dowel, you can make a fixture to do just that. If you are starting with, say, a ½-in. dowel, bore an oversized ½-in. hole through the center of a 1-in. by 3-in. by 12-in. hardwood block. Next, to support a gouge, glue and screw a smaller strip of hardwood onto the first one, with its upper edge along the centerline of the ½-in. hole. Lay a ⅜-in. or ½-in. gouge on top of this second strip, with its cutting edge overhanging the edge of the hole. Fashion a wood clamp as shown in the sketch, below right, to hold the gouge in place. Mount a ½-in. dowel in your lathe chuck, and insert the free end in the fixture hole. Run the lathe at slow speed and gently push the fixture along until it reaches the headstock. You don't need the tailstock, just support the free end of the dowel with your hand to keep it from whipping around. You'll have to fiddle a bit to find the gouge setting that produces the dowel diameter you want.

Finishing: For a high gloss, the old shellac finish is still ex-

---

R. Perry Mercurio, of Kingfield, Maine, is a retired plant engineer in the commercial woodturning industry.

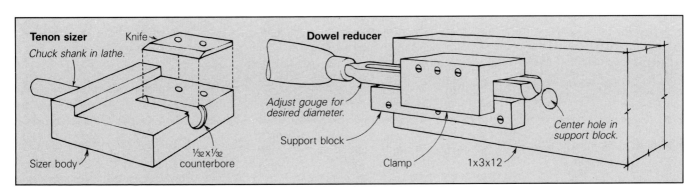

Tenon sizer — Knife — Chuck shank in lathe. — Sizer body — ⅟₃₂ x ⅟₃₂ counterbore

Dowel reducer — Adjust gouge for desired diameter. — Support block — Clamp — 1x3x12 — Center hole in support block.

cellent. With the work turning on the lathe, brush on thinned shellac until the brush starts to drag. Let the piece spin a while and repeat, being careful not to let the finish build up too much. When the surface is evenly coated and not absorbing any more shellac, let it spin a few minutes to set up. Then remove the work from the lathe and give it at least five hours to dry—overnight is best—before you smooth it with fine steel wool. Then apply paste wax, letting it dry thoroughly, and polish it on the lathe with a soft cloth.

You can obtain a fairly good instant finish by applying shellac or oil with the lathe running at high speed, and rubbing hard enough to generate heat for drying the finish. At first the surface will look glossy hard. But this method will not dry the finish that has penetrated the surface, and the interaction between the dry outer layer and the damp inner layer will eventually leave a matte finish.

Dust: Most mills have elaborate dust-removal systems. Do your lungs a favor by hanging the suction hose of your shop-vac on the lathe bed while sanding. The noise may be annoying, but it could keep you around for a few more years. □

A shop-built lathe duplicator

by Lawrence Churchill

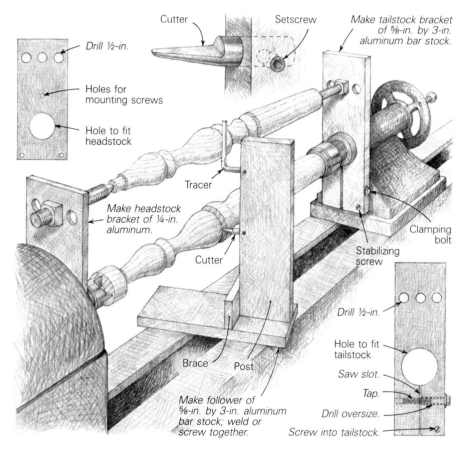

A considerable amount of my repair work requires replacing broken chair spindles and other such matching turned parts, so a duplicator is a valuable tool. In designing the one shown here, I wanted a jig that wouldn't interfere with normal lathe operation or require any elaborate setup. My duplicator isn't robust enough to trace a part from a square blank, but once the blank has been roughed to within ¼ in. of final size, this rig will finish the job nicely.

The duplicator consists of a pair of plates attached to the lathe's headstock and tailstock, and a follower that slides along the ways. The plates allow me to mount directly over the blank either a flat pattern or, by means of a pair of auxiliary spindles in the plates, the turning I want to duplicate. The follower is a post carrying a tracer that bears on the pattern or original turning. A cutter is mounted directly below the tracer.

First I replaced the headstock's original bearing cover plate with a piece of ¼-in. thick aluminum. This plate will hold the pattern about 4 in. above the turning axis. On some lathes you can use longer screws to attach the bracket over the original bearing cover. I made a similar bracket out of ⅝-in. by 3-in. aluminum bar to fit over the tailstock spindle housing. Aluminum bar can be jigsawn or bandsawn with ordinary woodcutting blades.

Drill the three ½-in. holes in the headstock plate as shown, then slide tailstock and its plate up to it and use dowel centers to transfer the holes. To hold the part you want to duplicate, mount a pointed length of ½-in. threaded rod in the center hole of each plate, with a nut on both sides. A flat pattern can be copied by cutting two tenons on each end and wedging these in the plates' outer holes.

The follower consists of two lengths of ⅝-in. by 3-in. aluminum bar, joined at right angles and rigidly braced. These parts could be heliarc-welded, but I just screw them together. At the lathe-center height, drill a ¼-in. hole for the cutting tool, then cross-drill and tap for a setscrew. Do the same about 1 in. below the pattern centerline, for the tracer. A broken ¼-in. diameter tap or an old drill ground to a pencil-shaped cone and then ground flat on top makes a scraping-type cutter. Make the tracer by bending a 4-in. length of steel rod to a right angle and grinding its vertical profile to the shape of the cutter. Mount and adjust these parts so that when the edge of the tracer touches the pattern, the cutter cuts that diameter.

Most old turnings to be copied are out-of-round (egg-shaped) and bowed. If you position the original with the bow up or down, it won't affect the reproduction; that's why the tracer is so long. The variation in egg-shaped parts is usually not significant, except on tenons, which should be gauged for a close fit.

Start with the regular tool rest and rough out the new part in the normal manner. Most turners can get pretty close by eye, and having the pattern near the work makes it even easier—you can sight directly down from the pattern to check your work. When the new part is roughed out, remove the standard tool rest and move its base off to one side. Then just guide the follower to trim the new turning to final size. Polish and wax the follower base to keep it sliding smoothly. In my shop, this simple system has turned those duplicating jobs from red ink to black. □

Lawrence Churchill works wood in Mayville, Wis.

Lathe speeds

by R. Perry Mercurio

What is the right speed for a lathe, and what can you do about it? Assuming you have the usual set of carbon-steel tools, speeds for spindle turning should range between 750 RPM and 2500 RPM. Ultimately, we are concerned with the speed at which the surface of the work is turning, not merely the speed of the lathe. Thus, the larger the diameter of the work, the slower the lathe should turn.

But surface speed isn't the only consideration. Let's say you have a stair baluster about 1½ in. in diameter and 30 in. long. Even though the diameter is small, you can see right away that the length should limit the speed, unless you want to risk getting a faceful of wood—a speed of 800 RPM will be fast enough. If you have a workpiece only about 10 in. long and perhaps 2 in. in diameter, you can go to top speed, unless the species of wood comes into play. Harder woods create more friction, quickly heating the tool, which will then require more sharpening. Go slower. Some woods, teak for example, contain abrasive minerals, and require slower speed as well as more frequent sharpening.

Add a countershaft: If your lathe has only the usual three or four speed possibilities and you are beginning to get serious about turning, you will want to add more speed changes. An easy way is to put a countershaft between the motor and lathe headstock, with a step pulley at each end, as shown in the drawing below. Belt one end of the shaft to the motor and the other end to the headstock pulley. The countershaft frame should be hinged and should also have a locking device. This will ease belt changes and cut down vibration. The motor mount should be attached in the same manner. With this setup you can change speeds easily and quickly.

A word of caution: it's surprisingly easy when switching belts around to end up with the opposite of what you thought you were doing. A large bowl blank revving up to 2500 RPM can give you quite a start. So figure out the speeds at various belt positions and make a chart to hang on the wall behind the lathe. The formula is simple: merely multiply the driver speed by the diameter of its pulley and divide the product by the diameter of the driven pulley. With V-belts and pulleys this method is approximate, but close enough.

Bowlturning can get you into a really low range of speeds, especially for larger bowls. You might want to choose a set of pulleys that get down to 200 RPM, or even less. A lot will also depend upon the rigidity of your lathe and how well it is anchored to the floor (*FWW #25*, pp. 80-81).

Reverse: It's a real help to be able to reverse the spindle rotation. Perhaps the most common benefit is being able to sand off laid-down fibers. But suppose you are making a dozen small bowls or bases that are being turned on a screw center. During the process of turning, sanding and finishing, you will have to mount and unmount each one several times. How easy it is to hit your switch either right or left to screw them on or off the headstock. When turning the interior of a bowl or dish, reverse allows you to work on the far side of the center, giving you improved vision and tool handling. Take care, however, that your work is securely fastened and that the faceplate is tight, else it might unscrew in the event of a dig.

Most motors can be reversed by swapping two wires in the junction box. Obtain a drum-type reversing switch from an electrical supplier and mount it over the lathe headstock. Connect it so that when the handle is pushed to the right, rotation is normal. Do not mount the switch where you could accidentally turn it on. Some professional turners like an on/off foot switch on the floor. This allows them to start or stop the lathe to inspect the work without losing hand position on the chisel. A foot switch and a drum-reversing switch can be wired so they work together. □

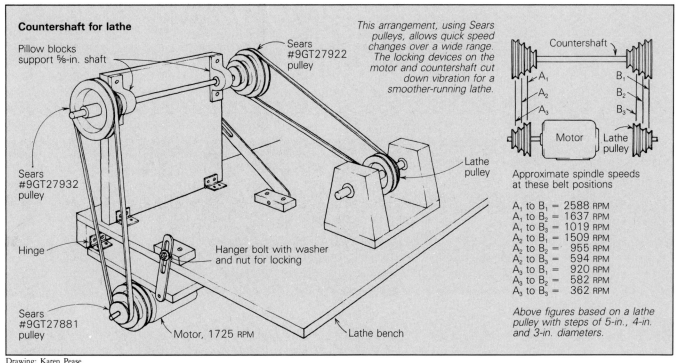

Countershaft for lathe

Pillow blocks support ⅝-in. shaft

Sears #9GT27922 pulley

Sears #9GT27932 pulley

Hinge

Sears #9GT27881 pulley

Hanger bolt with washer and nut for locking

Motor, 1725 RPM

Lathe pulley

Lathe bench

This arrangement, using Sears pulleys, allows quick speed changes over a wide range. The locking devices on the motor and countershaft cut down vibration for a smoother-running lathe.

Countershaft

Motor

Lathe pulley

Approximate spindle speeds at these belt positions

A_1 to B_1 = 2588 RPM
A_1 to B_2 = 1637 RPM
A_1 to B_3 = 1019 RPM
A_2 to B_1 = 1509 RPM
A_2 to B_2 = 955 RPM
A_2 to B_3 = 594 RPM
A_3 to B_1 = 920 RPM
A_3 to B_2 = 582 RPM
A_3 to B_3 = 362 RPM

Above figures based on a lathe pulley with steps of 5-in., 4-in. and 3-in. diameters.

Drawing: Karen Pease

Twist Turning
Traditional method combines lathe and carving

by Eric Schramm

Spiral or twist turning was introduced in Europe during the 16th century and was used widely for chair and table legs in 17th-century England. Today, the technique finds uses in antique reproduction and repair and for the Mediterranean-style furniture popular in the Southwest and West.

Spirals, solid and hollow, are not turnings in the true sense of the word because most of the work is really carving. A spiral resembles a screw thread; it has pitch and lead. Pitch is the distance from center to center of consecutive ridges or bines. Lead is the distance the spiral advances along the cylinder in each revolution. In a single-twist spiral, pitch and lead are the same. A spiral with a short pitch and great depth will be weak because much of the long-grain wood has been removed. A longer pitch will be stronger but less pleasing to the eye. I find that a pitch about equal to or slightly less than the cylinder's diameter produces the nicest effect. The precise pitch, however, is governed by cylinder length, if the spiral bines are to be spaced equally and are to start and finish their lead symmetrically.

To lay out a single spiral, you must divide the cylinder's circumference into four equal parts. A quick method is to wrap a strip of paper around the circumference and trim it so the ends just meet. Remove the paper and fold it in half once, and then in half again. The fold marks, which will quarter the cylinder, can be transferred directly to the workpiece with a pencil. With the cylinder on the lathe and the tool rest acting as a straightedge, draw four lines along the length of the workpiece passing through these marks (figure 1a).

Next divide the cylinder's length into spaces that are equal to or slightly less than the cylinder diameter (figure 1b). These marks are the pitch lines and represent the distance between the spiral's ridges. Pitch lines drawn, divide the space between them into four equal spaces. You can now sketch the spiral ridge by drawing a continuous line diagonally through one after another of the quarter spaces between the pitch lines. A scrap of sandpaper makes a good straightedge (figure 1c) for drawing the diagonal lines. If you've done things properly, the ridge line will cross a pitch line with each revolution. With the ridge line completed, draw in another line parallel to it to roughly locate the spiral's groove. The ridge line will remain intact through the carving process.

A double spiral, the most popular form, is layed out similarly. The pitch remains the same, but the lead doubles. So this time, divide the space between pitch lines into two instead of four sections. Draw one ridge line as before, passing diagonally through the squares. In the length of one diameter, this ridge line will traverse 180°. Start a second ridge line 180° from the first, and draw the diagonals so the line remains 180° from the first throughout the length of the cylinder. Triple spirals can be plotted by dividing the circumference into six parts and starting the ridge lines at 120° intervals.

Ridge lines can be drawn also by wrapping a strip of paper around the turning, leaving a slight space between turns. A pencil line is then traced through the spiral space.

Actual cutting of the spiral is tedious but not difficult. First make a saw cut on the line that represents the bottom of the groove. Start with a saw with a strip of wood clamped to it or some masking tape to indicate the depth of cut, which should be about a quarter of the workpiece diameter (photo A). Rotate the work slowly while cutting so the kerf will follow the line. After sawing, the space between the bines is shaped by making broad V-cuts with a sharp chisel or No. 2 carver's gouge (photo B). Use a round file to clean up these spaces (photo C), then dress up the rounds with a flat cabinet file. The spiral can be rotated in the lathe by hand to permit longer file strokes and smoother results. The ridge line should be preserved throughout the process. Finish the spiral with sandpaper or use a shop-made pinwheel sander such as that described in *FWW #30*, p. 67.

Another variation of the double or triple spiral is the hollow spiral where the bines of the spiral are separated by an opening. Hollow or open spirals generally lack sufficient strength for furniture legs, but are quite effective as candlesticks or lamp bases. The work is layed out as for the double or triple spiral, with the cutting line that represents the bottom of the groove used as a drilling line. A V-block is used when drilling to assure accuracy (photo D). The holes go through the turning and are best drilled half way through from each side to avoid splintering. Finish the shape with chisels, files and sandpaper (photo E). One of the best tools for cleaning out the inside is an ordinary sharp carving knife. Irregularities and tool marks can be removed with strips of sanding belt, pulled back and forth around the bines (photo F). Make the final strokes in the direction of the grain. A great deal of patience and skill is required for neat work. The wood used should be tough, hard, and free from defects.

Tapered spirals for flame finials are also possible. To lay out a taper, you must make the pitch vary so that it equals the diminishing diameter of the workpiece. Begin as above by striking four lines along the length of the taper. Then measure the diameter of the taper's large end and mark this distance on one of the four longitudinal lines. At this mark, measure the diameter again and mark this length along the taper. Repeat this process until you reach the end of the cylinder. Adjust the various pitch lines you have drawn so that they diminish proportionately. Draw in the ridge line and proceed with the cuts as in straight work. To make a flame finial, draw four ridge lines starting at 90° intervals from the large end of the taper. Use double ridge lines about ⅛ in. apart, and use gouges and files to remove the waste. I find a Moto Tool with a round burr a good tool for forming the flame. □

Eric Schramm designs and builds custom furniture in Los Gatos, Calif. Photos by Robert Schramm.

Fig. 1 Laying out the spiral

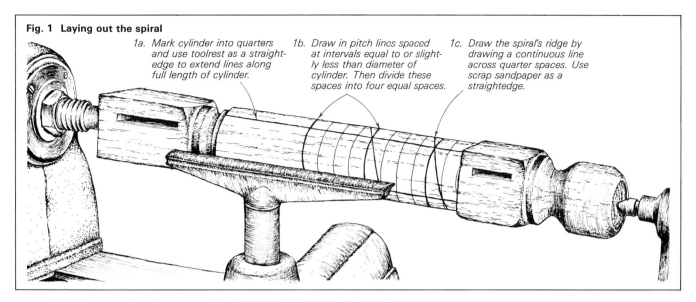

1a. Mark cylinder into quarters and use toolrest as a straight-edge to extend lines along full length of cylinder.

1b. Draw in pitch lines spaced at intervals equal to or slightly less than diameter of cylinder. Then divide these spaces into four equal spaces.

1c. Draw the spiral's ridge by drawing a continuous line across quarter spaces. Use scrap sandpaper as a straightedge.

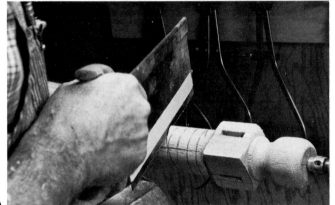

A

With the layout complete, use a backsaw to cut the initial kerf which will serve as a guide for carving the spiral's grooves.

B

Shaping the spiral is hard work. Start with a chisel or No. 2 carver's gouge. You can control the shape of the grooves and ridges by varying the angle of your chisel cuts.

C

After carving, use rasps and sandpaper to form the spiral in the shape you want. Here, sandpaper is wrapped around a rasp that acts as a sanding block to maintain the radius.

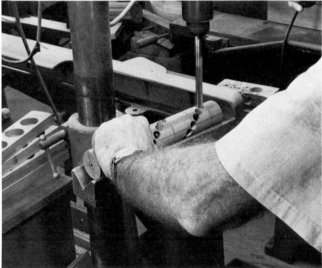

D

The hollow spiral layout is identical to that of the solid spiral. To waste the center of a hollow spiral, Schramm uses a drill press with the stock anchored against turning and slipping by a V-block.

E

After the drill press, it's back to carving by hand. The final shape of the hollow spiral is done with chisels, knives, rasps and sandpaper. Lathe-mounting allows the work to be positioned while carving.

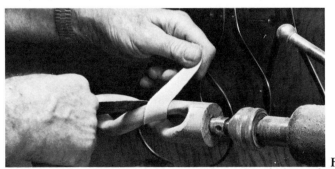

F

Cloth-backed sanding paper holds up well for sanding the bines of a hollow spiral. Old sanding belts can be cut into strips for this job. Use progressively finer grits to get a good finish.

A Mechanical Twist

The tablesaw can be used to lay out a helix and to cut its initial kerf at the same time. Then with a molding head on the saw and a guide pin running in that kerf, the bulk of the waste can be machined away. The basic method is to clamp an angled fence across the saw table just ahead of the sawblade, which is raised only ¼ in. above the table surface. A blank cylinder, lodged against the table and the fence and rotated over the blade, will feed itself along the fence regularly and automatically. The result is a helical kerf whose pitch is governed by the angle of the fence. A cylinder turned between square pommels, what you'd want for chair or table legs, can also be tablesawn in this way by screwing free-spinning end-blocks onto the stock, as shown at right. The end-blocks raise the stock off the table and away from the fence so its square sections don't interfere with its rotation.

As in all twist turning, the first step is to turn the blank cylinder, straight or between square pommels, depending on the application. There's uncertainty in these procedures so make five blanks if you need four legs. Then choose the pitch angle (α), which determines how quickly the helix rises—that is, its pitch, or lead, how far apart its ridges are. A pitch angle around 18° saws a helix whose lead (L) about equals its diameter (D). This pitch angle is set by locking the miter gauge at 72° (that is, 90° minus 18°), and using the gauge to locate the fence on the saw table. Whatever the angle, the fence should be located so that the center of the blank cylinder is directly above the center of the sawblade. Moving the fence forward or backward has the same effect as changing its angle. To saw a double helix whose ridges are still one diameter apart, use a pitch angle around 32°, which means set the miter gauge at 58°. Pitch angle (α), diameter (D) and lead (L) can be figured with the following formula:

$$\tan \alpha = \frac{L}{\pi D}$$

Always use a sturdy fence that's more than twice as long as the stock—a length of 2x4 is good. When the fence slopes away from the operator from right to left, the resulting helix will be like a left-handed thread. When the fence slopes away from left to right, the helix will be right-handed. Always feed the stock from the near side of the sawblade (the downhill side), always rotate it against the sawblade's rotation (so the blade doesn't self-feed), and always keep your hands well clear of the blade's path. For a double spiral, start the second kerf at a point 180° opposite the first.

After the helical kerf is cut, you can remount the stock on the lathe for carving, or you can further shape it with the molding head. Use coving knives in the head, and make a snugly fitting wooden insert for the tablesaw throat. Set a small dowel in the face of the fence (photo), just long enough to catch in the kerf. Fit this fence pin into the kerf and use the miter gauge (set as before) to locate the stock in relation to a molding knife. Clamp the fence to the saw table and rotate the stock into the molding head, slowly and carefully. The pin will automatically feed the stock. Shaping with the molding head has to be done in one pass because the cut removes the guide kerf. After the molding knives have done what they can, the helix can be cleaned up with carving tools, rasps and sandpaper. A strip of cloth-backed sandpaper in a bowsaw frame will speed the chore. —*Larry Green*

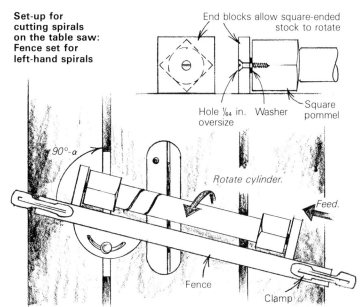

Set-up for cutting spirals on the table saw: Fence set for left-hand spirals

End blocks allow square-ended stock to rotate

Hole 1/64 in. oversize Washer Square pommel

90°-α

Rotate cylinder.

Feed.

Fence

Clamp

Position fence so stock center and saw arbor are vertically in line. Use miter gauge to set fence angle. Raise sawblade to cut ¼ in. into cylinder. Free-spinning endblocks provide clearance for square pommels, as shown in the detail at top.

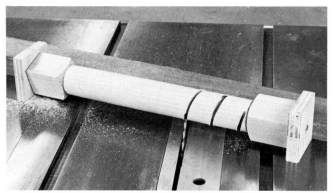

Rotate cylinder into the sawblade to cut helical kerf, above. It will feed itself along the angled fence.

Dowel pin set in fence will guide kerfed cylinder past molding head (right). Cut must be deep because a second cut is not possible (below). Go slowly to minimize tear-out.

Roller hold-in for resawing

Before I built this roller hold-in, I found myself using one hand to hold the work against the bandsaw fence and the other to steer and feed the stock. I didn't feel balanced and comfortable, and my hands were too close to the blade at the end of the cut. The roller fixture that solved these problems cost me $2.50, two hours of work and two trips to the hardware store.

The fixture consists of a base, two roller brackets and a roller. I made the base from plywood and glued and screwed it together for strength. Be sure to make the base large enough so you can clamp it easily to both the back and side of the saw table. I cut the roller brackets and turned the roller from maple. My version of the roller is about 1¼ in. in diameter and 5½ in. long, an ideal size for my 8-in. resaw-capacity bandsaw. I turned the roller and the ½-in. axles as a single unit. An enhancement that I didn't include on my roller fixture would be to point the axle ends to provide a low-friction bearing where the axle runs in the brackets. Attach the roller brackets and roller to the base with bolts, washers and nuts as shown in the drawing. Be sure to use bolts with a smooth shank where they pass through the brackets, else the brackets will bind on the bolt.

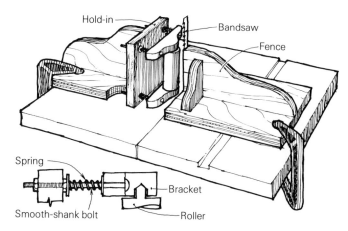

To use the hold-in, set the fence in position for the proper thickness of cut. Now bring the roller fixture into position and clamp so the roller exerts the proper pressure and touches the work just forward of the blade. If you use the narrow-faced fence shown in the sketch it is important to plane the stock between each resaw, because the narrow contact tends to duplicate any waviness or imperfection in the face of the stock. Reset the roller hold-in after each cut to regain the proper hold-in pressure.

—*Dennis LaBelle, Traverse City, Mich.*

Hold-in improvement

Fingerboards perform much more effectively if you screw them to tapped holes in the saw table rather than clamping them. Clamped fingerboards don't lie flat, and they can slip and lose pressure against the work.

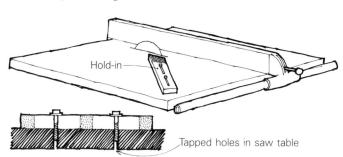

To make the fingerboard, saw kerfs ⅛ in. or so apart in the end of an angled 1x3. Rout two ¼-in. slots down the centerline of the fingerboard—one at the head, one at the tail. Now set the fingerboard in position on the saw, so it will exert pressure just ahead of the blade, and mark the center of each slot on the saw table with a punch. Drill and tap holes into the table at these points. Lock the unit in place with cap screws or bolts threaded into the tapped holes.

—*Ben Erickson, Eutaw, Ala.*

Outdoor workbench

I needed a small outdoor bench for fair-weather work outside my shop and demonstrations at the county fair. To make the bench I cut a beefy slice of oak tree and mounted it on three legs canted outward. For the "vise", I fitted the bench with holes for my cast-iron hold-down (available from Woodcraft Supply, 313 Montvale Ave., Woburn, Mass. 01888, and other suppliers). I bored a 2-in. hole into the top of the bench clear through to the bottom (so rainwater wouldn't collect in the hole). Then I plugged the top 2 in. of the hole with hardwood and centerbored the plug to fit the hold-down shaft. I flattened a place on the side of the oak slice and fitted a plug as above so I could use the hold-down to clamp work vertically. The arrangement works surprisingly well.

—*J.B. Small, Newville, Pa.*

Counterbalance improves belt sander

The belt sander can be a valuable tool in the production-shop world of tight schedules and competitive prices. But most belt sanders are designed with a flaw that renders them difficult to control: The motor hangs off one side, throwing the machine off balance. Unless you apply constant corrective hand pressure the sander will gouge or edge-scoop the work. A balanced machine will not scoop and allows the user to concentrate on direction and coverage.

To correct the imbalance I add wood and lead weights to my belt sanders. The amount of weight and position will vary with the sander. Fasten the weight under handles, knobs or whatever. The counterbalanced machines pass my test when they balance on a ¼-in. thick piece of plywood set under the centerline of the belt. —*Rod Goettelmann, Vincentown, N.J.*

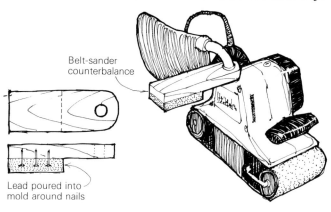

Belt-sander counterbalance

Lead poured into mold around nails

Woodturning on a Metal Lathe

Is there something different about Michelle Holzapfel's turned work? One turner, after learning how a piece was made, thought it appeared mechanical. She agrees: "My work has changed since I picked up this method. It has a removed quality which I like."

When Holzapfel first encountered the lathe, she knew she had found her craft. She began developing skills with the woodturner's usual selection of tools—keep the bevel rubbing, lift the handle, roll the tool, swing the handle. It's frustrating learning a delicate craft from books. "I can remember a few times having the feeling of being in control," she said, "but the effort to cut correctly diverted my energy from making the shape I wanted."

Holzapfel's lathe was assembled by her machinist father from odd parts, and it includes the cross slide and compound that metal-lathe operators use for precision work. When she tried these controls for shaping wood, she put her hand tools away forever.

Remember the drawing toy you had as a kid, with a screen and two little knobs? One knob made the stylus move up or down, the other moved it right or left, and you wound up with a sketch that looked like an etching. Remember the frustration in trying to draw a curved line? It took heroic concentration yet everything still came out with jagged corners. Controls on a machinist's lathe work the same way. The cutting tool is mounted rigidly in the mechanism and moved at right angles to the lathe bed by the cross-slide crank. The compound crank controls longitudinal movements. Holzapfel moves the controls simultaneously and independently to develop the graceful curves usually associated with freehand turning.

Many of us who turn wood are in love with the dance, those odd contortions we perform that echo the evolving shape on the lathe. Holzapfel's turning is more cerebral. She stands quietly in deep concentration, twirling a couple of cranks. Her control is as sure as any hand-turner's and her work is as fine. But she is free of worry about the tool digging in or catching in a crevice. "At first I missed the flexibility of using hand tools," she said, "but within a matter of days the machinery just fell away. I have no thought of bevels rubbing or anything but where the edge is and where I want it to be. I'm really free to concentrate on the shape.

"Because I don't have to hold the tool, I don't get tired. If I alternate sitting and standing, I can work eight, nine, ten hours a day."

Instead of the risk of working freehand, Holzapfel savors the adventure of working burls, crotches and spalted wood. Though her pieces are elegantly formed and superbly polished (two rubbed coats of tung oil and a third left to set on the surface), a bowl's contour may be interrupted by included bark, or the eye may be distracted from the delicate shape of a plate by a random spalt pattern. It is a harmonious discord that gives Holzapfel's work its vitality. "If a piece of wood is flawless," she said, "I don't know what to do with it. Working perfect wood bores me to tears."

With her husband, David, Holzapfel shares a shop, two children and a basic approach to wood. He makes tables of wildly shaped slabs in what he calls an "aformal" style. Their showroom in Marlboro, Vt., is called "Applewood," the translation of their German name.

"We have a common philosophy taking off in two completely different directions," said Michelle. "David believes in real randomness while I want to formalize things. But we both try to let the wood talk to us."

Reflecting on her technique, Holzapfel believes that handicapped persons could use it to gain access to turning. "A handicap is just a limitation. In a way, I consider myself handicapped. I can't build enough muscle to turn with hand tools for hours. I would have given up turning long ago, but through sheer luck I came upon a way."   □

The drive system of Holzapfel's lathe, above, harks back to the days of steam and lineshafts. The motor is mounted below the headstock and drives a jack shaft by means of a belt. The jack-shaft drives a second shaft above it, and pulleys on the two give twin speed ranges. The upper shaft has a four-step pulley that mates with a counterpart on the headstock shaft giving a total of eight speeds. An idler on the belt works through a ratcheted lever to engage and disengage the lathe from the motor. The idler will also work as a slip-clutch, allowing very low speeds when revving up heavy, eccentric chunks. Instead of hand-held gouges and skews, Holzapfel grinds her own tools from tool-steel blanks. Pictured at right are a parting tool, a left-hand cutter and a right-hand cutter. Each tool has its own holder. The tools, say Holzapfel, stay sharper longer than hand tools and require only a touch-up on the grinder once a week.

Richard Starr is a contributing editor of this magazine. Photos by the author.

Chucking up odd-shaped pieces, Holzapfel rounds them off as quickly as most turners would with hand tools. Standing to the side, above, keeps her out of the path of flying chips. Rounding off at low speeds, she runs the lathe slowly and since it's bolted to the floor, vibration is minimal.

Holzapfel uses a diamond-point tool, top, to shape a cherry vase. Having become accustomed to the machinist's lathe, she finds it easy to trace a contour while reducing its diameter, a feat of considerable coordination with a compound tool rest. Above, she uses a left-hand cutter to shape a vase's flaring top. Cross slides and compounds are available for many woodturning lathes and old metal lathes of all sizes can be adapted for woodturning.

The finest wooden turnings are possible on the metal lathe. At left, the vase's flare was intentionally interrupted by included defects, as was the thin-walled bowl, above. Metal-working tools leave fine ridges which can be removed quickly by 60-grit sandpaper. Holzapfel sands down to 600 grit before applying a tung-oil finish.

71

Dough Trays
The Southern tradition of handmade wooden bowls

by Delbert Greear

Though the handmade wooden bowl has an ancient and honorable past, it has become rare in modern times as people have turned to mass-produced substitutes. One form of wooden bowl, however, is still in demand—at least here in the South. This is the so-called dough tray—a large wooden bowl, sometimes round but more commonly oblong, that is traditionally used for the mixing, kneading and "rising" of bread dough. The dough tray has appeal for its charm, and it remains practical for making bread. The form, however, is not limited to this use. It can be large or small, and it can function as a salad bowl, a serving tray, a nut bowl, and so on. I have been making wooden bowls for several years, and here are some of the things I've learned.

The dough tray was an everyday item in the lives of our ancestors. Much of the tradition for it and other forms of wooden bowl came from Europe with the early settlers, but the tradition also owes much to the American Indian, who shared his knowledge of many crafts with his immigrant neighbors. Before the Europeans arrived, the first Americans used fire to help craft their bowls and worked with tools of stone and bone. Beavers' teeth were used for gouges. After trade with the settlers was established, metal tools were available to the Indians, and bowls became an important item of barter. The Cherokees of North Carolina still carve and trade very fine wooden bowls.

Choosing the wood—In the Southern Highlands forest and in the East, the choice of wood for bowls is large. Tulip poplar, river birch, wild cherry, black walnut, maple, basswood, buckeye and apple are all commonly used. Out West I made bowls from quaking aspen, and in the far north on the Yukon River, I used paper birch and northern poplar

---

Delbert Greear lives in Sautee, Ga., employing himself in country woodcraft. Drawings by Clay Johnston.

(cottonwood). Many other woods might also be chosen, so long as a few points are kept in mind. The grain should be smooth and closed. The wood should split straight and smell sweet, or at least not impart strong or bad flavors to food. And to make bowls, you need sound, whole logs several inches larger in diameter than the bowl you want to make, and of sufficient length to allow for cutting off checked ends.

There are several reasons I prefer to make bowls from green wood or from wood left as a whole log until I'm ready to carve. Green wood is much easier to carve than dry wood, and it splits cleanly into bolts of suitable size. When a bowl is properly made and finished from green wood, it will season nicely, retaining colors that kiln-drying destroys. If the grain is straight and free of large knots, warping (which can be a problem when using green wood) will be minimal. The hollow of the bowl lets the wood shrink and change shape slightly without cracking as it dries.

You can make a bowl from dry wood: it will be more uniform in texture and color than one made from green wood, and more stable. But it will also be much harder to carve. If you must postpone carving the green wood, or prefer to carve it dry, it is wise to season a piece quite a bit larger than the final blank desired. Crosscut the log about 6 in. or 8 in. longer at each end, to allow for checking. Then split the log in half with wedges or maul, and coat the ends with paraffin or beeswax, to minimize checking. To insure that the ends of the rim will be strong, cut away the pith of the wood and the first four or five growth rings. Then remove the bark. Some longitudinal cracking in the sapwood of the blank is to be expected. This can be minimized by cutting off some of the sapwood where the bottom of the bowl will be, thereby relieving pressure on the sides.

Doty or spalted wood is often used for contemporary bowls because of the beauty it reveals when carved. If you

choose to carve spalted wood, be sure your tools are extra sharp, as the wood tends to flake and is difficult to finish smoothly. I would not recommend it for very thin bowls, but it's fine for large, thick, decorative bowls, though you sacrifice some strength and durability with it as compared to green or properly seasoned wood.

A slight bulge in the side of a log can hide a flaw—a dead limb, for example, overgrown by sound wood. This can mean a hole in the wall of your bowl; on the other hand it can mean a handsome burl figure. Twisted grain or an offset heart with crowded growth rings to one side of the log means the finished product will twist as it dries. If you like freeform bowls, this can be an advantage. I like symmetrical bowls, and thus prefer a straight round log with the heartwood well centered.

Whatever your choice of wood, be sure to cut off all end-checks before starting to carve your bowl, and cut out

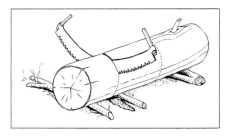

all radial cracks in the heart of the wood. Don't forget that a check extends a little beyond the point where you can see it. If you leave any part of a check in your bowl, it will spread when the bowl dries. For a full-size bread bowl—big enough for making four or five loaves of bread—you need a piece of wood that is free of defects, 20 in. to 24 in. long, 18 in. to 20 in. wide, and thick enough to allow 3 in. or 6 in. of depth in the finished product.

Roughing out the bowl—When you are starting with a fresh cut from a log, you first have to peel the bark (a step already taken with seasoned wood). Next split the log in half. Some judg-

Greear begins his dough trays by shaping the outside of the blank with a hatchet, above. Then he hollows the inside with a bent sweep gouge, supporting the blank in a cradle, as shown at right. With the inside excavated, he returns to the outside for a second cut, this time with a gouge, below, leaving a foot at the bottom and flares at the rim, which serve as handles. After more smoothing and sanding, the bowl is finished. Below right, bowls in foreground and in background were carved with heartwood down, contrary to the shape of the split log. The rest of the bowls were carved with heartwood up.

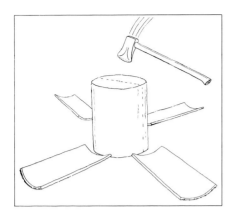

ment is necessary to choose the diameter for your split, as seldom is a log perfectly round. Good clean wood can be split with a solid stroke of an ax. Sometimes a maul and wedges are needed. If you lack confidence in your aim with an ax, you can use a froe to start the split square across the log. For twisted and knotty wood, you might need to saw the wood lengthwise with a chainsaw or a crosscut saw. However you go about it, your purpose is to halve the wood. Usually each half will make a bowl.

Once I have chosen and split a blank of wood, I stand it on a good solid chopping block and proceed to hew down the outside of the bowl. My tool for this job is a small hatchet with a gently rounded bevel on both faces. A hatchet beveled on only one face is right for hewing flat surfaces, but makes carving a round shape difficult. Ingenuity, balance and rhythm play a part in this operation, which with a large bowl may take several hours to accomplish. The ends must be rounded down to roughly the curve you want, and the bottom flattened so that the top is made level. Now and then you want to rest your bowl on something flat and stand back and look to see if it is coming out evenly. If you are striving for symmetry, you want to work from end to end, side to side, and around and around, taking off a little here and a little there to balance your bowl.

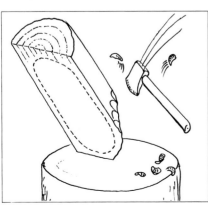

The shape you are working toward is a matter of design and personal taste. I like to leave a well-defined, undercut foot on the bottom of my bowls. This not only looks nice, it also allows the sides of the bowl to be cut to a more uniform thickness without sacrificing the strength and surface area of the bottom. A broad, flat bottom is traditional and makes for strength and stability. A shallow undercut, however, eliminates high spots upon which dough bowls are wont to rock and shift. For handles, I usually just flare the ends. Some people prefer protruding handles, and others, finger grooves for gripping the bowl.

Once the outside is roughed out, I proceed immediately to the inside. I use a long, bent sweep gouge and a wooden maul for this work; others use an adze. The trickiest problem is holding the bowl still while you work on it. The best solution I have found is a cradle made of two halves of a log just far enough apart to cradle the bowl, and fastened to a large thick board. It's quick to make, and gets more versatile

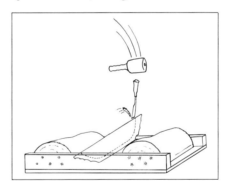

with use; and if you find that it doesn't accommodate itself to the size blank you want to work, it's easy to make another holder. With this rig I sit on a low stool in front of the cradle, and the blows of the maul force the bowl securely down into the cradle against the opposing log rather than propelling it all over the yard.

There is an alternative: you could carve the inside first. Dirk Rosse, who carves bowls for a living (*FWW* #32), roughs out the inside of a sawn blank first, which has the advantage of leaving the outside a regular rectangular shape that is easy to hold steady against an L-shaped stop on his workstump. I prefer carving the outside first, however. The flaws in the wood are more easily discovered and taken care of; the work goes quickly and the final shape is easier to visualize, making symmetry simpler to achieve. The solid block of wood,

roughed down on the outside, is a stronger structure to work on and seems less liable to check than the hollowed log you have if you shape the inside first. Once the outside is roughed to the desired shape and you have determined that the wood is sound, you can position the bowl right side up while carving the sides to the desired thickness—it's easy to run a hand along the rim of the work and feel its thickness. A quick glance tells you the relation of the outside to the inside. If the bowl is upside down, it must be turned over often, and you just can't tell thick and thin spots as readily.

Perhaps some of the advantages I find in this order of work have to do with the tools I prefer. Hollowing out a large bowl takes time, and though there is the temptation to think of shortcuts, I work entirely with handtools. Some people use a chainsaw and make a series of lateral cuts with the end of the blade in what is to be the inside of the bowl. The resulting blocks are easily knocked out with a hatchet, an adze or a gouge. I find this solution unpleasantly noisy, and the possibility for major error is great. Yet some people are real artists with a chainsaw, and you can't argue with success. I prefer the hand work because it keeps me in touch with the wood, and the shape evolves more pleasantly to the eye and mind.

Taking the slow approach, however, is tiring, especially for the arms and back. But anyone who has carved green wood can tell you what will happen if you stop very long while there is still too much wood on the inside of your bowl, or even on the outside. Cracking in the heart, checking on the ends and longitudinal cracks in the sapwood are likely if you don't get your blank well roughed out before leaving it for more than a few hours. When you do have your bowl roughed out, leave it in a shady, cool place, perhaps under a tarp, or sealed in a plastic bag.

Finishing the bowl—Once your bowl has been roughed out to the desired shape and to a fairly even thickness overall, you are ready for the finishing work. I use a long, bent, Swiss No. 7 sweep gouge for most of this process. A long, bent sweep of shallower profile—about a No. 2—is handy for smoothing out the deep cuts made by the No. 7 gouge. I also use the shallow gouge for all my final cuts, as it more nearly matches the curve of the bowl. I find that a small carving knife comes in handy for the bowl's top edge.

As a general rule, the outside is refined first, allowing more control over the final shape of the bowl. The thickness of the sides is determined by the final cuts on the inside. Of course, as you put the finishing touches on your bowl, you will be going around and around it inside and out, chipping away a little here and a little there until you finally decide you have done enough.

To shape the outside I start with the foot and cut smoothly toward the top. I leave a ridge of wood at the rim of the bowl; from this I make either handles or

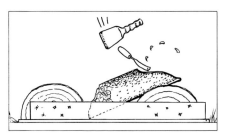

a graceful flare for gripping. It is important to work toward even thickness in the bowl sides; this will minimize the chance of warping and checking in the finished product.

For the final cuts on the inside, I hold the bowl in my lap and work the gouge in a rocking motion toward my body, using the maul only when necessary to remove thick high spots. The maul-driven gouge leaves a ridged surface; to smooth these ridges, you pull the gouge by hand. I start the inside finishing cuts at the rim, working around and then down to the bottom of the bowl, keeping a smooth working face, as on the outside. During this finishing work, you should stand back often and look carefully at your work. The true measure of your craftsmanship will be revealed at the inside bottom of the bowl. From both ends, both sides and all four "cheeks," your gouge cuts must come out smoothly and evenly to the same level. The final cuts need to be made across the grain, to avoid riving or tearing the long grain. This calls for a keen edge and steady hand. The best gouge for this work has a shallow sweep in its end profile and a bend along its length, so that the handle will not bump into the rim of the bowl as you work. A bevel on the outside of the gouge and a little extra upturn at its end is best, so that the tool draws itself back out of the wood. Most spoon gouges are simply too steeply bent to be useful here.

Final touches and care—Wait a few days before leveling the foot, for as the bowl dries it will twist and change shape slightly. If the relative humidity is low, you can wrap the bowl in cloth or paper to slow drying, but allow it some air, or mildew may result. After a few days, most wood has stabilized enough to proceed. In leveling the bottom of the bowl, a piece of lightly greased, flat

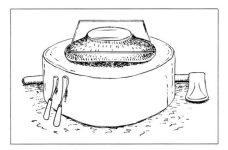

glass can be rubbed over it to show the high spots. A small plane is useful in this final leveling, though I often simply use a shallow gouge.

Sometimes, in spite of all your efforts, you will end up with a few seasoning checks or small radial cracks in the heart at the ends of the bowl; sometimes a hidden knothole will be revealed in the surface of the bowl. These are to be tolerated good-naturedly, though a little epoxy or glue mixed with sawdust will sometimes help.

The sap will continue to bleed out of green wood as it dries, and this will temporarily darken the wood and obscure the figure. After drying a few days, the bowl will be ready to sand, which will remove the stain left by the oxidation of the sap. I like to sand my bowls smooth enough so that the grain and figure of the wood show rather than the gouge marks. This smooth finish makes cleaning the bowl easy, and it takes oil well. A fairly fine sandpaper, 120-grit or finer, cuts green hardwood as well as a coarser grit would, without scratching the wood so badly.

I have found oil—animal or vegetable, applied when the sanding is finished—to be the best finish for dough bowls. Animal fat, properly rendered, makes an excellent finish that will penetrate better and last longer than vegetable oil. I've used groundhog, beaver and bear grease to good effect, as these are liquid at room temperature. Hog lard and beef suet are not as good, for they solidify and tend to get rancid. Of course, vegetable oils are more generally available to the modern craftsman and housekeeper than animal fat. I recom-

mend olive or safflower oil, as these penetrate better than corn, peanut or soybean oil. The bowl should be oiled often, especially after it is washed. For best results the oil should be rubbed in thoroughly with bare hands or a soft cloth. The heat from the hands and the friction from rubbing helps the oil penetrate the wood. Excess oil should be wiped off with a cloth.

I've heard from several sources that past generations used a small cloth bag containing salt to apply the oil. Perhaps the salt was believed to draw moisture from the wood, though I really don't know the reason for this interesting practice. At any rate, I have seen many old dough trays in antique stores and at auctions, and I believe a well-made one, if oiled and cared for, should easily last a generation, even with constant use.

*　　　*　　　*

The dough tray was once an important household item, likely to be installed in the kitchen when a couple first set up housekeeping, along with the cookstove, frying pan and cooking pot. It was a piece of family history—maybe

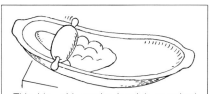

This big, old, poplar bowl is matched with a special rolling pin whose handles ride on the sides of the bowl. The rolling pin is pushed down the length of the bowl, flattening the bread dough along the bowl bottom. The dough is then folded over into a pile in the middle of the bowl and the rolling pin flattens it.

an uncle crafted it for his niece, a grandmother passed it to a granddaughter, or a newlywed husband carved it for his wife. Today the wooden dough tray has become a luxury instead of the household necessity it once was. Plastic, steel and mass-produced crockery bowls have replaced it. Bread is not made in the average home in the quantities it once was; and when it is made, the breadmaker will use an inexpensive enamel dishpan for mixing it and will knead it on a Formica counter. Yet this has not spelled the end of the dough tray. What is there that can grace the table so beautifully at Thanksgiving as a great wooden bowl full of bread, fruit or salad? Nostalgia is a strong force, and the wooden bowl represents a heritage and a fine old tradition. Whenever people recognize this, that tradition lives on. □

Linenfold Carving
Planes and gouges shape folds

by Rick Bütz

L inenfold carving creates in wood the effect of creases and undulating folds of cloth or parchment. The design seems to have originated with French and Dutch woodworkers around the year 1450, and was probably inspired by the shapes and patterns of draped altar cloths. Several surviving pieces show intricately carved borders reminiscent of the rich embroidery found on ecclesiastical appointments. During the late 15th century, linenfold was introduced into England, where it quickly caught on among the tradesman woodcarvers. The style became so popular that it is now the hallmark of Tudor-Gothic design.

Linenfold was usually carved on a rectangular panel, which was then fitted into a grooved framework. The design could easily be altered in length, and today can be seen as paneling in houses, public buildings and churches, including Westminster Abbey. Linenfold was also popular for paneled doors, chests, beds and other household furnishings of the 15th and 16th centuries. Although many of the early examples were realistic interpretations of cloth folds, the design eventually became quite stylized, and it is even found sideways at times, as if the idea of a hanging drapery had become quite forgotten. As tastes changed toward the end of the 16th century, linenfold carving was replaced by the elaborate floral themes of the early Renaissance.

There are many traditional designs to choose from. I've included drawings of a few to give you an idea of the range. The old woodcarvers varied each panel slightly, achieving a vitality that let them cover an entire room or hallway with linenfold without it seeming monotonous or repetitious. This variety sets the original Gothic woodcarvings apart from later imitations. So don't be afraid to modify the design, but keep in mind that it will be difficult to visualize the end result. Make precise drawings: a full-scale cross section and a clearly defined sketch of the end folds, as shown at right.

The carving of linenfold is basically a two-step procedure. The long folds and undulations are planed out, then the ends are shaped with various carving tools. One aspect that makes carving a linenfold panel so enjoyable and interesting is the variety of tools that are used. While you could use routers and circular saws, it's just as quick and more satisfying to do it with traditional hand tools. For cutting down the background and shaping the contours of the long folds and creases, use a rabbet plane, a plow plane, one or two round planes, and a small block plane (photo **A**, top of facing page). For carving the end folds, you will need one or two fishtail gouges of medium sweep and a back-bent gouge. If you don't own all of these tools, you can modify the design to suit the ones you have.

Rick Bütz, 34, makes his living by carving wildlife in Blue Mountain Lake, N.Y. Photos by Ellen Bütz, except where noted.

This linenfold panel, planed and carved in traditional oak, is ready to be let into a frame.

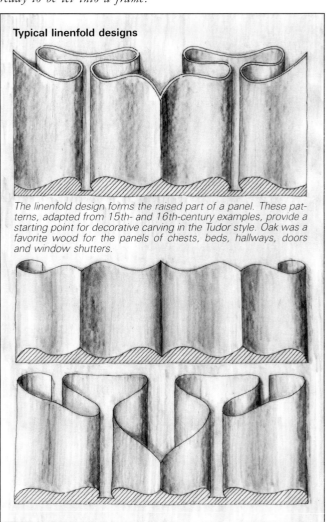

Typical linenfold designs

The linenfold design forms the raised part of a panel. These patterns, adapted from 15th- and 16th-century examples, provide a starting point for decorative carving in the Tudor style. Oak was a favorite wood for the panels of chests, beds, hallways, doors and window shutters.

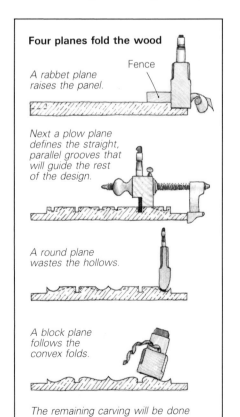

A

Four planes put back to work: The rabbet plane, at the left, lowers the background, and the plow plane grooves the guidelines; then the block plane and the round plane shape the curves.

Begin the linenfold by marking out the border with a marking gauge. Be sure to allow some extra material for a tongue, to fit the panel into a door or a furniture carcase. Next cut down the background along the edges with a rabbet plane (below). The most accurate way to set up the rabbeting is to clamp a fence, a smooth 1-in. by 2-in. board along the face of the panel, to guide the plane and keep the edges straight. As a general rule, the background should not be taken down any more than one-half the thickness of your panel. If you exaggerate the vertical scale of the drawing too much and go for a deeper relief, the

end folds will become fragile, which is a real problem in oak, the traditional Gothic wood.

When the background has been cut down and smoothed, mark out the ends of the panel by tracing a cross-section template from your plan. Make sure that your markings are symmetrical and that they line up on both ends of your board. I use a plow plane with a ⅛-in. iron to cut a series of grooves that exactly match the deepest parts of the cross section. The grooves will serve as a guide for hollowing out the undulations with a round plane, keeping the edges parallel and preventing the shaping from going too deep. This is important for a clean, crisp job.

Use a ¾-in. round plane, or something similar, and carefully hollow out the concave folds. The plane iron should be absolutely sharp and the sole of the plane should be waxed with either paraffin or a hard, cross-country ski wax. Ski waxes come in different colors to indicate their relative hardness and the kinds of snow they should be used on. I find that harder waxes, such as blue or green glider, make planing easy and keep the cuts true and clean.

Next smooth off the convex surfaces of the folds with a block plane, and then use a shallow carving gouge to eliminate any remaining ridges. A #5 sweep in a 12mm to 16mm width and a small flat chisel work quite well for this job. The rest of the shaping will be done with carving gouges and the lightest of finish-sanding.

Now make another tracing and template showing the shape and outlines of the outer end folds. Transfer this to the ends of the panel (photo **B**), and begin "setting in" with a mallet and gouges.

"Setting in" means to drive the tool down vertically with a mallet (photo **C**). Then make a horizontal cut to meet the curves. The sweep of the gouges should correspond to the curves of the lines. For this panel, I used an 8mm #5 and a 4mm #7 to set in all of the lines. Don't drive gouges too deep—they can break. When you set in, stop about ¹⁄₁₆ in. short of the background depth. This is important because the outlines will eventually be undercut in order to give the final piece a feeling of depth and separation from the background. If you drive the gouge down too far at this stage, the cuts will show after you undercut, leaving the work rough.

Using a 14mm #7 gouge, ease off the edge you have just set in. This is done by carefully carving a smooth bevel that extends from the inner fold line down to the outer fold line, leaving no

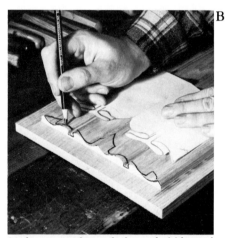

B

Make a template of the end folds and trace it on the work.

C

Set in by driving vertical cuts to within ¹⁄₁₆ in. of the background.

Four planes fold the wood

A rabbet plane raises the panel.

Fence

Next a plow plane defines the straight, parallel grooves that will guide the rest of the design.

A round plane wastes the hollows.

A block plane follows the convex folds.

The remaining carving will be done with chisels and gouges.

Linenfold paneling, an imitation of draped cloth in wood, evolved into one of the high points of Tudor design. This wall panel, from the Parnham House in Beaminster, England, is typical of much architectural woodwork of the 15th and 16th centuries.

D

Bevel between the lines with a gouge, leaving bottom edge of 'cloth.'

E

Outline the edges with a V-tool, cutting with the grain as much as possible.

less than $\frac{1}{16}$ in. of that contoured line (photo **D**). To begin setting in the inner folds, sketch in the line of the folds, then outline these edges with a 6mm V-tool (photo **E**). To prevent splintering when working across the grain, start each cut from the outer edges of the fold and work toward the center.

Make your horizontal cuts in from the end with a 5mm #3 gouge to clear away the waste, and use an 8mm #5 back-bent gouge to even up the outline (photo **F**). Undercut them slightly. A back-bent gouge is perfect for finishing up linenfold, but it can feel awkward if you are not used to it—the action is the reverse of the more familiar spoon gouge's. A straight gouge can also be used for undercutting, but be careful—the angle of cut may split the wood.

Use the small #3 gouge to clear away any waste, and smooth out the surfaces of the end folds. Use the back-bent gouge to undercut the original set-in line, and then clear away any background material that was left earlier.

As a last step, here's one of woodcarving's fine points: Take a small carving chisel, or shallow gouge, and cut a small bevel along the entire edge of the end fold lines, to reflect light so that the edge will shine (photo **G**). If this line were left sharp, it would disappear in most light and spoil the illusion of cloth folds captured in wood. Finally, lightly touch up any rough spots with fine sandpaper. Just be careful not to smooth over or obscure any edges that should be left crisp, and try to leave the tool-mark facets prominent. Gothic woodcarvings, particularly linenfold, should be boldly simple. Those old craftsmen cut right to the line. □

F

Undercut the folds slightly with a back-bent gouge.

G

Bevel the edges to catch the light, further defining the carving.

Grainger McKoy's Carved Birds
A wooden covey on springs of steel

by Roger Schroeder

Though they are wooden feathers that spread out in flight, metal feet that cling to brass foliage, and basswood bodies that seem to defy gravity, the birds carved by Grainger McKoy look alive. One of the finest wildlife artists in America, McKoy has spent ten years perfecting his art. He has a degree in wildlife biology and training in architecture from Clemson University, but he learned nearly all his techniques from his mentor, Gilbert Maggione, South Carolina painter and bird sculptor. Maggione showed McKoy how to create dynamic postures and how to avoid the static forms common to decoy carving. He taught McKoy how to insert individual feathers and how to give unerring attention to anatomical proportions and detail. McKoy now knows so much about his birds that, pointing to a bobwhite quail he carved, he can tell you how old the bird it represents would be, and why.

Since his two-year association with Maggione, McKoy has made more than 75 bird sculptures, some consisting of a number of birds. His and Maggione's works have been exhibited at the Museum of Natural History in New York, as well as in shows throughout the East and South.

McKoy's workplace on Wadmalaw Island, 20 miles outside of Charleston, S.C., is a tin-roofed country store converted to a workshop and an upstairs studio. Near a window is an old graffiti-covered student desk where he does much of his carving. He has few traditional carving tools, and his only standing power tool is a bandsaw. About his desk are large piles of Styrofoam blocks, which he uses to make models of his birds. When I visited him in the summer of 1980, he was working on a commissioned sculpture of a covey of quail: 15 bobwhites exploding into flight (p. 81). The uppermost quail soars four feet above the base. His most ambitious project thus far, it wasn't completed until the spring of 1981.

Though McKoy did make preliminary sketches of the covey, the drawings confined themselves to basic joinery and to the relative positions of the birds. He didn't do exacting sketches of his sculpture, claiming that too much planned detail would have bound him to a preconceived image. Rather, he let first the Styrofoam models and then the wood tell him how the sculpture would look. Each of the 15 birds began as a Styrofoam model. "They're easy to throw away," McKoy says, "just something you can play with." Cardboard wings can be variously positioned, and heads can be cut off, rotated and reattached with pins to test different postures.

Before McKoy could begin carving the individual quail, he had to see how they would be positioned in flight. On a turntable work surface that economized his own motions, he used thin, vertical steel rods that held chemistry-lab clamps, which in turn held pieces of brass tubing at right angles. A wood screw through the flattened end of this tubing could temporarily hold a bird, either Styrofoam or wood, in the air. These supports allowed McKoy to position the quail wherever he wanted until he was satisfied with the places they all held.

One of McKoy's preliminary sketches of his covey sculpture, showing the steel-ribbon understructure that supports each bird.

McKoy's solution to keeping the birds airborne, without hanging them like mobiles, is ingenious yet simple. The quail are joined together from the lowest to the highest, even if only by the tip of a feather. Yet how could solid wooden-feathered birds support each other when the uppermost life-sized bird is four feet off the ground? One answer is that the quail are not solid wood. McKoy bandsaws the bodies in half and hollows them with a #5 gouge before rejoining the halves. This reduces the weight by a third or more. The other answer is that the birds are joined from top to bottom by lengths of ⅛-in. thick by 1-in. wide steel, an annealed high-carbon knife-blade steel that can be bent, ground, welded and then hardened by heat-treating in a furnace. The hollowed bodies have another advantage, for a steel ribbon runs into the bird's body cavity where wood screws hold the metal to the wood. Another length of steel can then emerge from beneath a wing and end as a detailed feather, complete with

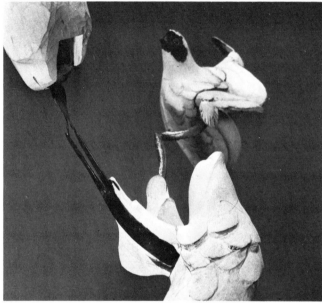

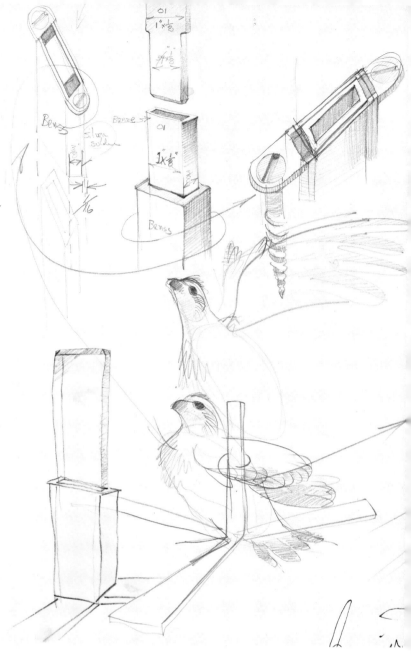

To make the bodies of the birds in his sculpture as light and structurally stable as possible, McKoy bandsaws them in two and hollows out the insides with a gouge (photo, top). Note the high-carbon steel ribbon that has been let into the wing and screwed in place. This is part of the understructure of the covey that supports the birds imperceptibly, presenting the illusion of flight. McKoy devised a tenon-and-socket joint (above) which allows the pieces to be disconnected when necessary. The basic joinery was worked out in sketches as at right.

rachis (quill) and barbs, those parallel fibers that stand out like the teeth of a comb. To this steel feather is welded the steel counterpart of yet another bird. The rest of the feathers are individually carved of wood. Using the branching steel ribbon, McKoy can have one bird giving support to two others above or beside it, one at each wing. Where bodies and not wing feathers touch, steel supports are concealed elsewhere in the anatomy.

The problem of disassembling so many birds for carving and detailing was solved with a socket-and-tenon joint. By making the steel ribbon in sections and brazing two flat pieces of brass and spacers to the end of one, McKoy was able to create a slot to accept the tenoned end of another section as shown in his drawing above. So even where the tip of a steel feather is permanently welded to the feather of another bird, its other end can slip into a slot carefully hidden among wooden feathers. As a result, McKoy can simply lift birds off one another, enabling him to work on them individually, then replace them.

After each bird was mocked up in Styrofoam, its wooden counterpart was shaped on the bandsaw, though McKoy had to rough out each one at least twice before he got what he wanted. He used basswood because of its stability and resistance to checking and cracking. It contains little resin and so it is easy to paint. He has in the past used poplar for feathers

because this wood can be cut extremely thin and still retain its strength. But poplar, McKoy points out, is fibrous, and thus is more time-consuming to work than basswood.

While the bone-and-sinew part of the wings was roughed out from thick stock and attached with screws to the quail bodies, the individual feathers began as ⅛-in. thick basswood blanks. After drawing an outline on the blank, McKoy carved with a 2½-in. pocket knife each of the bird's primary, secondary and tertiary feathers. These were then reduced in thickness with a hand-held, motor-driven, ½-in. by ½-in. sanding drum. The larger feathers could be held by hand, but for the smaller ones tweezers had to be used. For feathers that had to be bent, McKoy first heated the blanks on a bending iron and then bent or twisted them to shape.

Once shaped, the feathers needed barb details. For this McKoy used a burning tool that has a skewed tip—the Detailer, manufactured by Colwood Electronics (715 Westwood Ave., Long Branch, N. J. 07740). It is held like a pen and drawn forward, the slanted end of the heating element burning a straight line into the wood. He also used the Detailer for burning in feather detail on the birds' bodies.

McKoy's attention to anatomical detail is evident when one sees a wing disassembled into as many as 22 individual feathers. Yet he claims that if he reproduced them exactly as they are found on a bird, each feather would have taken him

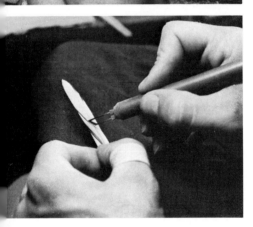

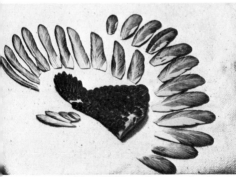

Top, McKoy shapes a feather in poplar using a sharp pocket knife. Next, he thicknesses the feather with a sanding drum in a Foredom rotary tool. Details (barbs and rachises) are then burned in with an electric hot knife. A wing may be made up of as many as 22 individual feathers (bottom photo). At right, the finished sculpture reveals an unexpected flurry of flight. Photo: Ted Borg.

For rough carving and shaping, McKoy uses a rotary stone in his Foredom power tool. The stone leaves behind a textured surface which enhances the expressiveness of the piece by deepening shadows.

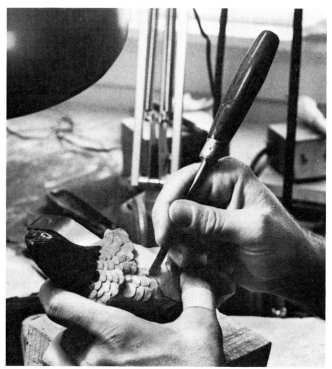

For fine carving—defining and undercutting the feathers and other features—he uses a skew chisel and holds it much as you would a pencil. This grip affords little power but maximum control.

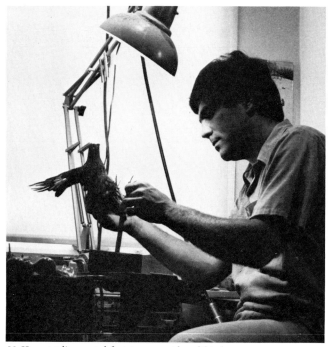

McKoy applies metal feet to a completed bird.

a day to complete, requiring, then, two years to do nothing more than the wing feathers of 15 quail.

McKoy's major tool for carving and shaping is the Foredom Series R rotary tool. Not only can the Dremel bits he uses work both Styrofoam and wood, but they can also add the details to a steel wing. For fine carving he uses a skew chisel which will undercut and define the feathers of a bird's body. But McKoy uses a rotary stone in his Foredom for coarse shaping. This setup will not produce sharp details. Instead, the stone will create a shadow effect that gives "expression, not duplication." This was of particular concern in the covey sculpture because the quail are meant to be viewed from a distance. Too much detail would look busy and detract from the overall effect.

The eyes of his birds are taxidermy glass, and the feet are brass, the metal being soft and easily worked. The toes of the quail, he solders on individually, and the completed feet are held in sockets in the birds' underbodies. The Foredom rotary tool again comes into play, with a carbide cutter used to form the scales on the birds' legs and toes. The feet of the still-grounded quail are brazed to lead plates in the base, which give the entire sculpture stability.

All of the quail were painted with oil-base paints, with the exception of the white areas, which were lacquered. He used lacquer because it could effectively cover the dark umber base produced by the burned-in details, which entirely cover the birds. Wings and feathers were removed, and painted with an airbrush to fill the smallest crevices. The final colors, however, were hand-painted. The process took an entire day for each bird. After the painting was completed, the feathers were glued into the wings.

About his sculpture, McKoy says, "This is the way a covey of quail might appear if frozen in flight by a stop-action photograph. But I didn't have any such photograph, and so I had to follow my instincts and intuitions in deciding how these birds look at the very moment they break from cover."

Remarkably portrayed are the instincts of flight and escape at the bottom, giving way to the natural grace of birds overcoming gravity at the top. It is a study in conflict that McKoy seeks to represent in many of his compositions. McKoy is a birdhunter and knows the habits of quail and other game birds. He is also licensed to collect game birds, and large drawers in his studio hold dozens of preserved birds, wings, and feet, all of which aid in his work. Yet, he does not want his works to look like taxidermy. His are wood sculptures in which anatomical accuracy must serve an expressive end. One recent piece, three weeks in the making, is what he describes as a pen-and-ink in wood. Out of a roughly carved basswood background emerges the body of an unpainted semipalmated plover—emphatically a composition in wood.

To McKoy the design of flight and escape are more important than carving technique or background. Over the years he has been de-emphasizing the habitats in his compositions, claiming that the background was dictating the piece and that they looked too much like museum dioramas. Always improving and simplifying his work, McKoy strives to avoid inert forms and excessive detail. Future works will probably include more examples like his pen-and-ink plover, where the concept of a bird as wood is clearly defined. □

Roger Schroeder, of Amityville, N.Y., is a woodcarver and freelance writer. Photos by the author, except where noted.

Burning-In Bird Feathers

by Eldridge Arnold

Man has had a long and varied experience with birds. He has envied them, worshipped them, painted and sculpted them and eaten them for dinner. Birds as symbols and motifs are everywhere, from King Tut's tomb to silver dollars, from pueblo petroglyphs to automobile ads. But the thousands of contemporary bird carvers in America trace the origins of their craft to the dinner table, and not to the making of feathered icons for hungry spirits.

Learning from the Indians how to make duck decoys with mud and rushes, American colonials soon began to carve decoys from wood and to color them with paint to achieve a lifelike quality. Anchored close to the hunter's blind, in shallow water, these wooden ducks attracted real ones, which made for good sport and tasty meals. These early decoys (those that have survived) are now collector's items and museum pieces. Decoys are still being made for hunting purposes, but most all of them are carved by machine or injection-molded from Styrofoam. And yet even with this great outpouring of machine-made models, the art of decoy carving is more widely practiced now than it ever has been before.

One branch of the craft, however, has evolved beyond just making decoys, and its practitioners find a special challenge in trying to reach absolute realism in their work. Not only do they pay closer attention to form and posture, but they strive to replicate the tiniest of anatomical details, down to the very barbs of the feathers. Texture is the subtlest and most difficult quality to get, created by a combination of carving, burning and painting.

Once the body of the bird is shaped and smoothed, and the parts for the feathers have been cut, you can pencil in the outlines of the individual feathers (photo, below left). Instead of carving around the feathers on the body, which gives them a shingled, layered look, I prefer to burn-in the edges, as well as the barbs. There can be as many as 300 barbs on a small ¾-in. long feather; so a good deal of practice with the burning tool is needed to get the required degree of control.

I use a couple of different burning tools—the Hot Tool, available from Hot Tools, Inc., 7 Hawks St., Marblehead, Mass. 01945, and the Detailer, made by Colwood Electronics, 715 Westwood Ave., Long Branch, N.J. 07740. The latter has a rheostat control, allowing you to regulate the heat; the Hot Tool also can be equipped with an accessory heat-control unit. The skewed tip of the tool must be kept sharp, and its beveled faces cleaned often during use. I use 320-grit wet/dry sandpaper tacked to a block of wood to hone and clean the tip.

The burning pen is gripped somewhat like a pencil, but is usually moved away from you in sweeping strokes. Pausing too long will make the line dark and deep, and stopping at the end of a stroke will create a dark blob where you want the line to be finest. To avoid this, follow through with each stroke and lift the tool, while it is still in motion, from the wood. With practice you can develop a rhythm that will make the work proceed efficiently, but even then it takes several hours to burn-in the barbs on ten or twelve feathers. Because the barb lines are so close together and because you can't interrupt the motion of the tool, intense concentration is required, and it's best to take frequent breaks to keep from ruining your work. Most lines on feathers are slightly curved. To get the curve, you have to rotate the tool minutely as you move along the line. Use only the point of the tip, not its whole edge, and avoid making absolutely straight lines. Every carver has his own style, and with practice you'll find your own.

Burning-in these details imparts a warm, vibrant texture to the wood, and gives it a lifelike quality you wouldn't get from carving or scratching. I like the brownish color of burned lines to show through the paint. It adds a subtle touch of realism to the finished sculpture, and it shows the craftsman's hand. □

Eldridge Arnold, a retired graphic designer, is now a sculptor in Greenwich, Conn. For further reading on this topic, see Pyrography, The Art of Woodburning, *by Bernard Havez and Jean-Claude Varlet, Van Nostrand Reinhold, 135 West 50th St., New York, N.Y. 10020.*

Using real birds and photos for models, Arnold pencils in the outlines for the body feathers on a mourning dove, above. Several feathers on the bird's flank have been undercut to give them a shingled look, something the author does judiciously. Working in his lap, right, Arnold burns in the barbs of the feathers he has just drawn. The burning pen is drawn away from the body in sweeping strokes, and the thickness and depth of each line is controlled by pressure and duration of stroke.

JOINERY

The Scribed Joint
Masking wood movement in molded frames

by Morris J. Sheppard

When moldings meet at an inside corner, as in framing a paneled door, they can be mitered by cutting each piece to a 45° angle. The joint is quick and it looks fine...until wood movement inevitably opens up the miter. Scribing the joint is an alternative to the miter. In this method, you cut the rail molding to the exact reverse section of the molding it will overlap on the stile. This allows the wood to move without breaking the joint. Where a center rail meets a stile the scribed moldings will slide and remain tight even with seasonal movement. In this article, I've used an ovolo molding or "sticking" on the frame parts, as shown in figure 1. However, any molding except those with undercuts can be scribed. Undercut molding must be mitered. A version of the scribe called the cope-and-stick joint can be done on the shaper or tenoner, but you can get excellent results by scribing with hand tools.

You'll need a small backsaw, chisels, a gouge and a miter template.

The scribe joint's overlapping moldings hide wood movement.

A commercially-made template is brass, about 5 in. long and cut to a 45° angle at each end. You can make your own out of wood, but make sure it is dead accurate. Ovolo sticking is scribed with an in-cannel gouge whose radius matches that of the molding. You'll need a gouge to match each size of molding you want to scribe. Put a keen edge on the in-cannel by working the inside bevel with a slip stone and then remove the burr by holding the outside of the tool flat against a benchstone. Don't double-bevel the edge as you would a carving gouge. If you do, it won't cut straight.

Prepare your framework as you usually do. In my shop, we mortise the rails and the stiles on the slot mortiser, then insert a loose tenon. You can use a dowel joint or a conventional mortise and tenon, but when cutting the rails remember that their shoulders fit to the bottom of the panel rabbet and not to the inside edge of the molding. Mill the molding and the rabbet along the full length of the rails and stiles.

Begin the scribe by cutting away the molding on the stiles where the rails meet them—at the stile ends and the center of the rail if a middle stile is used. The molding should be cut

back even with the depth of the rabbet and ought to align with the listel on the rail. To get an accurate mark, hold the rail against the stile and strike a knife line, as in figure 2. Then saw down with the backsaw, being careful not to go deeper than the rabbet's depth. Remove the waste by paring with a chisel or by bandsawing.

Now move to the rails. Place the miter template over the molding at the end of the rail as in figure 3. Align it so the miter cut will end exactly at the tenon shoulder; use the rail listel as a guide. Fix the template with a clamp and then use a sharp chisel to pare away the waste. On the final cut, rest the back of the chisel firmly on the miter template. With the miter cut, the contoured edge of the molding outlines the scribe cuts, which are then made perpendicular to the edge of the rail. Cut straight down with a straight chisel at the listel, and with the in-cannel gouge make the concave shape that will mate over the stile molding (figure 4). Several cuts may be needed but the trick is to make the last cut precisely at the mark outlined by the miter. It helps to stand directly above the work with light from the side, casting a shadow at the outlined edge. If the gouge is keen, it will be easy to place it right on the line, and a firm push will be all that's needed. Be careful with the thinnest corner of the scribed molding, as it is prone to damage. Hold the gouge square to the work or a gap will show in the finished joint. Use a small chisel to clean up the bottom of the cut.

The scribe joint will also work in frames with a groove for the panel instead of a rabbet. Then the molding on the ends of the stiles gets cut away to the bottom of the groove and one tenon shoulder is offset to accommodate the rear wall of the groove (*FWW #18*, p.88).

Cut accurately, the scribed pieces should slide together perfectly, as in figure 5. And they should stay that way through many seasons of wood movement. ☐

Morris J. Sheppard designs and makes furniture and cabinets in Los Angeles, Calif. Photo by the author.

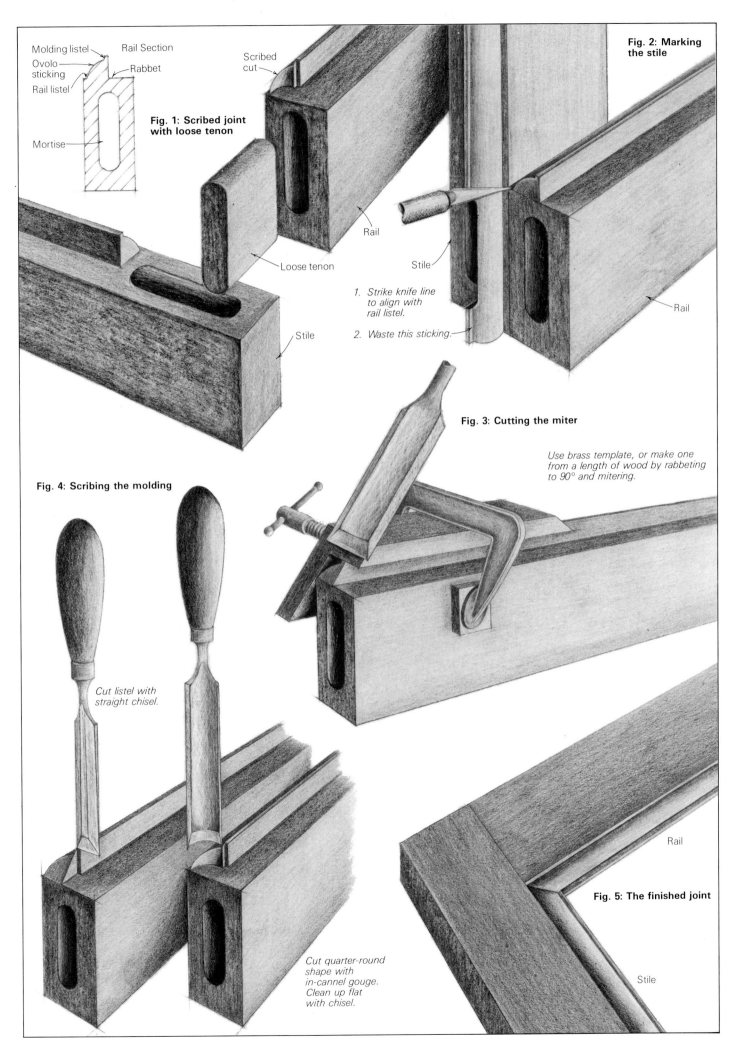

Molding listel — Rail Section
Ovolo sticking — Rabbet
Rail listel
Mortise

Fig. 1: Scribed joint with loose tenon

Scribed cut

Rail

Loose tenon

Stile

Stile

Fig. 2: Marking the stile

1. Strike knife line to align with rail listel.

2. Waste this sticking.

Rail

Fig. 3: Cutting the miter

Use brass template, or make one from a length of wood by rabbeting to 90° and mitering.

Fig. 4: Scribing the molding

Cut listel with straight chisel.

Cut quarter-round shape with in-cannel gouge. Clean up flat with chisel.

Rail

Fig. 5: The finished joint

Stile

Scribed mortise-and-tenon joinery in this 29-ft. trussed log bridge make all its parts securely interdependent.

Trussed Log Bridge
Scribed joints for structural strength

by Monroe Robinson

I hadn't thought of log work as being within the realm of fine woodworking until I saw the work of a master, Lee Cole, several years ago. After watching Cole work on a few jobs, I was ready to start a log project that had been offered to me eight years earlier: a 29-ft. trussed log bridge spanning a creek on a wilderness homestead at Lake Clark, some 140 air miles southeast of Anchorage, Alaska. The bridge was needed to connect the buildings that the owner had built on both sides of the creek. It needed to be strong and wide enough to support the front-end loader used on the homestead and to aesthetically complement the log buildings and the wilderness environment. It also required a rock foundation because the creek floods annually.

The project was started in the spring of 1978 when the creek flowed at its lowest. Two of us chipped through gravel and poured a concrete footing in water 18 in. below the water level in the creek. Before the spring breakup we built stone walls up above the high-water level of the creek. After we got the main logs, we finished up the walls about 8 ft. high and constructed a shelf on the top of each wall for the bridge to sit on. These had to be slightly different heights above the water line to accommodate the taper of the logs. All the rock, gravel and sand that we used we collected from the lake shore. Only the cement and reinforcing steel were flown to the site.

We obtained a permit to cut white spruce from federally managed land on Lake Clark, then selected, felled and peeled about two dozen logs. We skidded them into the lake, lashed together a raft with chain and towed it three miles across the lake to the homestead. Some of the 10-in. to 16-in. diameter logs we sawed into 4-in. thick decking boards using an Alaska chain-saw mill (see "Chainsaw Lumbermaking," p. 8). We squared up the sides but left the natural taper of the log to get maximum decking.

The three main logs (one chord for each side of the bridge and one in the center) were moved into place on rollers and oriented bow-side down to increase the bow during drying, since the objective was to have a bridge that would be level or just slightly higher at the center. The decking was temporarily laid upon these logs, and the remainder of the logs put on a rack. All the wood was allowed to dry for a year.

The following summer we removed the decking and turned the main logs over to have them bow-side up. We sawed a flat along the tops, making each log bow exactly ¾ in. Next we re-rounded the logs with a drawknife, leaving only a 2-in. wide flat along the top of each log for attaching the decking. A small flat leaves less area where water can collect.

The log joints in the bridge differ from the joints in a log house. In a house one log is set above its eventual resting place, scribed to match the contours of the log beneath it, rolled over, notched out to the scribed line and then rolled back into place. If the joint doesn't close up tightly, a log can always be notched a little more without affecting those already in place. When the fit is tight enough the builder goes on to the next log.

With a bridge, all the logs on each side are dependent on one another. None can be shortened, rotated or angled differently to help make one joint fit without affecting the fit of the other joints. As the drawing shows, the bridge has mortise-and-tenon joints at both ends of the brace logs and at the lower ends of the outer diagonal web logs. All-thread bolts run through the length of the brace and vertical web logs, and the joints between all the logs are scribed. These make construction rather more complicated than stacking the walls of a house. No part of the structure is really in place until all the parts fit.

Before any joints are cut, the centerline of each log must be determined. This establishes the path of the bore in those logs to be connected by all-thread and helps in laying out the joints and positioning the logs in relation to one another. Since the true centerline is concealed within the log, I projected it onto the outer surface. First measure across the end of the log from any four directions, marking a line at the center of each measure. With these four lines, a point can be picked that most closely represents the center of that end. Now using a carpenter's level, mark a plumb and a horizontal line through the centerpoint extending to the edges. Do the same on the other end of the log. Then snap four chalk lines along the length of the log connecting the lines on the log ends. These chalk and end lines can now be aligned with a carpenter's level to position the log precisely as desired—vertically, horizontally, or at any angle or rotation.

Next the vertical web logs and the braces are bored along

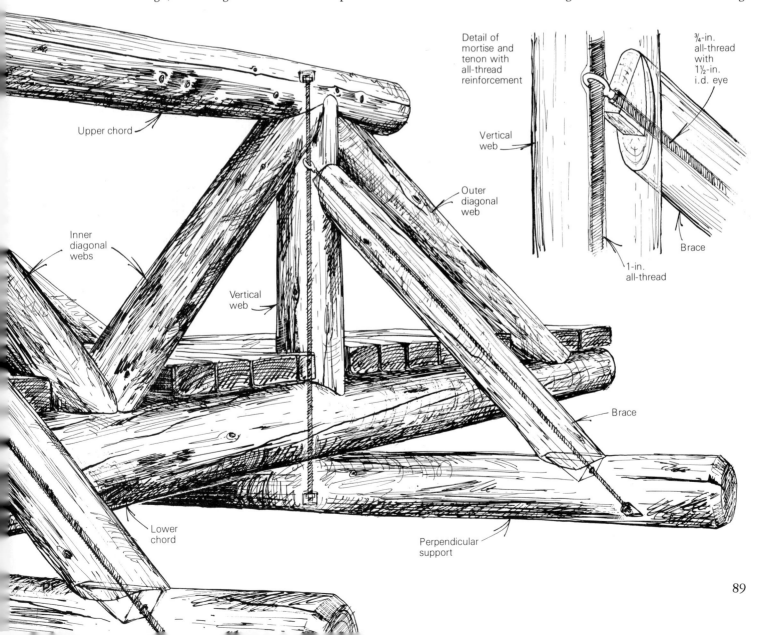

Upper chord

Inner diagonal webs

Vertical web

Lower chord

Perpendicular support

Detail of mortise and tenon with all-thread reinforcement

Vertical web

Outer diagonal web

¾-in. all-thread with 1½-in. i.d. eye

Brace

1-in. all-thread

Brace

Tammy Patrick

Author uses a ship auger with extensions to bore for the all-thread that secures the vertical web and brace logs, photo right. A pair of Starrett No. 85 dividers with a custom-made, adjustable target-bubble level, below, scribes the contour of one log onto the end of an adjoining log. The level helps keep the points of the divider plumb while scribing. Below right, Robinson has oriented the vertical web log horizontally to scribe its contour to the end of a brace log.

Tammy Patrick

their length to receive the all-thread. We used a ship auger with several extensions (photo, top) to drill 1½-in. holes for the 1-in. all-thread in the vertical webs, and 1¹⁄₁₆-in. holes in the braces for ¾-in. all-thread. To assure that the hole ran the center of the log, I drilled half the length of the log from each end, meeting in the center. Ream out the juncture by drilling past it. It's best to drill these holes in the rough logs before cutting any joints, so that if a log has to be scrapped because a hole went astray, you won't have put wasted work into it.

Now the ends of each log must be scribed to match the contours of the adjoining logs, and in the case of the braces and lower ends of the outside diagonal web logs, tenons must be cut. To scribe the contour of one log onto another, I used a pair of Starrett No. 85 dividers with an adjustable target-bubble level, which I had custom made (photo, above). You can get one from C. Norman Brown, S.R.A. Box 4008Q, Anchorage, Alaska 99507, or make one yourself with compasses and a bubble level. With the bubble adjusted so the tip of the steel point can be kept plumb to the tip of the pencil, an exact transfer of the contour of a horizontal log can be scribed to the end of an adjoining log, whether that log is plumb or diagonal. It requires positioning the log to be scribed within a few inches directly over the horizontal log.

We scribed the bottom ends of the vertical and diagonal logs first, positioning them exactly above the spot where they would sit on the lower chord or on the perpendicular log, and at the proper angle. Waste from the decking provided braces for the log while scribing. The contour of the horizontal log is scribed on the end of the adjoining log, and the waste is removed using chain saw, ax and gouges. In the case of the

Gouges are used to finish shaping the scribed shoulder of a brace log, above. The hole, which will receive the all-thread, was bored the entire length of the log before the tenon was cut. Below, a finished joint.

outer diagonal webs and braces, stock for tenons must be left. To lay out the tenon, we measured 1 in. on either side of the centerline for the cheeks, and 1½ in. on the other side of the centerpoint from the acute angle of the log's end for the edge of the tenon; the tenon has three shoulders. We used a handsaw to saw down the cheeks, and removed the waste with gouges and chisels (photo, top).

The mortise for this tenon is located using the chalkline on the horizontal piece (measuring 1 in. on either side of it) and the scratch from the steel tip of the dividers when the pencil end scribed the contour onto the adjoining log. This scratch marks the farther end of the mortise; the other end can be judged by eye. The photo above shows the relationship between the mortise and tenon.

The joints connecting the top ends of all the diagonal logs

to the vertical web logs are oriented perpendicular to the joints at the bottom end of these logs. Therefore the scribing technique using the bubble-level dividers cannot be used here; the bubble level only tells you when the divider points are plumb. Instead, I used two different methods to scribe these joints. For the joints between the outer diagonal web logs and the vertical web log and also for the joint between the lower ends of the inner diagonal web logs, I positioned the logs to be matched close together and held the divider points in line with one another, horizontally rather than plumb, without using the level. I set the dividers to mark ½ in. short of the final scribe, then notched out the waste and moved the logs closer for a more accurate rescribing and final fit.

For the other upper joints (between both the brace and inner diagonal web log and the vertical web log) I laid the vertical web log horizontal and then, using a carpenter's level, positioned the upper end of each diagonal log plumb above it at the proper angle. Then it could be scribed using the bubble-level-divider technique described earlier. I could have used this technique for the joint between the outer diagonal web log and the vertical web log, but the former is 10 ft. long and unwieldy to set up.

Before assembly all the joints and drilled holes were given numerous coats of creosote and a solution of pentachlorophenol in fuel oil. The all-threads were coated with grease, and the mortises were filled with enough grease to prevent water from being trapped if it ran in along a crack. The decking and exposed surfaces of the logs were treated with a mixture of 47½% fuel oil, 47½% creosote and 5% pentachlorophenol. Reading later about the health hazards of pentachlorophenol makes me leery about using it again.

To assemble, first the perpendicular support logs were positioned under the lower chord logs using temporary staging built on the creek bed. Then the vertical web logs were positioned, and the holes already bored in their length were used to guide the bit down through the lower chord log and the perpendicular support log. The braces were positioned, and the holes bored in their length were used to guide the bit down through the perpendicular support log and up into the vertical web log to meet the hole in its length. The brace was removed and gouges were used to enlarge the hole in the vertical web log to accommodate a 1½-in. i.d. eye that was coupled to the ¾-in. all-thread running through the brace. The eye was positioned in the mortise and the 1-in. all-thread passed through it, from the top of the vertical web log through the lower chord and perpendicular support logs, where it received a washer and nut for later tightening. The lower end of the all-thread running through the brace also received a nut that was tightened later. Next the outer diagonals were placed, then the inner diagonals. Mortise-and-tenon joints are unnecessary at the bottom of these inner diagonals because they wedge one another in place against the vertical web logs. Mortise-and-tenon joints at the tops of both inner and outer diagonals aren't needed either, because the upper chord log positions the others. The upper chord log was bored for the 1-in. all-thread and all nuts were tightened.

Within a year after construction the bow in the bridge had settled into levelness. ☐

Monroe Robinson is a woodcarver in Chugiak, Alaska, who also does architectural commissions. Photos by the author, except where noted.

The Torsion Box
How to make strong, light and stable panels

by Ian J. Kirby

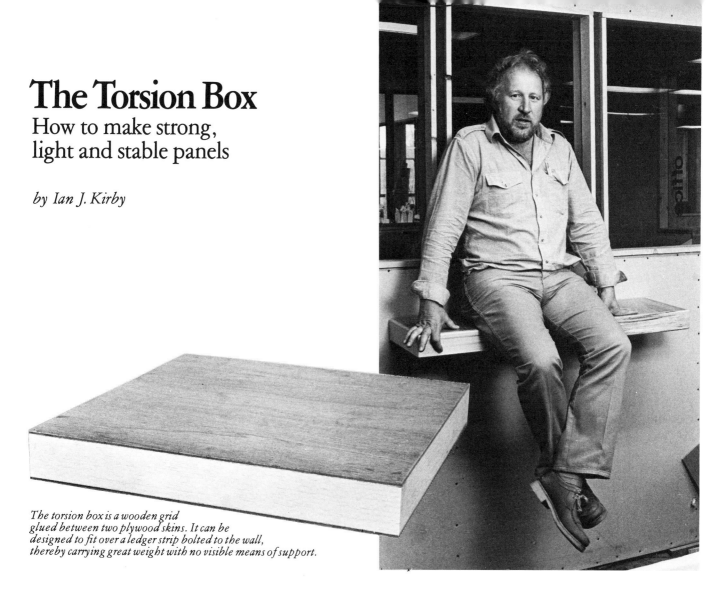

The torsion box is a wooden grid glued between two plywood skins. It can be designed to fit over a ledger strip bolted to the wall, thereby carrying great weight with no visible means of support.

Suppose you wanted to make a low bench about 18 in. wide and 4 ft. long, cantilevered out from a wall with no supporting structure underneath. In solid wood, you'd have to use a plank 2 in. thick or thicker, so this simple bench would consume at least 12 bd. ft. of wood, and it would weigh 40 lb. or more. Then you'd have the devil's own tussle figuring out how to hang it on the wall.

If you used a torsion box, you could make the same bench from less than 3 bd. ft. of wood and 12 sq. ft. of ¼-in. plywood. It could be any thickness you wanted, it would weigh about 10 lb., and it would be child's play to cantilever it from the wall. The torsion box is especially suitable for building high-quality veneered furniture, because it's both lighter and more stable than a conventional lumbercore structure. It's probably the simplest way to make a curved panel, and the ease with which the designer can manipulate the thickness dimension is truly liberating. At the same time, the torsion-box system is well within the technical reach of the amateur craftsman and the small professional shop.

As used in furnituremaking, the torsion box is two thin skins of plywood glued to a core grid of thin wooden strips. The resulting structure has strength not present in either the skin or the core alone—it's strong the same way an airplane wing is strong. In particular, a torsion box has tremendous resistance to twisting and bending forces. This is because the structure's geometry converts any applied force into shearing stress on the glue lines between skin and core grid. And a

Consulting editor Ian Kirby teaches woodworking and furniture design at Kirby Studios in North Bennington, Vt.

sound glue line is strongest in its resistance to shearing stress.

The concept behind the torsion box isn't new. Engineers use it for box beams as well as for airplane wings, and the same concept makes possible the structural steel I-beam. The system described here was developed in Europe during the 1960s for the manufacture of large wardrobes and other case goods for storage. The traditional way of making a wardrobe is to join four pieces of wood at the corners, firmly attach a back, and hang doors on the front. Although the back contributes a great deal to rigidity, the front corner of a 6-ft. wardrobe can still be lifted several inches off the floor with the other three legs remaining on the ground. Any unevenness in the floor will thus twist the case, jamming its doors and drawers. If a torsion box is used to make the back or sides, they will be absolutely rigid, and the rest of the wardrobe, if firmly attached to the torsion box, will also be rigid. The furniture industry hasn't made much use of the system, even though its applications extend far beyond keeping wardrobes free from twist. It can be used in practically every furniture form—storage cases, shelving units, tables, beds and all forms of seating, upholstered or not.

The torsion box is not a shoddy alternative to solid wood. It opens up design possibilities that simply cannot be achieved in solid wood. In the solid, you can usually find a board that's long enough, and the width can be glued up, but the thickness dimension is pretty much limited by weight and commercial availability to 2 in. or less, and you cannot eliminate wood movement. In terms of workmanship, the torsion box is fully as demanding as working in solid, and the result can be furniture of the highest quality. In fact, making a torsion box

Drawings: Ian J. Kirby

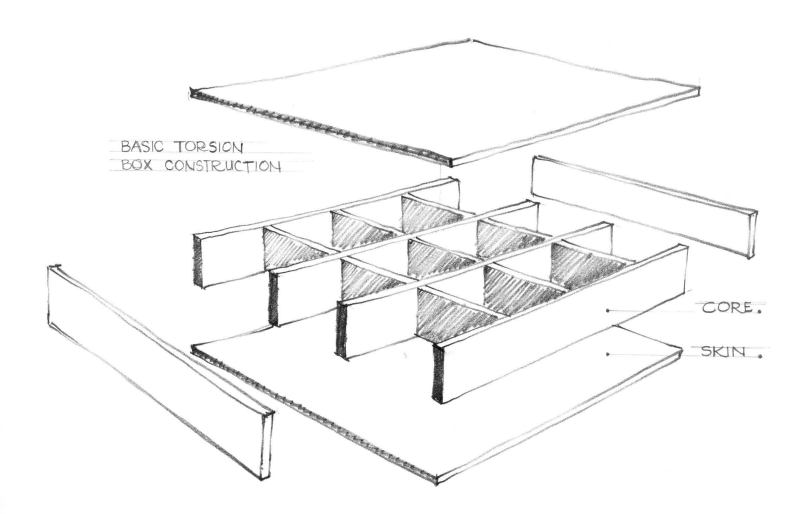

BASIC TORSION
BOX CONSTRUCTION

CORE.

SKIN

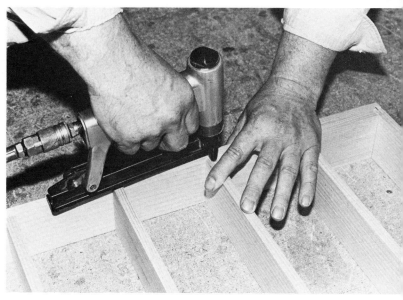

Here is the basic method for making a torsion box. Prepare stock for the skins and core (above), in this example ¼-in. plywood and clear pine sawn ⅜ in. thick by 2½ in. wide. Ordinary staples hold the core together until the skins can be glued on. Start with the outside pieces (right), and the long strips, then fill in the grid (below, left). Run a bead of white or yellow glue on one side of the grid (below, center), roll it out well, and carefully position the skin. Then flip the box over on top of the bench and clamp it down, using curved cauls to distribute the pressure (below, right). Unless you are using a veneer press, it's unwise to glue both skins at once.

requires more thorough planning than working in solid wood, for once you've glued up the box, you cannot change your mind and trim a half-inch off. There's no room here for inadequate design planning or for sloppy workmanship—quite the opposite.

A sample panel—The photo sequence on p. 93 and the following discussion are based on making a sample panel that's 2 ft. square and 3 in. thick, using ¼-in. veneered plywood for the skins and ⅜-in. by 2½-in. softwood for the core. The panel might be for a tabletop or for a shelf—it doesn't matter. The point is to establish the working principles involved. Once you understand the system, you'll see that the core grid and the resulting box can be virtually any shape you want, according to what your design requires. Later on I'll discuss surface and edge treatments, ways of joining two boxes together, and how to attach a torsion-box structure to a wall.

For the core we should use wood of practically any clear species, from poplar to maple, even pine, at 6% to 8% moisture content. But don't mix species in any one core. Differences in shrinkage can make the panel wavy. The thickness of each strip is as much a function of handling as of anything else. We could cut it down to ⅛ in. thick and build the grid on 2-in. centers, but we'd waste a lot of wood in sawdust. We'd also have trouble keeping the 24-in. long strips straight in one direction, and even more trouble handling 121 bits of wood, each 1⅞ in. long and 2½ in. wide, in the other direction. Even so, we could make a 4 sq. ft. core grid from 1½ bd. ft. of stock (not counting kerf losses), the 2-in. spacing would be enough to keep the plywood skin from sagging into the voids in the grid, and there would be about 78 sq. in. of gluing surface on each side—the panel would be plenty strong. If we make the core stock ⅜ in. thick, the strips won't be as numerous or as flexible. Spaced just over 4¼ in. apart, we'll have a 2-ft. square that still consumes less than 2 bd. ft. of material. There'll be 108 sq. in. of glue surface on each side, more than enough. At this point in the analysis we might decide that the grid spacing is too great for ¼-in. plywood, especially if it is to be veneered and used for a table. To keep the skin from dishing into the core voids, we could add a couple of core strips, or use ⅜-in. plywood for the skin instead. There is no hard rule—you decide according to the materials and the ultimate use of the box.

Whatever dimensions you choose, all the core material must be accurately prepared: it must be flat, uniformly thick, and cut off squarely. Both the width and the thickness can be got with a carbide-tipped saw, but it's better done through the thickness planer. Both skins should be made the same size, with their corners truly square, to the finished dimensions of the panel. The core grid, on the other hand, should be made a trifle large, say ¹⁄₁₆ in. over in length and width. Then after assembly it can be planed to meet the skin exactly.

If the finished box is to be veneered, the veneer should be glued onto the skins before they are cut to size. It's bad practice to veneer the assembled box, because the pressure of the press will tend to force the glue away from the core grid, making it puddle up over the voids. The box might end up looking like a lumpy checkerboard.

Joining the core grid—There are no joints in the core grid. The pieces are simply stapled together across the joint lines, top and bottom. Start by stapling together the four outside pieces, then run all the long strips in one direction, using crosspieces as spacers. Hold each piece firmly in place and staple. When all the long strips are stapled on one side, turn the grid over and staple the other side. Then fill in with the crosspieces. It's natural to imagine that staples can't possibly hold this thing together, that some joint must be necessary. Actually, the staples don't hold anything together. They merely stabilize the grid so it can be handled until the core can be glued onto it. The glueline between core grid and skin is what holds the box together. You would have to apply enough force to shear all that gluing surface before any core joinery would come into play.

Having now got the two skins cut to size and the core assembled, the next step is to put the three parts together. Any normal wood glue will do the job; I find it easiest to squeeze white or yellow glue along all the core edges, then to spread it out with a 1-in. paint roller. It is important to wet the entire surface of the core grid, since the skin goes onto it dry. Plant the skin on the core, register one long edge, then align an adjacent edge. If the core seems out of line, pull it into place using the skin as a try-square. Once one corner of the assembly is aligned, the rest of it will be aligned too. You can drive a couple of veneer pins or small brads through the skin into the core to hold it in place. Clamp or press the skin onto the core until the glue cures, then turn the box over and glue the second skin in place, being sure to work from the same edge and corner you aligned on the first side.

A veneer press is the ideal tool for gluing up the box, not because of the pressure it can exert, but because its bed is flat. In whatever shape you hold the torsion box while the glue is drying, that will be its final shape. If it is twisted while it cures, it will stay twisted forever. The veneer press also makes

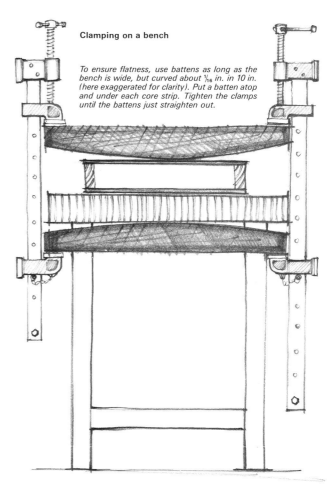

Clamping on a bench

To ensure flatness, use battens as long as the bench is wide, but curved about ¹⁄₁₆ in. in 10 in. (here exaggerated for clarity). Put a batten atop and under each core strip. Tighten the clamps until the battens just straighten out.

it practical to glue both skins onto the core at one pressing.

The best alternative to a veneer press is the top of your bench, but check it for flatness before you spread any glue. You can clamp the core to the panel (panel flat on the bench top) with standard quick-set clamps, as shown on p. 93. Use cambered battens to distribute the pressure. Be sure the clamps themselves don't twist the bench top; don't, for example, anchor clamps to the bench's understructure. The appropriate method is determined by the availability of a press or of clamps and a flat surface, and by the geometry of the workpiece. The important thing is to understand what has to be achieved and to respond accordingly.

Surfaces and edges—The torsion box is well-suited to the application of quality veneers and to the quality cabinetmaking techniques that go with veneering. As I mentioned earlier, it's best to veneer plywood skins before you assemble the box. There is nothing wrong with using pre-veneered plywood—the only drawback is that your choice of veneers is restricted. Applying your own veneers gives you easy access to the ebonies and rosewoods and other exotic species that can no longer be had in solid wood. I'll discuss veneering techniques in future articles.

Whether you apply your own veneer or use pre-veneered plywood, the edge of the torsion box needs to be finished. The most direct solution is to glue a solid wood lipping to the core, of the same species as the veneer or some contrasting species. Mitered corners always look good. If the lipping is to be flush with the surface of the box, it can be registered with a spline or a Lamello, or else it can be milled a little wide and planed flush after assembly. If the lipping must bear a load, a hinged door for example, it should be reinforced with a spline or tongue-and-groove. Grooves can be milled directly into the core of the box, and tongues onto the lipping stock. Of course the lipping can be shaped to virtually any profile. When the surface is an exotic veneer, you can make lipping stock by gluing three or four veneers together.

With the torsion box system, there is no reason to confine your design universe to wood. The stability of the skin allows

When the glue has cured, unclamp the assembly, clean off the glue squeeze and plane the core to the size of the skins. To assess the strength of the box you've just made, clamp one edge in the vise, grab the top corners and try to twist it.

What we've done up to this point is make the basic building brick of the torsion-box system. In order to use the system we must consider how to join two or more boxes together, and how to finish their surfaces and edges. These considerations are part of the design process, not afterthoughts, for most joining methods require some provision in the construction of the core. When you understand the system, the possibilities are limited only by your ingenuity.

you to cover it with virtually any sheet material. Thus you can develop your design with the colors, textures and properties of paint, leather, Naugahyde, cloth, Formica, ceramic tile, slate, metal tile or even sheet metal. There are special adhesives available for most of these materials. Tiles can be laid with adhesive and grouted. A traditional way to attach sheet copper is with decorative nails. Leather and Naugahyde are best stuck down with white glue. *(continued, next page)*

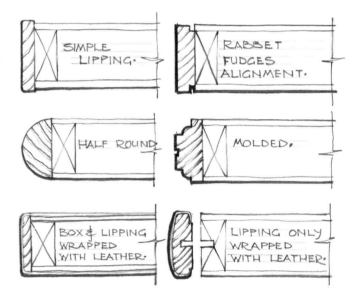

Rich Lippings

When the box is veneered, a leather-covered lipping will be quite rich in look and feel. An upholsterer would make up lipping stock by driving nails through one strip of wood, then gluing a second strip atop the nailheads to capture them. Trim this sandwich to width, profile its edges, glue the leather around it and then hammer it into position.

When the box is covered in leather or Naugahyde, neatly wrapping the corners can be most difficult. You can avoid the grief if you trim the leather exactly flush with the edge of the box, then glue on a solid wood lipping whose width is the thickness of the box plus surface material or even slightly wider, so it stands proud of the surface. The job will be especially rich if you make the lipping as wide as the panel is

thick without surface material, then plane the panel's top edge down by the thickness of the leather or Naugahyde. This planed margin should be about 1½ in. wide; it can be planed flat or round as shown. Glue on the surface material, trim it back flush, and use a spline to locate the lipping flush with the leather surface.

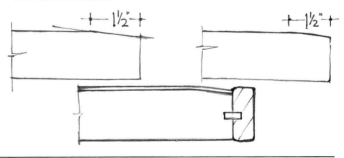

Joinery—The simplest way to join two torsion boxes edge-to-edge is to butt them together with glue. To keep the surfaces in line, use a loose spline or a Lamello spline (figure A). If you're in any doubt at all about the ability of the core to support the joint, double up the core stock in the joint area when you design the box.

A butt joint can also be used to join two boxes with their skins at right angles, as shown in figure B, but usually the core stock must be made doubly thick at the joint. The result will probably be more attractive if the skin of one of the boxes overhangs its core, so it can conceal the joint. Splines can be used to register the parts.

Alternately, the mating edges of the boxes can be mitered and glued (figure C), although once again enough stock must be provided for the miter cut when you are designing the

box. The miter is especially strong in this application, since the core strips both present long-grain gluing surfaces, not a near end-grain surface as is usually the case in solid wood. Some form of register is vital, and again a spline will serve.

There's a slightly different strategy for forming a right-angled joint with one box in the middle of another, for example a bookshelf or a wall system. It's best to glue and screw a ledger strip onto the surface of one box (the screws going into a core strip), and to build a pocket into the other box (figure D). The pocket then slips onto the ledger strip. It can be glued in place for permanency, or screwed. The lippings on the boxes will conceal the ledger.

Finally, an intermediate piece of solid wood can always be used at a corner, with the edges of the two boxes glued directly to it, as shown in figure E. *(continued, p. 98)*

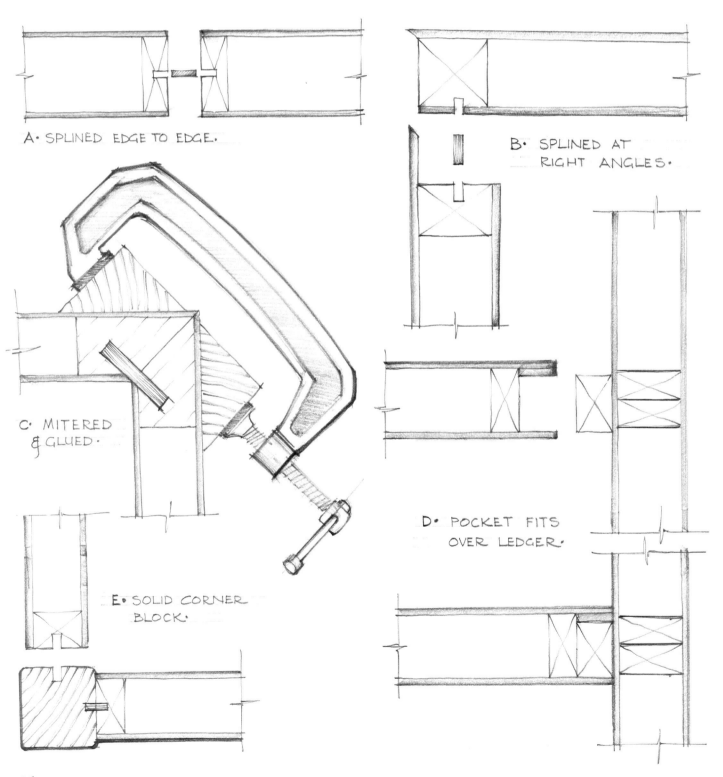

A· SPLINED EDGE TO EDGE.

B· SPLINED AT RIGHT ANGLES·

C· MITERED & GLUED·

D· POCKET FITS OVER LEDGER·

E· SOLID CORNER BLOCK·

Some applications of the torsion box, from work done at Kirby Studios.

Top: Three-part core grid made of medium-density fiberboard is 4 in. thick, 6 ft. wide and almost 15 ft. long. Designer-maker Mike Garner skinned each grid with ash-faced plywood, to build a trading desk that had been commissioned by a commodities investment firm.

Center: This four-module coffee table, shown in two of its many arrangements, could hardly have been built in solid wood. As the photo at left shows, each module consists of three torsion boxes. The flat top is veneered with Macassar ebony, the curved verticals are painted. Designed and made by Jim Van Etten (© 1981).

Bottom: David Schwartz joined his table by screwing ledger strips onto the vertical torsion boxes. The strips plug into sockets constructed into the box that is the tabletop.

Wall mounting—One of the attractive characteristics of the torsion box is the way it can be fastened to a wall and made to hold considerable weight with no visible means of support. The usual method is to bolt or screw a ledger strip to the wall, and to construct the box with a pocket at its back edge that exactly fits over the ledger (A). Screws hold the box to the ledger. Thus the whole thing can be removed from the wall. Or the box can be glued to the ledger, in which case the fixture is permanent (B).

The ledger should be a piece of clean, knot-free wood, preferably hardwood. The way it's fastened to the wall depends on the load it is likely to bear—No. 10 screws 1½ in. into the studs will support a telephone, but seating or shelves for such heavy loads as a television set may require bolts right through the studs. Use 2-in. Rawlbolts into masonry walls. Where the shelf goes into a corner, ledgers should be attached to both walls. Screws through the top skin into the ledger hold the box in place, but if the top skin is ¼-in. plywood it had better be doubled or trebled inside the pocket. Gluing extra thicknesses of plywood inside the flange that fits over the ledger will minimize the risk of the screws tearing out under load (C). This thickness may also permit countersinking and plugging to conceal the screws.

When you wish to eliminate any visible trace of holding screws but still want the box to be removable, you can profile the ledger with a dovetail as shown at D.

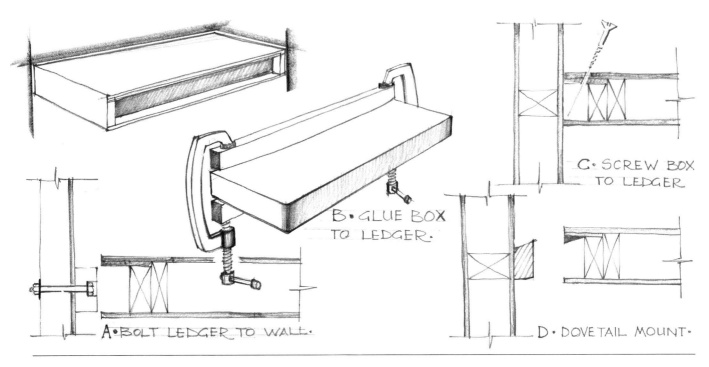

C·SCREW BOX TO LEDGER

B·GLUE BOX TO LEDGER.

A·BOLT LEDGER TO WALL·

D·DOVETAIL MOUNT·

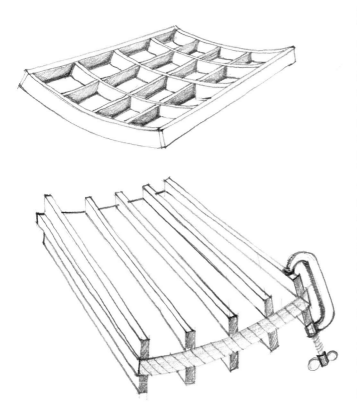

Curved panels—It's relatively simple to make a torsion box that's curved in one plane, such as for a chair seat or back. The method is to draw the curve full-size, then to cut out as continuous strips the core elements that form the curve. Don't try to use short curved pieces between continuous straight pieces, for they would be impossible to align. The outside straight pieces should also be continuous and attached to the end-grain of the curved pieces. This will aid in alignment and will also keep the core from twisting before the first skin is applied. It's best to skin the convex side first—if the finish is to be leather or paint, the skin can be glued and stapled or nailed. If the skins have a show veneer already, they'll have to be glued with the aid of battens and clamps. The battens should be slightly cambered, say ¹⁄₁₆ in. for every 10 in. of length. Place the battens in pairs, one over the other with a core strip between. Hardboard between the veneer and the battens will spread the pressure and keep the skins from scalloping.

In sum—The torsion box ought to be thought of as a building block within a system. In fact, the torsion box is the counterpart in man-made sheet materials, of the frame-and-panel in solid wood. Both are systems that have developed in response to the dimensional instability of wood. Either system brings its own limitations and liberations, but these depend mainly upon the designer-woodworker's imagination. □

Often maligned as unsafe and inaccurate, the radial-arm saw actually is able to cut neat, complex joints like those in this three-leg table. Erpelding cut the dovetail mortises in the legs as shown on page 102. The tenons on the triangular stretcher assembly, composed of bent laminations, were scribed from the mortises, then cut with a back saw—an efficient interplay of hand and power tools. Photos: Steve Young.

Slip Joints on the Radial-Arm Saw
Getting accurate results from a versatile machine

by Curtis Erpelding

Most discussions of power-tool joinery focus on the table saw, the router and the bandsaw, and neglect the radial-arm saw. Many insist that the radial-arm saw is inherently dangerous, and impossible to adjust accurately. I find neither argument convincing. Caution and common sense go a long way in reducing potential hazard, and the saw's ability to do precise work is almost completely in the control of the operator. My saw is a mid-60s vintage 10-in. Sears Craftsman. The guides for the rollers are worn and pitted, the indexing pins less than tight, and the arbor has a slight amount of run-out. Nevertheless, I've been using this saw for five years to cut close-fitting joints, and would hesitate to replace it with a new industrial model. As a good marksman knows how to deal with the idiosyncracies of his rifle to group his shots, so the canny woodworker knows how to compensate for slop and play in his radial-arm saw.

In making slip joints, the radial-arm saw offers several advantages over the table saw. First, the workpiece remains fixed during the cut, and because there is less slop in an old radial-arm saw than in most new tenoning jigs (homemade or otherwise), the cuts are more precise and easier to control. Second, the column-raising mechanism on the radial-arm saw lets you make very fine depth-of-cut adjustments for paring a joint to final fit. You'd have a hard time adjusting the fence on a table saw in such small increments to make the same cuts. Finally, the radial-arm saw imposes no real limits on the length of the pieces being joined, as long as the ends are supported. With the table saw, cutting joints on members more than 4 ft. long involves a precarious balancing act, which will adversely affect the accuracy of the joint, particularly if the free end runs afoul of a ceiling joist or light fixture in a shop with a low ceiling.

Cutting a slip-joint mortise and tenon on the radial saw requires, as in hand work, careful marking out. But you need to mark out only one joint, which becomes the reference from which the saw is set to cut the others. After the members are

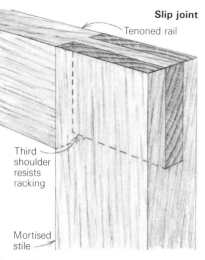

Slip joint

Tenoned rail

Third shoulder resists racking

Mortised stile

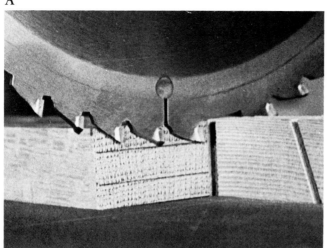

A

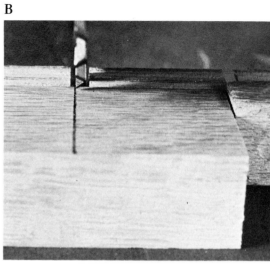

B

Cutting slip-joint tenons on the radial-arm saw begins by properly setting the blade to cut the shoulder line. Set the depth of cut by aligning the blade with the marking-gauge line that delineates the tenon thickness on the end grain (**A**). Then align a tooth that has outside set with the shoulder line (**B**). Sawing the cheeks requires rotating the blade to its horizontal position and positioning the stock using a 7-in. high substitute fence, a spacer and an auxiliary table (**C**). For safety, make several passes, advancing the work into the path of the blade between passes. The waste piece is left attached and broken off by hand before the cut is completed (**D**).

D

E

To complete the tenon, a third shoulder (**E**) adds, resistance to racking and hides imperfections in the mortise. Author cuts mortise for slip-joint with saw in horizontal position, using substitute fence, spacer, and auxiliary table, as in cutting tenon cheeks. A dowel in a thin piece of wood (**F**) stops the workpiece to control the depth of the mortise.

C

F

Photos, except where noted: John Switten

thicknessed and cut to length, they are positioned in what will be their final orientation. The triangle marking method (*FWW* #11, pp. 50-53) is a way to avoid confusion.

The tenons—The tenoned members (rails) are marked first. For the shoulder lines, set the cutting gauge (see p. 38) to the width of the mortised member and score the lines on both faces and on the inside edge as well. With a marking gauge, mark out the tenon thickness on the end grain, letting the gauge ride against one cheek and then the other. This ensures a perfectly centered joint. Where the tenon must be offset, use a mortise gauge and set the two points to the thickness of the tenon, then set the fence the appropriate distance from the face side. When the rail has been marked for the shoulders and for the tenon thickness, take a sharp pencil and make the lines more visible.

Cut the shoulders to the appropriate depth first. Set the height of the saw so that the teeth just touch the top mark on the end of the piece (photo **A**). Then line up the piece so that a tooth with outside set just touches the inside of the shoulder line (**B**). Clamp a block on the fence to hold this setting. Cut the shoulders, first one side and then, by flipping the piece over, the other.

Of all the operations, cutting the shoulders square requires the most accuracy on the part of the saw. And adjusting it to cut consistently square to the fence seems to be the major bugbear concerning the tool. If you simply can't get your machine to cut square, don't despair. Cut 1/32 in. shy of the shoulder, and then trim to the line with a rabbet plane.

But before you decide that your saw won't cut square, make all the usual initial adjustments to align it, and then practice pulling the blade into a piece of scrap that's been scored a number of times at 90° to the fence. Vary the way you pull the saw carriage over the work, observing the results of each cut. Because the blade will respond to very slight lateral pressure on the carriage handle, it could be your operating habits that keep the tool from cutting square consistently. Once you find the proper stance, the arm and the shoulder movements that make for repeated square cuts, practice until you can get it right every time.

To cut the cheeks of the tenon, turn the saw to its horizontal position. Remove the regular fence and replace it with a 7-in. high auxiliary fence on the right-hand side of the blade. This is adjusted square to the table, and so that the sawblade just touches its edge. An auxiliary table is necessary to elevate the workpiece. I use a piece from an old solid-core door; it remains reasonably stable throughout seasonal changes. Finally, clamp a block of 8/4 maple to the fence as a spacer so that its edge just touches the blade when the saw is pulled through (**C**). The spacer prevents the blade from contacting the workpiece when the saw is fully retracted.

Set the blade about 1/32 in. above the mark for the tenon. Advance the workpiece about an inch at a time, and pull the saw through. Don't try to make the whole cut in one pass or try to feed the workpiece into the saw as it cuts, or you'll overload the motor and risk a dangerous kickback. Also, don't complete the cut at this point, but leave the waste slightly attached (**D**). Remove the workpiece and break the waste off by hand. Then make the final pass, setting the shoulder line even with the edge of the maple spacer block.

Using even a 40-tooth carbide-tipped blade, cutting into tough end grain causes the blade to vibrate and leaves a cut that's less than clean and accurate. So cut all the tenons first to this 1/32-in. margin; then trim them later with a final light cut to the gauge line, which you can make in a single pass. In operation, hold the workpiece firmly with your right hand at a safe distance from the blade. When guiding the saw carriage into the cut, keep your elbow stiff and pull by pivoting your upper body rather than by bending your arm. This helps keep the saw from self-feeding and stalling.

Though not a common practice in making slot mortises, cutting a third shoulder on the underside of the tenoned member will add strength to the joint, making it more resistant to racking. Also, the third shoulder will hide any imperfection on the inside bottom of the mortise. All that's involved is taking a slice off the bottom edge of each tenon (**E**). Set the saw to cut 1/8 in. into the tenon. Set the shoulder slightly behind the edge of the spacer block so the blade cuts just shy of the line, then chisel the remaining end grain flush with the shoulder.

The mortise—The next step is cutting the mortise. When both pieces are the same thickness, the width of the mortise can be marked out with the marking gauge at the same setting used for the tenon. The depth of the mortise is gauged from the width of the tenon and a line is scored on each edge with a knife. Continue the line across the inside and outside edges and make a slight notch with a knife on the corner edge. This notch, when lined up with the edge of the spacer block, determines the depth of cut. A long, thin piece of wood with a dowel sticking vertically out of it is clamped to the tabletop as a depth stop. With the workpiece resting against the upright dowel, there is clearance for the saw to pass (**F**). Set the stop so that the saw cuts just shy of the gauge line.

Lower the saw to cut 1/32 in. above the bottom line of the mortise layout. As in cutting the tenon, advance the workpiece only an inch or less with each pull of the saw. Make the final cut with the workpiece registered against the dowel of the stop block. Flip the piece over and repeat the process. On small pieces with narrow mortises, you can clean out the waste with the saw, but on larger members I cut the waste out with a coping saw, after which I clean up the bottom of the mortise by chiseling to the gauged line.

Return the piece to the saw and lower the blade so that it cuts just to the bottom line marked on the end grain. Lowering the blade in tiny increments after each set of cuts will widen each mortise until the respective tenon will snugly slip through. Note the word "respective." The triangular marking system pays off here by eliminating a great deal of confusion (and probable error) by showing which mortise belongs to which tenon.

Theoretically, the final saw setting should produce mortises of identical width in each member, and each tenon should fit with the same snugness. Theoretically. In practice I've found that it's better to make the necessary adjustments to fit each joint separately. It takes only a little longer, and inspires more confidence in the strength of the finished assembly. A tenon offset with respect to its mortise or vice versa will not allow you to flip the piece over to make the second cut at the same saw setting. Rather, after cutting one kerf in each piece, you have to pause to make a new saw setting. Fine-tuning this second cut widens the mortise to fit its tenon.

At this point a skeptical reader might wonder how, if you can't expect the saw to cut precisely square to the fence, can you ever expect it to cut truly horizontally (in line with the workpiece)? Well, you can't. You just try to take advantage of this. Indeed, whenever I confront a situation where I doubt achieving the required accuracy, I try to determine on which side of perfect it behooves me to err, in order to obtain the best results. In this case, a snug joint and a frame that won't twist or wind will result if certain parts of the joint have a little looseness and other parts are correspondingly tight. Because there is some play in the horizontal indexing pin on my saw, I can manipulate the angle of error. By pushing up on the left side of the blade and then tightening the locking knob, I can minutely incline the blade. This will produce a tenon that will narrow ever so slightly from front to back, and a mortise that will widen ever so slightly from top to bottom. These "errors" make for a joint that looks, in a much exaggerated view, like that shown in the drawing at right. In actuality, the amount of deviation from horizontal amounts to less than half a degree ($\frac{1}{64}$ in. end to end), and the corner of the joint is tight and snug.

Before gluing up I always plane the rails clean on both sides. This removes the triangle markings, which you still need, so transfer them to the outside edges or lightly re-mark them immediately after planing. Also plane all inside edges on both rails and stiles. Apply the glue to both the mortise and the tenon, assemble the frame and draw it up first one direction and then the other with a bar clamp. If the shoulders were cut square and the bottom of the mortise pared true, and if the outside corner edge of the joint is tight, there is no need to leave the frame clamped up, especially since clamps can throw the frame out-of-square or in winding. Having checked for squareness (*FWW* #31, Nov.'81, p. 89), clamp the cheeks of each mortise with two C-clamps, one at each "loose" area. Use pads to protect the work. When the glue is dry, plane the stiles flush with the rails.

The dovetail slip joint—Shown at the top of the facing page, this joint is well suited to being made on the radial-arm saw. The first step is to make a cradlelike fixture to hold the rail (tenoned member) at the proper inclination for cutting the tenon cheeks and shoulders. As shown in figure 3, the fixture is made from two pieces of $\frac{3}{4}$-in. plywood and a couple of stretchers. The angle of inclination shown at *a* is the slope of the dovetail. This angle will vary, of course, depending on the dimensions and proportions of the stock. Two members joined with their edges in the same plane (figure 1) will not require as steep a slope as two members joined with their faces in the same plane (figure 2). A slope of 10° from the vertical will do in the former case, while a slope of 3° to 5° seems appropriate for the latter.

Marking out the pieces proceeds in basically the same manner as with the slip joint. Start with the rail and mark the shoulder lines.

The dovetail tenon—With a sliding bevel and a scriber, mark out the dovetail tenon, making it no less than $\frac{3}{16}$ in. thick at the top edge. The sawblade will normally remove at least this

much from the narrow part of the mortise. Also remember that at the widest part of the mortise the cheeks are the narrowest, so leave enough wood here for a strong joint, something to consider when laying out the tenon. As a last step, witness-mark the outside edges of all the members.

Now place the fixture on the saw table, its high side against the fence on the left side of the blade. Place a rail, outside edge out (facing you), in the crotch of the fixture, and set the saw to the proper depth for cutting the shoulders (**G**). Clamp a stop block to the table for repeated cuts (**H**). To cut the opposite shoulders on the rails, you must reverse the fixture, placing the low side against the fence. Because in this position there is no back stop to hold the rail, you have to nail a strip behind the workpiece or devise some other means of holding it firmly in place. Don't try to make this cut without securing the work, or the blade will snatch the piece from your grasp and send it flying.

When you have cut all the shoulders for the tenons, tilt the saw to its horizontal position, and arrange the fence, spacer and auxiliary table in the same manner as for the slip joint. Set the fixture's high side against the fence, and place the workpiece face edge out in the crotch (**I**). Adjust the blade $\frac{1}{32}$ in. above the top line scribed on the end grain for the tenon, and cut the tenon on one side; again advance the workpiece an inch or so at a time between passes, and stop the cut $\frac{1}{4}$ in. shy of the shoulder. Break the waste piece off by hand and complete the cut. Cut the other side by reversing the jig and flipping the rail (**J**), taking the same cautions as before to secure the workpiece. Now, lower the blade $\frac{1}{32}$ in. to the gauge line and trim the tenons to final thickness. To cut the shoulder at the bottom of the tenon, reset the saw and hold the piece directly on the auxiliary table.

The dovetail mortise—Gauge the depth of the mortise from the width of the tenon, and continue the mark across the entire edge of the stile (or leg). Notch the corner edge to determine the blade setting for the depth of the mortise. Lay out the shape of the pin on the face edge and continue the lines across the end-grain surface.

Set the sawblade now at the correct angle, using the sliding bevel (**K**). Unplug the saw before removing the guard; then replace the guard after making the setting. As in cutting the slip joint, you can tension the dovetail mortise and tenon by inclining the blade slightly, so that the tenons will narrow from front to back and the mortises widen from top to bottom. To get the correct setting—a fraction of a degree over the angle of the fixture—some trial and error is required. Use a test piece.

After fine-tuning the tilt angle, you must readjust the fence and maple spacer so that the teeth of the blade will just touch their edges. Line up the notch on the corner edge of the stile with the edge of the maple spacer, and clamp the stop block to the table. Adjust the blade to cut just above the bottom line marked on the end grain of the piece. Because the blade is set at an angle, you cannot cut the piece in increments, but must make the entire cut in one pass. This means that the blade will want to push the piece away, and so you must pull the saw into the cut very gradually, and with the utmost caution. When you have established kerfs on both sides (**L**), a coping saw removes the waste, and a chisel cleans the bottom of the mortise. Trim the mortise by lowering the saw in small amounts until the respective tenon slips snugly

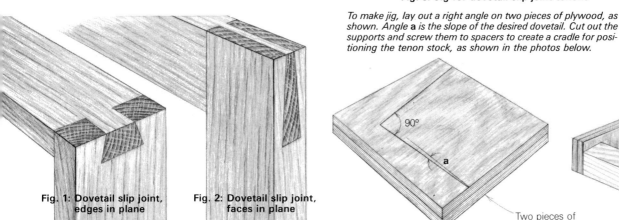

Fig. 3: Jig for dovetail-slip-joint tenons

*To make jig, lay out a right angle on two pieces of plywood, as shown. Angle **a** is the slope of the desired dovetail. Cut out the supports and screw them to spacers to create a cradle for positioning the tenon stock, as shown in the photos below.*

90°

a

Two pieces of ¾-in. plywood

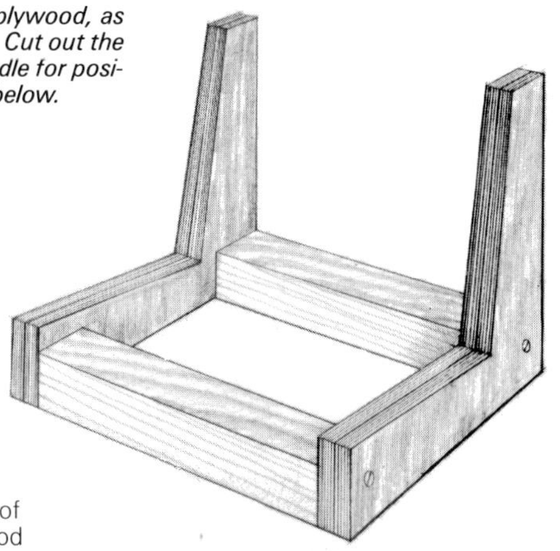

Fig. 1: Dovetail slip joint, edges in plane

Fig. 2: Dovetail slip joint, faces in plane

G

H

*To cut the tenon for a dovetail slip joint, author uses a cradlelike fixture, the construction for which is shown in figure 3, above. Place the scribed stock in the fixture and set the depth of cut for the shoulder (**G**). Then clamp a stop block to the saw table and cut the shoulders for one side of all your stock (**H**). To cut the shoulders on the other side, reverse the cradle so its low side is against the fence.*

I

J

*When all the shoulders are cut, saw the cheeks on one side of each piece (**I**): tilt the saw to its horizontal position, set the fixture's high side against the fence and adjust the blade just above the scribed line on the end grain. To saw the cheeks on the other side, reverse the jig and flip the workpiece (**J**). Saw in a series of passes, advancing the workpiece between passes and breaking off the waste before completing the cut.*

*To saw the mortise for the dovetail slip-joint, the stock is positioned horizontally, and a sliding bevel is used to set the sawblade at the correct slope (**K**). Because the blade is tilted, the mortise cheeks must be sawn to full depth in one pass, necessitating extreme caution, lest the blade throw the work. The substitute fence, spacer and auxiliary table, used for cutting the simple slip joint, are used for this operation too. Flip the board to saw the other cheeks (**L**), then remove the waste with a coping saw and chisel.*

K

L

Variations on the slip-joint that the radial-arm saw can make include the dovetail slip-joint with two half-pins and a full tail (right) rather than with two half-tails and a pin, as described in the previous pages. Below is a dovetail three-way case joint for the four top corners of a frame-and-panel cabinet. The double dovetail pins on the front horizontal member are cut by hand.

Curtis Erpelding

in. If you have made correct settings, the joint will be tighter at the top corner than at the bottom. This tension actually forces the tenon into the mortise.

Other joints—In addition to the two joints described here, other variations are possible, either using part of the method or adapting it to different requirements. Instead of joining two members with a dovetail pin (tenon) and two half-tails, you could use the same fixture to cut a joint that consists of a full tail (tenon) on one member and two half-pins on the other, as shown in the drawing at left. In some situations such a joint might be structurally or visually preferable.

Sometimes it's not possible or even desirable to cut the entire joint on the saw, as was the case with the curved-stretcher table shown in the photos on p. 99. Because the stretchers (rails) are curved, and glued together in a triangular fashion before the tenons are cut, I couldn't hold them on the saw table, certainly not in the fixture. I cut the mortises in the legs using the radial-arm saw, marked out the tenons from the mortises, clamped the stretcher assembly in my vise and cut the tenons with a backsaw.

I used a dovetail three-way case joint (photo, left) for the four top corners of a frame-and-panel cabinet. First I cut the dovetail slip joint in the regular way and then cut the two sockets in the mortised members, all on the radial-arm saw. From the two sockets I laid out the two dovetail pins on the third member, and cut these by hand. Next, I glued up the slip-joined members and cut the tenon flush with the socket walls to receive the pins.

The angled fixture pointed the way to an even more specialized joint—a knockdown, through-mortise-and-wedge joint, which I used to connect the stretchers to the legs in my "Orientable" (*FWW* #20, Jan. '81, p. 59). The fixture held the stretcher at the proper angle while the tilted saw cut a tapering dovetail mortise. A compound tapered wedge draws the stretcher tight against the crossmember of the legs. I later applied the same joint to a knockdown shelving unit. □

Curtis Erpelding makes furniture in Seattle, Wash.

On exposed joinery

Architect Louis Kahn once said that the joint is the beginning of ornament. He was talking about architecture of course, but the same can be said also about cabinetry and furniture. Until the Arts and Crafts Movement in England (*FWW* #26, Jan. '81, p. 54) the history of furniture design had been a history of hiding the joint. There are some notable exceptions to this generality. The American Shakers, whose religious scruples proscribed ornament, relied on visible joinery to give their simple designs character and presence. English country craftsmen, who inspired Ernest Gimson and others in the Arts and Crafts Movement, cared chiefly about the practical utility of their furniture, and had no reason to conceal its structural integrity beneath floral decoration and classical moldings. After Gimson and the Barnsleys, exposed joinery became, for better or worse, a design principle. Through wedged tenons and through dovetails attest both to the skill of the craftsman (if it's going to show, it had better be sweet) and to the honesty of the design.

The modern craftsman has the advantage of using power tools which greatly facilitate the speed and accuracy with which open joints can be made. And these tools do this, I think, without sacrificing any measure of handmade quality. Exposed joinery can be the signature of a craftsman or shop, an important design detail, and a record of the piece's manufacture. Industry cannot economically use exposed joinery as a design element to any great extent. The few examples—machine-cut dovetails and finger joints in chair frames—usually lack the crispness, the clarity, and the careful proportioning that the individual craftsman can bring to a piece. When the joint fits really tight, when no gap shows and even the glueline disappears, the end-grain and flat-grain surfaces set up a visual vibration, a dancing of surfaces. Conceptually there's magic in the tight geometrical mating of two elements, the triangular interweave of dovetails, the knotlike locking of mortise and tenon. Joinery can indeed be the beginning of ornament, but it can be the culmination of it as well. —*C.E.*

Dovetail Jigs
We test three fixtures for routing carcase and drawer joints

by Paul Bertorelli

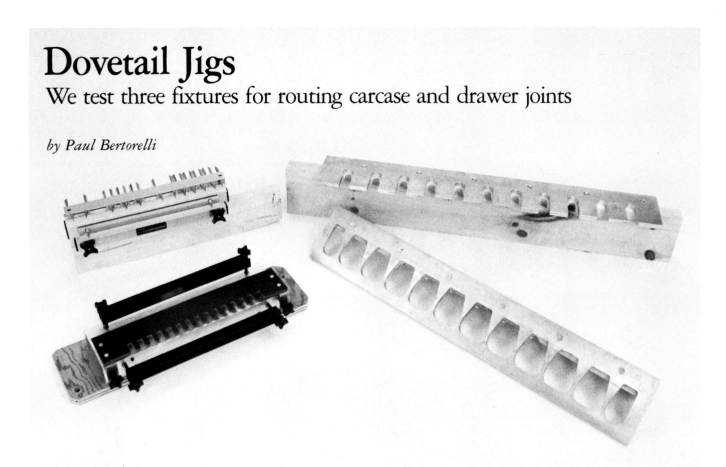

Router dovetail jigs are available in three types. The Sears jig, left foreground, will cut fixed-spaced half-blind dovetails for drawers or small carcases. Behind it is the Leigh tool, which will cut variably-spaced through dovetails. Keller's two-piece aluminum template, right, is designed for routing large dovetails in carcases. Pin spacing can be varied by shifting this tool.

Machine-cut dovetails have always gotten a bum rap. They're either too fat or too thin, or the angle is off, or something else is wrong that only cutting them by hand seems able to avoid—provided you've got the time and skill. These complaints, valid or not, have inspired the invention of router jigs that attempt to solve the problem.

Three basic types of dovetail jigs are now on the market—a large one for cutting through dovetails in carcases, and two smaller ones for through and half-blind dovetailing of drawers and smaller carcases. We bought one of each and I spent several days trying them out.

I wasn't surprised that I had to fuss to get the jigs to work well, but once router and jig have been accurately set up using test pieces, all three jigs will cut joint after joint with good results, providing that the stock has been planed accurately and cut off squarely. I was surprised, however, to find that I could join boards as well with the cheapest jig as with the most expensive.

Two of the jigs tested—David Keller's $325 two-piece aluminum tool and Leigh Industries' $149.50 adjustable device—are recent inventions. They were designed partly to address the common complaint that machine-cut dovetails lack visual excitement because the angle and spacing of the pins and tails don't vary. With either of these two jigs, the pin angle is determined by the router bit, but you can change the look of the joint by varying the pin-tail proportions and spacing. Both of these jigs cut only through dovetails. Keller's is for large carcase joints, while the Leigh jig is for drawers. Sears' jig, the third type I tested, cuts only half-blind dovetails, and the space between pins and tails is fixed. At $45, its design and price are representative of jigs by at least three other manufacturers—Porter Cable ($68), Black and Decker ($68), and Bosch ($82), all of whom sell through local distributors. Bosch also makes a large jig (for $94) that will dovetail boards up to 16 in. wide.

Keller jig—David Keller, a Bolinas, Calif., woodworker, began selling his dovetail jig in 1976. When first conceived it was made of Plexiglas, and later of phenolic plastic. The version he sells now is made of two ½-in. thick, 36-in. long, machined aluminum plates—one for the pins and one for the tails. A pair of bearing-equipped ½-in.-shank router bits (a 1-in. diameter, 14° dovetail bit and a ¾-in. straight bit) are included in the jig's $325 price. The templates can be repositioned, so there's no limit to how wide the stock can be. Boards ranging in thickness from ⅝ in. to about 1¼ in. can be joined. The dovetail bit, however, has a limited depth of cut, so for stock thicker than ⅞ in., the pin board must be rabbeted.

To use this jig, you need a beefy router with a collet that will mount ½-in.-shank bits—I tried a 2-HP Milwaukee and a 2¾-HP Makita. The templates are first screwed to backing boards. These give you a way to clamp the tool to the work, and they keep chunks from being torn out of the stock as the bits exit from the cut. If the jig's built-in 3-in. spacing is used, it's simple to lay out the joint. The tail-cutting template is clamped to the end of the board, and the tails are milled with the dovetail bit. The template is removed and the tail locations are scribed directly to the pin board, as in hand-dovetailing. It isn't necessary to scribe each tail. If two or three are located accurately, the jig automatically lo-

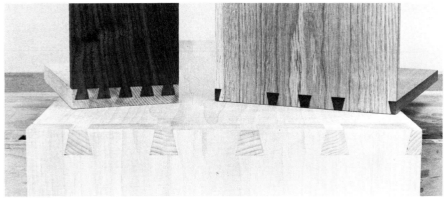

A near-perfect joint is quickly attainable with all three of the jigs tested. Above foreground are the large dovetails with pins on 3-in. centers made with the Keller jig. The joints made with the Sears fixture, left, are of fixed spacing, giving them the unmistakable look of machine-made dovetails. With its variable pin spacing, the Leigh jig makes dovetails, above right, that come closest to looking handcut.

The Keller jig is furnished with bearing-guided router bits that follow the template more accurately than the guide bushings used with the other two jigs. This photo shows how the bearing guides on the template to cut the pins. And it also illustrates how close the bit comes to the templates, a condition that requires constant vigilance when using any of these jigs.

cates the others. The straight bit is used to cut the pins. If you prefer, the fixed spacing can be ignored and you can put the pins anywhere you like. In that case, the templates must be moved after each cut, and all the tail locations must be scribed to the pin piece, a tedious and inaccurate routine. You might as well dovetail by hand.

To tighten the joint, you make wider pins by moving the edge of the template toward the work; moving it away shaves them down and loosens the joint. Keller suggests you experiment with mounting the template on its backing board until a good fit is produced. But I found it handier to set the jig up to make a tight joint, and then loosen it with masking-tape shims.

Of the three jigs tested, Keller's was by far the simplest to use. Once I had it set up correctly, I could make tight dovetails that were attractive, but somewhat square and clunky-looking for my tastes. I like to start and end a dovetail

series with a half-pin, and by departing from the jig's fixed spacing I was able to do that, with only a minor loss of accuracy. The alternative is to let the pins fall where they may, as in the photo above, or to design in widths that are multiples of the jig's 3-in. spacing.

Avoiding tearout with this jig requires some care. After the backing board has been used a few times, too much material is cut away for the board to offer much protection as the bit exits. Slower cutting, or a new board, helps.

This jig does its job, but its price and size limit its appeal. Keller says it is aimed at small production shops that don't have the time to hand-dovetail carcases, or the capital to buy specialized machinery. The weekend woodworker should be wary—dovetailing with this jig calls for experience with large routers. I was reminded rather violently of the risks. As I was finishing cutting the pins on one test piece, I inadvertently tilted the router. The bit grabbed the

corner of the jig. The confrontation snapped the router's shaft and hurled the collet and bit out the bottom of the machine, shattering the Bakelite base as it went. I suffered a shrapnel wound in the face. While I don't see this jig as being more dangerous than other power tools, it does demand undivided attention and careful movement, along with good eye and face protection.

Keller's jig is available direct from him at Star Route, Box 800, Terrace Ave., Bolinas, Calif. 94924.

Leigh jig—Ken Grisley, an English boatmaker now living in Canada, designed a jig that will make pins and tails with variable spacing. Earlier this year, he formed Leigh Industries Ltd. to manufacture and market this device, the only small jig we could find that can make randomly spaced, through dovetails.

The Leigh jig consists of ten pairs of movable, die-cast aluminum fingers mounted on a heavy aluminum extrusion. The boards to be joined are clamped to the jig, pin board on one side, tail board on the other. The aluminum fingers project over the stock to guide the router bit through the cut. The fingers can be positioned anywhere along the extrusion and are locked in place with socket-head screws. The pin side of each finger pair is angled at 15° to match the dovetail bit used with the tool (bits aren't included in the price). The opposite or tail side of the fingers is straight. The jig is intended for making drawers, since it works best cutting through dovetails in stock up to ½ in. thick and 12 in. wide. But by cutting a rabbet in the pin board, it's possible to dovetail stock up to ¾ in. thick.

Instead of bearings to guide the bits through the wood, a guide bushing is attached to the router base and the bit is centered inside the bushing's bore. Bushings tend to be less accurate than bearings because it's difficult to get and keep the bit concentric.

Setting up the jig involves loosening and retightening 20 socket-head screws (two for each finger pair) to achieve the desired spacing. It takes time. For the effort, though, you get pins and tails where you want them, and you can start and end the joint with a half-pin, no matter what the width. You can also vary the width of pins and tails. I used a 1-HP Sears router and ¼-in.-shank carbide bits to test the Leigh jig: tails first with the dovetail bit, then pins with a

$\frac{5}{16}$-in. straight bit. Since the fingers automatically locate the pins on the piece clamped in the other side of the jig, no scribing is necessary. Leigh supplies a stack of $\frac{1}{64}$-in. paper shims for adjusting the tightness of the joint. The shims fit under an aluminum plate to which the pin board is clamped. Removing shims moves the work closer to the jig, thus tightening the joint.

After some confusion over finger spacing, I was able to cut tight dovetails in both hardwoods and softwoods. Once I got the hang of it, changing the spacing was easy. The biggest problem I had with this jig was tearout. As the bits leave the cut, a ragged edge often results. Backing the cut with a strip of wood clamped between the work and the jig corrected this, but I had to replace the strip frequently.

For all its complexity—it has some 25 separate parts—the Leigh device held its adjustments throughout the day I used it to join a batch of drawers. The last corners I made were as tight as the first. The tool seems robust enough for a small production shop. But it may be pricey for the woodworker with just a few drawers to dovetail; and besides, in the time it takes to adjust the jig, you really could chop quite a few hand dovetails. Moreover, I found that having to rabbet the pins in stock thicker than $\frac{1}{2}$ in. limits the tool's versatility.

The jig is sold through mail-order tool distributors; Leigh Industries (Box 4646, Quesnel, B.C., Canada V2J 3J8) has a full list.

Sears jig—Singer Motor Products Division has made the Sears dovetail jig for more than 20 years. It consists of a phenolic template machined with fingers and mounted on aluminum channel iron. The pieces to be joined are clamped at right angles to each other under the template. The router (through a guide bushing) cuts half-blind pins and tails in a single operation with one cutter—a $\frac{1}{2}$-in. diameter dovetail bit. Boards up to 12 in. wide and from $\frac{3}{8}$ in. to about 1 in. thick can be joined. The dovetails made by this jig are square-dimensioned and closely spaced, with tails undercut on the inside face. Another template sold separately ($13) can be fitted to the jig to make $\frac{1}{4}$-in. half-blind dovetails in stock as thin as $\frac{5}{16}$ in. Though intended only for half-blind dovetails, the Sears fixture can cut through dovetails. It requires routing perilously close to, or

Pin spacing can be varied with the Leigh jig by moving fingers locked down by socket-head screws. Fit of the joint is determined by the pins' width, which is controlled by adding $\frac{1}{64}$-in. thick paper shims stacked behind an aluminum plate between work and jig. The plate at left fastens over fingers to give the router a smooth surface to ride on.

The Sears dovetailer is the quickest to use because both pins and tails are milled in one operation with the same bit. The workpieces are clamped together, limiting tearout and making joints consistently clean.

even into, the aluminum base of the tool, however. And the ill-fitting, half-round pins thus produced are hardly worth the effort.

Pin and tail spacing is fixed with this jig, so set-up involves little more than ripping the stock to width and squaring the ends to be joined. The critical and most difficult task is getting the joint tightness just right. You do it by changing the router's depth of cut, lowering the bit to tighten the joint, raising it to loosen it. With the crude rack-and-pinion depth control on a Sears router, adjustments take lots of trial and error. A router with a better depth control, I suspect, would simplify this job.

Once set correctly, though, the Sears jig is faster and easier to use than the other two because the 15° dovetail bit mills pins and tails at the same time. No

bit or jig changes are needed. The boards are clamped tightly against each other during the cut, thus backing the bit's exit and eliminating tearout.

The performance of this jig surpassed my expectations. I once bought a cheaper version, and after using it twice with mediocre results, tossed it back behind the scrap pile. The version I tested, though, is better made yet still priced low—well within the budget of most woodworkers. True, the pin-tail spacing can't be varied, but the precise regularity of the joint made by this jig has a certain appeal. It looks exactly like what it is—a machine-made dovetail.   □

Paul Bertorelli is an assistant editor of FWW. *For more on dovetails, see issues #2, p. 28; #15, p. 20; #21, p. 73; #22, p. 21; and #27, p. 68.*

Joinery Along Curved Lines
A general method for template routing

by Jim Sweeney

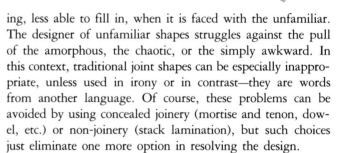

Bearing on router-bit shank solves curve-tracing problem.

We woodworkers are fascinated by joinery. Often we'll examine a piece of furniture to see how it's put together, even before we consider how it looks or functions. Exposed joinery is particularly satisfying. Through its visible joinery, a piece speaks of the fact that it is wood, and of all the possibilities and limitations of assembly which that implies. In this article I'll discuss a general method for extending exposed joinery from the ordinary linear joint to joints that follow almost any arbitrary curve. Using only a router and a few combinations of straight cutters and bearings, complex but precise curved joints become available to anyone willing to apply some ingenuity.

In making furniture with non-traditional shapes, it's particularly valuable to have a vocabulary of curved, exposed joints that are analogous to the lap, bridle and dovetail of rectilinear joinery. The principal lines in contemporary furniture often are not straight; the maker tries for a coherent whole using the rhythms and tensions of curved lines and planes. But in a non-traditional shape, as in an unrhymed poem, the sense of rightness is elusive. The eye is less forgiv-

ing, less able to fill in, when it is faced with the unfamiliar. The designer of unfamiliar shapes struggles against the pull of the amorphous, the chaotic, or the simply awkward. In this context, traditional joint shapes can be especially inappropriate, unless used in irony or in contrast—they are words from another language. Of course, these problems can be avoided by using concealed joinery (mortise and tenon, dowel, etc.) or non-joinery (stack lamination), but such choices just eliminate one more option in resolving the design.

It's not surprising that the tool used to cut curving joints is the router. The other joinery tools that have evolved—saw, chisel, plane, and their machine counterparts—cut flat planes. The router, unlike these older tools, does not need to refer to where it has just been to determine where it is going. At any instant it is free to move exactly where we guide it. The problem of curved joinery thus becomes how to guide the router to cut the precisely matching negative and positive curves that will unite to form some particular joint.

The main tactic for doing this is to shape templates of some durable material (plywood, Masonite, aluminum) and to transfer the shape to the work, by using a straight two-flute router bit with a ball-bearing mounted above its flutes. There are thus three parts to the problem of cutting curvilinear joints: first, how to make precisely matching negative and positive templates of a chosen shape; second, how to transfer these shapes into the workpiece; and third, how to make this transfer occur exactly where we want it in the finished work. Though this third aspect of the problem may at first seem trivial, it often calls for the biggest bag of tricks, and is the least susceptible to any kind of general solution.

Let's first consider the second problem, that of transferring the curve from a template to the work, because it best introduces the use of bearing-cutter assemblies. My technique descends directly from two common techniques, so I'll start by describing them and their disadvantages.

In one standard technique the router is guided, as it is fed through the cut, by its subbase being pressed against a template or fence that is clamped to the work. In a more flexible version of this method, a template guide-collar is attached to the subbase of the router and run against the template, while the router subbase rides atop the template. The cut may go completely through the work, or only partly into it. But in either case there is one problem: concentricity, or rather, the lack of it. The router bit is reasonably concentric with the motor, the motor is somewhat loosely housed in the base, the subbase is aligned with the base by some hopeful screws, and finally, the guide collar fits into a hole in the subbase. All of these attachments are governed by the initial imprecision of manufacturing as well as by subsequent wear. We should not be surprised when this chain of vagueness does not yield pre-

Bridle joint with curved shoulder.

cise concentricity. The cutter changes position whenever the router is rotated relative to the template. So the worker must try to keep the same point of the subbase, or guide collar, against the template throughout the cut—a hopeless task when so much else compels his attention.

In a second standard method, the guiding surface is built into the cutter, so that concentricity is guaranteed and overall accuracy is limited only by the precision of the cutter assembly itself. This technique employs a flush trimmer bit—commonly, a $\frac{1}{2}$-in. straight cutter with a $\frac{1}{2}$-in. ball-bearing at its end—with the bearing rolling against a template that is attached to the work on the face opposite the router. This method is limited mainly by the position of the bearing: we can trace through work only as thick as the cutting flutes are long, and we must always cut completely through the work. The first limitation is not serious because you can find trimmer bits as long as 2 in., though they are fragile. The second limitation, always cutting through the work, is very restrictive—a mortise cut this way, for example, must always be a through mortise. You cannot use a trimmer bit to cut the negative part of a half-lap or a bridle joint.

Furthermore, trimmer bits themselves contain a subtle source of error. Because they are designed so that the bearing can roll against a vertical, Formica-covered surface while the cutter trims the adjacent horizontal surface, the diameter of the cutting circle is usually 0.005 in. to 0.010 in. smaller than the bearing. This minute difference can become significant when you make a template from a series of intermediate templates, because the errors accumulate. You can sometimes compensate with a layer of tape on the template.

There is another technique for transferring a curve from template to workpiece, but it requires a pin router. A template fixed to the underside of the workpiece can run against a pin the same diameter as, and directly below, a bit entering the workpiece from above. For more about pin routers, see *FWW* #29, p. 63, and p. 143.

The system I consider optimum combines the best features of both standard techniques: a bearing on the bit for concentricity, but placed on the router side of the cutter, on the shank above, rather than below, the cutting flutes. This bearing will follow a template exactly, yet the cut can stop at any desired depth. The outside diameter of the bearing is ordinarily the same as the cutting diameter, but it can also be larger. This simple idea, it turns out, unlocks a host of joint designs that can be as simple or as complex as the craftsman wishes. Any pair of fitted shapes that you can make in $\frac{1}{4}$-in. hardboard can be transferred into solid wood, either completely through the workpiece or to any depth, although it is sometimes necessary to juggle template thickness and cutter length.

Router bits with bearings mounted on their shanks, unfortunately, are not stock items. And although router bits are made in a wide range of sizes, ball-bearings are not. The woodworker must devise bearing/bit combinations that will do the work at hand, and find a mill supply house or industrial hardware dealer who stocks or can get the parts. For

Author's open-sided chest-of-drawers relies upon curved bridle joint for visual continuity. Chest is under construction in photo below, and finished in detail photo on facing page. Scalloped template (shown standing at right) straddles the chest's vertical spine to rout the curved shoulders of the bridle joint. A mating template attaches to the horizontal arms that hold the drawers, and the ends of the arms are routed to fit the spine. Inset drawer pulls are shaped with the same template techniques; a similar handle is explained in detail on page 114.

most of my work, and in the examples that follow, I use either of two bit/bearing combinations: a $\frac{3}{4}$-in. diameter cutter with $\frac{3}{8}$-in. diameter shank plus a bearing of $\frac{3}{8}$-in. ID and $\frac{3}{4}$-in. OD (for example, New Departures' #77R6AB), or a $1\frac{1}{8}$-in. diameter cutter with $\frac{1}{2}$-in. shaft plus a bearing of $\frac{1}{2}$-in. ID and $1\frac{1}{8}$-in. OD (for example, TRW's MRC R8ZZ).

The only limitation here is that the smallest radius of curvature in the joint must equal or exceed the radius of the smallest bearing. With my $\frac{3}{4}$-in. combination, a $\frac{3}{4}$-in. diameter washer must be able to roll along the curve and touch every point of it. You can get around even this limitation by using unmatched bearing/bit combinations, $\frac{3}{4}$-in. to $\frac{3}{8}$-in. for example, with appropriate offset in the template.

Usually the bearings simply slide onto the bit shank until they are stopped by the metal of the cutting flutes. If there is any resistance, apply force to only the inner race of the bearing. In extreme cases, expanding the bearing with heat and

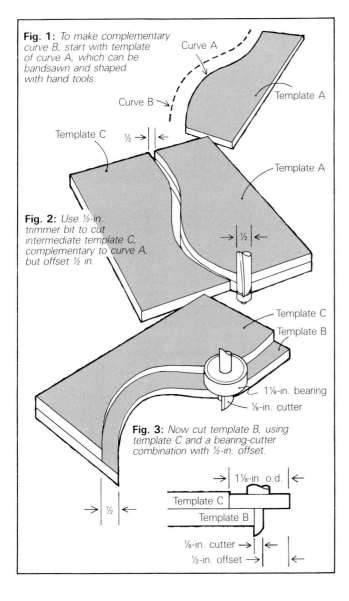

Fig. 1: *To make complementary curve B, start with template of curve A, which can be bandsawn and shaped with hand tools.*

Curve A

Curve B

Template C

Template A

½

Template A

Fig. 2: *Use ½-in. trimmer bit to cut intermediate template C, complementary to curve A, but offset ½ in.*

½

Template C

Template B

1⅛-in. bearing

⅛-in. cutter

Fig. 3: *Now cut template B, using template C and a bearing-cutter combination with ½-in. offset.*

1⅛-in. o.d.

Template C

Template B

½

⅛-in. cutter

½-in. offset

contracting the shaft by freezing will help. On the router end, the collet itself stops the bearing from sliding up on the bit shank. A drop of Loctite will hold it fast.

Of my two bearing/cutter combinations, the smaller is best for inside cuts (that is, when the bit is surrounded by wood), where control and power are most important. The larger is for outside cuts, where good surface finish and freedom from tear-out are necessary. Bear in mind, though, that even a powerful router is an ineffective hogging tool, because the counterforces developed in a heavy cut make precise control difficult. Whenever possible, it's best to use the router as a trimming tool, with some other tool—drill press, gouge, dado blade, or bandsaw—removing the bulk of the waste.

Now that we have a way to trace a template curve down into the workpiece, let's return to the original problem of fitting two pieces of wood together along some curve—that is, how to create two matching templates, one negative, the other positive. Let's assume we already have an arbitrary curve A and we wish to create the matching curve B (figure 1).

Clamp or tack a piece of template material on top of template A, leaving plenty of this template material on the off side of the curve. We will cut an intermediate curve, C, which will be exactly like the desired curve B except offset ½ in.—too small or too large, depending on whether it is concave or convex. We can do this by tracing along curve A with

an accurate ½-in. trimmer bit, as though creating a copy of A. What we want, however, is the fall-off (figure 2).

This is the only stage in the process where we are at risk, because any deviation by the bearing from perfect contact with A will result in a defect in curve C, which will be inherited by curve B. You might need several tries to get it right, but the price of failure is low—a wasted piece of hardboard.

Now, to obtain curve B it's necessary to cut a curve parallel to C but offset ½ in. in the other direction. Tack C onto a piece of template material, and cut out B by rolling along C with an unmatched bearing/cutter combination, one with a bearing 1 in. larger in diameter than the cutter. One such combination would be a 1⅛-in. diameter bearing on a bit with a ½-in. shank and ⅛-in. cutting diameter (figure 3).

Although in theory this would work perfectly, in practice ⅛-in. diameter cutters are fragile and easily broken. I therefore had a machinist turn a bushing with a 1⅛-in. ID and 1¼-in. OD, and press it onto a ½-in. ID by 1¼-in. OD bearing. This maneuver created a 1¼-in. bearing that I could mount on a ¼-in. cutter. The difference in radii is the desired ½ in. Another way to achieve the transition from C to B is to make two setups with a 1⅛-in. bearing on a ⅝-in. cutter, first using C to cut an intermediate curve, D, and then using D to create B. This tactic achieves a ½-in. displacement by adding two ¼-in. displacements. A number of other combinations will also work as well.

Curve B should fit precisely into curve A—unless, of course, something went amiss, which it frequently does. One source of error is any difference between the diameter of the cutter and the diameter of its bearing, likely if the bit has ever been sharpened. A discrepancy can be corrected by applying tape along curve A, as close as possible in thickness to half of the difference between cutter diameter and bearing diameter. Masking tape, packing tape, duct tape, and ordinary Scotch tape all have usefully different thicknesses.

Before going on to consider the third part of the curve-fitting problem, that of using these templates to rout our matching curves exactly where we want them, I should mention a few ways to generate curve A. Bandsawing and hand-sanding work, though it's difficult to maintain a perpendicular edge. If the edge isn't perpendicular to the face of the template, you have not one but several curves, all vaguely close to A, depending upon which cross-section the bearing rides. A drill press with sanding drum, or better still a spindle sander, is more effective. A good way of generating curve A in the first place is to combine several sub-curves already on hand, for example circles of various diameters (cut with lathe or drill press), straight lines, or french curves, tracing out the various components one at a time with a bearing and bit, all the while maintaining fairness where they merge and overlap.

To the third problem, that of positioning the matching curves in the work, I can give no general solution. Each joint requires its own tricks. Perhaps it will be useful to discuss a joint, the trick for which occurred to me suddenly as I was riding on top of a crowded bus to a dive in Moorea, dodging coconut fronds, and certainly not thinking about woodworking. Suppose we have templates A and B, with which to cut boards I and II, so that they may be joined in a lap joint, as shown in figure 4.

A template can be aligned on board I by making the respective edges flush and by making some point on the curve coincide with some point on the edge. But board II has no

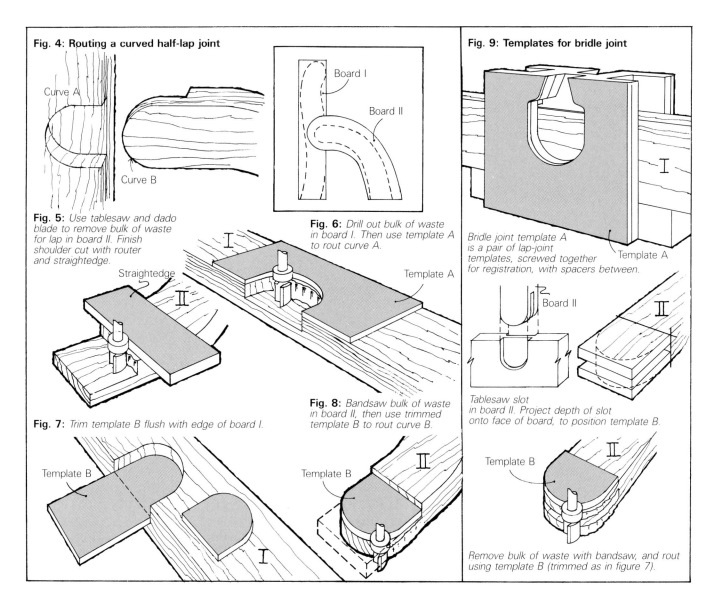

Fig. 4: Routing a curved half-lap joint

Curve A

Curve B

Board I

Board II

Fig. 5: *Use tablesaw and dado blade to remove bulk of waste for lap in board II. Finish shoulder cut with router and straightedge.*

Straightedge

Fig. 6: *Drill out bulk of waste in board I. Then use template A to rout curve A.*

Template A

Fig. 7: *Trim template B flush with edge of board I.*

Template B

Fig. 8: *Bandsaw bulk of waste in board II, then use trimmed template B to rout curve B.*

Template B

Fig. 9: Templates for bridle joint

Template A

Bridle joint template A is a pair of lap-joint templates, screwed together for registration, with spacers between.

Board II

Tablesaw slot in board II. Project depth of slot onto face of board, to position template B.

Template B

Remove bulk of waste with bandsaw, and rout using template B (trimmed as in figure 7).

straight edges, and it will be difficult to position the template to cut a half lap so that curve B has the same relationship to the lap's shoulder as curve A has to board I's edge. Do we cut the lap first, or curve B first? Proper cutting sequence is crucial in curved joinery, because each curve cut eliminates one more straight line from which to index.

In this case, it makes sense to cut the lap shoulder first. Start by scribing a line on board II for the lap shoulder. This doesn't have to be exact, as there is some allowance for waste, but the closer it is, the less waste there need be. Rough out as much wood as possible with tablesaw and dado blade, cutting to the finished depth but not to the lap shoulder line. Because of the curvature of board II, it would be awkward, though not impossible, to cut this shoulder on the saw. Instead we turn the work over and use a router with a straight-edge template to finish the shoulder (figure 5).

Now mark out curve A on board I, and drill out most of the waste. Clamp template A to board I, lining up the edges, and cut curve A into board I with the router (figure 6).

Now, and this is the crucial trick, slide template B into the A-shaped cutout you just made in board I, and tack it tightly. Then trim template B flush with the edge of board I (that is, the edge that ultimately will butt against the lap shoulder in board II). Use either an accurate trimmer bit, with the router base riding on the cut-out face of board I, or a bit-with-bearing-above-cutter, with the router base riding on the face opposite the cutout (figure 7).

Tack this truncated version of template B tightly against the lap shoulder in board II. The lap shoulder of board II will fit against the edge of board I exactly as tightly or as loosely as template B fits against the shoulder. Cut template B's shape into board II using a cutter with same-size bearing above its flutes (figure 8).

In the very corners, the bearing will bump into the lap shoulder, leaving an area where B is not traced down. A few minutes with bandsaw and file, or chisel, or spindle sander, cleans this up for a perfect fit.

Though procedures like these may become convoluted, care will always yield a perfect fit. Sometimes, of course, I choose to work at risk, not to seek the tedious but foolproof solution. But at other times, when my ultimate concern is the accuracy and strength of the finished joint, I use techniques like the ones I've described here, ignoring the automatic censor that won't allow things of great difficulty to suggest themselves. New joints can emerge from design processes that are integral with and complementary to the lines of the piece as a whole. Such an exposed, routed joint can be the whole focus of an otherwise simple piece of furniture.   □

Jim Sweeney makes furniture in San Francisco.

Relying on the Router

Three tricks from San Rafael

Unlike woodworkers in the European tradition and, to a lesser degree, those on the East Coast, many woodworkers on the West Coast came to their profession with a minimum of formal training. Thus there has developed among us a heavy reliance on the electric router for doing quite a few jobs that the old school would have done with other tools in other ways. Never mind that a sharp chisel could do a job well, we're more fluent with the router. A lot of us have spent the better part of a day—or even a week—perfecting a jig or a template that will harness the router to the task at hand.

Often this router technology is enormously efficient, allowing us to repeat processes quickly and accurately. At other times the router work is mundane, just another way of doing an ordinary woodworking job that could be done by other tools. But not surprisingly, the router is also capable of making many cuts and shapes that no other tool can accomplish.

Those of us who rely on the router in our everyday work are the ones who are likely to discover the creative things it can do. Many times it seems that the router jig itself is our final product, rather than the piece of furniture. Sometimes we miss out on the sound of a sharp blade slicing into the wood; instead we put on ear protectors to mute the whine of the three-horse Stanley. Nevertheless, the router technology we've evolved allows an economical efficiency that the professional woodworker cannot overlook in his struggle to make a living. I share shop space with two other craftsmen, Dale Holub and Bruce McQuilkin. The following pages demonstrate what I mean about the router by explaining three of the things that have evolved here in San Rafael: an inlaid wooden handle that Holub routs into his drawer fronts, the quick mortising method that I use, and a nifty wooden hinge that McQuilkin uses for desks and cabinets. —*Grif Okie*

Holub's inlaid wooden drawer pull

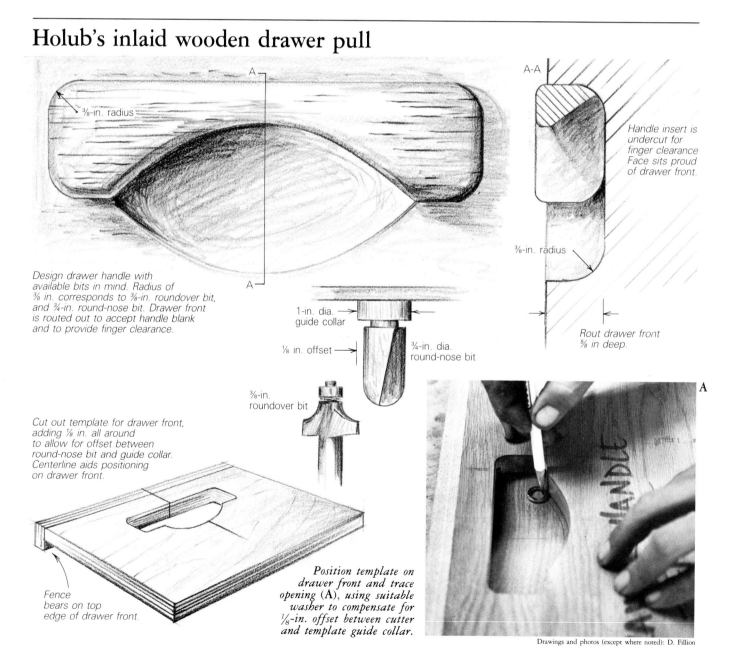

⅜-in. radius

Design drawer handle with available bits in mind. Radius of ⅜ in. corresponds to ⅜-in. roundover bit, and ¾-in. round-nose bit. Drawer front is routed out to accept handle blank and to provide finger clearance.

A-A

Handle insert is undercut for finger clearance. Face sits proud of drawer front.

⅜-in. radius

Rout drawer front ⅝ in deep.

1-in. dia. guide collar

⅛ in. offset

¾-in. dia. round-nose bit

⅜-in. roundover bit

Cut out template for drawer front, adding ⅛ in. all around to allow for offset between round-nose bit and guide collar. Centerline aids positioning on drawer front.

Fence bears on top edge of drawer front.

Position template on drawer front and trace opening (A), using suitable washer to compensate for ⅛-in. offset between cutter and template guide collar.

A

Drawings and photos (except where noted): D. Fillion

B

C

Drill the outlined area ½ in. deep (**B**). In general, waste as much stock as possible with other tools before routing to the line. Clamp template to drawer front. With a ¾-in. round-nose or corebox bit set to cut ⅝ in. deep, begin routing in a circular motion from the center of the opening (**C**). With a clear area in the middle, check the depth of cut, adjust if necessary, then rout out the entire area. Clean up with a gouge, and sand the top edge.

D

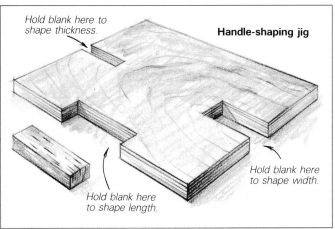

Hold blank here to shape thickness.

Handle-shaping jig

Hold blank here to shape width.

Hold blank here to shape length.

E

Plane, rip and crosscut handle stock to size. Shape the underside of the blank on the router table, using a ⅜-in. roundover bit with guide bearing (**D**), and a jig for holding the work (drawing). Alternatively, if you are making a number of handles, you can rip and shape a suitable length of stock to width and thickness, then crosscut individual blanks to length for further shaping. A routed handle blank is shown at left (**E**). Clean up edges with a drum sander, and try the fit. Transfer the curve of the finger allowance to the face of the handle. Bandsaw the curve of the handle and undercut the finger space (**F**). Sand the edges. Chamfer or round over the show edges, then glue the handle in place (**G**). The finished drawer pull is oak inlaid into a koa drawer front.

F

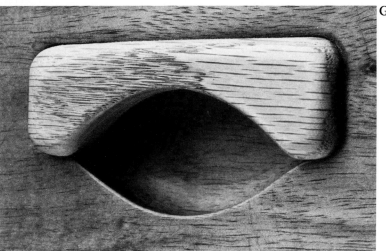

G

Joel Schopplein

Okie's quick jig for routing mortises

This jig for routing mortises is simple to build, and it produces an accurate joint that's easily repeated. It does, however, make a round-cornered mortise. The corners can be squared off with a chisel, or the tenon can be rounded over to match. But you can also rout equal mortises in both pieces of wood and then insert a separate, spline-type tenon. Tenons can be ripped by the running foot, then routed with a roundover bit of the appropriate radius to fit into the round-cornered mortise.

The jig consists of two shoulder blocks clamped onto the wood, with four pieces of hardboard tacked onto them to confine the travel of the router's template collar. The template can be a rectangular hole cut into a single piece of hardboard; I find it easier, however, to make each jig anew to fit the thickness of the stock I'm using, by assembling the jig right on the stock. First decide on the length, width and depth of the mortise you want, according to the strength needed as well as the bits and template guide collars you have. The best mortising bits are either spiral endmills or straight, two-flute cutters, carbide or steel. Lay out the mortise on the stock, then clamp the shoulder blocks to

Okie's mortising jig, for use with router and guide collar, is expeditious. First lay out mortise, then clamp shoulder blocks to faces of stock, and tack hardboard template parts to blocks. Size of opening depends on offset between cutter and guide collar.

the adjacent faces. Make sure that the shoulder blocks are wide enough, of sufficient length, and flush with the surface to be mortised. Now tack or glue the hardboard strips to the shoulder blocks, far enough away from the layout lines to account for the difference in radius between your router bit and its guide collar. With the jig in place, tip the router into the cut and run its guide collar around the inside of the opening you've made, proceeding in suitable increments to the full depth.

Two things make this type of cut easier: a template opening that's wider than the guide collar, and template

hardboard that's thick enough to contact and align the guide collar before the bit gets into the wood. A plunge router (*FWW* #30, p. 90) is ideal. Walk the router clockwise around the mortise, in the bit's direction of rotation.

I use this method enough to have settled on the mortise widths and tenon thicknesses appropriate for my work and my tooling. For each width of mortise, I make up a bunch of hardboard template end-plates with tongues, as shown. Then making a new jig for each new mortising situation is only a matter of cutting the side plates to length, and nailing them to shoulder blocks.

McQuilkin's inlaid wooden cabinet hinge

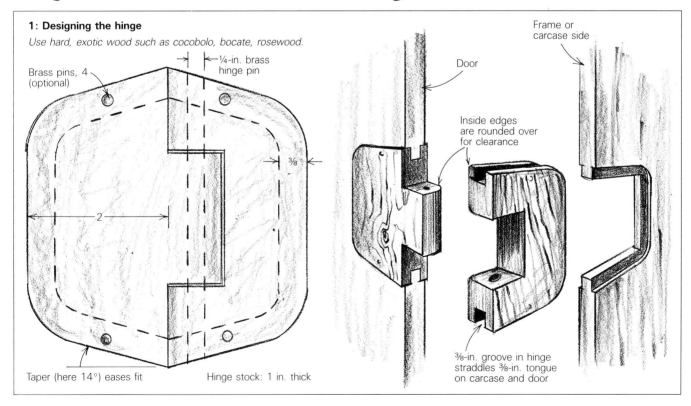

1: Designing the hinge

Use hard, exotic wood such as cocobolo, bocate, rosewood.

Brass pins, 4 (optional)

¼-in. brass hinge pin

2

Taper (here 14°) eases fit

Hinge stock: 1 in. thick

⅜

Frame or carcase side

Door

Inside edges are rounded over for clearance

⅜-in. groove in hinge straddles ⅜-in. tongue on carcase and door

2: Routing the opening

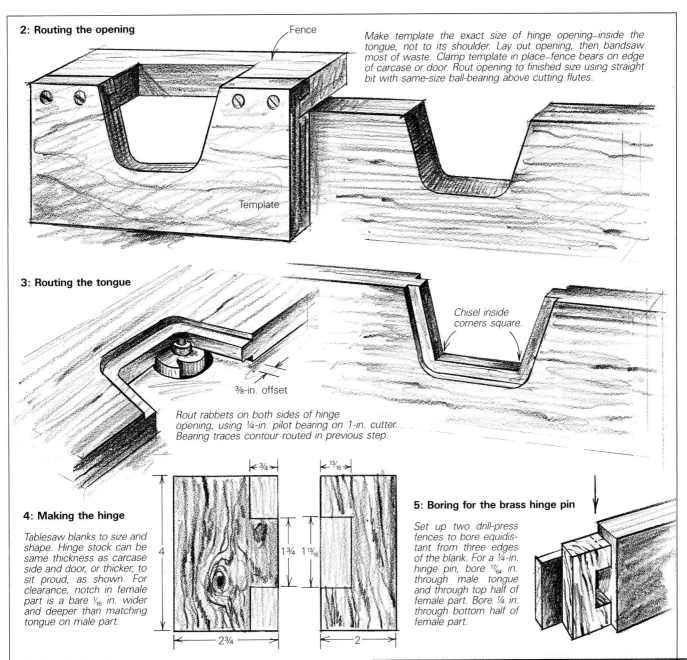

Fence

Template

Make template the exact size of hinge opening—inside the tongue, not to its shoulder. Lay out opening, then bandsaw most of waste. Clamp template in place—fence bears on edge of carcase or door. Rout opening to finished size using straight bit with same-size ball-bearing above cutting flutes.

3: Routing the tongue

Chisel inside corners square.

³⁄₈-in. offset

Rout rabbets on both sides of hinge opening, using ¼-in. pilot bearing on 1-in. cutter. Bearing traces contour routed in previous step.

4: Making the hinge

Tablesaw blanks to size and shape. Hinge stock can be same thickness as carcase side and door, or thicker, to sit proud, as shown. For clearance, notch in female part is a bare ¹⁄₁₆ in. wider and deeper than matching tongue on male part.

5: Boring for the brass hinge pin

Set up two drill-press fences to bore equidistant from three edges of the blank. For a ¼-in. hinge pin, bore ¹⁷⁄₆₄ in. through male tongue and through top half of female part. Bore ¼ in. through bottom half of female part.

6: Shaping the hinge parts

Make a plywood template (positive) that exactly fits rabbets routed in carcase and door. Attach a hold-down mechanism (DeStaco clamps, for example) to position the hinge blanks for shaping on the router table, with 1⅛-in. flush-trim bit and top-mounted guide bearing. Bearing runs on plywood template.

7: Final shaping

Tablesaw ³⁄₈-in. groove around hinge blocks. For safety, dado cutter should tightly fit slot in saw's throatplate. Use ³⁄₈-in. roundover bit to shape inside edges of hinge and carcase for clearance. Glue hinge in place. The finished hinge at right is bocate, let into a rosewood door.

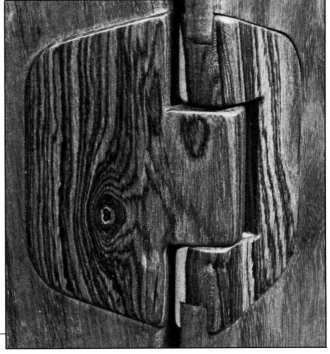

Drawings: D. Fillion

Three Decorative Joints

Emphasize the outlines with contrasting veneers and splines

by Tage Frid

I've been a craftsman and designer for 53 years and a teacher for more than 30, but I'm still learning. My students keep me on the ball by always asking questions. I experiment to come up with new ideas and simpler or better ways to do things. Students usually don't ask for help until they are in trouble. By then they have a big investment in time and materials, and we have to figure out some way to fix the mistake so it does not stick out like a sore thumb.

Dovetails are difficult for the beginner, and I have many times shown how to fix a badly fitting dovetail by inserting a piece of veneer. When I thought more about this trick, I realized you could outline the whole joint with veneer of a different color for a nice decorative effect. The technique also works on other joints, such as the mortise-and-tenon slipjoint. Another kind of decorative joint is a three-way miter where the strengthening splines are also emphasized in a contrasting wood. This is an attractive joint for framed cabinets, tables and stools. Here is how to make these three joints.

Outlined dovetails—The joint is laid out, cut and fit in the same way as a regular through dovetail. The veneer inlay that will outline the base of the pins and tails is glued onto the inside face of the mating pieces before the joint is cut. The rest of the outlining is done after the joint is glued together. Gauge the usual depth-lines around the ends of both pieces. To house the inlay, cut shallow rabbets up to the gauge line on the inside face of each piece. If you cut the rabbet on the tablesaw, set the blade as high as the gauge line (the thickness of the dovetailed pieces). Then set the fence to cut the rabbet slightly shallower than the thickness of the veneer.

The grain of the veneers should run in the same direction as the grain in the pieces to be dovetailed. It's easier to trim the inlay flush after the glue has set than to fit it perfectly before. So cut the veneer slightly oversize. Be sure the joint is perfectly tight where the end grain of the veneer meets the solid wood, especially on the pins piece because the veneer will be visible on both edges. Glue and tape the inlay in place

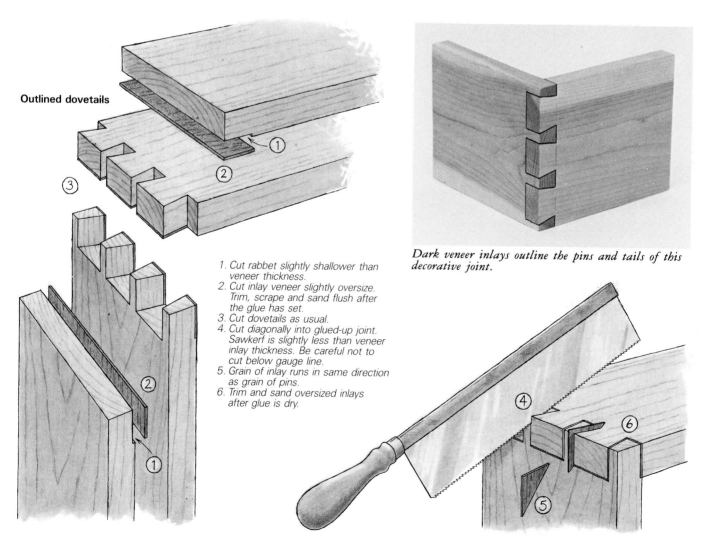

Outlined dovetails

1. Cut rabbet slightly shallower than veneer thickness.
2. Cut inlay veneer slightly oversize. Trim, scrape and sand flush after the glue has set.
3. Cut dovetails as usual.
4. Cut diagonally into glued-up joint. Sawkerf is slightly less than veneer inlay thickness. Be careful not to cut below gauge line.
5. Grain of inlay runs in same direction as grain of pins.
6. Trim and sand oversized inlays after glue is dry.

Dark veneer inlays outline the pins and tails of this decorative joint.

Drawings: Roland Wolf

and clamp it tight. When the glue has dried, lightly scrape and sand the inlay flush.

Now cut and glue up the dovetails. The veneer will line the base of the pins and tails. To add the veneer that will complete the outlining of the joints, saw diagonally along the line of the joint between tails and pins. Use a saw that cuts a little thinner than the thickness of the veneer inlays, and be sure the sawcut doesn't go below the gauge lines. Cut triangular pieces of veneer for the inlays. Orient the cuts so that when the pieces are glued in, their grain will run in the same direction as that of the pins. To fit the inlay pieces in the thinner sawkerf, you need to compress them a little by hammering them or by squeezing them in a steel vise.

Now put some glue in the kerf—not on the veneer. Rub it into the sawcut, using your finger to force it in deep. Slide the veneer into the kerf. It will pick up moisture from the glue and swell for a perfect fit. When all the inlays have been inserted and the glue has dried, cut off the veneer with a sharp chisel and finish-sand.

Outlined mortise-and-tenon slipjoint

—This joint can also be decorated with inlay, in the same way as dovetails are. Before you cut the joint, rabbet the inside edges of each piece for veneer. If you cut the rabbet on the tablesaw, use a backing block for more bearing surface against the fence. Flush off the glued-on veneer, then cut and glue up the joint as usual. To complete the veneer outline, saw diagonally down the line between tenon and mortise. Cut veneer triangles slightly larg-

er than finished size, and compress them to fit the kerf. Rub in glue as for the dovetail; you can use a mechanics' feeler gauge to get the glue all the way in. Slide the veneer in, trim it and finish-sand the joint when the glue is dry.

A surer, easier way to make this joint is to glue the veneers on the two cheeks of the tenon before the joint is put together. Rabbet and veneer the inside edges of the two pieces as before. Then cut the tenon and glue the veneer onto its cheeks. Allow for the veneer thickness when laying out the tenon thickness. Cut the mortise to fit the veneered tenon and glue up the joint as usual. For dovetailed or slipjointed pieces made of thicker wood, the inlay could be thicker too.

Decorative splined miters

—There are other ways besides a veneer outline to emphasize joints. A strong, decorative and quite simple joint to make is the splined miter frame, as shown on the next page. I made this three-way miter frame joint with wood that is square in section. For demonstration, I made only one corner joint—in a table you might have four, in a cabinet, eight (one at each corner of a cube). Glue together the joints of the mitered frames. I use hot hide glue because it sets fast. Next, cut the grooves for the decorative splines. If you cut the grooves for the splines on a tablesaw, use a cradle to hold the piece at a 45° angle to the table. I cut a notch in a 2x4 to make a cradle. For strength and decoration I put in several splines.

Clean up the surfaces after the glue has dried, then bevel or miter one side of each frame along its length so they will

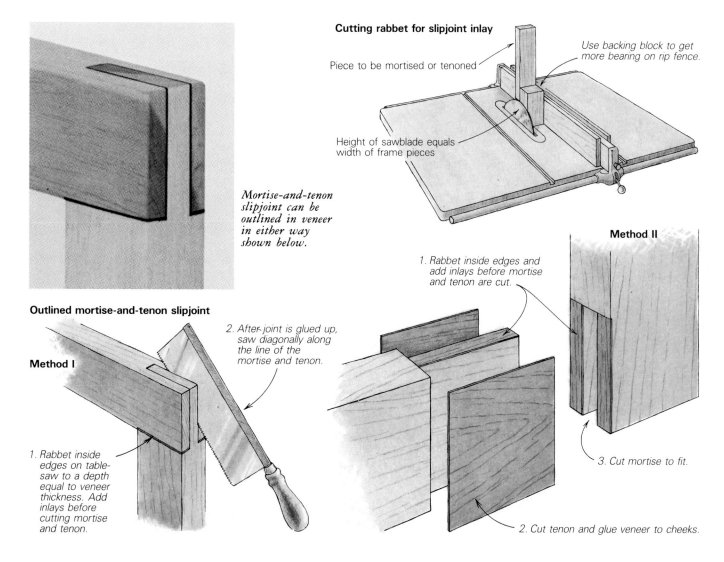

Cutting rabbet for slipjoint inlay

Piece to be mortised or tenoned

Use backing block to get more bearing on rip fence.

Height of sawblade equals width of frame pieces

Mortise-and-tenon slipjoint can be outlined in veneer in either way shown below.

Method II

1. Rabbet inside edges and add inlays before mortise and tenon are cut.

3. Cut mortise to fit.

2. Cut tenon and glue veneer to cheeks.

Outlined mortise-and-tenon slipjoint

Method I

2. After joint is glued up, saw diagonally along the line of the mortise and tenon.

1. Rabbet inside edges on tablesaw to a depth equal to veneer thickness. Add inlays before cutting mortise and tenon.

Three variations of the decorative splined mitered joint. Piece with angled faces, at right, is the most difficult of the three to make.

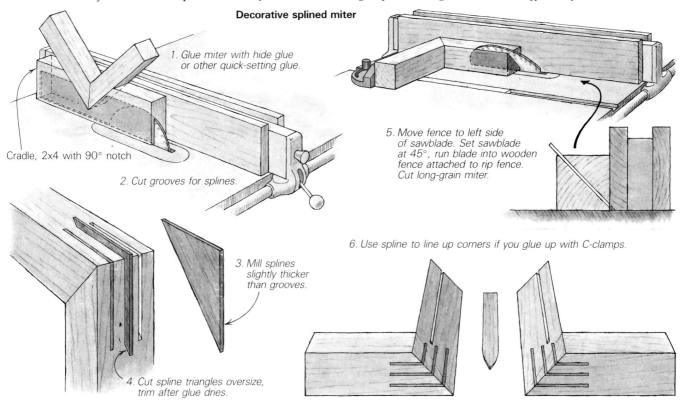

Decorative splined miter

1. Glue miter with hide glue or other quick-setting glue.

Cradle, 2x4 with 90° notch

2. Cut grooves for splines.

3. Mill splines slightly thicker than grooves.

4. Cut spline triangles oversize, trim after glue dries.

5. Move fence to left side of sawblade. Set sawblade at 45°, run blade into wooden fence attached to rip fence. Cut long-grain miter.

6. Use spline to line up corners if you glue up with C-clamps.

fit together. You can do this with a hand plane or with the tablesaw. With the tablesaw, mount a piece of wood on the rip fence, tilt the blade to 45° and run the blade slightly into the wooden fence. Use trial and error to find the right setting of blade and fence. You can leave a $\frac{1}{32}$-in. shoulder on the mitered piece, to bear against the fence beyond the sawcut. Plane this shoulder off before gluing up, or lose it later by rounding the edge. Don't stand directly behind the blade when you make this cut—the waste can be thrown backward.

Next make a groove in the mitered side for a hidden or blind spline, using the tablesaw or an electric router. The joint is long-grain to long-grain, so this spline is not for strength but for getting the corners to align if you glue up using clamps. If instead you wrap strips of inner-tube around the joined pieces, stretching it as you go, the corners will align and the spline won't be necessary. I have also used $\frac{1}{2}$-in. surgical tube; it's inexpensive and works better.

You can round off the corners, as in the photo, top center, before gluing up. I shaped the curves on a disc sander and dry-fit them to make sure they lined up at the joint.

For an interesting effect, you can put an angle of about 15° on the faces of the frames, as in the photo, top right. This joint is more difficult to make. Before gluing the frames together I ripped one face of each piece at a 15° angle. These bevels all should be on the front faces (in the same plane). You can use the same kind of tablesaw setup as for ripping the miters. These cuts must be very accurate. Finish-sand these faces before mitering and gluing up each frame. Then cut the sawkerfs and glue in the splines.

Next miter a long-grain side of each frame and cut the groove for the positioning spline if you are gluing up with clamps. Then rip the outside faces of each frame (that is, where the decorative splines appear) at 15° and finish-sand them. Finally, glue the two frames to each other. I like this joint and am going to use it in a frame-and-panel cabinet—when I get the time. □

Tage Frid is a contributing editor to this magazine, and the author of Joinery: Tools and Techniques *and* Shaping, Veneering, Finishing, *available from The Taunton Press.*

Bermudan dovetailing

by James Bump

Bermuda is a lovely semitropical island about 600 miles off the Georgia coast. Today it is a center for tourism, international banking and a couple of "country club" military bases. I was surprised to find, on this 20-square-mile paradise, a distinctive tradition of cabinetmaking. From the 17th century, Bermudan craftsmen carried on an individual style of decorative, cogged dovetail uncommon in either Britain or America.

Settled in 1609 by shipwrecked British sailors, Bermuda has been a British colony ever since. Early accounts cite plentiful supplies of timber as the island's only natural resource. Its cedar trees were used in furniture, in musical instruments, and in the Bermuda sloop, this seafaring community's lasting contribution to shipbuilding.

Bermudan ornamental dovetailing evidently had its origins in medieval Moorish workshops. It then spread to Spain and finally to Bermuda. To my knowledge, fancy dovetailing was used in Bermuda only for chests-on-frame. Early island cabinetmakers used Bermuda cedar (*Juniperus bermudiana*), now blighted and struggling against near-extinction. Today, Bermudan craftsmen import what they call Virginia cedar. Both cedars are aromatic, close-grained and knotty, and they finish to a gorgeous red-brown color.

Each cabinetmaker in Bermuda probably had his own individual designs for dovetailing. I made my own and found that templates were necessary. I cut the joint like a lap dovetail, the tails cut through, the pins blind. This leaves material for decoration on both pieces, which I shaped with a fretsaw, chisels and files. Test-fitting the joint is nearly impossible. The two boards have to be cut accurately before they will fit together at all.

Since there is so much room for error in the first attempts, I used pine to make my dovetails. I am a lutemaker, not a cabinetmaker, and I struggled a bit with the joint. Someone handy with dovetails should have no difficulty.

Bryden Bordley Hyde's fine book on Bermudan furniture, *Bermuda's Antique Furniture and Silver,* published by the Bermuda National Trust, shows examples of this sort of work. You can get it from the Maryland Historical Society, 201 West Monument Street, Baltimore, Md. 21201. □

James Bump lives in Hampden, Mass.

The early Bermudan chest-on-frame at left displays two patterns of cogged dovetail. The author designed his own pattern for his pine box at right.

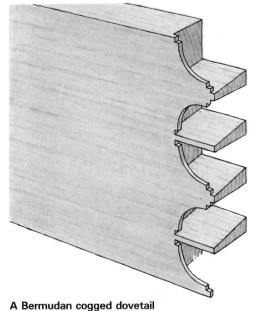
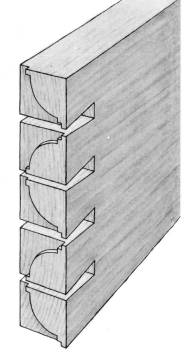

A Bermudan cogged dovetail

Cut joint as for lap dovetails, trace around templates to set out decoration.

Photos: J. Bump, Don Eaton; drawing: Roland Wolf

Routing splined miter joints

This router-based method for cutting the slots in splined miter joints is easy to set up and guarantees an accurate fit. First miter the panels in the normal fashion on the tablesaw and clamp them face-to-face as shown in the drawing below. Wide or bowed panels may require the addition of a stiffener clamped below the miters. Now chuck a spline-sized bit (⅛-in. or ³⁄₁₆-in. for ¾-in. stock) into the router and set the depth of cut (¼ in. to ⅜ in.). Adjust the router guide to be about

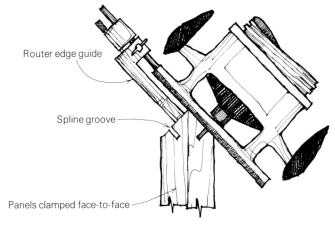

Router edge guide

Spline groove

Panels clamped face-to-face

¾ in. from the bit. Absolute accuracy in depth and guide settings is irrelevant. Rest the base of the router on the peak formed by two panels and rout a spline slot in each panel. To cut a stopped spline slot, just plunge the router.

Although the whole process can be accomplished with little more than eyeball measurement, the right angle formed by the two miters and the constant offset of the cut all but guarantee success. —*Warren H. Shaw, San Francisco, Calif.*

Portable benches

Shown below are two valuable additions to my shop. The sawhorse on the left is fitted with a small bench vise. I keep small power tools in the tray, and store hand tools in the drawers below. Because of the three legs and the extra weight

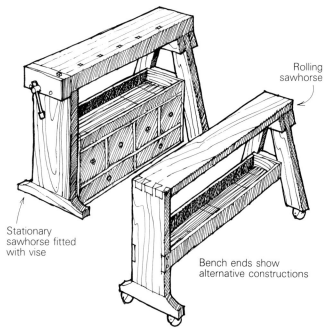

Rolling sawhorse

Stationary sawhorse fitted with vise

Bench ends show alternative constructions

the horse is very stable. A short board can be clamped between the dogs. For longer work, the caster-fitted second horse rolls easily into position to support the distant end.
—*S. Grandstaff, Happy Camp, Calif.*

Routed miter joint

I recently had to make two 24-in. long splined 45° miter joints to join a coffee-table top to its sides. Since the tabletop was too large for me to use my table saw, I devised a way to cut miters and spline grooves with my router and a simple homemade jig.

To make the jig, select a 2x4 slightly longer than the required joint and, using a carbide-tipped blade for smoothness, rip the board at 45°. Glue and screw the smaller piece to the main piece to extend the face of the jig, as shown in the sketch. Rip a ¼-in. groove a little less than 3 in. from the pointed edge of the jig and install a spline in the groove. The spline serves as a straight-edged guide for the router's base.

To use the jig, rough-cut the workpiece at 45°, leaving it about ⅛ in. long. Position the jig exactly on the cut line and

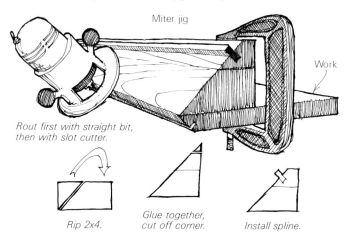

Miter jig

Work

Rout first with straight bit, then with slot cutter.

Rip 2x4.

Glue together, cut off corner.

Install spline.

clamp in place. Chuck a double-fluted carbide straight bit in your router and feed the router along the jig slowly and carefully. The ends are especially delicate. After the mitering cut is complete, leave the jig in position, chuck a slot cutter in the router and rout the spline slot. For a blind spline just stop the cutter an inch or so from the end. Repeat the process on the matching 45° piece. If the jig is made accurately, you'll be amazed how perfectly the joint will turn out.

—*Paul Darnell, Phoenix, Ariz.*

Mini-drawknife

This mini-drawknife is as small and handy as a spokeshave but can slice away a good deal of wood on each draw. It is great for getting in close to the bench and for use in tight quarters where neither of its brothers could perform.

To make the tool, start with an old 6-in. jointer knife and slowly grind the handle tangs as shown in the illustration. Grind the tangs at a slight angle back from the cutting edge so that the handles wedge on the tangs and stay tight when the tool is pulled. Turn the handles to any comfortable shape, and fit the tangs. For a perfect fit, glue up the handle blanks with paper between. Turn, split apart, and groove each half to fit the tang. Then glue the halves together.

—*Jim Clark Jr., Bridgeville, Penn.*

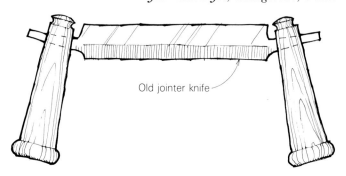

Old jointer knife

Plate Joinery

We test two machines that make fast, tight joints

by Paul Bertorelli

Doweling is a quick and strong way to make carcase and frame joints, but the problem with dowels is accuracy. Even the best jigs maddeningly tend to misalign the holes in a way that isn't evident until after the joint is glued and driven home, with no hope of adjustment.

Faced with that trouble with dowels, a Swiss cabinetmaker named Herman Steiner during the 1950s tried substituting spline-like, eye-shaped plates of compressed wood. Instead of a drill and jig, he used a small circular saw to scoop out a short kerf, into which he could insert the thin plates. The joint proved quick to cut and to assemble. More important, the parts could be slid along the slot into alignment after assembly. The compressed beech plates then absorbed moisture from the glue and swelled, making the joint tight and strong.

Steiner's invention developed into biscuit or plate joinery, a technique widely used in Europe but just becoming known in North America. Plates can connect carcases or frames in solid wood or in plywood, and especially in particleboard. Plate-joining machines are as portable as routers and require very little set-up. When making large carcases whose components may be difficult to pass through machines, plate joiners can be brought right to the job.

Steiner Lamello Ltd., the firm that sprang from Steiner's tinkering, has marketed its system in the United States for the past ten years. This summer the German tool firm Elu will offer a similar system. The Lamello machine (called a Minilo) costs about $580, the Elu about $300. Both companies say their machines are best suited for small shops where hand methods can't keep pace but where heavier equipment isn't justified. In my experience they've pegged the market. I used the Minilo in a small production shop for nearly two years and found that it worked well as a substitute for doweling, tongue-and-groove or even mortise-and-tenon. I recently borrowed an Elu machine from that firm's U.S. outlet for testing and found that, with some qualifications, it too makes an attractively quick and simple joint.

The plate does it—Steiner tried various sizes and shapes of wooden inserts, and even dabbled with plastic ones. He final-

Plate joints are made by inserting a beech biscuit into slots milled with a specialized portable plunge cutter. The cross-hatch pattern on the biscuit holds glue and speeds the biscuit's swelling, thus tightening the joint.

ly settled on three plates of the same thickness and shape (their edges are arcs of the same circle) but of different lengths and widths. Elu calls them biscuits, but the beech plates sold by both firms are virtually identical. Both make the same three sizes: No. 0 (about ⅝ in. wide and 1¾ in. long), No. 10 (¾ in. wide, 2⅛ in. long) and No. 20 (1 in. wide, 2½ in. long). The plates are die-cut from beech blanks with the grain running diagonally to the plate's length. Thus they are nearly impossible to snap across their width. The plates are compressed and embossed with a cross-hatch pattern that holds the glue, which you squirt into the slot before assembly. At first the plate fits its slot loosely. But as the compressed beech absorbs moisture from the glue, it swells in its slot. This swelling action is what makes the joint so tight and reliable. If there's enough glue in the slot, the joint tightens to maximum strength every time. Any water-based glue seems to work, sometimes even a little too quickly. I once misassembled a plywood carcase and tried to pull the yellow-glued Lamello joints apart after just ten minutes. I ended up with a lot of broken plywood.

Both machines consist of a high-speed motor powering a 4-in. carbide-toothed sawblade through a right-angle drive, attached to an adjustable base. Both machines have a spring-loaded mechanism that keeps the blade inside its base until you plunge it into the work to make the cut. Then the spring slips the blade back out of the wood and into its guard, while you move on to the next slot. The Minilo motor and blade move in a straight line, while the Elu swivels on a pivot; otherwise they both mill slots the same way.

Apart from speed, the big advantage of plate joints is being able to slide assembled parts into alignment. The machines cut a slot slightly longer and deeper than the actual dimensions of the joining plate. This tolerance allows the entire joint to slide along its length by as much as ⅛ in. The slot width is critical and is fixed at ⁵⁄₃₂ in. Spacing of the biscuits depends on the joinery situation, although the closer together they are, the stronger the joint. For maximum strength, the plates can be end-to-end (on about 2½-in. centers) and side-by-side (in stock thicker than about ⅝ in.). In most applica-

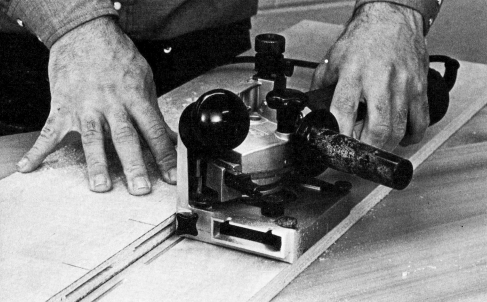

To cut slots with the Elu, above left, the cutter index is aligned with each pencil mark and the motor-cutter assembly is pivoted, plunging the blade into the stock. The edge of the mating board acts as a fence and must not be moved during the plunge, or an oversize slot will result. Slots in the mating part are cut by repositioning the machine, left. Above, glue has been squirted into the slots, and the beech plates inserted. The metering nozzle and glue bottle sold by Lamello are on the bench. Now the joint is assembled and pulled up tight with clamps, screws or nails. Clamps can be removed in as little as 10 minutes, because the plates swell, locking the joint.

tions, you cut the mating parts as if for nailing or butt-joining. You bring the parts together and strike pencil marks about 5 in. apart across the line of the joint. Then cut the slots in both parts by setting these marks to a centerline on the base of the machine. Add glue and the plates themselves, and assemble. The joints can be pulled up tight with clamps, screws or nails and need be held tight only until the plates swell. As with any joint, the final position of the parts must be marked accurately. And you have to hold the machine and its positioning guide rock-steady while cutting, or the slot will splay out and will be too wide for the biscuit.

Despite its versatility, the plate isn't always the best joint. When joining boards edge-to-edge, for example, a spline or an accurately placed dowel will draw warped or bowed surfaces into plane. Until the glue swells it, the plate is too loose in its slot to align two surfaces. I've tried to use plate joints to edge-join slightly bowed plywood panels and found that the method won't get the faces within a veneer thickness.

The plate joint can substitute for a mortise and tenon in a frame, but within limits. The rails have to be at least 1⅞ in. wide, the length of the No. 0 biscuit slot, or else the

edges of the slot will show. A protruding plate can be trimmed flush, but the result is never as neat as a well-made mortise and tenon. In frame stock thicker than ⅝ in., two plates should be used side-by-side.

Controlling the amount of glue in the slots is important. Too little and the plate won't swell. Too much and you get a messy river of squeeze-out. Lamello sells a bottle with a split nozzle for metering glue, although at $20 it seems overpriced.

I've seen no data comparing the strength of plate joints with traditional joinery. So I assembled a few test joints in poplar with dowels, stub tenons and plates. I was surprised to find that only the plate-joined piece couldn't be wrenched apart by hand, although it did succumb to a swift kick that broke the wood, not the glue line.

Comparing the machines—Both the Elu machine and the Minilo are well-crafted. But after I used each in the shop for a few hours, I found the Elu system to be generally less refined. The Swiss-made Minilo has a slick, detent-type depth adjustment, a real help when you want to switch plate sizes. I had to struggle with the Elu's stiff, threaded stop for depth set-

These frame joints were cut by placing the parts together and marking them, as with doweling. Using two plates in stock thickness makes for a stronger joint.

The Minilo's front fence can be set at 45°, making it the better machine for slotting lengthwise miters. Spring-loaded pins in the machine's front guard lock the Minilo against sliding during the plunge, a feature lacking in the Elu.

The Elu and Minilo are similar in size and weight. The plates, center, are sold in the same three sizes by both manufacturers.

ting. To locate the plate in the wood's thickness, Lamello uses a flip-down fence that rides atop the stock. A simple plastic snap-on template accommodates thinner stock, and also does double duty as a guide for plate spacing, typical of this machine's thoughtful design evolution. Elu's base rides on the bench top, which means there must be no debris under the stock, and it uses a tedious screw to adjust the cutter to the stock's thickness.

Both machines are at their best when making carcase joints. For cutting frame joints, the Minilo is handier than the Elu. Its front fence flips down and locks parallel to the cutter, and gives you plenty to hang on to while making the plunge. The Elu has no front fence, making it tough to hold both stock and machine at once, unless you clamp the stock down.

The Elu does have one feature the Minilo lacks. With a clamped guide or side fence (sold with the machine), it can cut a continuous groove faster and cleaner than a router does. Set to its full depth, the Elu could even be used as a panel saw for stock up to ⅝ in. thick.

The real difference between these machines is price. When I bought my Minilo, it was the only game around, so I winced

and paid the $580. It turned out to be worth it. The machine paid for itself every day by speeding carcase and frame joinery, and I soon wondered how I had ever gotten along without it. Yet, after trying the Elu, I'm sure it is more than half the machine for half the money. And despite its design shortcomings, I'd put up with its relative crudeness—particularly if I weren't going to use it in production every day.

The decision whether to buy a plate joiner ought to be guided by clear purpose. If you enjoy creating complicated, fussy joinery with little regard for time, one of these machines would only take some of the joy out of your woodworking. But if you find joinery a chore anyway, the plate joiner will make you wonder why you ever bothered with many traditional joints. A plate joiner is fast—a specialized power tool for doing lots of work quickly.   □

Paul Bertorelli is assistant editor of this magazine. The Lamello system is available through local tool outlets. It is imported by Colonial Saw Inc., 100 Pembroke St., Kingston, Mass. 02364. The Elu will be sold by Elu Machinery, 9040 Dutton Dr., Twinsburg, Ohio 44087.

PROJECTS

To make ten of Sawyer's chairs, left, one for each of us in the workshop, we started with a 6-ft. length of an 18-in. dia. white oak log. After quartering this with wedges to see the lay of the grain, we bucksawed lengths for chair parts. At top, two students saw a bolt for rungs. Steadying the log are Country Workshop sponsor Drew Langsner and his daughter Naomi. Above, teacher Dave Sawyer demonstrates drawknifing a rung on a dumbhead shaving horse.

Green Woodworking
How I split and shaved a chair at Country Workshops

by Rick Mastelli

Last summer, amid the Blue Ridge Mountains of North Carolina, I attended a week-long chairmaking workshop that changed my ideas about working wood. Ten of us had come because we were interested in learning to make chairs in an old way. We put aside our electric tools and surfacing machines, and we kicked the habit of using mill-sawn, kiln-dried wood. We retreated from the cabinetmaker's craft, with its jointing and smoothing planes and sandpaper. Instead, we adopted the tools of the country joiner, who rives the wood and shaves it into sticks and panels.

The joiner's craft has been practiced for centuries in peasant communities, where everyone, for at least part of the year, produces food, shelter, clothing, utensils and furniture. Originally a homely craft, it evolved into a specialized profession, which in parts of this country is being revived as part of the modern-day homesteader's diversified livelihood. The country joiner does not employ a sawmill, but goes directly to the local tree and, treating wood like the bundle of fibers that it is, pries it apart with wedges, gluts and froes. He shapes this riven wood with drawknives and spokeshaves, retaining the

126

Sawyer produces as many as 50 ladderback chairs a year without using jigs. "In my power-tool phase," he said, "I made some very fancy jigs. But it turned out to be mindless.... And I'd be looking for them and fiddling with them, and they'd end up in the fire." So now Sawyer just clamps the posts to the bench, shims to "close enough" and guides his brace and bit with a T-bevel and his eye.

continuity of the fibers that a rip saw would sever. Riven wood is stronger than sawn wood, easy to work while green, and more resistant to the deterioration of age and weather. Its grain and figure can be felt, not just seen as in planed and sanded wood. Its texture is rich and varied. And when you rive and shave wood, there is no dusty air to breathe. Green woodworking relies upon simple tools, cheap materials and direct processes. The result can be as useful, beautiful and inspiring to make as the chair pictured here.

Our classroom was an old tobacco barn on Drew and Louise Langsner's 100-acre homestead in Marshall, N.C. To get there, you drive along increasingly rural roads, till the last half-mile or so of the Langsner's driveway, which is best walked. "When you come to Country Workshops," remarked Langsner as his truck bounced us up to within reach of the farm, "you come to the country." Each summer, the Langsners sponsor as many as five week-long workshops in country crafts, alternating their workshop responsibilities with their farm chores. We helped a little with those chores, ate three bountiful meals a day of farm produce, and slept in our own tents. We worked long days and into the night, not exploring our individual bents, but practicing craft in the age-old sense. We did not design, for instance, but copied a traditional design. And though we initialed the parts we made, we didn't take the identification too seriously—on the first day we shaved more than a hundred rungs and threw them into a communal pile. In this way we concentrated on acquiring skills and minimized prideful fussing, making extra parts when we were finished with our own, and sharing them readily.

The workshop reflected the character of its teacher, Dave Sawyer, a 45-year-old New Englander who now lives in East Calais, Vt. Sawyer has an M.I.T. degree in mechanical engineering, but he retired from that career at age 28. "If I'd lived a hundred years ago," he said one evening in the barn, while tenoning rungs at the pole lathe to help some of us catch up, "I'd have done fine in mechanical engineering, because then people built what they thought up." The rhythmic slap of the lathe punctuated his words. "But thinking's pretty far from doing nowadays in that field." So Sawyer tried restoring old cars, he spent a half year in Bolivia in the Peace Corps Craft Program, and he worked for a while with the Amish. His turning point was the summer he spent working in the shop of Daniel O'Hagan, another sometime teacher at Country Workshops. O'Hagan's example encouraged Sawyer to do direct, simple woodwork. In 1969 he put together his own shop, and he has been making furniture and utensils from green wood ever since.

The ladderback chair we made is little changed from the first one Sawyer made ten years ago. He took the measurements from the first comfortable ladderback he'd found, a factory-made chair from the 1920s that he saw in an antique shop. After some minor changes in the way he made the first six, Sawyer had his product and his procedures down. I asked him, while he was showing us how to shape the back slats, if he was ever tempted to vary the design, to make a fancy chair with carved slats, for instance. "No," he said, "I don't believe in art. I never carved anything in my life, and I don't believe I ever will." Why, I asked? "Because I have no imagination," he said. "I never got into that individual expression bit, and I never made anything original. I work on the Volkswagen theory. You stay with something that works, and you make little improvements as you see them. I tried making an arty

Top, Sawyer marks the end of a bolt for splitting with a froe. The finished rungs have to be ⅞ in. in diameter, and Sawyer lays out squares only ⅛ in. oversize. He controls splitting by arranging to split relatively equal proportions (figure 2, p. 132), by splitting slowly, and if the split begins to run out, by exerting pressure against the heavier side of the split (figure 3, p. 132). Above, a student splits rung blanks in a small brake—two boards mounted like scissor blades to hold the work. By the end of the workshop's first day, we had shaved more than a hundred rungs, trying various styles of shaving horses and drawknives. The two horses, top right, are roughed out from thick slabs; the large stone holds them steady. At right, Sawyer loads the rungs into an oil-drum kiln.

chair once. I prefer being productive." I remembered that Drew Langsner had warned me on the way to the farm: "You're going to meet a lot of reactionaries here, people who figure rough woodworking is just fine."

Sawyer's ladderback *is* fine. It is just as strong-lined and as comfortably proportioned as you'd expect a chair to be that has been unchanged through ten years and hundreds of copies. Its high back is well balanced by the thickening of the back posts below the seat. Sawyer steambends at the thickest part of the legs to increase the chair's stability and to angle the back comfortably. Other ladderback chairs, John Alexander's, for instance *(FWW #12, p. 46)*, bend above the seat at the thinnest part of the back posts. Sawyer's chair is stouter than Alexander's elegant rendition. Sawyer's is a professional chairmaker's pre-industrial product, and he makes 20 to 30 of them a year, sometimes as many as 50. It takes him 12 hours

from tree to finished chair, and he gets $115 for each. When he needs more money he makes wooden hayforks for $17 apiece. He once made 200 hayforks in two months.

So we learned how to make chairs in batches. For a week we became a green-wood chair shop. Our industry was interspersed with demonstrations and learned, talky meets; the ten of us went home knowing not only how to bust a chair from a tree, but also how to do it efficiently within a daily work rhythm. We began by making rungs because they are easiest to make, and because they want to be drier than the posts into which they are mortised. After assembly, the tenon absorbs moisture from the post and swells while the mortise shrinks, locking the joint firmly. It took us a day to split and shave the rungs, but by the end of that day, the best among us could shave a rung almost as fast as Sawyer, in under 3 minutes. While the rungs dried in a jury-rigged kiln—a

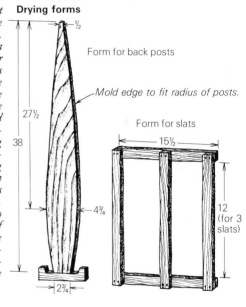

The chair parts are bent without steel straps. First we boiled the 1½-in. to 1-in. diameter posts in water for a couple of hours (the boiler rests between cement blocks in the background of the photo top left). Then we coaxed the bend into shape on the shaving horse. A pad under the horse's head prevents the stock from being marred. The posts are muscled in pairs onto drying forms, above, and held in place with leather thongs while they set overnight. The slats, left, were also boiled, but only for a half hour or so, then bent on the horse and over the knee until they fit on their own drying form. Plans for the forms are given at right.

Drying forms

Form for back posts

Mold edge to fit radius of posts.

Form for slats

½

27½

38

4¾

2¾

15½

12 (for 3 slats)

70-gal. oil drum perched over a smoldering campfire—we split and shaved the posts. By the third day we were dumping the back posts into a smaller drum full of boiling water to prepare them for bending. We flexed the hot posts on a shaving horse, then strapped them to simple forms and laid them in the kiln to set their curve while we split and shaved slats, which went through the same process. All the parts made, we bored the mortises for the front and back rungs and chopped the mortises for the slats. The evening of the fourth day we turned tenons on the ends of the rungs.

We assembled our batch of chairs on the workshop's last day, banging them together with a lead-filled rawhide mallet wielded over a hefty stump. It was heady stuff. First we pounded the front rungs into the front posts, then the back rungs and slats into the back posts. In these sub-assemblies, we bored the mortises for the side rungs, nicking the front

and back rungs so the side rungs would interlock with them, like Lincoln logs. Tension was high as each of us brought our sticks to the assembly stump, sticks that represented a week's shaping and scraping. Driving oversize tenons into slender posts means real fear in that moment when the mallet is poised between blows. Yet chair after chair popped into being. I asked Sawyer why he preferred this daring finale to a project so painstakingly prepared—why not use clamps? It was easier and faster this way, he said, but also the experience should be intense. "If you can get a chair together without splitting, it's not going to split afterwards," he said. "Assembly is the worst time. It's like being born. If you can survive that, chances are you'll last another fifty years."

*   *   *

For most of us, the workshop was over that fifth night. Whether or not we stayed on for Sawyer's optional seat-

Assembly is tense. Under that lead-filled mallet a week's work might end up a pile of broken sticks. Everyone went home with a chair.

weaving demonstration the next morning, each of us went home with a chair, and that alone was worth the workshop's $175 tuition. But the real value was in what we'd learned, and the chair was there to remind us of that. I left with an appreciation for green woodworking that continues to grow. It was not the first time I'd sat on a shaving horse, but it was the first I'd done enough work on one to get sore. You learn a lot this way, subtle understandings along with plain, common sense. Surrounded by others to watch and new tools to try, the revelations come, and the horse gets comfortable. Here is some of what I learned.

Measuring—There's nothing novel about cutting a number of parts to size and checking one against another. It's faster, easier and more accurate than measuring each individually. But many of us feel we need drawings covered with dimensions to be able to build anything. We didn't need a drawing to build Sawyer's chair, and there weren't many numbers to worry about either. All we needed to know was recorded on the two sides of a flat stick. It didn't get wrinkled and messy in the shop, and it was always handy to place on the wood to

lay out tapers, bores, mortises or whatever. Figure 1, on the facing page, represents Sawyer's chair stick, and it's all the blueprint you need to make his chair.

Getting the most out of the wood—We split enough wood for ten chairs from a single white oak veneer-quality log 18 in. in diameter and 6 ft. long. We could get a back post and a front post, four short rungs, three long rungs or various other combinations out of the length. With wedges we split the log into quarters, then we read the grain to make best use of the wood. We crosscut the quarters into bolts, pieces the length of the various parts. Then a froe, that long-bladed, long handled, clumsy-looking tool, dimensioned the blanks

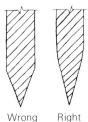

Wrong   Right

faster, neater and more efficiently than a saw could. We were splitting blanks for rungs ⅛ in. oversize, blanks for posts ¼ in. oversize, and rarely having to reject a piece. The secrets of the froe are as follows: First, it doesn't need a sharp edge, but the bevel must be properly shaped. The bevel on a new froe is usually

Scribing a back leg for final trimming.

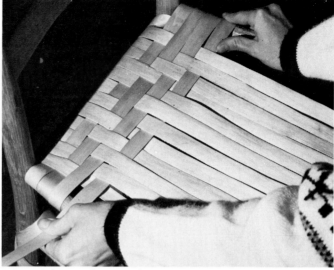

To weave the seat, first wrap the warp in one continuous strip from front to back, splicing your material underneath. Bark and splints shrink as they dry, so leave the warp overnight, then push it tightly together to fit another round or two of warp. The weft can create any number of patterns, here a diamond-shaped herringbone. The triangular spaces at the sides of the seat will be filled with short lengths woven into the weft.

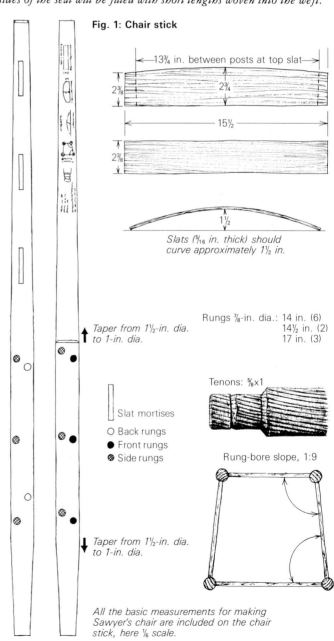

Fig. 1: Chair stick

13¾ in. between posts at top slat

2¾

2³⁄₈

15½

2³⁄₈

1½

Slats (⁵⁄₁₆ in. thick) should curve approximately 1½ in.

Taper from 1½-in. dia. to 1-in. dia.

Rungs ⅞-in. dia.: 14 in. (6)
14½ in. (2)
17 in. (3)

Tenons: ⅝×1

Slat mortises
○ Back rungs
● Front rungs
◉ Side rungs

Rung-bore slope, 1:9

Taper from 1½-in. dia. to 1-in. dia.

All the basic measurements for making Sawyer's chair are included on the chair stick, here ⅙ scale.

too blunt and too angular. It should be no more than 30°, and it should blend smoothly into the sides of the tool to form a single, convex surface. A facet, as in a chisel or plane-iron bevel, tends to stick in the wood and does not rock smoothly during levering.

Second, the froe must be properly placed on the bolt. When you have to make a number of splits in one bolt, don't start at one end and work across, but start in the middle and then again in the middle of each of the halves, and so on (figure 2, next page). With equal portions on either side of the split it's easier to control its direction. The handle of a good froe is about 16 in. long, the blade about 10 in. Make sure the whole edge is in full contact with the wood before you strike— you're liable to shift the froe if it is slightly angled off the surface. Once you start a split (give it a good rap) you have to follow through, so make sure you begin in the right place.

Now, put down your mallet. One or two blows are all that's needed—the rest is levering not severing. You need a rigid, fork-like arrangement of boards or logs, called a brake, to hold the bolt while you bear on it. If the wood begins to split unevenly, place the heavy side of the split down, and use your

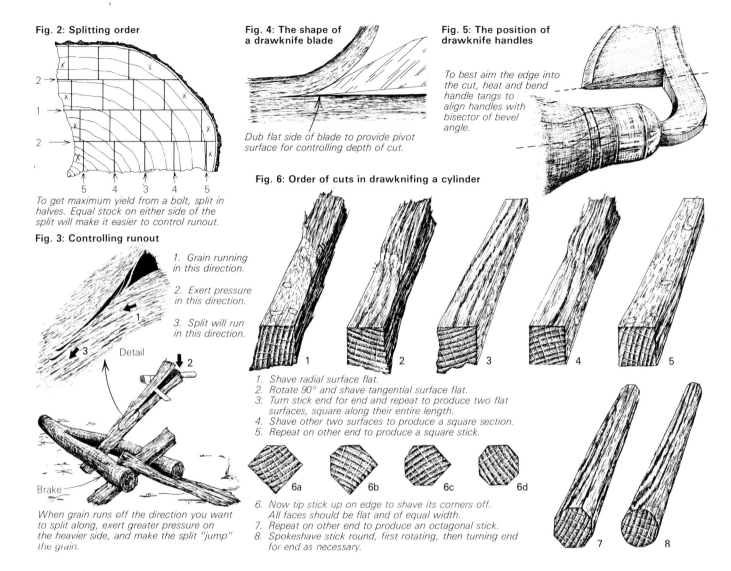

Fig. 2: Splitting order

To get maximum yield from a bolt, split in halves. Equal stock on either side of the split will make it easier to control runout.

Fig. 3: Controlling runout

1. Grain running in this direction.
2. Exert pressure in this direction.
3. Split will run in this direction.

Detail

Brake

When grain runs off the direction you want to split along, exert greater pressure on the heavier side, and make the split "jump" the grain.

Fig. 4: The shape of a drawknife blade

Dub flat side of blade to provide pivot surface for controlling depth of cut.

Fig. 5: The position of drawknife handles

To best aim the edge into the cut, heat and bend handle tangs to align handles with bisector of bevel angle.

Fig. 6: Order of cuts in drawknifing a cylinder

1. Shave radial surface flat.
2. Rotate 90° and shave tangential surface flat.
3. Turn stick end for end and repeat to produce two flat surfaces, square along their entire length.
4. Shave other two surfaces to produce a square section.
5. Repeat on other end to produce a square stick.

6a   6b   6c   6d

6. Now tip stick up on edge to shave its corners off. All faces should be flat and of equal width.
7. Repeat on other end to produce an octagonal stick.
8. Spokeshave stick round, first rotating, then turning end for end as necessary.

hand to bend the heavy side away from the split. Go slowly. You need time to see which way the split is going and to direct it. If you have split firewood only, where you strike a single blow with a maul and pick up the odd pieces, you will be surprised at the control you have with a froe. Sure, wood splits along the grain. But by bending the wood away from the split, you can cause the plane of failure to jump the grain (figure 3 and front cover).

Shaving wood—If I never work another piece of green wood, I will still use my new drawknife and the shaving horse I recently built. These tools are surprisingly handy for all kinds of work. The shaving horse quickly clamps stock of various shapes and sizes so you can shave it, plane it, scrape it, or (heaven forbid) sand it. It doesn't take long to coordinate hand and foot: clamp down, take a stroke, release pressure, move the stock, and clamp down again. You can't do this sort of thing as fast with a bench vise. Your whole body works on the shaving horse, not just your hands and arms. The harder you pull with your knife, the more you push with your leg, and the tighter your stock is clamped. And all the while you're on your butt, building a chair while you sit.

I tried a number of different shaving horses and I like the dumbhead horse best (FWW #14, p.4). I tried different drawknives too, and it seems most can be made to work well, if properly sharpened (FWW #25, pp.93-94). The angle of the bevel should be relatively small, between 28°and 32°. I

dub the edge on the flat side, the sort of thing that you'd never do to a plane iron. A plane iron is positioned in relation to the surface of the work by the sole of the plane. Only the edge of the blade touches the work and dubbing the back dulls that edge. The drawknife, having no sole, is guided by the back of the blade sliding on the wood (figure 4). You can regulate depth of cut—from ½-in. thick slabs to paper-thin shavings—simply by tilting the handles. To best aim the edge and control the cut, the handles should be parallel to a line that bisects the bevel angle (figure 5). You will have to heat the upper portion of the tangs and rebend the handles of most drawknives to establish this relationship. Some drawknives work better bevel-side down, as this surface provides something to rock the blade on. I find that dubbing the flat face produces a fine pivot surface for sensitive work.

Sawyer showed us how to hold the knife diagonally to the stroke, and to slide it sideways, slicing as we pulled it. He liked long, consistently thick shavings from long, even pulls. As we worked, he would wince at the crackling sound of badly cut wood. Good shavings whisper off the knife.   □

Rick Mastelli is associate editor of Fine Woodworking. *This summer's Country Workshops will include hand-tool techniques, with Willie Sundqvist; basic country woodcraft, with Daniel O'Hagan; and chairmaking, with John Alexander. For details write Country Workshops, Route 3, Box 221, Marshall, N.C. 28753.*

Two plywood dollies

Struggling with sheets of plywood is a real strain on my back, so I built this plywood dolly that makes handling those sheets easy. When I bring plywood to my shop in my pickup truck, I wheel the dolly up to the back of the truck with the cradle locked in the horizontal position. Then I slide the plywood from the truck onto the dolly with the long edge of the sheet resting against the foot. To tilt the cradle for transporting I just tap the locking bar with my foot to allow the cradle to swing to the vertical position. The cradle, when loaded with plywood, is almost evenly balanced but with a little more weight on the side with the foot. That way the cradle always tips the right way. When I wheel the plywood up to the saw, I tilt the cradle back to the horizontal position where the locking bar falls into a notch and locks. Since the dolly is the same height as my saw I can feed the plywood directly into the saw from the dolly.   —*R.W. North, Burbank, Calif.*

I've used the dolly sketched below right for years to handle large, heavy panels. I use it to tilt the panels up to the top of my table saw and unload panels from my truck. It also serves as a roll-around stepladder and a portable work surface.
     —*Ben James, Jacksonville, Fla.*

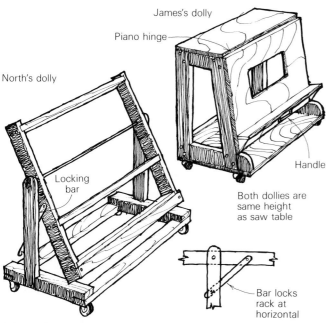

James's dolly

Piano hinge

North's dolly

Locking bar

Handle

Both dollies are same height as saw table

Bar locks rack at horizontal

Two-level rolling worktable

I made this rolling worktable to ease the logistics of constructing a full set of kitchen cabinets in my small (18-ft. by 18-ft.) workshop. Since then I have found it to be the ideal companion to the traditional cabinetmaker's workbench when space is limited. Built square, level and strong it provides an excellent base for moving cabinets and furniture into or out of the work stream. Or, with the crossbars in place, the worktable can be used at waist height for moving production pieces from machine to machine. As a bonus, it stores away without taking up much room.

Four 360° heavy-duty casters support a 40-in. by 40-in. finger-joined or dovetailed frame of 2x3 hardwood, gusseted with ¾-in. plywood at each corner. Add a couple of 1x3 crossbraces if needed. Screw and glue the ¾-in. plywood top to the frame, then paint and wax it to make it easy to clean up spilled glue and finishes. Next add two pockets on each of the two opposite sides, as shown, to accept the ends of the four hardwood 1x3 uprights. Slot the top of each upright to slip into the two appropriately notched crossbars. These four

uprights and two crossbars can be assembled in about 30 seconds to produce a table height workhorse.
     —*Norman Odell, Quathiaski Cove, B.C.*

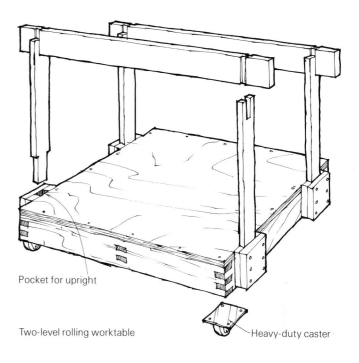

Pocket for upright

Two-level rolling worktable

Heavy-duty caster

Hold-in improvement

The molding head for the tablesaw is a valuable tool. But without the proper hold-ins it is practically impossible to shape thin stock without chattering. The hold-in fixtures I use to overcome this handicap consist of an auxiliary fence and a horizontal hold-in. The auxiliary fence is a maple 1x3 that screws to the saw's rip fence. Since this fence may cover part of the rotating cutterhead, it's a good idea to cut a recess into the fence beforehand by raising the cutterhead into the fence. The top of the fence is fitted with an adjustable pressure shoe that holds the work to the saw table.

Make the pressure shoe from a stick of maple by sawing two (or more) sawkerfs from opposite ends. This gives the shoe some spring, allowing it to adjust to minor variations in thickness and to damp out any chattering.

The horizontal hold-in is simply a slotted arm fitted with another pressure shoe. It holds the work firmly against the fence. The arm locks in place with cap screws that fit tapped holes in the table.

Design the fence and hold-in so you can reverse them and use them on either side of the saw's rip fence. This will allow you to take full advantage of both left-hand and right-hand cutter designs.   —*Walter O. Menning, LaSalle, Ill.*

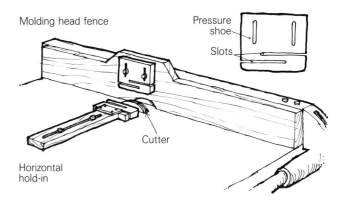

Molding head fence

Pressure shoe

Slots

Cutter

Horizontal hold-in

On Making Chairs Comfortable

How to fit the seat to the sitter

by Alan Marks

Many contemporary chair designers seem more interested in innovation than in good seating. The imagination must be indulged, but should the end product please the eye at the expense of the body? Dr. Janet Travell, who was once therapist to President Kennedy (it was she who prescribed the rocking chair as back therapy) points out, "You wouldn't dream of buying shoes that don't fit you. But have you ever stopped to consider whether the chairs you sit in are right for you? One can go into most homes and not find a single chair that's properly designed to support the framework of the human body."

The industrial designer, in his eagerness to take advantage of new production techniques and materials, may mistakenly assume that human flesh and bones will conform to the same configurations as plastic and steel. Discomfort, however, is not always a deficiency. Thonet's most successful bentwood chair, employed by generations of avaricious Parisian cafe owners, is sufficiently uncomfortable that customers rarely dally after eating. But getting people back on their feet in a hurry is not what this article is about.

Ideally, a chair used by only one person ought to be custom-fitted, like a tailored suit or custom shoes, especially if the owner will be spending a lot of time in it. The fit of an office chair, for instance, can make the difference between productive workdays, and uneasy ones. Bad chairs create back problems. As there are few mass-produced chairs designed for very tall or very short people, and since even the most "average" person is still an individual, I custom-fit the chairs I design. I interview the client at home and take measurements from chairs he or she considers acceptable, often taking a width measure from one chair and a height from another and so on. I work in centimeters because they scale up easily *(FWW #31, p. 56)*; the inch sizes given here are approximate.

The *Humanscale* seating guide, along with a number of other ergonometric guides worked out by Henry Dreyfuss Associates (MIT Press, 28 Carleton St., Cambridge, Mass. 02142, 1974, $37.50) provides a wealth of information for the designer. In it are worked out the critical angles and measurements for the entire range of chair types for men or women of average, large or small build. For each possible combination, a rotating dial gives optimum seat height, depth and angle, backrest height and angle, and armrest height. If you build custom-fitted chairs, this guide is a real time-saver, although individuals in each of the five given categories will still vary.

The seat—Begin designing your comfortable chair by considering the seat's height, width, depth, shape and the material to pad it. If this is a one-off chair to be used by more than one person, it is safer to use the measurements suitable for the average person. If you, like me, mistrust statistics, turn to the nearest suitable human reference—yourself, for example.

I am about average height, and the distance from the floor to the underside of my bent leg is about 50 cm (19¾ in.). For the average person, then, the front edge of the seat has to be lower than this to avoid pressure on the sensitive arteries that feed the lower leg. If you are designing the average dining chair, choose a front edge height of 45 cm (17¾ in.).

Seat depth, the distance from the front edge to the back, is critical. If too deep, the sitter will be forced to slouch or else will suffer the discomfort of pressure on the back of the leg, which cuts off blood circulation and cramps tendons. If the depth is too shallow, discomfort may result from the decreased area over which body weight is distributed.

Most commercial sofas have a seat depth of between 53 cm and 56 cm (21 in. to 22 in.). According to *Humanscale*, however, depths greater than 43 cm (17 in.) will be uncomfortable for most small women and for at least half of all men. These people have to forgo back support, either sitting ramrod-like toward the front edge or sliding their pelvises forward and slouching. The sofa is therefore an in-between piece of furniture—not really comfortable for sitting nor well suited for lying down. The similarity between the words "couch" and "slouch" seems more than coincidence. For the average person, the distance between the rear of the bent lower leg and the plane of the lower back is 44 cm (17¼ in.). I generally subtract 2 cm to 4 cm (¾ in. to 1½ in.), for a seat depth that allows freedom of movement.

The seat of a dining chair should be wider at the front than at the rear, so the sitter's legs can spread. Good widths are 46 cm (18 in.) at the front and 36 cm (14¼ in.) at the rear.

A flat, hard seat is rarely comfortable for long sits. A contoured wooden seat, even if it faithfully reproduces the imprint of all the bones, muscles and curves of a resting derriere, is not comfortable either; the smallest shift in position causes misalignment. A seat must provide support over as wide an area as possible. A deep bucket seat such as found in sports cars does this well. It does not, however, permit the change in back position needed to relieve muscle strain. The most comfortable contour is the ever-changing one made by the sitter adjusting position on a cushioned surface. Only the most general sort of contour for the cushion underlayment is needed—at most a 20-mm (¾-in.) depression for the buttocks. A ridge in the middle of a seat is a real pain.

To counteract "foam pinch," caused by too much soft polyurethane (the deeper the sitter sinks, the more pressure is exerted on the sides of the thighs and buttocks), try laminating different densities of foam together. The portions of the chair bearing the most weight should have the highest density foam. The parts of the body most sensitive to pressure, such as the back of the knees and the bony portions of the upper back, should rest on softer material. I prefer to keep dining and office chairs as firm as possible, with perhaps an inch of high-density foam over a contoured plywood base. Most plas-

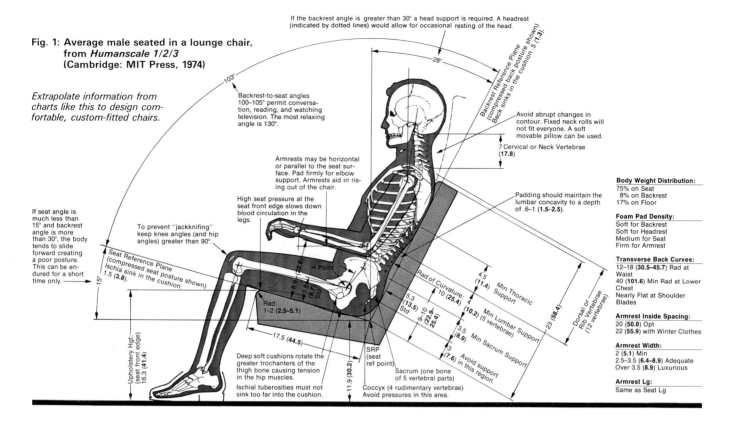

Fig. 1: Average male seated in a lounge chair, from *Humanscale 1/2/3* (Cambridge: MIT Press, 1974)

Extrapolate information from charts like this to design comfortable, custom-fitted chairs.

If the backrest angle is greater than 30° a head support is required. A headrest (indicated by dotted lines) would allow for occasional resting of the head.

Backrest Reference Plane (compressed back posture shown) Back sinks in the cushion .5 (**1.3**)

28°

103°

Backrest-to-seat angles 100–105° permit conversation, reading, and watching television. The most relaxing angle is 130°.

Avoid abrupt changes in contour. Fixed neck rolls will not fit everyone. A soft movable pillow can be used.

7 Cervical or Neck Vertebrae (**17.8**)

Armrests may be horizontal or parallel to the seat surface. Pad firmly for elbow support. Armrests aid in rising out of the chair.

High seat pressure at the seat front edge slows down blood circulation in the legs.

Padding should maintain the lumbar concavity to a depth of .6–1 (**1.5–2.5**).

If seat angle is much less than 15° and backrest angle is more than 30°, the body tends to slide forward creating a poor posture. This can be endured for a short time only.

To prevent "jackknifing" keep knee angles (and hip angles) greater than 90°.

Seat Reference Plane (compressed seat posture shown) Ischia sink in the cushion 1.5 (**3.8**).

15°

H Point

Rad: 1–2 (**2.5–5.1**)

Rad of Curvature: 10 (**25.4**)

4.5 (**11.4**) Min Thoracic Support

5.3 (**13.5**) Std

9–10 (**22.9–25.4**) Std

4 (**10.2**) Min Lumbar Support (3 vertebrae)

3.5 (**8.9**) Min Sacrum Support

3 (**7.6**) Avoid support in this region.

23 (**58.4**)

Dorsal or Rib Vertebrae (12 vertebrae)

Upholstery Hgt: (seat front edge) 16.3 (**41.4**)

17.5 (**44.5**)

Deep soft cushions rotate the greater trochanters of the thigh bone causing tension in the hip muscles. Ischial tuberosities must not sink too far into the cushion.

SRP (seat ref point)

11.9 (**30.2**)

Sacrum (one bone of 5 vertebral parts)

Coccyx (4 rudimentary vertebrae) Avoid pressures in this area.

Body Weight Distribution:
75% on Seat
8% on Backrest
17% on Floor

Foam Pad Density:
Soft for Backrest
Soft for Headrest
Medium for Seat
Firm for Armrest

Transverse Back Curves:
12–18 (**30.5–45.7**) Rad at Waist
40 (**101.6**) Min Rad at Lower Chest
Nearly Flat at Shoulder Blades

Armrest Inside Spacing:
20 (**50.8**) Opt
22 (**55.9**) with Winter Clothes

Armrest Width:
2 (**5.1**) Min
2.5–3.5 (**6.4–8.9**) Adequate
Over 3.5 (**8.9**) Luxurious

Armrest Lg:
Same as Seat Lg

---

tic foams can be readily cut with a bandsaw, and can be laminated using contact cement either brushed or sprayed on.

You might want to try a relatively new type of foam patented and manufactured by Kees-Goebel, 4954 Provident Dr., Cincinnati, Ohio 45246. Called Temper Foam, it is both viscous and elastic, almost like a marshmallow. Body heat softens it so that it conforms to the sitter's shape, distributing body weight evenly over the entire contact area. After use, it slowly regains its original shape.

At the bottom of the pelvic girdle two knobs of bone jut out. You can feel the pressure these two knobs exert if you sit on your hands. They're about 13 cm (5 in.) apart and 13 cm (5 in.) from the plane of the back. If these bones bottom out in sitting, most of the body weight is supported by two tiny areas barely 6 mm (¼ in.) square each. This hurts. A two-layered cushion—high density foam on the bottom, medium density on top—is one way to deal with this problem. Another way is to add webbing at critical points covered by a single layer of foam. With a circle cutter set to a 12-cm (4¾-in.) diameter cut two holes in the flat plywood seat, centered 13 cm (5 in.) from the rear edge and 6.5 cm (2½ in.) on either side of the centerline. Round the edges with a rounding-over bit to prevent chafing of the webbing, which should be tacked in Xs over the holes. Using this technique, as little as ½ in. of the proper foam padding makes the seat quite comfortable.

Nylon-reinforced rubber webbing, such as available from Constantine, 2050 Eastchester Rd., Bronx, N.Y. 10461, has replaced the traditional jute variety. Besides being strong and durable, it is elastic. I have used it in both sofa and easy-chair construction. You can tack it to wooden seats, or use special metal clips that fit into routed grooves, making installation quick and eventual replacement easy.

A cheap alternative to rubber webbing, which apparently possesses all its strength and springiness, consists of longitudinal latex cords wrapped and tied with synthetic threads and covered with a thin bonding layer of latex. Because this web-

bing comes in several strengths, various grades can be combined to achieve the chair support needed for maximum comfort. In attaching it, the material is stretched to twice its original length, so the frame must be sturdy enough to withstand this constant tension. It can be obtained from Sanglatex USA, Inc., PO Box 269, 921 Baker Road, High Point, N.C. 27261, and from Mateba Webbing, 715 Pine St., Dunville, Ontario N1A 2M4.

The back—Again, to design a comfortable chairback, we must consider some basic human anatomy. The spinal column consists of 24 vertebrae that form a reverse curve. The lower five, the lumbar vertebrae, comprise the concave curve of the small of the back. They attach to the sacrum, the broad triangular bony structure of the pelvis. The twelve segments above the lumbar are the thoracic or dorsal vertebrae, forming the convex dorsal curve. Above them come the seven cervical vertebrae of the neck, a concern in specialized seating. In addition to the curve along the length of the spine, there is the curve across the width of the back made by the rib cage, shoulders and waist. Any comfortable chair must consider this curve too.

The spine has two functions that concern us here. It supports the body and it enables the body to twist and bend. Because the weight it carries continually shifts during normal motion, it must flex in all directions. This flex is permitted by tough yet elastic ligaments which fasten the vertebrae to one another. The entire spine is balanced and held in position by pairs of muscles in the back, abdomen and hips. If a muscle contracts to a new position, its complementary muscle must relax enough to allow it to do so. To hold the body in any one position against the force of gravity, both muscles tense. Thus even when the body seems at rest, muscles can become fatigued if body weight is not supported by the chairback.

The two sources of back discomfort are stretched ligaments and fatigued muscles. The ligaments that can cause the most pain when stretched are the two that run front and back the

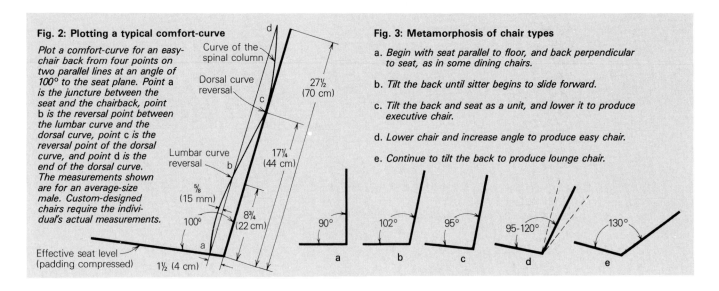

Fig. 2: Plotting a typical comfort-curve

Plot a comfort-curve for an easy-chair back from four points on two parallel lines at an angle of 100° to the seat plane. Point a is the juncture between the seat and the chairback, point b is the reversal point between the lumbar curve and the dorsal curve, point c is the reversal point of the dorsal curve, and point d is the end of the dorsal curve. The measurements shown are for an average-size male. Custom-designed chairs require the individual's actual measurements.

Curve of the spinal column

Dorsal curve reversal

27½ (70 cm)

Lumbar curve reversal

17¼ (44 cm)

⅝ (15 mm)

100°

8¾ (22 cm)

Effective seat level (padding compressed)

1½ (4 cm)

Fig. 3: Metamorphosis of chair types

a. *Begin with seat parallel to floor, and back perpendicular to seat, as in some dining chairs.*

b. *Tilt the back until sitter begins to slide forward.*

c. *Tilt the back and seat as a unit, and lower it to produce executive chair.*

d. *Lower chair and increase angle to produce easy chair.*

e. *Continue to tilt the back to produce lounge chair.*

90° — a

102° — b

95° — c

95-120° — d

130° — e

entire length of the spine: the anterior and posterior longitudinal ligaments. Too much curve at the small of the back, too small an angle where the back meets the seat, or sitting upright in too low a chair can deform the spinal curve, stretching the anterior ligament. Too little support will allow the spine to bow, stretching the posterior ligament. A comfortable chairback must be designed to keep these two ligaments free of tension.

The other cause of discomfort, muscle fatigue, can be alleviated in one of two ways. You can try to relieve weight from the lumbar region by increasing the angle between the chairback and the seat, and providing a suitably cupped cavity for supporting the upper body. The farther a chairback reclines, the less weight the muscles have to balance and the more important the cushioning of this cavity becomes. The second way to deal with fatigue is to allow for movement rather than locking the muscles into a single, tiring position. Back muscles should constantly change their state of tension, as in walking. The most comfortable stool I ever designed was one whose legs and seat flexed to permit twisting and swaying. Avoid deep lateral curves in straight, upright chairbacks; they cause fatigue by inhibiting sideways body movement.

I use four reference points to plot the basic comfortable curve for the back of an easy chair: the juncture between the seat and the chairback (point *a* in figure 2), the reversal point between the lumbar curve and the dorsal curve (*b*), the reversal point of the dorsal curve *(c)*, and the end of the dorsal curve *(d)*. Draw a straight line between points *b* and *c*, and a concave curve from points *c* to *d*. The convex curve drawn from points *a* to *b* not only provides lumbar support, it creates a slight pocket for the buttocks to expand into. A comfortable chair does not crowd the sitter here. If the chair seat is padded, measurements must be taken with the padding compressed, as it will be in use. This is the effective seat level.

Little weight rests on the chairback except in the most laid-back chairs. Cushioning for the lower back should be generally firm; for the upper back, soft. The lateral curve can be achieved with curved back rungs or shaped upholstery.

The armrests—We have all sat in chairs with armrests so high that shoulder muscles are tensed. Armrests that are too low feel awkward, encouraging the sitter to slouch. Ideally, armrests should take half the weight of the arms, while the remaining half is taken by the shoulders. The average adult re-

quires an armrest 22 cm (8¾ in.) above effective seat height. The distance between arms should be at least 49 cm (19¼ in.). Large people will need more width.

The seat/back angle—To understand the variations possible for the angle between seat and back, consider the metamorphosis of an imaginary chair through the range of chair types, from dining chairs through executive and easy chairs, ending with the lounge chair (figure 3). The basic comfort-curve built into the back remains constant throughout, though neck and head support must be progressively added as the sitter's weight shifts back. The three factors that do change are the angle between the comfort-curved back and the seat, the angle between the seat and the floor, and the height of the seat from the floor.

In the dining chair, the seat is parallel to the floor and the back is vertical (a). If you now, in imagination, hinge the back where it attaches to the seat and slowly tilt it (b), you reach a point at which the sitter begins to slide forward—about 102°. To prevent this, the entire chair must tilt as a unit (c), while maintaining a seat/back angle of 95° or less, which is a good, standard angle. This, however, raises the front edge and creates uncomfortable pressure at the back of the knee. To relieve this pressure, we lower the chair toward the floor (executive chair). Continuing to tilt and lower the chair reclines the body enough for the seat/back angle to be increased again (d), since a forward slide has been forestalled (easy chair). Any further recline is now accomplished by increasing the pitch of the back (e). Metamorphosis complete, we end up with a lounge chair.

Pat measurements such as from *Humanscale* can lead to a good chair, but there's more to it. I remember a fellow student asking Carl Malmsten how he knew that a chair he'd drawn would be right. Malmsten looked askance at the youth and retorted that he had been designing chairs for fifty years, that was how he knew. Designing a comfortable chairback has much to do with experience and a lot to do with instinct. Given comfort as a criterion, there still remain endless possibilities for expressing individuality and originality. A designer should welcome at least some limitations. They are rather like the weights a diver uses to explore the ocean floor. □

Alan Marks wrote on how to develop ideas for chair design into working drawings in FWW *#31, Nov. '81.*

The Three-Legged Stool
Furniture turned on the lathe

by David W. Scott

The three-legged stool is the essence of casual furniture, good for a brief perch in the kitchen or shop or for a longer sit when the body is leaning forward and partly supported by a desk or counter. For a turner, the stool may serve as an introduction to joinery and a chance to go beyond the usual turned work.

The idea of individual turnings coming together to form a finished piece of furniture is fascinating. Building furniture and doing production lathe work in a small shop, I have long been intrigued with the structure of the three-legged stool—the variations on its simple theme seem endless. Free-form slab seats in the style of Wharton Esherick (*FWW* #19, pp. 50-57), seats that are turned and then carved, other rung configurations and legs at other angles, even different angles in the same stool, all open up new design possibilities.

I make stools between 25 in. and 28 in. high, a good size for general use. A 25-in. stool with legs angled at 78° has feet about 17 in. apart—graceful and stable in appearance and in use. I determine the placement of the rungs according to appearance, intended use of the stool, and the user's leg length. If the rungs are too low, the stool looks clumsy; if too high, it begins to look storky. Two-rung stools, like one of those in the photo at right, have the rungs' mortises all at the same height from the floor. Three-rung stools have rungs staggered in height 1 in. to 1¾ in. so as not to weaken the legs. In order to be able to choose the rung heights and lengths for each stool individually, I turn the seat first and then the legs. The legs join the underside of the seat in 1-in. diameter holes about 4 in. to 5 in. from the seat center. I mark and drill the holes in the legs for the rungs, test-assemble the legs and seat without glue, and measure the lengths of the rungs. Then I turn and finish the rungs, take care of details and glue the pieces together.

Making the seat—Usually, I turn the seat from 6/4 or 8/4 stock, 12 in. to 14 in. in diameter, mounted inboard on a Glaser center-screw chuck on the lathe (*FWW* #25, pp. 84-85). I bought the chuck, which lets me mount and unmount the seat blank quickly and precisely, for $70 from Turnmaster Corp., 11665 Coley River Circle, Fountain Valley, Calif. 92708. My preference is seats made all from one board, but seats glued up to get that width look fine too. First I drill the hole for the center screw on the seat-blank underside, then, using a protractor, I mark three lines radiating out from the center at 120° intervals. Then I bandsaw the rough shape, mount the blank on the lathe, and pencil-mark a circle that sets the distance the legs will be from the center. This ensures that the legs will center up with the finished seat. The holes for the legs must be drilled before the seat is turned, because the top's final shape may not lie flat on the drill-press table without wobbling. I tilt the table to 78°, and drill 1-in. dia. holes in the bottom of the seat

Two graceful and perky stools: turned furniture.

blank, making sure that the holes angle out from the center. Multi-spur bits make clean holes. You can make holes only 1 in. deep or so, if you don't want the legs to come up through the top of the seat.

Legs—I turn legs from 8/4 stock. With my production stools, particularly sets, I use a router and a homemade duplicator, a long, open-ended box that fits over the lathe. It's similar to one I saw in *FWW* #25, on p. 22. The router rides on the flat top of the box, and a ½-in. dia., 2½-in. long, double-fluted straight carbide bit makes a shearing cut on the side of the spindle as it turns. The router collar rides against a template of ⅛-in. hardboard cut to the final leg shape, and mounted just above the stock. I rip the leg blanks octagonal on the tablesaw before turning, to minimize stress on the router and bit, and I take a number of end-to-end passes to work down to template size, working from the tailstock to the headstock on each pass. The final pass leaves a rough surface, which I clean up later with a gouge or skew, when I turn the details of the feet and the top tenons.

Rungs—Because most stools have rungs at different heights from the floor, the rungs will vary in length. I turn rungs from 4/4 stock. Conventionally, rungs taper to ½ in. or ⅝ in. at the ends, and this diameter enters a mortise in the leg. This is the weakest link in the stool's structure, however, since the rung is vulnerable to the concentrated weight of a careless

To strengthen the stool's weakest joints, Scott turns shouldered, round tenons that will be pinned in the legs.

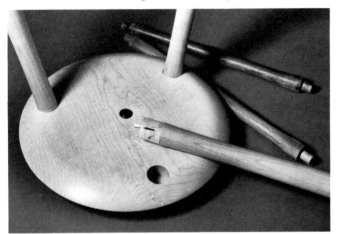

This fox-tailed wedge will lock the leg to the stool. The rosewood plug in the center of the seat fills the single hole left by the chuck's center screw.

When easing a stool together dry, Scott makes sure the joints all draw up at the same time, or the last pieces will be difficult to get into place.

person. To beef up this area without removing too much material from the leg, I turn each rung with a double-diameter end—in effect, a shouldered, round tenon. The larger diameter, $\frac{7}{8}$ in., penetrates only $\frac{1}{4}$ in. into the leg, while the $\frac{1}{2}$-in. tenon goes a full 1 in. deep. Size the rung ends carefully and check them in a sample hole; they should fit snugly.

Assembly—The legs are now ready to be drilled for the rungs. The placement of these holes will determine the height of the rungs from the floor, the angle of the rungs to the legs (the same as the angle of the leg hole in the seat), and the relationship between adjacent rungs, which should be 60°.

Adjust the drill-press table to the same angle used for boring the leg holes in the underside of the seat. Then clamp a long V-block to the drill-press table. Fix an adjustable stop-block at the lower end, at the distance one of the rungs should be from the foot of the leg. With the stop thus set for the proper hole height, drill one shouldered, round mortise in two of the legs for the lowest rung. You need to drill two holes in the same place, the larger, shallower one first and then the smaller, deeper one. Dry-assemble these two legs and one rung (the longest) with the seat to ensure that the angles are going in the right directions. Now move the stop block 1 in. farther from the drill bit to set the height of the next rung, and drill a hole in the remaining leg. Leave this stop block in place on the drill press. The next steps will determine the proper relationship of the remaining three holes to these first ones.

Dry-assemble the legs and seat with the lowest rung in its holes in the back legs. Placing your forehead against the front leg opposite the hole you have drilled in it, sight with one eye to either side of the leg directly across to the leg adjacent. This will locate the center point of that leg for the fourth hole to be drilled. This point could also be located by using a piece of dowel with a pencil lead in one end, but the eye produces an accurate result. After marking the point, drill it using the same setup as for the third hole.

Finally, drill the holes for the third rung, using the same procedures as before, with the stop blocks moved to allow for the new distance from the floor.

Dry-assemble the entire stool to get the feel of how it must go together during glue-up—you must ease all the joints together simultaneously, or you won't be able to get the last pieces into place. You will have to flex the rungs into place in any case—and a rubber mallet will help drive them home—but be sensitive to their breaking points. While the stool is still dry-assembled, wax around all the joints to protect the wood against glue squeeze-out.

The wedges that hold the legs in the seat should be perpendicular to the grain line of the seat. For further security, the rungs should be wedged too, or else cross-pinned. If you use wedges in the ends of the rungs, orient them perpendicular to the leg grain. I cross-pin the rungs into the legs using a small finishing nail set in a shallow $\frac{1}{4}$-in. dia. counterbore. I then cut $\frac{1}{4}$-in. decorative plugs with a plug cutter, turn their ends while I hold them in a drill chuck on the lathe, and leave them proud to cover the pins. To cover the screw-chuck hole in the seat bottom, I turn a rosewood plug. □

David Scott is a full-time woodworker. He and his wife, Kathy, are also caretakers of the Museum of North Carolina Handicrafts, in Waynesville. Photos by the author.

Stools: A slightly different angle

by Jim Cummins

Ron Curtis doesn't "relate" to his tablesaw, a 16-in., 5-HP beauty, though he respects it. "You just can't slow it down," he says. He's an established woodworker in Bloomfield, Conn., with a one-man shop full of good equipment. Curtis has been building furniture and stools he describes as "free-form construction with sound joinery" since 1968, and these days he's able to make his living from his work.

But he's not a tablesaw type of woodworker, the kind he defines as thinking square and parallel all the time. Not that he doesn't build square himself, when that's his intention, but he usually feels a little looser than that. He'll use any jig that makes his work easier or better, but he'll eyeball everything he can.

Mostly with power sanding equipment, Curtis shapes the top of his stool seats freely. But he leaves at least the middle of the bottom flat, so it will bear against his leg-angle jig: a tapered piece of wood about 8 in. long made from a 2x4 that he clamps to the drill-press ta-

ble. He drills clear through from the top at locations he works out with a compass—he'll wedge the tenons later. The jig for the stool in the photos is 17°, but he uses 15° as well.

Curtis takes leg blanks that he has pre-cut with a taper jig on the tablesaw, and makes the tenons with an adjustable hollow auger that he bought at a garage sale. With the three legs stuck in the seat, he stands the stool up on an assembly table and proceeds to his other jig: a plain board with drilled holes for the feet of the stool. With all three legs locked into the seat at the top, and two legs fixed at the bottom by the jig, he measures the height for the first rung, then eyeballs the direction for the holes.

With a Stanley ½-in. Powerbore bit, shortened so the electric drill can fit between the legs, Curtis drills from the outside until he feels the point of the bit coming through. Then he drills back through the hole from the other side, so as not to tear out chunks at the exit hole. He drills the second leg like the first. If the holes do not line up perfect-

ly, he says it just puts a little tension on the rung and helps tie the stool together.

For stretchers, he makes up octagons (he likes the way they catch the light in the finished stool), gauges them by eye for length against the legs while they are still in the foot jig, and then uses the hollow auger to make long tenons. He bandsaws the rung to a taper that will meet the tenon smoothly, then removes the marks with a drum sander.

Curtis is quick to give Wharton Esherick credit for the inspiration behind his type of stool, and Sam Maloof credit for the finish: beeswax and oil over a sealer that's part polyurethane. But when it comes right down to it, Curtis's eye makes each stool. □

Instead of tilting the table, Curtis uses this angled block. He sets the seat blank on it when he drills the holes for the legs.

Ron Curtis eyeballs a mortise as his foot jig steadies the work, left. The stool has an elm top and legs, and is about to be fitted with ash rungs. Curtis prefers native woods and will go out of his way to get them, but admits, 'I usually cut up some South American stuff for the wedges.'

The stools sell for $195 at Pritam and Eames Gallery in East Hampton, N.Y.

139

Folding Stool With Tray
Knockdown design for a dual-purpose project

by Tage Frid

I was asked to design a folding stool that would be light, take up little space when folded, and serve as the base for a tray. In addition, any parts broken during service would have to be easily replaceable. When the stool was finished it weighed 4½ lb., and measured 1¾ in. folded. Nothing has broken yet, so I haven't had to take it apart, but I could if I wanted to and it would go back together good as new.

I made the stool from ash. If I had used a weaker wood, I would have added to the thicknesses and widths for strength. The seat can be either leather or canvas. The one shown is canvas, with a single row of stitches to make a hem at the edges and a double row to hold the 3-in. overlap.

The stretchers can be held to the legs with either T-nuts or barrel nuts and ³⁄₁₆-in. stove bolts. The stool shown here has T-nuts, which leave the holes in the stretchers open. Barrel nuts would have filled the holes and looked like metal plugs. Where the stretchers butt against the legs there's a hidden dowel (or a steel pin) that keeps the stretchers from turning. A washer between the legs where they cross allows the stool to fold easily, and double nuts are locked together so they don't have to be drawn too tight. If a tight single nut were used, the stool wouldn't fold. Washers under the bolt heads protect the wood.

The legs are identical except for the angle on the foot—the angle makes it a right leg or a left, to keep the dowel holes inside. Mill the leg blanks, square them and cut them to exact length. Set up the drill press with stops to locate the holes, and then drill them all. Notice that the holes for the dowels

or steel pins don't go through—make these holes ⅜ in. deep. After you've drilled the holes, taper the legs with a taper jig on the tablesaw or on the bandsaw. Cut a little wide so you can run the edges over the jointer to remove the saw marks, and then cut the foot angle.

The stretchers are all the same length. I made the bottom stretchers ⅛ in. wider than the top because people have a tendency to put their feet on them when they sit on a stool, but the stretchers could be all the same size. Mill them out and cut them to length, then use a stop on the drill press to make the holes for the T-nuts or barrel nuts. For T-nuts, make ⅝-in. holes; for barrel nuts, use ½-in. holes. Of course, regular nuts could be used if the others aren't available, but barrel nuts are easy to make. My students and I use them a lot—they make an attractive and strong joint if a piece has to be disassembled. They can be of ½-in. cold-rolled steel, aluminum, brass, or other rod stock. Cut the nuts to length, so they will be flush with the surface if you want them to show, or shorter if you want to use them in a blind hole. File and sand the ends, then drill and thread holes for the bolts. Use a V-block jig in the drill press to bore the hole. Remember to countersink these holes so the bolt will start easily—when it comes time for assembly, you can wiggle the nut until you feel the bolt start to engage. If you use barrel nuts or regular nuts for the stool, use a ³⁄₁₆-in. stove bolt, 2½ in. long. For T-nuts, use a 2-in. long bolt. Tilt the drill-press table to 90° and clamp a jig to hold the stretchers while you drill the holes

The taper in the legs of this stool cuts down weight, leaves the wood where it's needed, and allows the stool to close up to a snug 1¾ in. T-nuts in the stretchers allow disassembly. You don't have to store this stool in the closet when you're not sitting on it—make a tray that converts it into an occasional table or server, as shown above.

Photos: Roger Birn

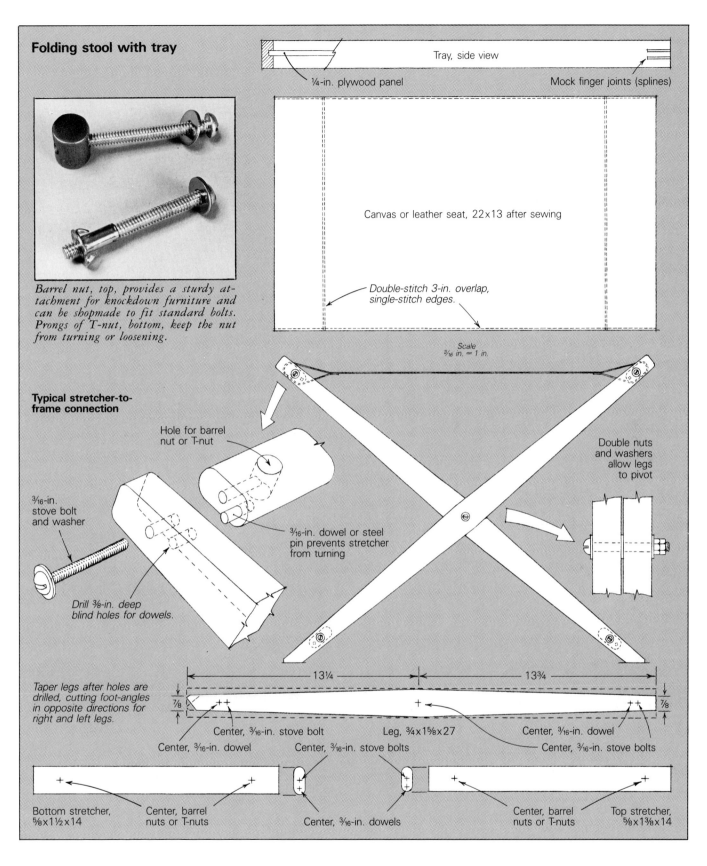

Folding stool with tray

Tray, side view

¼-in. plywood panel

Mock finger joints (splines)

Barrel nut, top, provides a sturdy attachment for knockdown furniture and can be shopmade to fit standard bolts. Prongs of T-nut, bottom, keep the nut from turning or loosening.

Canvas or leather seat, 22x13 after sewing

Double-stitch 3-in. overlap, single-stitch edges.

Scale
³⁄₁₆ in. = 1 in.

Typical stretcher-to-frame connection

Hole for barrel nut or T-nut

³⁄₁₆-in. stove bolt and washer

³⁄₁₆-in. dowel or steel pin prevents stretcher from turning

Double nuts and washers allow legs to pivot

Drill ³⁄₈-in. deep blind holes for dowels.

Taper legs after holes are drilled, cutting foot-angles in opposite directions for right and left legs.

13¼

13¾

⅞

⅞

Center, ³⁄₁₆-in. stove bolt

Leg, ¾x1⅝x27

Center, ³⁄₁₆-in. dowel

Center, ³⁄₁₆-in. dowel

Center, ³⁄₁₆-in. stove bolts

Center, ³⁄₁₆-in. stove bolts

Bottom stretcher, ⅝x1½x14

Center, barrel nuts or T-nuts

Center, ³⁄₁₆-in. dowels

Center, barrel nuts or T-nuts

Top stretcher, ⅝x1⅜x14

for the bolts and dowels. The stool is now ready to be assembled, but first chamfer all the edges with a router or a plane, then sand and finish the pieces.

Don't make the tray before you have assembled the stool and measured it to be sure that the tray will fit. This one is an ash frame with a panel of ¼-in. walnut plywood in a groove. I didn't use solid wood for the panel because, to remain stable, it would have had to be ³⁄₈ in. thick, and that would have made the tray too heavy to carry around. There's

no trick to making the tray—I cut the corners to 45°, rubbed them together with hot glue, then strengthened them with a mock finger joint, which I learned from that wonderful book by Tage Frid. □

Tage Frid is professor emeritus of furniture design at Rhode Island School of Design, and the author of Joinery: Tools and Techniques *and* Shaping, Veneering, Finishing, *both of which are available from The Taunton Press.*

Jointing wide planks

Here's a way to joint those monster wide planks that are impossible to true on a jointer no matter how strong you are. Clamp your raggedy edged board over a long, straight guide-stick and trim the edge square with a big (1½-HP, ½-in. collet) router fitted with a flush-cutting spiral trimmer. Position the workpiece to overhang the guide-stick slightly so the whole edge gets machined in one pass. With a hardboard template the same setup can be used ro smooth contours.

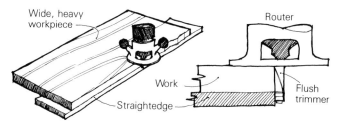

Ocemco (1232 51 Ave., Oakland, Calif. 94601) makes a dual-bearing, ½-in. diameter, flush trimmer with two spiral flutes that's ideal. The trimmer, which sells for about $30, is 1½-in. long, limiting its use to 6/4 stock.
—*Patrick Warner, Escondido, Calif.*

Jointing on the radial-arm saw

Lacking a jointer here's an improvised radial-arm-saw setup I devised to joint the thick oak boards I used in two butcher-block tabletops. First rip a thin board the exact thickness of the saw kerf of the blade you're using. Tack the thin board to the saw fence behind the blade. Bring the blade up against the fence and adjust so that the blade and the piece you've added to the rear fence are flush. If your setup is accurate, your fence is long and straight and your blade has 60 or more carbide teeth, you should get perfectly jointed edges ready to be glued up. —*Dale Snyder, Duluth, Minn.*

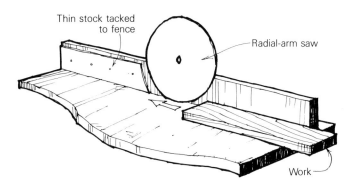

Solution to tear-out problems

If your planer or jointer tears out crossgrained wood, sponge on a light coat of water. The water swells and softens the fibers, packing them tight together to give the cutting edge a little more to push against. Where the grain is steep, more water is absorbed—just where you need it. After applying a light coat of water, wait a minute and take a light cut. If the grain tears out, add more water and let it soak in longer. Since most of the wet wood is planed away, there is little chance of warping the wood.

This trick works best with hardwoods but is occasionally successful with softer woods. Tear-out problems in hand-planing also respond to this treatment, but you must wait until the surface is completely dry before scraping.
—*John Leeke, Sandford, Maine*

Planing thin stock

I have found that the following procedure for preparing small pieces of veneer works well. Bandsaw a ⅛-in. thick slice from the desired veneer stock which has already been planed. Then glue the slice to a scrap board with rubber cement. Apply the rubber cement to both the scrap board and the smooth side of the ⅛-in. thick slice. Press the two pieces together after the cement has dried. With the scrap as a base you can hold the work securely for planing to final thickness. To remove the veneer insert a putty knife between veneer and scrap; then slide it along the scrap. Rub the veneer with a rough cloth to remove the remaining rubber cement.
—*Alan U. Seybolt, Harwich, Mass.*

Here's how I safely smooth resawn veneer on the jointer. I secure the veneer to a flat back-up board with double-stick carpet tape. The back-up board holds the veneer flat and gives it the stiffness it needs. If the veneer is short or narrow I tape scrap of the same thickness to the back-up board to keep it from tipping. Set the jointer for a light cut and proceed slowly. —*Rock Thompson, Centerville, Utah*

Skewed jointing

When you're jointing wavy-grained, contrary woods like curly maple, a skewed cutting angle will often produce smoother results with less tear-out than a straight-on cutting angle. To take advantage of this effect simply attach a long wedge to the jointer fence. —*M.W. Uresti, Bryan, Texas*

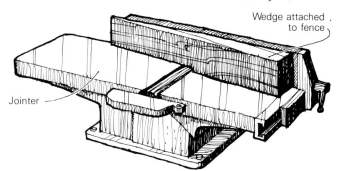

Thickness-sanding on the belt sander

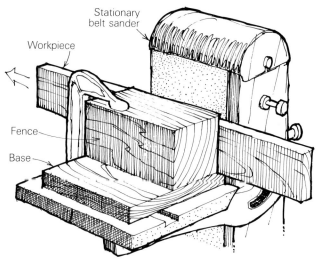

Lacking a commercial thickness sander, I use my standard 6-in. stationary belt sander as shown to face-sand thin strips of resawn stock. The base of the fixture touches the sanding belt. The fence is slightly angled, to provide a wedging effect for pressure. Cross-grain sanding removes wood fast, and the work can't kick back.—*William B. Allard, Tacoma, Wash.*

Designing for Machine Craft
Desmond Ryan's route to handsome boxes

by Roger Holmes

For nearly ten years Desmond Ryan has been making little wooden boxes—boxes for all sorts of things, from jewelry worth fortunes to sentimental trinkets. He makes boxes one at a time and in batches of ten or twenty, with traditional hand tools as well as with modern machinery. His favorite machine has become the overarm router that stands in the middle of his shop; Ryan has learned to use this router with the sensitivity usually associated with a handtool, and his designs capitalize on the machine's strong points. He's succeeded in blending craft with industrial design, handwork with machine work—he is toolmaker, jigmaker and old-fashioned bench craftsman all rolled into one.

Last fall I visited Ryan at his shop, in a 176-year-old paper mill in the town of Maidstone, 37 miles east of London. The mill sits in a tight wooded valley, and Ryan's shop, a long narrow room lit by a wall of windows, is on the second floor of a timber-clad building. It is a large shop for one man, but Ryan prefers to work alone. The extra space is for making furniture, a side of his work overshadowed by the success of his boxes. "Nobody actually needs boxes," he told me, "they aren't necessary like tables, chairs and cabinets. But it is surprising how many people indulge themselves."

Few craft woodworkers have exploited the router as thoroughly as Ryan has for his boxes. Almost every woodworker has a router; they are cheap, take up little space, and can perform a bewildering array of operations. The router can replace whole chests of molding planes, hollows, rounds, gouges and more. It works quickly and precisely—sometimes too easily. The unwavering accuracy of a routed surface doesn't complement

every design. Ryan therefore designs with the router in mind. He derives the basic shapes and joints of many of his boxes from it, and often a routed detail will tie a whole design together. The jewelry box pictured at the top of p. 145 is a good example. A coved rabbet frames the ends of the box when closed, and it connects with the routed handles on the four trays when they are set into the open box for display. "It is one object closed and a different object when open," explained Ryan. "I usually try to do this with boxes. I try to keep them simple on the outside, and when you open them, there is a more complex but visually harmonious interior."

One-off boxes need a lot of handwork. Ryan's batch-production boxes are almost entirely machine-made, and usually routed out of a solid block of wood: no assembly necessary. Some of his production ideas develop from one-off commissions, like the paint box (p. 145) and some of his game boards; others come while playing around with ideas and with the machine itself.

Batch production has different requirements for design, production and materials than one-offs. The designer must eliminate complicated, time-consuming constructions or details. These can be absorbed when done once, but are prohibitive when they must be repeated over and over. A logical succession of simple, quick and accurate operations is the key to successful production, and there isn't much margin for error. "You have got to have an absolute sure-fire way of controlling production operations," says

Some of the items that Ryan machines in small batches on his router, drill press, lathe and other machines. In the back is a board for the old English game of Nine-Man's Morris.

Photos, except where noted: Maggie Ellis

143

Ryan's drawing board and workbenches share the same room, where he often works well into the night. Small machines line the windows: a bandsaw, router, drill press, 5-in. jointer and disc sander. He hoards scraps of exotic woods in the 70 or so cardboard tubes on the left—raw material for boxes. Router jigs hang on the far wall. The other end of the shop is taken up by a 10-in. Wadkin table saw, a metal lathe and a massive, aged, 12-in. over-under thickness planer. Downstairs in a

musty room, Ryan keeps a three-platen veneer press, a couple of disassembled machines and his lumber store. Ryan's overarm router, left, is not a heavy-duty production machine, but a Watford 18,000-rpm router body bolted to an overarm stand. The throat is 24 in., and the table, moved up and down by foot, has four adjustable stops that can be preset for a sequence of cuts at different depths. Slip-on collars, placed over the pin, determine the size of the openings.

Ryan. "If you work to the sort of precision possible with the machine and you fit one piece into another, the consistency has got to be there."

Ryan chooses his materials as carefully as he constructs his jigs. "When I'm doing a production piece," he says, "I don't see individual pieces of wood. With the hexagonal boxes (p. 147), for example, I wasn't trying to create interest in the wood. I used walnut or rosewood for their color against which I contrasted an interesting wood, amboyna, which is decorative in itself, but is a bit like wallpaper. One box lid was different from another, but it was really the color and texture I was after, not a specific piece of wood."

I wondered if he couldn't just as easily make his boxes from metal or plastic. "I suppose I use wood rather than metal because I like the warmth and feel of it. It also machines well, handles easily and can be worked with hand tools." The ideal wood? He laughed, "I suppose it would be something like a firm cheese that you could work and harden up afterwards."

Having worked on the design, made the first jigs and started a half dozen prototypes, Ryan is liable to abandon the project. "That happens quite a lot. Either I reject them because I am not happy with them visually, or I feel that the price is going to be too high to justify finishing them off. It is very costly."

A box that has made it past these obstacles must still prove itself. "I like to leave boxes lying around and observe people handling them," Ryan said. "The longer they keep one in their hand, perhaps turning it over absent-mindedly while talking, the more successful the box."

Ryan's pleasure in the boxes is designing them, figuring out the jigs, and wrestling with the machine, seeing what he can make it do. "The trouble," he confesses, "is really that I lose interest when I've made all the jigs and done the first one. My production pieces are never in that high a production, usually tens or twenties. I spend perhaps two or three weeks with a pro-

duction piece, take it to a certain stage and then it gets left and taken on to the next stage later. There is never enough time between commissions to finish them." They are not, therefore, great money makers. Friends, steady clients and exhibitions take most of them off his hands.

Recently, Ryan has spent more time making furniture, a change from boxes that he finds stimulating. "Boxes are an isolated thing and fit into whatever scheme of decoration people have," he says. "Furniture has got to fit in with what is already there." At first glance, his chunky furniture seems much different from his precise boxes. But the same functional economy and attention to detail is there. Other ideas carry over, too. He doesn't want the wood to compete with the form, in boxes or furniture, so he builds table tops, for instance, of thin strips of wood rather than wide, figured boards.

Ryan is interested in doing more with decorative effects, but he's wary of them. Game boards whose surfaces are necessarily decorative were an easy first step. "But I can't bring myself to use decoration much on furniture," he said. "I want to use a decorative surface without destroying the form. Perhaps I'm afraid of it and don't want to push too hard in case something strange comes out." He has firm beliefs about furniture, and if they seem old fashioned, they are nevertheless sound. "You make furniture to be used. There are similarities with sculpture, painting, and so on, but I can't accept furniture that doesn't do what it should—be useful."

Ryan has been interested in furniture since he was a boy; after technical school, he studied furniture and industrial design at Beckenham Art College and at the Royal College of Art, where he received a masters degree in 1965.

All this college training—eight years studying design—may seem odd to Americans who are more likely to knock together a bench, buy a few tools and open for business, picking up design and woodworking skills as they go. The British

A museum in Munich, Germany, commissioned this rosewood box (19½ in. by 16½ in. by 9 in. when closed) to display as well as to store its changing collection of jewelry. Ryan wove the function of the box together with its appearance. The reveals on the end frames set off the panels against the seamless surface of the box. When the box is open, the upper of the two panels in each half can be removed, and the four trays positioned by brass pins. The curve echoes throughout the box: the coved rabbet bends around the mitered corners, the handles flow into the trays—even the hinges, lock plate and dead bolt are radiused.

The characters of production and of one-off work contrast in these two paint boxes made by Ryan. The one at right (unfinished) is his most complicated production piece, requiring several cutters, jigs, router-fence settings and about five hours to machine. It was designed to serve the basic needs of any watercolorist. The box below was commissioned by a professional painter to hold exactly what he needed for his tramps around the countryside. Though there is as much machine work in this as in the production box, it has more personality than the production box.

Photos of jewelry box and of paint box, left, by Ken Adams.

Ryan's dressing table, commissioned in 1975, is really three boxes on a stand, but boxes and stand have merged—the rails of the stand are also the sides of the boxes. The table is 42 in. long when closed, 13½-in. wide, 29 in. high and is finished with cellulose lacquer.

have always followed a more formal path. Until the 1960s, many makers of craft furniture endured an apprenticeship of five or even seven years, or else spent several years as a paying student in a workshop. During the last twenty years, however, students from art and design colleges have chosen to make, as well as to design, for their livings.

Ryan was one of the first of this generation. A year in industry followed college and convinced him that making was as important to him as designing. "Industry was too restrictive," he said. "Designing on paper at drawing boards is like composing music that is never played. I strongly believe that you should design as much in the workshop as on paper, by making mockups and prototypes as well as finished pieces."

He is a self-taught woodworker and doesn't think of himself as a craftsman. He said, "I suppose designer-craftsman is the closest one can get to a classification. What fascinates me most is problem solving: linking the object's function to its appearance and juggling them to get the most exciting result with the least compromise."

Like many designer-craftsmen, most of Ryan's work is commissioned. "I think people like to buy something from the person who has made it," he said. "They are buying a bit of somebody's life, almost."

Today, at 41, Ryan is established and earns a living from his workshop. But it has been a long time coming. He subsidized his work for many years by part-time teaching, but he found that this proved to be a distraction that took the edge off his business drive. Each time he dropped a day's teaching his own work improved. Still, it wasn't until 1978 that he could afford to work wood full time.

I asked him about all the eager newcomers setting up workshops today, what were the prospects for them? He thought that a lot of them would fall by the wayside. "It's not just training you need, you have got to be right for it, it's more of a vocation. It's got to be a vocation to work for the money you get and the long hours you put in." He paused and continued, "Every job that I take on, I treat as if it is the one and only thing in my life, and I've got to do it to the utmost. This isn't necessary if you just want to make a living, but it is if you want to say anything. That is what I want to do—it is a means of expression, I suppose." Momentarily embarrassed by his own profundity, he fussed with his pipe and added with a smile, "though I don't know what it is I'm trying to say...."

Whatever it is, his clients get the message: "One of the nicest comments I've received was from a client who said, 'You know, Des, every time I come down in the morning those objects of yours give me pleasure and I see something new in them.' All the effort that I had put into things that seem so simple paid off." ☐

Roger Holmes is assistant editor of this magazine. For more on pin routing see FWW #29, p. 63.

The top of this huge pine table—11 ft. long, 3 ft. wide and over 2½ in. thick—rests on hefty trestles uncluttered by any additional underframing. The table has the commanding presence of the medieval tables Ryan admired as a student. But instead of the wide boards of the old tops, which he felt distracted from the overall form of the tables, Ryan glued up narrow strips, side by side and end to end, to break up the color and strong grain pattern of individual planks.

How Ryan makes hexagonal boxes

Ryan is a master at coaxing precise work out of his overarm router. His secret is accurate jigs. A jig may be just a piece of wood clamped to the router table or it may be a more complex construction that guides the cut by means of a template. Either way, careful preparation and set-up are essential.

Much of Ryan's work is pin-routed, clamped to a baseboard which is attached to a template. The template guides the cut by running against a pin set into the router table; the pin's centerline is the same as the cutter's above it. With a rise-and-fall table, this set-up is ideal for excavating solid blocks of wood to make boxes.

The little hexagonal box pictured here is made in batches of ten or twenty, and takes advantage of production economies even at that small scale. Ryan pin-routs the inside of the solid block, and routs the foot and the lid rabbet against a fence. He uses the disc sander like a milling machine to grind the outside surfaces of box and lid to size while keeping their edges sharp. The lid is about 1/64 in. undersize (for what Ryan calls a "rattling good fit"); it closes with a satisfying click. Here are some tips on making jigs like Ryan's.

Preliminary jigs: Use rough-and-ready jigs to test rough-and-ready designs. You can even nail or screw the prototype blank to the baseboard and make the template from wood—the jig will be used only once or twice. Work from the design to the jig and back again to eliminate small errors and inefficiencies—they make a big difference when repeated tens or hundreds of times.

Production jigs: After the bugs have been worked out and the final design has been decided, make production jigs. They need not be expensive or complicated, just sturdy and accurate—they must produce exactly the same cuts time after time. Jigs should be heavy enough to help counteract the router's torque and large enough to keep hands well away from the cutter, but they should not be unwieldly. Chipboard is ideal for baseboards. The template gets the most wear; good template materials are mild steel and Formica.

The template size: The size of the template is determined by the sizes of the router cutter and the pin. If the pin and cutter are the same size, the routed shape or opening will be exactly the size of the template. If the pin is smaller than the cutter, a routed opening will be larger and an outside shape smaller than the template by the difference in their respective diameters. For example: A 1/4-in. pin and a 1/2-in. cutter will produce an opening 1/4 in. larger than the template. Likewise, a pin larger than the cutter will produce a smaller opening.

Pin collars: Ryan routs different sized openings in the same piece, without changing cutters, pins or jigs, by slipping collars of various diameters over a single pin. The smallest collar produces the largest opening, and larger collars produce the smaller openings.

The cutter: Ryan uses high-speed steel router cutters. A carbide edge lasts longer, but a high-speed steel edge can be honed. Sharpening a fluted cutter minutely alters its diameter, so check this regularly and alter the jig to compensate. Ryan hones both face and bevel of the cutting edges with a triangular Arkansas slipstone. He sharpens after every four or five boxes for such hard stuff as rosewood, to produce surfaces that require only light sanding or scraping to finish.

The design of this rosewood and amboyna hexagonal box takes advantage of the overarm router's production strengths.

Different sized collars (above) can be slipped over the router's pin. By bearing against a template, they control the size of the rabbet or box opening as shown below.

Hexagonal box router set-up

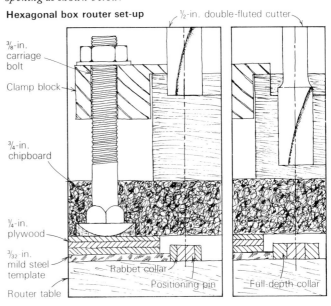

3/8-in. carriage bolt

Clamp block

1/2-in. double-fluted cutter

3/4-in. chipboard

1/4-in. plywood

3/32 in. mild steel template

Router table

Rabbet collar

Positioning pin

Full-depth collar

The jig

To make the router jig for his hexagonal box, Ryan started with the template. First he laid out the exact size of the template in the center of a piece of ¼-in. plywood. He positioned the ³⁄₃₂-in. metal strips, each the width of a box side, and screwed them in place. Taking the strips off, he cut a slightly oversized hole in the plywood so the strips would project slightly beyond the opening. Next he screwed the strips back in place, tapping them into exact position. He ran epoxy glue around them to ensure against movement. Finally he flushed off the strips and screwed two additional ones at the two ends for stability (photo **A**).

To make the baseboard (**B**), Ryan positioned the clamping block and its two hanger bolts, transferring the template position to the baseboard top by measurement. The box blank must be held directly over the template, and the clamp bolts must clear the router, yet be close enough to exert direct pressure on the blank. Ryan bolted the hard maple clamping block in place, and routed out its center by guiding the template on the pin collar for the box's rabbet—the largest opening to be routed. Then he enlarged this hole to comfortably fit a blank, chopping to within ¼ in. of the clamp's top surface. The fit need not be tight—three chisel-pointed panel pins embedded in the baseboard keep the blank from twisting while it's being routed.

A

B

The box

Ryan starts a batch of boxes by bandsawing the blanks about ³⁄₁₆ in. oversize, from selected rosewood or walnut blanks planed to final thickness. He drills the waste from the center of each blank, then clamps it to the jig. He places the first (smallest) collar on the router pin and routs the rabbet for the lid to its full depth in one cut (**C**). Using the second (largest) collar and three depth stops, he routs the inside of the box to its full depth (**D**). Safe depth depends on the wood, the cutter size and sharpness, and on the power of the machine. With the final collar, minutely smaller than the second, he takes a finishing cut of a couple of hundredths of an inch to remove tears and burns left from the heavier cuts. As before, he goes to full depth in three steps.

All router work should be moved into the cutter against the direction of rotation, otherwise the cutter self-feeds and grabs the work. Sometimes difficult grain requires feeding in the same direction as the router rotates—in tough spots like these, Ryan hogs the waste in small bites and finishes by careful back-cutting, making sure his clamps are tight and his hands well clear.

With the inside cuts completed, Ryan moves to the 12-in. disc sander to shape the outside (**E**).

The sanding jig is glued up from two pieces of ¼-in. plywood the exact size of the box rabbet, but one of them has radiused corners to fit the routed opening. Inserted into the box, the sharp-cornered piece forms the jig's template. It is pushed against a brass strip that is fixed to the edge of a board clamped on the sander's worktable. The distance between the strip and the disc determines the thickness of the box's walls.

Ryan sands around the box several times, taking care not to overheat the wood. When the boxes have all been sanded with 80-grit, he changes the disc to 120-grit and moves the board with the brass strip fractionally closer to the disc for a finishing pass.

C

D

E

Back at the router, Ryan clamps a fence to the table, sets a depth stop and routs a foot on the bottom of the box using a double-fluted cutter ground to a very small radius (F). This completes the machining.

Ryan hand-sands the outside faces with two grades of fine paper glued on opposite sides of a flat board. He draws the box across the paper, taking care not to lose the sharp edges, then sands small, crisp chamfers. He removes small ridges on the inside with tightly-rolled sandpaper.

F

The lid

To make the box lid, Ryan planes, thicknesses and bandsaws to size solid padouk blanks, aligning the points of the hexagon with the grain direction. He veneers the blanks top and bottom with amboyna, the richly figured burl wood of padouk. After veneering, the lids are rough-sanded on the disc (G) to remove glue and tape—a difficult and risky operation when hand-holding such a thin piece.

G

He shapes the lid on the disc sander the same way he shaped the box. A plywood jig (H) is cut the exact size of the lid; it should allow for slight shrinkage in the box. A rabbet in the jig forms the template and lets the jig clear the brass fence and just touch the sanding disc. Small radii worked on the points on the underside of the template fit the lid to the box rabbet. Four tiny pins set in the jig hold the lid in place during the machining—their holes are lost in the wild figure of the amboyna.

H

On the router, Ryan works a decorative rabbet around the top of the lid (I), using the rounded cutter that routed the box foot. As he routs, he works around each corner with a series of small cuts, keeping the edge of the lid hard against the fence. Any difficult grain is back-cut—very carefully.

I

Next he routs a stopped rabbet on two adjacent sides of the bottom of the lid (J). Pushing on this corner pivots the lid on the rabbet stops and pops it up for removal. Ryan uses the same set-up as before but moves the fence so the width of this rabbet will just exceed that of the ledge in the box. The depth remains the same. Pencil lines on the baseboard mark where to begin and end the cut. This rabbet starts 3/16 in. from one point of the hexagon and moves through an adjacent point, ending 3/16 in. from a third. It includes two sides that run across the grain direction of the veneered padouk so the thin division between the lid's upper and lower rabbets will be end grain and not weaker edge grain.

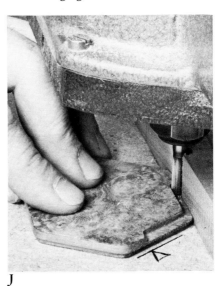

J

Ryan finish-sands the lid on the fine-paper boards and then he lightly chamfers its edges. Finally he wipes the box and lid with teak oil, keeping the oil clear of the bottom where the suede must be glued, then he stamps his name on the bottom. —R.H.

Oval Boxes

How to make steambent containers

by Tom McFadden

I designed my oval boxes and carriers after studying Shaker examples. Typically, the sides of Shaker boxes were made of maple and splayed into three or more tapered fingers in the area of the scarf joint, where the two ends overlap. In my boxes the sides are of cherry, maple, madrone, mahogany, oak, ash or walnut, and I leave the outside overlapping end square, instead of cutting fingers on it. All these woods steambend easily in a thickness of ⅛ in. Before bending, the inside end involved in the scarf joint is tapered to produce a smooth surface when assembled. I fasten the joint with copper tacks and yellow glue, and attach the handles on carriers using the same. (The tacks are available from Fasco Fastener Co., 2023 Clement Ave., Alameda, Calif. 94501.) The pine tops and bottoms fit into the bent sides of the box and rim, and I secure them with round-head brass brads. The completed pieces are finished with two coats of polyurethane followed by an application of paste wax. I make the boxes in seven sizes and the carriers in five sizes.

When selecting stock for bentwood boxes, you should use only straight, even-grained wood for the side pieces. Imperfections such as curl, knots (sound or otherwise) or slanting grain may cause the pieces to break or to bend unevenly. You can use kiln-dried stock, but lumber that has been air-dried to 10% or 12% moisture content will respond to the steam more readily and produce more consistent results. Resawn, a good 4/4 board will yield three side pieces.

Before resawing, crosscut each board to within 3 in. or 4 in. of its finished length; then joint one face and edge, and plane the unjointed face. Now rip the boards to width, then resaw and plane them to produce blanks ⅛ in. thick. Take ten of the ⅛-in. blanks, align and stack them one atop another and tape them together with masking tape. Mark out the narrow part of the outside end of the scarf joint and the location of the tacks by laying a pattern on top of the bundle. The ends of the pieces can now be stack-sawn to shape and the ¹⁄₁₆-in. dia. pilot holes drilled for the copper tacks. Smooth the end-grain edges with a stationary belt or disc sander.

Next separate the pieces and with a hand plane taper the inside end of each overlap down to ¹⁄₆₄ in. over the last 6 in. After tapering, sand each side piece inside and out with a 100-grit belt in a belt sander, and round the edges by hand slightly with 120-grit paper. Mark the inside of each piece with a pencil so you'll know which way to bend it after it comes out of the steam box. The completed side pieces are again taped into bundles to await steaming.

I made the bending forms for the boxes and their tops from stacked ¾-in. hardwood plywood, sanded and varnished to facilitate removing the completed side pieces. I use hardwood plywood for the forms because of its stability in the

Author's Shaker-style oval boxes and carriers are steambent from various hardwoods, glued and nailed at the splice. Boxes nest one inside another. Below, rack of dowels inside steambox holds the stock, sawn and planed to about ⅛ in. thickness, on edge for a 15-minute soak in unpressurized steam.

Tom McFadden, a woodworker by trade, lives near Navarro, Calif. Photos by the author.

For seven sizes of box, McFadden has made seven sizes of mold, plus seven more slightly larger molds for their lids. The molds are hardwood plywood, sanded smooth and varnished. Stainless-steel plate let into each mold is an anvil against which first row of tacks may be clinched.

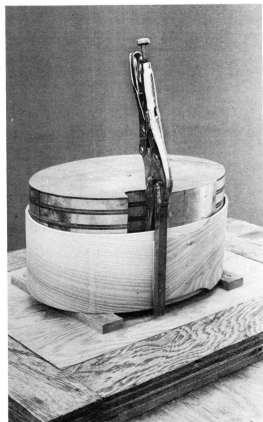

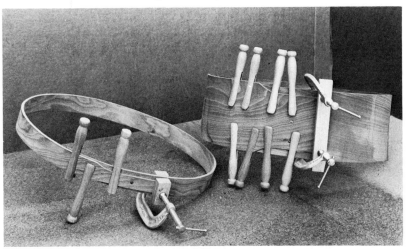

After steaming, box sides are wrapped around the bending form and clamped in place, above. The clamp shown here was made by welding two steel bars to the jaws of a Visegrip pliers. When the piece has cooled enough to retain its shape, the scarf joint is glued and minimally nailed, then clamped with C-clamps and clothespins, upper right, until the glue has dried. At right, author drives and clinches the remaining nails against an anvil made from 1½-in. galvanized pipe. Below, one of McFadden's boxes, with carved lid.

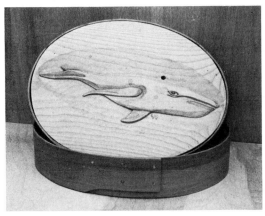

face of temperature and humidity changes. Each form is fitted with a stainless-steel plate in the area of the scarf joint that lets me drive tacks through the wood without damaging the form. Stainless steel is used to ensure against staining the steamed wood. The plate is let flush into the surface of the form and attached with stainless-steel screws. At one end of the plate the form is notched to accept an adapted Visegrip which clamps the steamed sides in place while they cool and are glued and riveted with the tacks. Further, each form is mounted on a plywood base plate which fits interchangeably into a frame screwed onto a table. Two cleats hold the form ½ in. above the base plates so that the completed sides can be easily gripped from below and slid upward off the form.

The side pieces are placed in the steam box and subjected to unpressurized steam for 15 minutes. After steaming, quickly remove each piece from the box, wrap it tightly around the form and clamp it with the adapted Visegrip. After the piece has cooled enough for its shape to set, remove it from the form. Apply glue to the scarf joint and then re-clamp it on the form for tacking. Only the center vertical row of tacks is driven at this time; these will fix the size of the oval and will hold the overlap in place while the side is removed from the form and the overlap is clamped with C-clamps and clothespins. Drive the remaining two rows of tacks after the glue has dried. The points of the first row of tacks are turned over and mushroomed against the stainless plate in the bending form; the remaining tacks are hammered in against an anvil made from 1½-in. galvanized pipe. The finished side pieces are hand-sanded with 120-grit paper to remove the raised grain caused by the steaming.

Handles for the carriers are resawn and shaped in the same manner as the side pieces. They are steamed and bent around

Rack keeps carrier handles bent while they cool and dry.

a form, then placed in a drying rack until they are attached to the sides with glue and copper tacks.

Cut the tops and bottoms from pine (quartersawn is best) with a moisture content of 6% to 7%. It is essential that this material be very dry or it will shrink away from the side pieces and leave ugly gaps. Place the side piece for the box on the pine bottom, trace the inside shape and bandsaw along the line. Make final adjustments in the fit with a disc sander. Round the edges of the pieces slightly, and sand them. Use dividers to mark the location of the brass brads that will hold the top and the bottom in place. Then drill the pilot holes through the side pieces, and drive the brads. □

Shaker Carrier
Dovetail box, steambend handle

by John Kassay

This not-so-difficult-looking project offers two challenges—the hand-cut, through-dovetail corners and the sculptured, steam-bent bail (handle). Carrier is the Shaker name for a box fitted with a bail. Those carriers that exhibit pleasing form, fine construction, and quality craftsmanship were made for the Shakers' own use, whereas carriers made for sale in Shaker stores, though well crafted, look mass produced. With the exception of the manner in which the bail is fastened, this carrier is a fine example of one made for communal use.

To make the carrier, thickness-plane enough pine (wood species is optional) to make the sides (A), ends (B) and bottom (C). All surfaces should be hand-scraped and sanded. Those surfaces that will be on the inside of the carrier should be finished surfaces and so marked. Now lay out the sides and ends and add 1/32 in. to their widths and lengths, and cut accordingly. The extra length allows the ends of the dovetails to project minutely beyond the outside surfaces. After the sides and ends are assembled, these projections are planed or sanded off, resulting in a better appearing dovetail joint. The extra width is used for truing up the edges at the top and bottom of the carrier, again after assembly.

Mark out and cut the bottom ¼ in. longer and wider than the overall length and width of the carrier sides and ends. Sand the inside surface and shape the upper edges as shown in the drawing. Nail the bottom in place—a nice touch here would be to use ⅞-in. fine-cut headless brads (available from Woodcraft, 313 Montvale Ave., Woburn, Mass. 01888).

Nailing the bottom onto the carrier sides may seem to contradict all we have been taught about wood movement, but it is the way the Shakers did it—and they had central heating too. It has been suggested that the bottom ought to be let into a groove in the sides, like a frame-and-panel. However, I have rarely seen good results from altering a Shaker design. In this particular case, inletting the bottom would eliminate a characteristic Shaker form, the molding created by the protruding bottom, and it would greatly complicate the carrier's joinery. I think that when the bottom worked loose, the Shakers would just nail it on again.

The bail is made of ash; red or white oak or hickory could be used instead. Mill straight-grained stock to overall thickness, width and length (detail 2), then steam it and bend it around a mold before tapering it to shape. Although it's difficult to shape the bail after bending, it's more frustrating to lose a pre-shaped bail during the bending process.

The photo on the facing page shows my bending jig, with a back-strap made of four strips of 24-gauge galvanized sheet steel, spot-welded together at the center *(FWW #8, Fall '77, p. 40, and #30, Sept. '81, p. 84)*. This apparatus will bend

John Kassay is the author of The Book of Shaker Furniture, *available for $40 from University of Massachusetts Press, Box 429, Amherst, Mass. 01004.*

kiln-dried white oak that's been steamed for about two hours under low pressure (5 PSI to 10 PSI). If you use split-out green wood, the chance of a successful bend is greatly increased; you can probably substitute an ordinary band clamp for the steel back-up strap and end blocks. I leave the bent stock on the jig to set for a couple of days. When removed, it springs back just the right amount to fit the carrier.

Now make a full-size pattern of half the length of the bail, trace it onto the bent wood and cut out the shape. With a block plane and a scraper blade, taper the bail in thickness from the center to the ends, as shown in the edge view, then spokeshave it to the cross-sections shown. Note that the undersurface is rounded, while the outer surface is left flat. Both ends of the bail are flat where they attach to the carrier ends, and chamfered on their outer corners. Fine-sand all the surfaces and ease any sharp corners, except those where the bail meets the carrier. Fasten the bail with four brass rivets and washers, two at each end; you could substitute counter-sunk flat-head woodscrews.

The inside surface of the original carrier was protected with a wash coat of yellow milk-paint, while the outside was left natural. The bail was varnished.   □

Wedges hold bent stock against bending form while it cools and sets. Steel back-up strap with end blocks helps make the bend, but once bent, the strap can be tipped away from the stock, as shown.

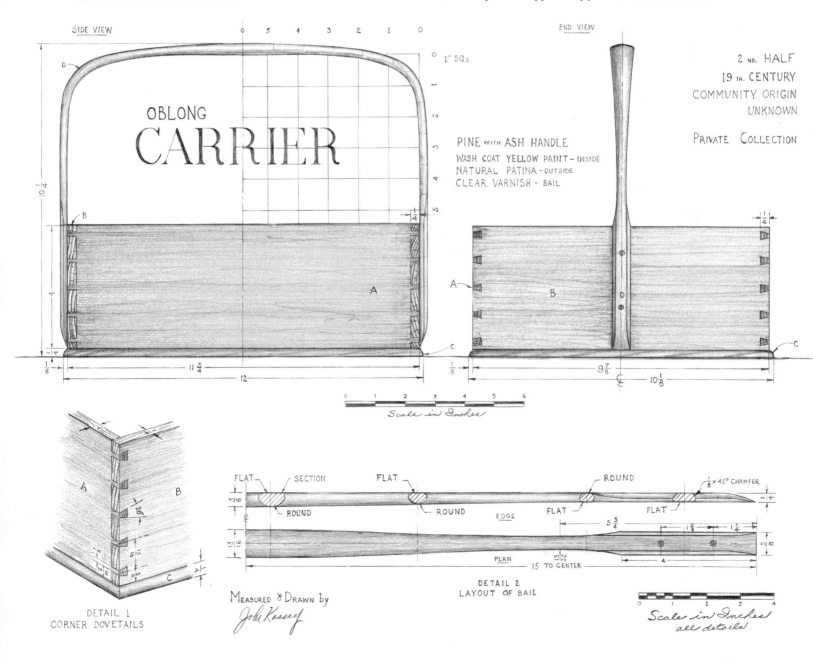

SIDE VIEW

OBLONG
CARRIER

END VIEW

2 ND. HALF
19 TH. CENTURY
COMMUNITY ORIGIN
UNKNOWN

PRIVATE COLLECTION

PINE WITH ASH HANDLE
WASH COAT YELLOW PAINT - INSIDE
NATURAL PATINA - OUTSIDE
CLEAR VARNISH - BAIL

Scale in Inches

DETAIL 1
CORNER DOVETAILS

MEASURED & DRAWN by
John Kassay

DETAIL 2
LAYOUT OF BAIL

FLAT   SECTION   FLAT   ROUND   ⅛ × 45° CHAMFER
ROUND   ROUND   FLAT   FLAT
EDGE
PLAN   15 TO CENTER

Scale in Inches
all details

Stereo Equipment Cabinets
Take the heat off your audio gear

by Carl Spencer

Housing audio and electronic equipment in specially designed casework is not a new idea. Thomas Edison's first commercially available phonographs came complete with their own wooden cases, and even Marconi's early radio sets had their own boxes. The casework was originally devised to protect the fragile gear from damage, and the consumer from electric shock. Retailers quickly learned that the appearance of the package was often more of a selling point than the sound of the equipment.

Even today there is lively competition at antique shops for the beautiful old AM-shortwave radios from the 1920s and 1930s. That some of the old radios still operate is only a portion of the appeal. Modern stereo furniture—for which there is a growing market—has its roots in the prepackaged high-fidelity consoles first marketed just before World War II. With the advent of FM radio and stereophonic sound, the console became common in the American home. By the 1950s, the console had evolved into a tuner, phonograph, amplifier and two speakers all permanently installed in a single wooden cabinet that fit the decor of the day. Many even incorporated television sets. Consoles remain popular, probably because they combine and conceal, with a minimum of wires and controls, what some people see as unsightly and confusing equipment. The console's advantage, an all-in-one package, proved to be its weakness as well. If the amplifier or the television died beyond repair, one could only replace the entire unit or limp along indefinitely with half of an entertainment system. Some old consoles could be retrofitted with new gear, but variation in case construction and proportions made that remedy costly in money and trouble. The console's shortcoming teaches a valuable lesson to the designer of modern stereo cabinets: good casework will outlast the electronics, so it makes sense to design for equipment changes.

By the 1960s, "component" audio systems confronted consumers with more storage problems. The audiophile could buy separately the best amplifier, tuner, speakers and turntable—each from a different manufacturer. While some people didn't care about the resulting tangle of patch cords, others wanted their systems to look as neat as the old consoles did. Thus the modern stereo cabinet industry was born.

The early 1970s saw a resurgence of the console approach as stereo "racks" began replacing the cinderblock and pine board shelving that had been pressed into service by early

This RCA record player/radio combination was a forerunner of modern audio equipment cabinets. This cabinet, constructed of veneers and solid wood, was closed up to hide and protect the electronics.

component fans. The racks were supports that organized the equipment with maximum exposure—for better or for worse. Little attention was paid to good equipment placement, tidying up the wires, or dustproofing and ventilating the electronics. The racks were more attractive than boards and bricks but still offered little protection for sensitive equipment. As the "baby boom" kids of the 1950s began having their own children, they found that nothing can so thoroughly devastate a phono stylus or decorate a room with yards of magnetic tape quite like a two-year-old. Audio equipment also needs protection from thieves; it is easily stolen and resold. Equipment racks are simple to spot in a room, and some even have casters. A burglar can just unplug the system and roll it out to the trunk of his car—a perfect 60-second crime.

The problems of designing cabinets for stereo components can be solved in ways that improve the appearance and function of the equipment while protecting it from children and thieves. Wires can be run out of sight, panels can be installed for dustproofing and ventilation, and all of the equipment can be housed in attractive cabinetry that permits quick changes when the system is replaced or updated.

Case design and equipment placement—The shape and style of stereo casework is up to the aesthetic bent of the client and the maker. Vertical designs are generally superior to the traditional horizontal layouts. Few people "drive" their audio gear like a car, nor do they sit in front of it while using it. Adjustments are made after the listener has walked up to the equipment so it is sensible to assume the user will be standing. Vertical formats are also less expensive to build: there is no finished countertop to add to the carcase.

Heat is the bane of electronic gear, and ignoring it can shorten the life of expensive systems. Always locate the receiver, amplifier and other heat-producing components near the top of the case. This keeps the rising heat away from the other units, and also puts the various scales and controls at eye level, easy to read. Other frequently adjusted equipment that can be set by ear or by feel can be mounted wherever convenient. If the system you are housing has both amplifier and tuner, mount the tuner below the warmer amplifier. Some systems use preamplifiers and they ought to be mounted below but as near to the main amplifier as possible. This will ensure short patch cords and a clean signal between the units. Some systems solve this three-component problem by combining all three units in a receiver. If so, the receiver should be mounted above the other units.

Turntables should be as close as possible to waist height. Mounted too low, one's view of the turntable is blocked by the shelf above it, making it difficult to put a record on the spindle. If it's too high, the oblique view makes it equally hard to operate, and the inevitable result is scratched records. Leave enough room for opening the turntable dust cover if you mount it on open shelving. Never put turntables on pull-out platforms. Turntable designers go to great lengths to produce balanced, vibration-free equipment. The sloppiness in even the best ball-bearing drawer slides will defeat this sophisticated engineering for which you've paid so dearly.

Cassette recording decks are available in both front-load and top-load designs. They should be mounted as near to eye-level as the case and amplifier placement permit. If frequent taping of records is anticipated, the deck could be placed on a fixed shelf at the same level as the turntable.

Televisions complicate stereo cabinet design because they compete for the ideal equipment locations, and they are nearly always wider and deeper than stereo components. Usually, it's best to keep the TV elsewhere, but if it must go in the stereo cabinet, the best position seems to be centered at sitting eye level. Horizontal formats favor television-stereo combinations because they permit more spacing between the heat-producing components. Don't mount any equipment above televisions; they generate large amounts of heat.

Mounting, dustproofing and ventilation—Stereo equipment can simply sit on a shelf or it can project through a vertical panel mounted in the front of the cabinet. Shelves should be cut to allow for wire runs and for cooling ventilation, either by leaving a 1-in. space between the back of the shelf and the carcase back or by boring holes in the shelf. To panel-mount equipment, an opening the exact size of the component chassis is cut in the panel and the unit is slid in, supported behind the panel by shelves or cleats to keep the weight of the gear from bulging the panel. Panel mounting looks neat, and the equipment is less available to thieves. What thief has time to extract equipment from something that looks so intimidating? I've had customers who have lost their speakers, televisions and silver to burglars, but so far none have lost stereo components that I've set into panels. Another tip on security: don't bother with locks on stereo cabinet doors. If a burglar encounters a locked cabinet, he'll assume there's something really valuable inside and break the doors with a crowbar, perhaps leaving the equipment anyway.

Besides improving security, panel-mounting aids dustproofing and ventilation. Dust finds its way into cabinets and settles on equipment heatsinks, reducing cooling efficiency and shortening equipment life. Closely fit panels seal out the dust and actually improve ventilation by suspending the equipment in a cooling bath of moving air. Panels should be mounted so they can be removed from the rear of the case, and modified for new equipment.

Cabinets with open compartments can be fitted with false backs to give a finished appearance. The actual cabinet back should be removable and have an access panel to permit equipment installation and connection.

Cabinets can be ventilated by drilling a row of 1-in. diameter holes in the lower back of the equipment compartment to draw in cool air and to exhaust heated air out the top through a slot. The ventilation flow should be baffled to force the air to turn a corner on its way out—this keeps dust from filtering into the equipment compartment when the system is off. Higher-powered equipment (more than 50 watts per channel)

Vertical cabinets can have shelving for turntables and top-loading cassette decks. Other components are panel-mounted for protection against dust and theft.

may need a "whisper" fan mounted in the top of the case to draw hot air out. A commonly available 55-cfm fan can cool the largest amplifier. Figure on using a fan if the temperature inside the cabinet when the stereo is on is more than 10° warmer than the room temperature.

Books, records or additional equipment can be stored behind doors, on open shelving or in drawers. Store record albums at the bottom of the cabinet where it is cooler. Their weight will add to the stability of the case—an important consideration here in earthquake-prone California.

All of the design requirements I've mentioned can be altered to suit special equipment or the whims of builders and clients. Rapid-fire innovation in electronics, in fact, is changing the shapes and sizes of components faster than ever, allowing cabinet design to develop too. There's a constant demand for cabinet work both for the protection of the equipment and for the convenience and satisfaction of those who have it in their homes. *(continued next page)*

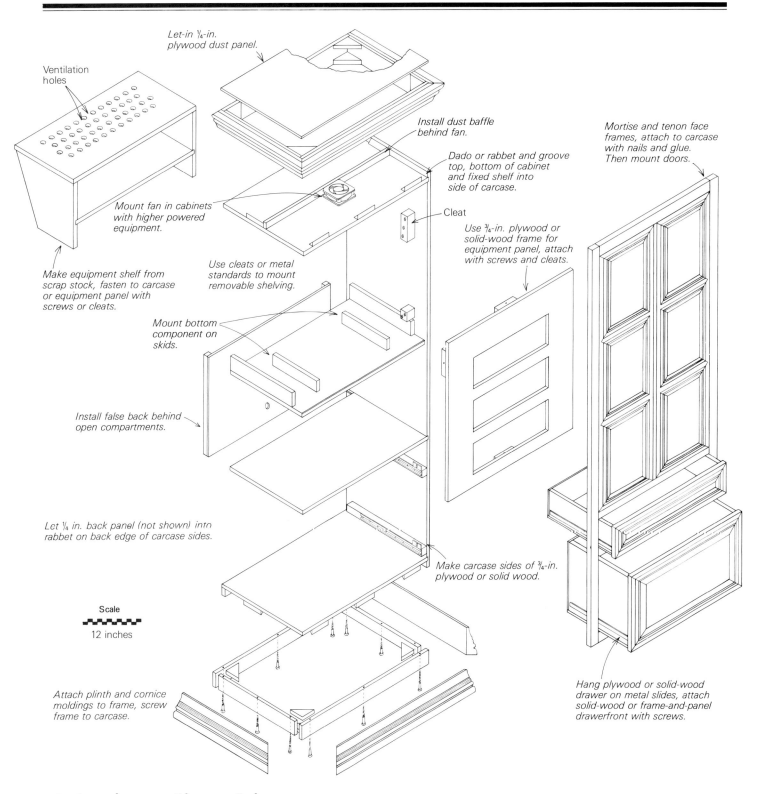

Ventilation holes

Let-in 1/4-in. plywood dust panel.

Install dust baffle behind fan.

Dado or rabbet and groove top, bottom of cabinet and fixed shelf into side of carcase.

Mortise and tenon face frames, attach to carcase with nails and glue. Then mount doors.

Mount fan in cabinets with higher powered equipment.

Cleat

Use 3/4-in. plywood or solid-wood frame for equipment panel, attach with screws and cleats.

Make equipment shelf from scrap stock, fasten to carcase or equipment panel with screws or cleats.

Use cleats or metal standards to mount removable shelving.

Mount bottom component on skids.

Install false back behind open compartments.

Let 1/4 in. back panel (not shown) into rabbet on back edge of carcase sides.

Make carcase sides of 3/4-in. plywood or solid wood.

Scale

12 inches

Attach plinth and cornice moldings to frame, screw frame to carcase.

Hang plywood or solid-wood drawer on metal slides, attach solid-wood or frame-and-panel drawerfront with screws.

A basic audio cabinet

Stereo cabinets can be made of solid wood or plywood, with traditional joinery or the simplest knock-up construction. Whatever way, the placement of the equipment governs the cabinet's size and shape. I make five or more cabinets at once in small production runs using what's basically kitchen cabinet construction: plywood carcases with solid-wood face frame and door frames. I measure the equipment that will go into a case, leaving room for accessories that might be added later.

First I cut parts for the face frame from 5/4 lumber planed to 1 1/16 in. thick. The frames are mortised and tenoned together, but dowels could also be used. I make the face frame 1/16 in. wider than the plywood case and trim it flush later, so I won't have to sand the veneer. While the face frame is in clamps, I cut the door rails and stiles from 3/4-in. stock, and join them with mortise and tenons. I glue 1/4-in. plywood to the back of the frames for panels, but you can float the panels in 1/4-in. grooves milled in the rails and stiles.

Cabinet access and ventilation

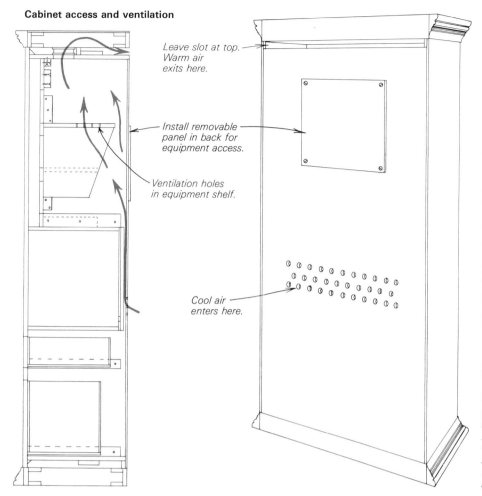

Leave slot at top. Warm air exits here.

Install removable panel in back for equipment access.

Ventilation holes in equipment shelf.

Cool air enters here.

A removable shelving unit, made from plywood scraps, supports the equipment. The shelf is attached with screws or wedged between cleats. Holes in upper shelf are for amplifier ventilation.

Next, I rip the major carcase components—sides, top, bottom, shelving and equipment panel—from ¾-in. A-2 cabinet plywood. You can use solid wood, or substitute cheaper plywood or even particleboard for unseen parts, like the carcase top and bottom.

I join the top, any fixed shelves, and the bottom to the carcase sides with fully-housed dado joints that are nailed and glued. This joint is quick, and it has proven to be strong enough for the stresses involved. Before assembly, I rabbet the back edges of the carcase sides for the ¼-in. plywood back, which can later be attached with screws.

With the case squarely assembled, I attach the face frame with glue and nails and make certain the edge of the frame is flush or slightly proud of the plywood. When the face frame is cured and cleaned up, I trim the doors to size before hanging them. These can be lipped, flush or overlay doors. Hang the drawers with metal slides, particularly if they're intended to store weighty record albums. Record drawers need at least 100-lb. slides.

The equipment panel is next, and you must carefully measure the components going into it. Some have front bezels slightly larger than the chassis. If so, cut the panel openings to fit the chassis and slide the gear in from the front. Otherwise, cut the panel openings to fit the exact outside of the bezel. I plunge-cut these openings on my tablesaw, but a saber saw or router would also do the job. I slide the completed panel in from the back of the case so it's 2 in. from the back of the face frame. This leaves clearance for equipment knobs. The panel is held in place with screws so it can be removed for equipment additions. I make a removable shelf unit from scrap wood that supports the equipment inside the case (photo above). The shelf unit slides in from the back and is held in place between two cleats. Shelves must be level, or the equipment will project unevenly from the openings.

Test-fit the equipment by sliding it in. Rubber feet mounted on some chassis may have to be removed. I've found it unnecessary to attach the equipment to the cabinet, but for extra security, it could be blocked or wedged in place. If there's a fan or built-in lighting, install these next. Plan on connecting them to switched outlets on the stereo gear so they'll go on and off when the equipment does; it's a heat-insurance policy for the components.

Next fit plinth and cornice molding. I make up frames to which I can then attach the molding—this allows me to cut the plywood carcase sides shorter, reducing waste. The molding could, of course, be glued and nailed directly to the case. After filling all the nail holes and sanding the case, I spray-lacquer the cabinets, rubbing them by hand between coats. Any finish is suitable, however, including oils and varnishes, whatever suits the needs of the client. Move the cabinet to its location before installing the equipment, to avoid damaging the gear. Make the connections through the removable access panel just before you set the cabinet in the room. □

Carl Spencer owns Presidential Industries, a stereo cabinet manufacturing company in Riverside, Calif. He is the author of Designing and Building Your Own Stereo Furniture, *published by Tab Books Inc., Blue Ridge Summit, Pa. 17214. Photos, except where noted, by Carl Spencer.*

SPECIALTIES

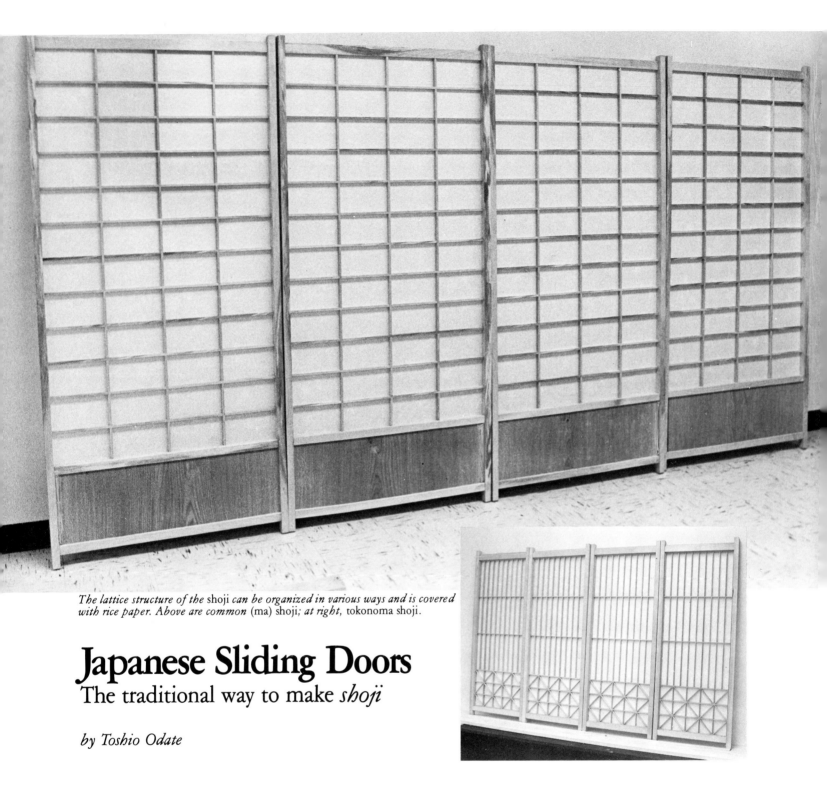

The lattice structure of the shoji *can be organized in various ways and is covered with rice paper. Above are common* (ma) *shoji; at right,* tokonoma shoji.

Japanese Sliding Doors
The traditional way to make *shoji*

by Toshio Odate

The traditional Japanese house allows for very flexible living. The house is post-and-beam, with the spaces between posts filled by doors, most of them sliding. Thus any wall, interior or exterior, can at different times become an entrance or an exit, a window or an open space, as the people desire. In this article I am going to show you the authentic way of making a sliding door. Although there are many kinds of sliding doors, the kind that Westerners associate with Japan are called *shoji*. This type of door consists of a softwood frame filled by a light latticework of thin wooden strips (called *kumiko*), to which is glued a layer of rice paper. The rice paper filters the light from outside into the home, for the people to enjoy.

When I was 16 years old, I was apprenticed to a *tategu-shi*, a maker of sliding doors. My master and I would carry the tools on our shoulders from house to house and place to place. We often worked out-of-doors, under an overhang, or in a vacant cowshed. Everywhere we went we made the planing boards, beams and horses on which we could prepare the customer's materials, and when we were done, this equipment remained with the customer. We would stay at a single job for as short a time as one week, or as long as three months, working from dawn to dark, whatever the weather. After seven years of this, I could call myself *shokunin*, which means craftsman. Such an apprenticeship is the only way to acquire a skill in Japan, for these kinds of knowledge are nowhere written down and never pursued as hobbies. I don't imagine you can become *shokunin* simply by reading my article.

For that matter, I am no longer *shokunin*. I have been in America 24 years now, and my commitments are different.

But I am still a skillful person, and because of my unusual life I can be a bridge from the traditional Japanese way to the American craftsman who wants to understand. You may find new uses for *shoji* and other ways to make them. Each craftsman has his own experience and training. I can not tell you how to make American *shoji*, but I can describe for you how the *tategu-shi* has always made Japanese *shoji*. If you know where the design comes from, even if you change it to suit your own life, you will know what you are doing.

Varieties of sliding doors—*Shoji* is only one of the many kinds of sliding doors. The outermost door of a Japanese home is a wooden storm door (*amado*) which is closed tight every evening and left open during the day. Behind the storm door is a glass door in a wooden frame (*garasu-do*). The *shoji* is next. Often there is a narrow veranda, 3 ft. to 4 ft. wide, between the glass door and the *shoji*. This hallway borders the living space and is used to pass from one room to another (figure 1). Sliding room dividers separate the interior spaces. These room dividers can be *shoji* (with translucent rice paper), *fusuma* (with opaque paper and a very thin frame), *itado* (with wood panels), or a combination of *shoji* and *itado*. A living/dining room is commonly converted into a bedroom at night. Dining tables are folded flat, and beds are soft mattresses that are folded and stored every morning. Most rooms have a built-in closet with sliding doors (*fusuma* or *itado*) for household supplies.

The seven traditional styles of *shoji* are shown in figures 2 and 3. The one I will describe how to build is the common (*ma*) *shoji*, whose frame contains three vertical *kumiko* and either nine or eleven horizontal *kumiko*, with a hipboard (*koshi-ita*) at the base. This *koshi-ita* is a solid wood panel and is called "hipboard" perhaps because it is the height of your hip when you sit on the floor. The size of the hipboard varies according to the total height of the *shoji*, but the spacing between the horizontal *kumiko* depends on the two sizes of rice paper available: 28 cm wide and 25 cm wide. The edges of the paper overlap on top of the horizontal *kumiko*. The wider paper is used with the nine horizontal *kumiko* to produce the classic *mino* proportions. The narrower paper is used with the eleven horizontal *kumiko* to produce the more contemporary *hanshi* proportions. These two variations, and more, are possible in all the styles of *shoji*.

Rice paper (*shoji gami*) sometimes is watermarked with a pattern, commonly of plum trees, blossoms, pine trees, bamboo leaves or chrysanthemums. Sometimes these patterns are realistic, sometimes abstract. Because they are watermarks, you can see these patterns best from the inside of the room when daylight passes through the paper. The effect is like sitting with a beautiful garden outside, the pattern on the paper like the shadows of trees and flowers. Bringing nature inside the home is characteristic of the Japanese. The cultivation of miniature trees, *bonsai*, is another example of this.

Preparation—It is a common saying among Japanese craftsmen that when an apprentice can accurately prepare door materials he knows how to make a simple sliding door. People see the finished product and they say, "He is neat," or "He has skill," but actually most of the quality of the work is in the preparation of the materials. For typical dimensions of the parts, refer to figure 3. I begin with the hipboard. If you do not have stock wide enough to make it out of one piece,

Fig 1: Floor plan of a traditional Japanese house

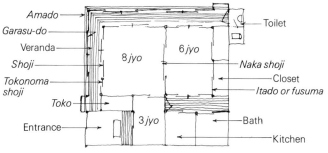

Sliding doors allow for a flexible living area. Jyo is 6 ft. by 3 ft., the size of the grass mats (tatami) *used to cover the floor.*

Fig 2: Varieties of *shoji*

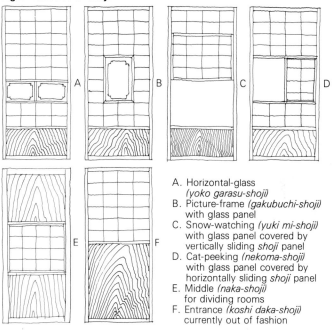

A. Horizontal-glass
   (*yoko garasu-shoji*)
B. Picture-frame (*gakubuchi-shoji*)
   with glass panel
C. Snow-watching (*yuki mi-shoji*)
   with glass panel covered by
   vertically sliding *shoji* panel
D. Cat-peeking (*nekoma-shoji*)
   with glass panel covered by
   horizontally sliding *shoji* panel
E. Middle (*naka-shoji*)
   for dividing rooms
F. Entrance (*koshi daka-shoji*)
   currently out of fashion

Fig. 3: A typical *ma-shoji*
There are two alternate top rail designs. The rail can be 1⁵/₁₆ in. thick and rabbeted to fit the track it slides in, or ³/₄ in. thick, unrabbeted. The thicker rail looks more finished, because the rabbet covers the track. The thinner rail is stronger, because the tenon can be wider.

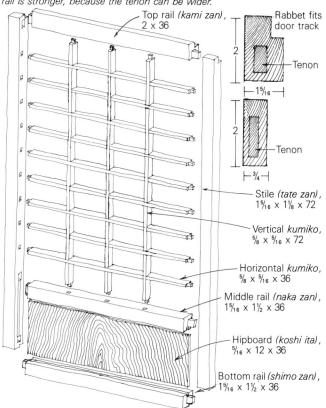

The tategu-shi *(sliding-door maker) begins by planing his stock to size, left. He uses planes that cut on the pull stroke, and he supports the wood on a kezuri-dai, that is, a beam held at one end by a triangular support and lodged against anything sturdy at the other. A nail driven into the beam stops the work against the pull of the plane. Traditionally, the kezuri-dai is fashioned at the work site and left behind when the craftsman finishes the job and moves on. Layout, above, is done with a thin, narrow square and a marking knife. Similar pieces, here both stiles for one shoji, are clamped together and layout lines struck across the stack.*

Fig. 4: Two tools for sizing *kumiko*

Splitting gauge splits kumiko *strips without kerf-waste.*

Block, $1^{3}/_{16}$ × $2^{1}/_{2}$ × 7

Hollow-ground
splitting knife

Beam, $^{1}/_{2}$ × $1^{1}/_{2}$ × $8^{3}/_{4}$

Wood strips tacked to edges of plane sole regulate thickness of kumiko.

you begin by gluing it up. This way the glue will be dry when it comes time to plane the hipboard and cut it to size.

Next I prepare the stiles. The front face, which will face out of the room and receive the paper, must be planed flat and free of twist. Next plane the inside edge perpendicular to the front face, but instead of being straight along its length, it should bow slightly. This will hold the stile tight against the *kumiko*. The large tenons of the rails will be made to fit tight in the mortises of the stile—so tight that they will have to be hammered home. But the *kumiko* are delicate. Bowing the stile to press gently against the *kumiko* shoulders, instead of making the tiny mortises and tenons hold the parts snug, I call the "thoughtfulness of the craftsman."

Once the front face and inside edge are planed, gauge the width of the face with a marking gauge and plane the outside edge. Then gauge the thickness of the edge and plane the back face. This is the face that will show in the room. All the frame parts of the *shoji* are planed in this order. Plane the *kumiko*-facing edges of the top and middle rails and the inside edge of the bottom rail to bow in. Now I cut the stock to rough length and turn to the *kumiko*.

Apprentices being trained today use a tablesaw and a thickness planer for preparing *kumiko*. The hand method I describe here is the one I learned. I begin by planing perfectly flat a 1-in. thick redwood board, 6 ft. long. Mark it to ⅝-in. thickness, and plane the back face to the mark. Plane the edges of the board square to the face.

Now I use a splitting gauge (figure 4), which is like a marking gauge but larger and heavier. I score the board, first one face, then the other, until I can snap off the *kumiko*. I plane the edge of the board again, then split off another *kumiko*, repeating the process until I have plenty of extra pieces.

Next I wet the knifed surface of each piece with a damp

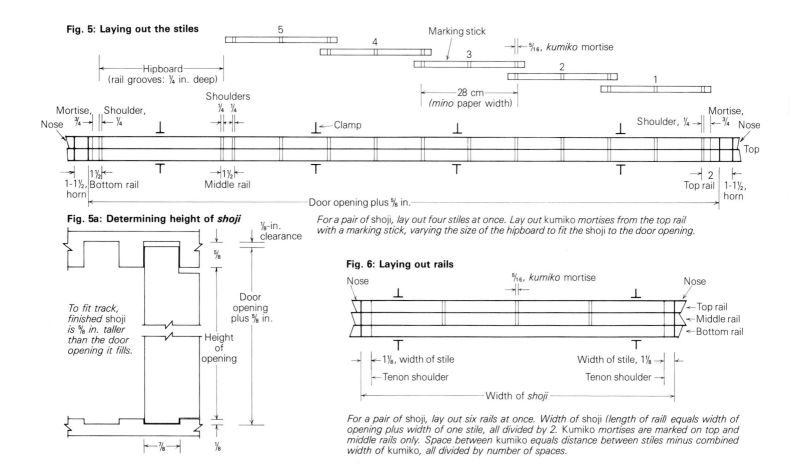

Fig. 5: Laying out the stiles

5

4

Marking stick

3

⁵⁄₁₆, kumiko mortise

Hipboard
(rail grooves: ¼ in. deep)

28 cm
(mino paper width)

2

1

Shoulders
¼ ¼

Mortise,
Nose ¾ →

Shoulder,
← ¼

⊥

← Clamp

⊥

⊥

⊥

Shoulder, ¼ →

Mortise,
← ¾ Nose

Top

1-1½,
horn

→ 1½ ←
Bottom rail

T

→ 1½ ←
Middle rail

T

T

T

Top rail

→ 2 ←

1-1½,
horn

Door opening plus ⅝ in.

Fig. 5a: Determining height of shoji

⅛-in.
clearance

⅝

Door
opening
plus ⅝ in.

To fit track,
finished shoji
is ⅝ in. taller
than the door
opening it fills.

Height
of
opening

← ⅞ →

⅛

For a pair of shoji, lay out four stiles at once. Lay out kumiko mortises from the top rail
with a marking stick, varying the size of the hipboard to fit the shoji to the door opening.

Fig. 6: Laying out rails

Nose

⁵⁄₁₆, kumiko mortise

Nose

⊥

⊥

← Top rail
← Middle rail
← Bottom rail

T

T

→ 1⅛, width of stile

← Tenon shoulder

Width of stile, 1⅛ →

Tenon shoulder →

Width of shoji

For a pair of shoji, lay out six rails at once. Width of shoji (length of rail) equals width of
opening plus width of one stile, all divided by 2. Kumiko mortises are marked on top and
middle rails only. Space between kumiko equals distance between stiles minus combined
width of kumiko, all divided by number of spaces.

cloth, to relieve the pressure made by the knife. If you don't do this, the *kumiko* will eventually swell after they are assembled, and cause trouble. I lean the *kumiko* against a wall so the air can move around them until they are dry, and then plane the split edges square. To make sure they will be exactly the same width, I plane three or four *kumiko* at once, using a plane I reserve for this purpose. It has wood strips tacked to the bottom to stop the cut (figure 4).

Laying out the joints—The wall opening and tracks built by the house carpenter determine the outer dimensions of the *shoji*. The width of the rice paper determines the spacing of the horizontal *kumiko*. Marking out this spacing from the top rail determines where the middle rail goes, and thus the *tategu-shi* finds the height of the hipboard. All other measurements are according to the discretion of the craftsman. The measurements in the drawings are typical.

For speed and accuracy you lay out similar pieces, both stiles for instance (or four, when one opening requires two *shoji*), at the same time. Use clamps to keep the pieces aligned. The *tategu-shi* uses his clamps mostly for layout, almost never for assembly. I strike finished mortise heights and tenon shoulders across the width of the stock, using a square and a marking knife. Pencils and pens are not so accurate as the knife, and are used only for marking to rough length. I mark the stiles first, then the rails, then the *kumiko*. *The stiles*: It is customary to orient the stiles the way the wood grew in the tree. So, I make sure the largest growth rings are at the bottom of the stiles when I start to lay them out. Clamp the stiles together, inside edge up, and mark the finished height of the *shoji*, ⅝ in. longer than the height of the opening it will fill. The extra length fits the tracks, top and bottom, in which the *shoji* will slide (figure 5). Next I make a

mark for the horns, 1-in. to 1½-in. past the finished height on either end. Most of the horns will be cut off later, but for now they keep the stiles from splitting when the rail tenons are driven into their mortises, and they also protect the ends of the stiles from damage during the work. Mark the width of the top and bottom rails next, and within those widths mark the mortise height.

Next I mark off the mortises for the *kumiko*, using a marking stick. The stick carries the width of the paper and the position of three *kumiko* in relation to that width. Figure 5 shows the layout of *kumiko* mortises for the *mino*-size paper, 28 cm wide, which gives nine horizontal *kumiko*. The stick has two *kumiko* mortises marked just inside the paper width, plus one centered between them. I begin at the mark for the top rail, overlap it the width of one *kumiko* mortise, and knife off the other two mortises. Reposition the stick to overlap the last mortise marked, and mark the next two mortises. I continue in this manner five times, until I have marked off nine *kumiko* mortises, and then I mark off the top of the middle rail. Finally I mark the width of the middle rail, and within it the mortise height. I square all these knife marks across all four stiles, saw off the noses (the waste beyond the horns), unclamp the stiles and chamfer the ends against damage.
The rails: When two *shoji* fill a door opening, they overlap each other by the width of a stile. The width of each *shoji* thus is figured by adding the width of a stile to the width of the opening and dividing by two. The final rail length will be shy of this dimension, because the tenon is not quite a through tenon, but for now, I clamp the rails together, inside edge up, and mark their length as the *shoji* width (figure 6). Next I mark off the width of the stiles, which locates the tenon shoulders. The mortises for the vertical *kumiko* are marked next, equally spaced between the two stiles. I use a

Fig. 7: Laying out vertical *kumiko*　　Lay out two kumiko from stile, use these to lay out others.　　Mark top end.

Stile　　Lay out three vertical *kumiko* for each shoji from the two marked ones.

Clamp

³⁄₈, tenon　　　　　　　　　　　　　　　　　　　　³⁄₈, tenon

Chamfer corners.　　Finished *kumiko*

Odate clamps the kumiko *(the thin strips that form the* shoji *grid) together in a stack and saws the notch shoulders a hair more than halfway through. A piece of scrap starts the saw correctly.*

To break out the waste Odate pulls the corner of a flat chisel along the kerf (top). Then he clears the waste with a mortise chisel run in the notch, bevel-side down (above).

With the kumiko *still clamped together, Odate makes their tenons. First he saws the shoulders, then breaks off the waste with a chisel pushed in from the end grain (top). The index finger on the bottom of the chisel acts as a stop to protect the shoulder. He cleans up the tenons by paring with the chisel across the grain (above). When all the tenons have been formed and their top and bottom corners chamfered with a few strokes of a plane, he unclamps the stack, fans out the* kumiko *and chamfers the other two corners (below).*

marking stick, as for the horizontal *kumiko*. Lastly I saw off the noses squarely, and unclamp the rails.

Vertical kumiko: To lay out the tenons and the notches for the half-lap joints on the vertical *kumiko* I transfer the layout lines from one of the stiles to two of the *kumiko*, and then from these two to the rest of the *kumiko* (figure 7). I clamp the two marked *kumiko* on either side of the stack of unmarked *kumiko* to strike the layout lines across the stack. It's a good idea to make two extra *kumiko* and not use the marked *kumiko* in the finished *shoji*. The vertical *kumiko* get notched alternately front and back. So I square every other notch around the underside of the stack. Last, I mark the tenon shoulders and lengths.

Now, while the vertical *kumiko* are still clamped together, I saw the notches and the tenons (photos, facing page). You cut both shoulders of one notch first, using a piece of scrap to start the saw correctly. Saw a hair more than halfway through the *kumiko*, break out the waste with a chisel, and clean up by running a mortise chisel, bevel-down, along the bottom of the notch. I insert a scrap of *kumiko* in this notch as security in case a clamp shifts while I'm cutting the other notches.

Next I cut the clamped *kumiko* stack to final length. To cut the tenons, square the shoulder lines around all four sides of the stack. Gauge the tenon on the end grain of the stack and on the faces of the two outside *kumiko*, then saw the shoulders. These are small tenons, so instead of sawing in from the end grain to meet the shoulder, I use a chisel to break off the waste. My index finger on the underside of the chisel acts as a stop to keep the chisel from damaging the *kumiko* shoulders. In all but the straightest-grained stock, I break a little bit wide and pare the tenons to the line.

Before removing the clamps, I chamfer the upper and

Fig. 8: Laying out horizontal *kumiko*

Lay out two kumiko *from rail, use these to lay out others.*

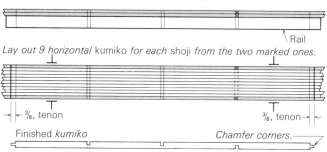

Rail

Lay out 9 horizontal kumiko *for each shoji from the two marked ones.*

³⁄₈, tenon   ³⁄₈, tenon

Finished kumiko   Chamfer corners.

lower edges of the tenons. Then I remove the clamps and fan out the stack to chamfer one corner, then the other. The vertical *kumiko* are now ready.

Horizontal kumiko: Many people think that the *kumiko* overlap, every other one, as if they are woven. But *kumiko* will not bend that much. They are only partly woven. When there are three vertical *kumiko*, for instance, the notches in the horizontal *kumiko* are two, adjacent, on one face, one on the other (figure 8). They are marked out and cut exactly like the vertical *kumiko*.

Cutting the joints—The *kumiko* notches and tenons have been cut while the *kumiko* were clamped up for layout. The joints on the stiles and rails are now cut on the pieces individually, mortises first, then tenons. Cutting the tenons last lessens the danger of damaging them. The quality of a craftsman's skill is judged by his speed and accuracy. It is considered most important to make each cut with the saw or chisel the final cut—you go directly to the layout line. The

Like the planes, Japanese saws cut on the pull stroke. The long handle is usually held with two hands, spaced well apart for maximum power and control. There are three basic sawing stances, each suited for a different sort of cut. For crosscutting, left, Odate supports the stock on two low horses, holds it steady with his foot, and saws through. For sawing shoulders, as at top left of facing page, Odate sits so he can see where *the cut has to stop. And for ripping, as for tenon cheeks, center and right, he supports the stock on one horse so he can see the layout lines on the near edge and on the end grain at the same time. To avoid cutting into the shoulder, Odate saws on an angle into the near edge first, then turns the stock over to cut into the opposite edge, finishing with the saw straight up and down.*

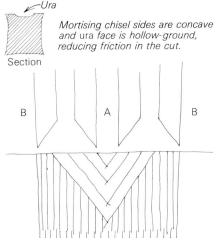

Fig. 9: Mortise chisel/chopping method

Mortising chisel sides are concave and *ura* face is hollow-ground, reducing friction in the cut.

A: Begin in the middle of the mortise and chop out toward the ends, alternating sides, always with the *ura* face toward the middle.
B: At ends of the mortise, turn *ura* face around.

The tategu-shi *sits on the wood to steady it while he mortises it, above, stabbing his chisel frequently in a box of cotton wadding soaked with vegetable oil, to reduce friction. The chisel has three concave sides and a hollow-ground face (figure 9 and photo, top of facing page). He chops from the middle out, always with the face toward the middle of the mortise, except for the final cuts at either end of the mortise. These are angled slightly from the perpendicular (photo, right, includes a square for illustration only) to taper the mortise for a tight fit when the tenon is driven in.*

least contact lessens the chance of error and keeps the work crisp. Should the *shokunin* make a mistake, no matter how small, his error remains in the work, and even if only he knows it, it is a permanent reproach. Nothing can be done about it. So you learn not to make mistakes.

Japanese mortises are somewhat different from Western mortises, and so are some of the tools used to cut them. To get maximum strength in a delicate frame, the *tategu-shi* shapes his mortises with walls that taper in, to compress the fibers of the tenon without crushing them. The natural springiness of the wood enhances the mechanical strength of the joint. He works to very close tolerances: a shaving here or there makes all the difference. It is thought coarse to show end grain, so through-joints are used only in heavy entrance doors, rain doors, and doors that carry glass. For strength and refinement, the main joints of the *shoji* must be as deep as possible without going through. The bottom is paper-thin, thin enough for light to show through. But no mark must show on the outside. One slip and the wood is ruined.

You gauge the mortise width, making sure the fence is always on the front face of the stock, then chop your mortises with a chisel exactly as wide as the mortise. Japanese mortise

chisels are rectangular in section and will not turn in the mortise. Three sides are slightly concave, and the face, called *ura*, is hollow-ground (figure 9 and photo, facing page). This reduces friction in the heavy cuts. Stabbing the chisel frequently into a box of cotton wadding soaked in vegetable oil further reduces friction. The edges of the chisel scrape and true the long-grain sides of the mortise.

The *tategu-shi* strikes his chisels with an iron hammer, not the wooden mallet used in the West. He works from the middle of the mortise out, alternating cuts at either end, the *ura* always facing toward the middle. As the chisel cuts, it follows the bevel, so each cut shears toward the middle. As you near the ends of the mortise, you turn the *ura* around and chop straight down. The last cut at each end is with the chisel tilted slightly into the mortise. This tapers the walls just enough to pinch the tenon when it is driven in.

The *tategu-shi* does not lever waste out with the chisel as he chops, as does a Western woodworker. Instead he uses a small harpoon-shaped tool called *mori-nomi* (photos, facing page). Its face is flushed against the mortise wall, and the tool is tapped down and quickly jerked up. Its hook catches the chips and clears them out. Chopping, alternately with the mortise chisel and the *mori-nomi*, proceeds quickly until the final depth is approached. Then you slow down and gauge the depth with a piece of *kumiko* cut to length. Score the remaining wood with the chisel, and remove the last fibers from the bottom of the mortise with a *sokozarai-nomi*, another tool I have not seen in the West. It is a thin, goose-necked tool with a small spade-like bend at its end. This tool is not tapped with a hammer, but used like a scraper, with one or two hands, to level the bottom of the mortise.

The *kumiko* mortises need not be as deep as the mortises for the rail tenon because the bow in the stiles and rails holds them tight. The *kumiko* mortises are too small to be scraped in the usual way. So, you chisel to within ⅛ in. of the final depth and use a small steel rod to tap the wood down for clearance (about 1/16 in. deeper than the length of the *kumiko* tenon). This method works best in softwood.

The tenons on the rails are cut in much the same way as they would be in the West, although the *tategu-shi* holds his work differently and uses Japanese saws which cut on the pull stroke. First extend the shoulder lines (marked on the inside edge when the stiles were clamped together for layout) around the other three sides of each rail. Gauge the tenon thickness on the two edges and on the end grain. Saw the shoulders first, on all the rails, then line the rails up to saw the cheeks. The photos on p. 165 show how to proceed, sawing with the stock supported at an angle, so you can see the lines on both the end grain and the edge of the stock. Saw at an angle to the near edge of the shoulder, then turn the stock over to finish. This way there is less danger of oversawing into the shoulder. To cut the narrow third and fourth shoulders, you should not saw the shoulder right on the line, because the set of the saw can damage the first two shoulders sawn. Instead, saw a little wide of the shoulder and trim with a chisel. All shoulders cut, saw the length of the tenon ⅛ in. to 1/16 in. less than the depth of the mortise. Finally, chamfer the end of the tenon so it will go in easily.

Last, plow-plane the grooves that will hold the hipboard, and rabbet the bottom rail (the top too, if you are using the thicker top rail), so the *shoji* can fit into its track in the wall opening (figures 3, p. 161, and 5a, p. 163).

Assembly—The Japanese prefer natural surfaces. The *shoji* receives no finish except a final planing of all its parts, to clean them from handling. The finish plane takes off the slightest shaving, with only one or two passes. Pressing the plane hard against the stock burnishes the surface and brings the wood to a warm glow.

Cut and plane the hipboard to fit, allowing room for the wood to move across the grain, finish-plane its two faces, and chamfer all its edges. Finish-plane all other exposed surfaces of all other parts and lightly chamfer the edges of the main frame parts, except the inside front edges, where a chamfer would create a gap between them and the *kumiko*. Now at last, you're ready to assemble. I use rice glue that I make myself, so the *shoji* can be taken apart if it ever needs repair. Any starch glue, like wallpaper paste, will do.

Assemble the *kumiko* first. Group the horizontals together and the verticals together to make quick work of applying the rice glue to the shoulders of all the notches. Do not put any glue in the bottom of the notches, because glue here would prevent the *kumiko* from fitting tightly. Tap the *kumiko* together using a hammer. Fit the assembly into the mortises

The tategu-shi's *mortising tools. From left to right, a mortising chisel, with hollow-ground face (*ura*); a* mori-nomi, *whose harpoon-like hook is tapped down and jerked up to remove chips; and a* sokozarai-nomi, *which scrapes the mortise bottom flat and also lifts out chips. Last is a steel rod for tapping flat the bottoms of small mortises.*

Removing chips with the mori-nomi.

Scraping the bottom of the mortises with the sokozarai-nomi.

The kumiko *lap joints alternate, above, and must be eased into place. Below, Odate holds a small* shoji *he made for demonstration at a recent workshop.*

in the top rail. No glue is needed here. Fit the hipboard into the groove of the middle and bottom rail, and fit the *kumiko* assembly into the mortises in the middle rail.

Now you are ready to add the stiles. First take a hammer and tap around the mortises so the edges of the rail shoulders will fit tight. Then apply glue to both stiles at once. Tap the rail tenons into one of the stiles, stopping when the *kumiko* tenons just begin to engage, then start the other stile in the same way. Make sure both stiles are going on straight, and tap them home with a hammer. Hammer on a small block of wood with chamfered edges to avoid damaging the stock. When the tenons fit tight, check to be sure the *shoji* is square and flat. Tap and twist it into shape if it is not.

Installation—With assembly, the tense part of the *shokunin's* challenge is accomplished. Installation is the joy of displaying your work. Place the *shoji* on the outside ledge of the bottom track and check the stiles against the door frame for alignment. Cut the bottom horns as close to the bottom rails as possible, but if necessary at slightly different heights to align the stiles parallel to the door frame. Rabbet the horns, like the bottom rail, to fit the groove in the track. Now put the *shoji* back on the ledge (not in the groove yet) and press the top of the *shoji* up against the outside of the top track. Make a mark on the inside face of each horn where the track meets it, add ⅝ in. to this mark, and you will have the length to which the top horns should be cut. Once they are cut, rabbet them to fit the track.

Applying paper—Rice paper has a smooth side, which is on the inside of the roll, and this should face out when the paper is applied to the screen. The horizontal strips are pasted to the *shoji* with rice glue, and they overlap one another like shingles, so the seams will not collect dust. Paper is traditionally applied by the housewife and customarily changed during the last week of the year, so that the paper is bright white for New Year's Day, signifying a fresh start. Old paper is easily removed by moistening it.

Besides the traditional *mino* and *hanshi*-size rolls, paper companies now make rolls one meter wide to be pasted on vertically in one piece. This opens up many possibilities in the spacing and patterns of the *kumiko*, which have always been carefully positioned to accommodate the traditional-size papers. This kind of change creates freedom in design, but it raises questions about pride in craftsmanship.

* * *

Well, finally you have finished and neatly installed a pair of *shoji*. You can appreciate now their character. The *shoji* paper draws in not only light, but light's warmness, softness and taste. The frames and *kumiko* that support the paper are not heavy or coarse. You open and close the *shoji* gently. The *shoji* has everything you need to feel peaceful. You retreat from the bustling world outside, you take off your shoes when you enter your home, and you sit down on a thin mattress in a room of *shoji* walls. You can call this place an oasis of life. □

Toshio Odate was trained as a tategu-shi *(sliding-door maker) and is now a sculptor, living in Woodbury, Conn. This article was prepared with help from Audrey Grossman. Odate wrote on sharpening techniques in* FWW #29; *his work appears on the back cover of* FWW #26. *Drawings by the author.*

Framing Pictures
Choosing and making suitable moldings

by Jim Cummins

Picture frame construction

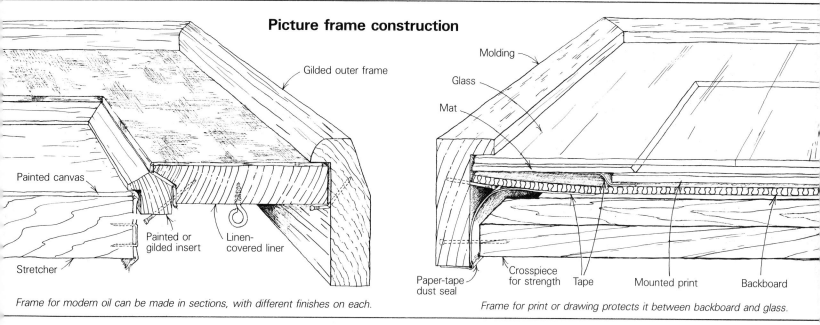

Gilded outer frame

Painted canvas

Painted or gilded insert

Linen-covered liner

Stretcher

Frame for modern oil can be made in sections, with different finishes on each.

Molding

Glass

Mat

Paper-tape dust seal

Crosspiece for strength

Tape

Mounted print

Backboard

Frame for print or drawing protects it between backboard and glass.

Illustrations: E. Marino III

Department-store frames, mass-produced, rarely succeed at matching up with works of art that are made one at a time, nor do they readily suit rooms and tastes that are personal and distinctive. Custom-made frames, on the other hand, seem extravagantly priced, and there's no guarantee of satisfaction there, either. You and the framer can pick a molding that suits the picture just fine, but in your home it may not look quite right. The next time you need a frame, you might try making your own. You can end up with something you're satisfied with, save money, and perhaps develop an interesting sideline. After all, none of the separate operations involved in framing a picture is very difficult.

Frames are commonplace because they're necessary. Once we realize what's required of a frame, we are on the way to making one, because a frame's functions determine both its construction and its visual design.

Function and design—Design in framing is related to function—not only physical function, but also the visual and emotional function the frame plays as it affects the picture, the room, and the viewer. Consider four functions as you choose a frame: protection, enrichment, focus and transition.

Protection: A watercolor cannot be cleaned, so it is sealed up behind glass in its frame. Pastels need protection not only from dirt, but also from physical contact, because they smudge easily. Needlepoints can go either way; while cleaning them may mean restretching them, glass does interfere with the appreciation of their texture. An oil painting should be cleaned every 20 or 30 years and is protected by its removable coat of varnish. Glass in this case is not only unnec-

essary, its hardness and reflection would diminish the texture and lucidity of the painting. Hence oils are left unglazed. The frame may still protect an oil by preventing the wooden stretcher the canvas is mounted on from warping or by actually holding together multiple panels (as in the case of some Renaissance paintings). In the same way, the frame protects a flimsy piece of paper by providing a stiff mat to which the paper is attached. The strength and size of the frame depend somewhat on the weight of the picture, although in the case of a large poster—in its pure form a piece of artwork originally meant to be pasted to a wall without a frame at all—the frame may be made with hidden supports that allow its visible part to be minimal.

Enrichment: Stone-age cave paintings have no formal edge, the cave itself is the frame for the art. Egyptian or Greek murals were framed by the rooms in which they were done. Picture frames, as we think of them today, began in the Renaissance: the artist scooped out a board to paint on, leaving the edge full for stiffness—frame and painting were one piece. Painting was then regarded as more of a craft or a science than an art, and the frame was within the artist's sphere of work. The workmanship in the gilding, inlay, carving and design of the frame reflected his general competence, and encouraged a good price for the art. Eventually, artists left the framing to others; by the time of the High Renaissance, it wasn't unusual for the frame carver and gilder to make as much money as the painter himself. The artist, however, probably designed the frame. Money aside, a frame still reflects on the art in it. Paintings rich in color and subject matter, suggesting opulent times, require complementary frames;

rustic frames suit rustic subjects. Most drawings look best with a mat and narrow frame, but a Picasso line drawing, just a few strokes, can have all the richness of an oil, and be able to balance an ornate gold frame without losing its character. *Focus:* Since the style of a painting, its color, texture and period, should be balanced by the frame's design, the frame, in effect, makes the painting into a larger object. The frame's continuity provides a visual field that defines the subject matter and directs the eye into it. The regularity of the frame first draws the eye to it, then sends it into the picture. A frame therefore should attract the eye—with gold leaf or fancy carving, for example, or a mat under glass. The proportions are important. Visual effects that are too much the same, such as a 2-in. frame with a 2-in. mat, trap the eye. Too colorful a mat or too bright a finish will do the same, which is why some frames are made to look faded and old. Many modern works of art are designed to catch the eye without much of a frame. A broad, uninterrupted wall may be all that a strong oil painting needs to be seen at its best. The frame merely covers unsightly staples, tacks and ragged canvas at the picture's edges. Lack of focus is the reason that lumberyard moldings don't work well for frames. They are designed to shoot the eye along, to make it wing outward in order to enlarge rooms and break up flat, blank walls. This is the opposite of what a frame should do.

Transition: While a painting is an object with merit of its own, a framed painting doesn't do well without reference to the room in which it hangs. This is why paintings in museums often look absurdly overframed. Their period frames need period rooms. The frame's color, reflection, richness or simplicity, even its width, must relate to and be seen along with its surroundings. A room without a framed painting is no worse off than a framed painting without its room.

Measurements

If we look at a basic frame we can start to tie the abstract and the practical together. Look at a frame from the back, and note the different ways it can be measured.

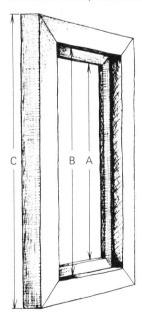

A is "sight size," what you'd see from the front. B is "glass size" or "rabbet size," the size to which the mat, glass and backing are cut. We normally call a frame by its rabbet size, although the rabbet is cut $\frac{1}{16}$ in. or so larger than the mat and glass, to allow a comfortable fit for standard-size glass. If the frame is too tight, the mat and backing will soon buckle, and the glass may break or force open the corners of the frame. Frames for oil paintings are usually made $\frac{1}{4}$ in. oversize, room for pegging out the stretcher that keeps the canvas free from ripples and sags. C is "overall size," but the term can be misleading because the length of the molding needed for a frame is the sight size plus double the width of the molding. An 8x10 frame (rabbet size) made from a 2-in. wide molding needs sides that measure about 12 in. and 14 in., so instead of 3 ft. of molding, you actually need almost $4\frac{1}{2}$ ft. because of the waste at the miters.

Cutting miters

Professional framers have specialized machines for making miters. These include guillotine choppers that cut a 90° notch, making two miters at once, Lion trimmers that neatly slice one miter at a time, 45° cutoff saws, radial-arm saws, and industrial pneumatic and hydraulic monsters weighing tons. But you can cut a perfect miter on a tablesaw, if you forgo speed and automatic accuracy.

First, check that the sawblade is parallel to the miter-gauge groove in the table. A blade that is not parallel will seem to work fine when the gauge is on one side, but on the other side it will force the molding away during the cut, changing the angle. And vice versa. This is one reason for making sample cuts and checking that two pieces meet to form a 90° angle. If the molding is forced away from a nominal 45° on one side, then the other side (the side that will cut the true angle) must be fudged to compensate. Worse, moldings of different widths and profiles will be pushed different amounts along the gauge fence, so no single gauge setting will work for all shapes if the blade itself isn't parallel to the table grooves. Carbide blades, with their wide teeth, allow a little latitude if the cut can be completed before the molding contacts the side of the blade. Set the blade high, and push the molding only as far as necessary to complete the cut.

Check that the miter gauge is a good fit in the groove. Sometimes the grooves themselves are different sizes. I've had to peen the slide to fit one groove, and file the other groove wider. If the gauge wobbles, you can't expect an accurate cut. If the gauge binds, even a little bit, you can't tell if the work is binding—a potential disaster. Once your gauge runs smoothly, you can improve it further by adding a backup fence that's L-shaped in cross-section. It will support both the back and the bottom of the molding as it is being cut. Make the backup fence long, then cut off its ends at 45°, with the gauge sliding in its grooves. The fence ends now mark the

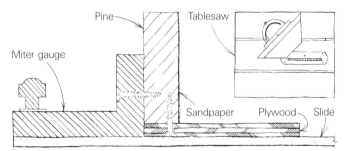

line of cut. Glue fine sandpaper or non-slip tape to the fence so the molding won't slide while you're cutting it.

Never trust the angle indicator on the gauge, since any error will be multiplied by the number of cuts in the frame. Instead, make a template for setting the gauge. Either scribe lines right on the saw table (*FWW* #26, p. 80), or take a piece of 8 in. wide plywood that's long enough to contact the full miter-gauge fence, and lay out a square and its diagonal on one end. With the gauge set to its nominal 45°, nibble toward the diagonal line, adjusting the gauge until the cut is exactly on the line. This is a perfect 45° cut—from now on you can use it to set the miter gauge. With the saw turned off, raise the blade as far as it will go. Place the template against the miter fence and slide it over to the sawblade. Rotate the miter gauge until the diagonal evenly meets both the front and the back of the blade, then lock it. Flip the template over to reset the gauge for the opposite cut.

Instead of resetting the miter gauge every time you make a

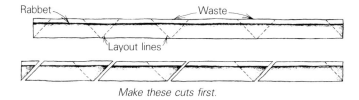

Make these cuts first.

corner, saw all the right-hand miters at once. If you are taking more than one piece from a length of molding, mark it to make sure the miters go in the right direction and that you are leaving enough for waste. It's easy to come up short, and embarrassingly easy to cut a miter that goes the wrong way. Remember that every cut will leave the piece larger on the side away from the rabbet. Locate and draw the first miter on the back of the molding, and make a clear mark inside the rabbet where the miter line meets it. Then write the rabbet size to be cut on the back of the wood. This helps avoid cutting three 24-in. pieces and one 30-in. piece for a 24x30 frame—another familiar pitfall. Carefully lay out the rest of the rabbet marks and sketch in the miter marks as you go. When you saw the molding, cut on the marks in the rabbet— the drawn miter lines are just reminders.

Some moldings won't sit flat on the saw table, and special pains must be taken to keep them from rocking during the cut. Make blocks and wedges as needed. Extra-deep moldings (like some shown in the box on page 67) may be too high for your saw. Cut these flat on the table, with the blade tilted to 45°, and the miter gauge set to 90°, as shown in the drawing below. Always use a sharp, fine-tooth blade. Dull blades will only force the molding away, while coarse ones won't leave a good gluing surface.

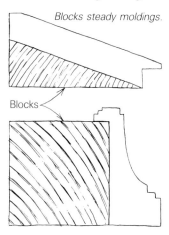

Blocks steady moldings.

Blocks

Joining frames—In spite of perhaps a dozen other methods that can be used, nearly all picture frames are joined with glue and nails. You start by making two Ls, and then join the Ls. In our shop, the process goes like this:

We put one side in a machinists' vise (padded), and hand-hold the other side in position to drill holes for the nails. This allows the corner to tighten to the maximum when we set the nails. We don't use those 90° vises that hold two sides together for gluing and nailing, because the corners will never be tighter than you can set them in the vise. If you make it a habit always to put the long side in the vise and glue the short side to it, you can avoid joining the sides in the wrong

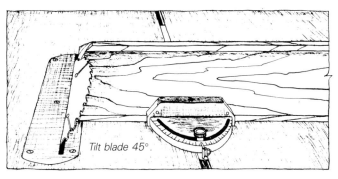

Tilt blade 45°.

order, which results in a diamond shape instead of a rectangle—if you can get the miter together at all. Put glue on both miters to be joined. We use ordinary yellow glue. If you prefer to use white glue, let it thicken first; as it comes from the store it's too thin for miter joints. Apply enough glue so that it squeezes out along the entire glueline when the joint is nailed, then wipe off the excess with a wet rag.

If you are right-handed, support the short side with your left hand, and pick up an electric drill with your right. Drill holes for the nails or brads, not allowing the corner to shift. We use 1x18 brads for small frames, 4d finishing nails for larger frames, and up to 10d where extra length is needed. In soft woods such as pine, use a #56 drill bit for the brads, and a #50 bit for all finishing nails. Angle the holes a little to get the most purchase. A common mistake is to start the nails too close to the corner, which results in no gripping power at the head. Use your three-dimensional imagination to keep wood around the nail. If a 4d nail seems a little short, and a 6d nail might split the wood, just set the 4d nail deeper. On very wide frames, where even a 10d nail is too short, you

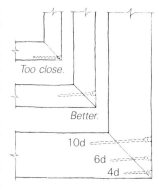

Too close.

Better.

10d

6d

4d

can hold the inside of the miter tight while the glue dries by stapling it from the back in addition to the nails.

Support the weight of the loose side while it's in the vise. At no time should the free side hang by the nails. We rarely nail across corners from both sides, because it's the glue that keeps the corner together, not the nails. If a corner pulls up tight when the first nails go in, that's all that's necessary. Cross-nailing, or using elaborate metal fasteners, can weaken a corner by imposing additional strain and shock. Force applied to pull up a corner just builds stress into the joint, and sooner or later it will crack.

Repeat the process with the other two sides, and then join the two Ls. If the frame is not too heavy, just support the free L as you did the free side. Handle the Ls carefully—you have a good, tight corner when you set the nails, but until the whole frame is joined any shock or twist will open it. We have a tilting vise that lets us support heavy Ls on the table. You can block up the free end; but it's usually easier to hold things than to set up blocks or to tilt the vise. Helpers are rarely any help.

Join a complete frame at once, don't let the Ls sit around and take the wrong set. If you finish joining the frame before any of the glue has dried, the stresses will even out, the frame will be stronger, and it will dry square. Clean the glue from the rabbet, or it may break the glass when the picture is being fitted into the frame.

Glass—Glass comes in several varieties. Ordinary window glass weighs about 19 oz. per sq. ft. Picture glass is 15 oz. to 17 oz. per sq. ft.—more expensive, slightly clearer, and usually available only in frame shops. The trend is to use window glass for most frame jobs. Non-glare glass has been surface-treated to reduce reflection, and is best used in direct contact with the art—any separation, as caused for instance by a double mat, will blur the image. Allowing glass to contact artwork is chancy because moisture condensation can cause

Photos: Karen Sahulka

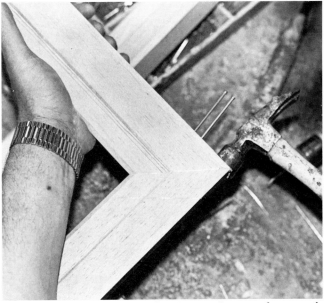

Predrilling nail holes guards against splitting, ensures good starts in the right direction for maximum purchase. One side of the frame is held in a machinists' vise, the other is steadied from underneath by hand, the forearm resting on something solid.

Cabinet joints evolve to meet changing requirements for strength. In picture framing, the nailed miter continues to hold its own.

Free side of the frame must be hand-supported at all times until the corner comes out of the vise. Nails pull the miter as tight as it will go—tighter than a corner vise can be set.

damage. Non-glare glass, incidentally, won't perform miracles in really bad situations—it has an overall "bloom" which you can't see through at all. Try changing the height of the picture or letting it tilt out from the wall. If your frame is very large, your local hardware store may stock the size only in double-strength window glass—too heavy for framing. You would be better off using Plexiglas.

Matting—Artists' supply stores sell matboard, differentiated from cheaper illustration board by its surface finish and light-colored paper core. Standard matboard sizes are 30 in. or 32 in. by 40 in., and 40 in. by 60 in., with a smaller color range in the larger size. Until recently, colored matboard was made by gluing cover sheets to a pulp center that contained acids left over from the paper-making process. These acids would gradually seep out through the cut bevel, and nearby portions of the art would turn brown. Museums and collectors don't like that at all. Instead, they use board made from 100% cotton fiber (rag), and processed without acid residues. A new type of matboard, called Alpha-mat, is chemically buffered to have a long, acid-free life, and comes in over fifty colors.

Sometimes artwork is simply laid on top of a matboard (to show the edges of the paper), but usually, after a color has been chosen to suit the artwork and its surroundings, an opening with a beveled edge is cut in the board. This bevel can be cut by hand or by machine. In our shop, we use utility knives (with a new blade for each mat) and a metal straight-edge. Lay out and cut matboard from the back. Make neat corners by overshooting the mark—a slight overcut won't be obvious. The mat border is usually from 1 in. to 4 in. wide. A stiff backboard (usually corrugated cardboard or acid-free Fome-Cor) protects the back of the art and keeps it flat in the frame. The art can be attached to it using small hinges or straps of acid-free paper and paste at the top edge, so it hangs and can expand or contract in the frame. Don't use masking tape—it will soon dry out, turn brown and stain through to the front of the paper.

Mounting—Posters, eye-catching outdoor advertising, were designed to be pasted to walls without frames at all, so they don't require fancy mats. But posters are typical of many lightweight papers that need mounting (pasting to a heavier board) to keep them from wrinkling badly. Valuable works of art should never be mounted—collectors and museums insist on maintaining the paper in its original condition. But for most of us, wrinkles interfere with our enjoyment of what we hang on our walls. There are many modern mounting systems using special-purpose adhesives and boards that will stiffen artwork without damaging it. A frameshop can advise you whether or not to try a particular mounting job yourself. If you want to try, it's a lot like veneering and just as difficult to fix when something goes wrong. Use wheat paste, dampen the print, countermount a similar paper on the back of the board to equalize tensions, weight the art down while it dries, and make sure it's really dry before removing the weights.

Stretching—Often, instead of gluing something down, you can stretch it. Oil paintings on canvas are usually stapled to stretcher bars. If you are stretching an oil, make sure the stretcher is square, then staple pieces of cardboard to the back corners to keep it square while you work. It is more important to keep the tension even than to try to get the painting

A mat cutter's grip presses the backs of the fingers against the surface to hold the bevel angle. Practice canting the knife until the blade travels straight, pulled by the entire body, not the arm. Once the grip is mastered, a straightedge can be used for peace of mind. Blades are cheap—use a new one for every mat.

super-tight. Stretch needlepoints and crewels around heavy cardboard or ¼-in. plywood. If you stretch a crewel over artists' stretchers, put matboard behind the fabric, otherwise the wood may show through the stretched-open weave.

Fitting and hanging—Putting the picture into its frame is called fitting. The sandwich of glass, mat and backboard is usually held in by the pressure of small brads in the rabbet.

Twist.

Go through twice.

Oils can be toenailed into their frames. Weight adds up—if regular screw eyes don't seem strong enough, try mirror hangers, or fasten a sturdy crosspiece behind the frame. Double the picture wire if you can't find any heavy enough. Most pictures that fall off walls do so either because the hanger failed in the wall or because the frame was split when the screw eyes were being installed. Drill a hole before you force the screw eye—splits only get worse.

Set the screw eyes about a quarter of the way down from the top of the frame. The lower they are, the more the picture will tilt from the wall. Wind the wire twice through the screw eye (so it won't slip), and don't make the wire too tight—a tight wire has only about half the strength of a loose one.

Wherever you hang the picture you have framed, make sure that there is enough light to see it, and enough room to stand back and enjoy it. Having done all this work on the frame, I'm afraid that you will never be able to see it the way others will. To them it should be almost invisible. "Is that a new painting?" is the best thing visitors can say about your framing. "What an interesting frame..." means that you haven't quite got it right. □

Jim Cummins, an assistant editor at FWW, *has owned the Vasco Pini Frame Shop in Woodstock, N.Y., for 15 years.*

A tablesawn molding

The tablesaw is a versatile machine, even if you don't want to invest in a molding-head cutter. You can make most of the moldings shown in the box on p. 175 with a regular 10-in. blade. You can also make good copies of many other designs that strike your fancy. One customer recently brought in a painting from the 1920s, still in the frame in which it had won a national award. I copied the frame as shown in the photos on the next page.

I used sugar pine because it machines and finishes well. Harder woods can be used, but work should go slower, especially when making coves. Wood must be dry, or you're wasting your time—miter joints open up quickly if the wood moves much, often within a week of when the heat comes on in the fall. A 60-tooth carbide combination blade leaves a surface I hardly need to sand. This blade can't be hurried, but you shouldn't let it burn the work either. Ripping with a coarser blade would be much faster, but I'd rather make the cuts right than sand and fuss with the molding later.

I don't like to do careful ripping like this on pieces that are more than 6 ft. long. There isn't enough control. In making this frame, one long side and one short side added up to about 4 ft. in length, so I worked with two 4½-ft. pieces. For a large frame, I make all the sides separately. I joint the stock square on two sides and then cut it to width and depth on the tablesaw. I make one extra piece, to see the results of each saw setting before risking the frame itself. This piece can be saved and used as a template for saw settings when you want to duplicate the molding. I make the piece about 2 ft. long to start, even though the final template can be as short as an inch or two. For the time being, the extra length allows you to cut off the ends as you go along if you don't like the way a test cut starts. Instead of measuring angles and doing a lot of mathematics, I usually sketch the profile on the end of the test piece and then set the blade and the fence to cut just shy of the line.

I make cove cuts with a shopmade adjustable-angle fence, which is shown at the bottom right on the following page. To get the idea of how it works, lay a board at an angle across the saw table, with the blade up about an inch and the saw turned off. Imagine that this board is the fence; sight along it and change the angle. Notice how the blade's profile changes from a circular cross-section (with the board at right angles to the blade) to a deep, narrow elliptical shape when the blade and board are almost parallel. If you run the work across the blade at any one of these angles, the shape you see is the shape of the cove you get. A smaller blade will give you a tighter curve, and tilting the arbor will make one side of the curve steeper. You can make molding without making the adjustable fence, by clamping the board to the table, but adjustments are tedious and difficult to duplicate.

Start with the cove on the outside edge. A cove cannot be made taking a heavy cut. Once you have adjusted the blade height and locked the fence angle to conform to the drawing on your test piece, you must lower the blade until it barely clears the table. Then take away only about ⅛ in. or less on each pass until the cove reaches the depth you want. The test piece will quickly tell you if you are trying to do too much at once: if the stock rides up, or won't feed without pressure, or if the blade is being forced to bend, you must retreat, lower the blade, and try again. Your last cut should be especially slow and fine, to minimize sanding.

The straight cuts are all made with the regular rip fence. Notice that we leave good bearing surfaces for later cuts as we go along. This makes the work safer and more accurate.

Watch out that you don't trap narrow cutoffs between the blade and the fence—I've had them shoot out of the saw and stick into the wall behind me.

Save your scraps, you can build up other molding shapes from them later. Cut the rabbet last, then watch how a light sanding brings the profile to the line.

1. *Cove starts with a shallow cut using the angled fence shown at bottom right.*

2. *Five passes bring cove to its full depth.*

3. *Three straight passes begin to define the decorative rises.*

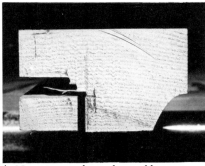

4. *Next pass takes salvageable waste.*

5. *Cove on lip, of tighter radius, requires two passes over a 6½-in. blade.*

6. *Angled top is removed with one cut.*

7. *Starting a decorative step on the outside. A second pass will deepen it.*

8. *Adding one more rise to the face.*

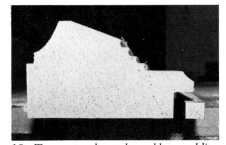

9. *Removing sharp point with a light cut.*

10. *Two cuts clear the rabbet—molding needs only light sanding to soften rises.*

Adjustable-angle fence allows a range of coves to be easily set and duplicated on the tablesaw using regular sawblades.

Moldings you can make

Many moldings can be copied on the tablesaw in a straightforward way. For those that can't, even intricate curves can be achieved without a molding-head cutter by chewing close with lots of linear cuts, and then fine-shaping with gouges and sandpaper. One advantage of making your own molding is that you can adjust the size to suit the job. You could frame anything, from a wedding announcement to the shotgun that inspired the marriage, by varying the proportions of these basic molding shapes, combining them and rearranging them. Wider moldings are frequently carved, finished with stain or gold-leafed. Interiors of boxes, and many liners, can be covered with fabric. —*J.C.*

When all else fails, chew down near the line, finish with ingenuity.

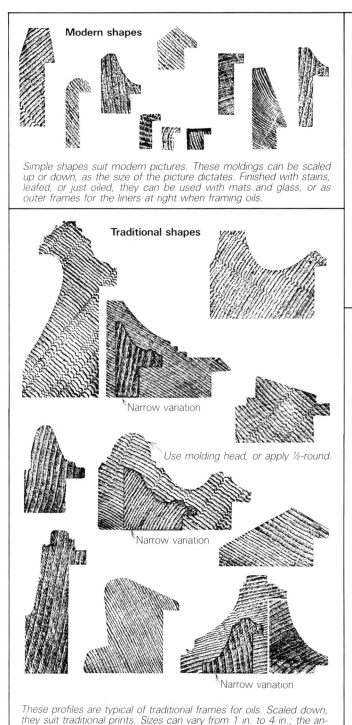

Modern shapes

Simple shapes suit modern pictures. These moldings can be scaled up or down, as the size of the picture dictates. Finished with stains, leafed, or just oiled, they can be used with mats and glass, or as outer frames for the liners at right when framing oils.

Traditional shapes

Narrow variation

Use molding head, or apply ½-round.

Narrow variation

Narrow variation

These profiles are typical of traditional frames for oils. Scaled down, they suit traditional prints. Sizes can vary from 1 in. to 4 in.; the angles steepen and the shapes simplify as the size becomes smaller.

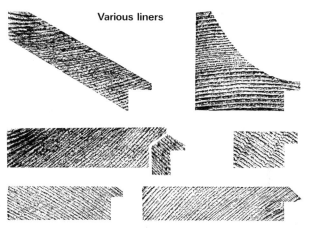

Various liners

Liners vary in width, are usually fabric-covered, and can take the place of mats for oil paintings. Use narrow liners (¾ in. or 1 in.) with wide frames as a visual separator; use liners up to 3½ in. wide with narrow frames. Liner and frame should not be the same width—it's a visual trap that distracts from the picture.

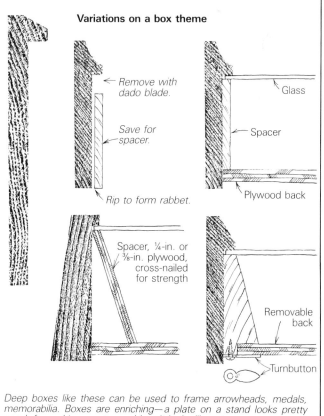

Variations on a box theme

← *Remove with dado blade.*

Save for spacer.

Rip to form rabbet.

Glass

Spacer

Plywood back

Spacer, ¼-in. or ⅜-in. plywood, cross-nailed for strength

Removable back

Turnbutton

Deep boxes like these can be used to frame arrowheads, medals, memorabilia. Boxes are enriching—a plate on a stand looks pretty good; framed in an octagonal box it looks like a treasure.

All moldings shown approximately half size.

Fly Rods from Split Bamboo
With a hand plane and lots of gadgets

by L. U. Beitz

The anonymous craftsman who in 1859 tried fastening a split-bamboo tip to the butt of a hickory fishing rod started a revolution in rod technology and craftsmanship. Charles F. Murphy of Newark, N.J., soon became the first builder to make a complete six-sided split bamboo rod of Calcutta cane. Previous rods were turned and shaved from the springiest woods available: lancewood, greenheart, ash, hickory. They were heavy by any standard, up to 15 or 20 ounces, and positively limp compared with bamboo.

A typical flyfishing rod before bamboo was about 12 ft. long, consisting of two or three sections connected by thread wrappings or metal ferrules. The rod would have been turned round to about ¾-in. diameter just above the handgrip, and would have tapered smoothly to about ⅛ in. at the tip. When they discovered bamboo, last century's makers reproduced the shape of the rods they already knew. To do this, they split and planed Calcutta cane into triangular sections, tapering in length, then they glued the strips into a hexagonal shape. People tried turning the rods on the lathe to round them, but quickly discovered that turned rods lacked strength—the cane is weakest toward its pith, and every precious fraction of its outside surface must be conserved. You can't sand away protruding edges when you make fly rods. If you do, the rod will be stronger in one direction than in the other, resulting in an erratic action. For the tip of a fly rod, a four-foot sliver of bamboo has to be beveled to a perfect equilateral triangle, and tapered from ⅛ in. to 1/32 in. Then five other pieces have to match it exactly—all this using a material that, ounce for ounce, resembles wood less than it does steel (see Bamboo, p. 178).

A fishing rod is basically a spring used to store energy. In spinning or baitcasting rods, the energy is transmitted to a relatively heavy lure that then pulls the light line from the reel. In flyfishing, however, it is the weighty line itself that is cast (almost like snapping a whip), and the nearly weightless fly goes along for the ride. A good caster is able to put as much energy into a long cast as he would into driving a railroad spike—just about all he has. Sometimes that's what it takes to get the fly to the wily trout. A thick rod suffers too

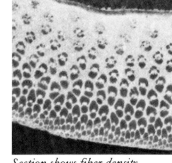

Section shows fiber density.

much from air resistance. A weak rod can't store enough energy for decent casts—it merely breaks. The test of strength-for-weight makes bamboo the finest natural material for fly rods. Its only competition comes from man-made materials (fiberglass and graphite) that closely imitate its structure—long, stiff fibers in a binding matrix.

Rodmakers since Murphy's day have refined their techniques and their concepts of what a good fly rod should be. The old rods were long: 12 ft. to 15 ft. was not uncommon. Length, in a wooden rod, compensated for weakness—if you couldn't make a long cast, the rod got you halfway there anyway. The early bamboo rods were nearly as heavy as wooden ones. They were way overbuilt, but fishermen took generations to get used to a weak-looking rod. Toward the end of the century, progressive makers (Hardy in England, Leonard in America) introduced lighter and shorter rods at every opportunity. Then Tonkin cane replaced the weaker Calcutta cane. By the mid-forties, fifties, and sixties, master rodcrafters and designers such as Everett Garrison, "Pinky" Gillum, Lyle Dickerson, George H. Halstead and Jim Payne, were making the finest rods ever produced in the world. Their rods are now collector's items, selling for four figures. About a dozen companies are still engaged in bamboo rodcrafting. Although their output is excellent in quality, many people have had a hand in the making of each rod. Some of these production rods are priced in the $500-$600 range. Today, a few dedicated builders carry on the tradition of the hand-split, hand-planed, precisely balanced split-bamboo fly rod. In this article I'll describe the building of such a rod. I've included the taper specifications of a rod by Garrison, from which I made the 7½-footer shown along the bottom of these pages. At the end there's a source list for the materials and equipment you need to try these methods yourself.

Selecting and splitting the cane—Let's start building a two-piece (butt and tip), 7½-ft. fly rod, plus an extra tip. Alternate use of two tips prolongs the life of the rod, and if one tip is damaged while fishing, the angler isn't cast adrift.

The Tonkin cane pole, or culm, runs a standard 12-ft. length, with a diameter of 1¾ in. to 2½ in. Its nodes—humpy rings around the circumference—are closer together toward the bottom, about 10 in. apart, spreading to near 16 in. at the top. It is from the thin-walled top that we plot out the

Author's 7½ ft. split-bamboo fly rod shown actual size, with ebony ferrule plug.

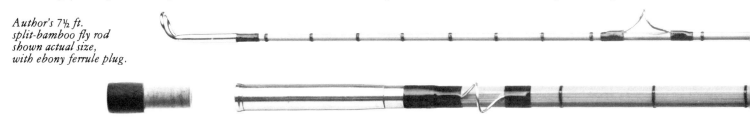

176

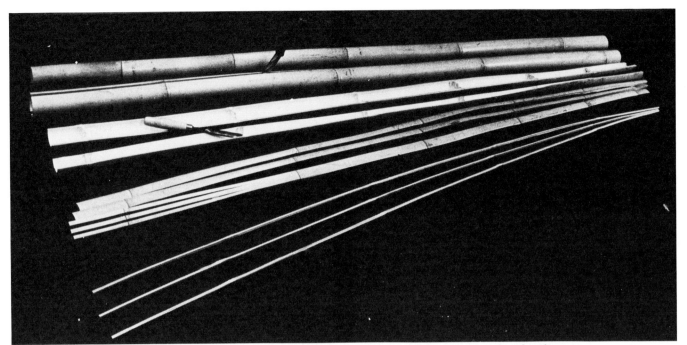

The long fibers in Tonkin cane allow it to be split into many narrow strips that retain lightness, strength and resiliency.

Fig. 1: Strip arrangement

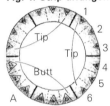

A. To arrange the strips that will become the finished rod, split the culm into at least 18 pieces (dotted lines), choosing pieces for each butt and tip section from adjacent parts of the culm. Tapered triangular strips will be planed from the dense outer part of the culm.

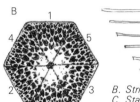

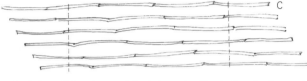

B. Strips will be alternated for balanced action in the glued-up rod.
C. Stagger the brittle nodes to avoid weak spots, then trim rough sections to length before filing and planing.

sections of a 7½-ft. rod. The stouter end can be used for making an 8-ft. or 8½-ft. fly rod; these use thicker strips.

Saw the 12-ft. culm into two 6-ft. lengths. Put aside the thicker piece and place the other piece on the bench to be split up. We'll aim to split strips the full length of the piece, and it's not hard to do—the fibers run very straight.

Study the culm carefully, planning to avoid scuffs, scars, water stains and other imperfections. A few minor water blemishes are bound to show up, since only one culm in a thousand is absolutely perfect in all respects. Look for an overall light-straw color. Greenish culms, or deep yellow ones should be allowed to season several months longer.

Now using a stout knife split the culm down its length into halves, starting at the thicker end. Be careful—bamboo edges can be glass-sharp. Along the U-shaped split half, at each node, is a solid interior wall or dam which must be cut out with a gouge before further splitting. After you've leveled the inside of the culm, split each half into three preliminary pieces, each about 1 in. wide. Then split each of these 1-in. pieces into three or four strips—you'll need at least 18 good strips for the three rod sections. These strips are considerably wider than they will be after planing. Because the culm structure varies slightly in density around its circumference,

number each strip so you can make each rod section from adjacent parts of the culm, as shown in figure 1A. To even out irregularities and keep the rod's action uniform, strips that were adjacent in the culm should be placed opposite each other within each rod section (figure 1B).

Next, stagger the nodes. Lay the six strips that will comprise the tip section of the rod in their proper sequence on the bench. The first strip stays put. Move the next strip about 2 in. along the length of the first. Shift the following strip another 2 in., and so on (figure 1C). This will stagger the nodes in a helix along the finished rod. Check the positions of the nodes along the entire length of the tip. If any are too close together, move the strips a little to balance them out.

Now mark and cut all the wood to length. Cut the 12 strips for the two tip sections to 47 in. long, the butt strips to 46½ in. These lengths allow 1 in. to be cut off each end after the strips have been glued together.

Filing and straightening the nodes—The 18 split strips are considerably oversize at this stage. Before proceeding with the planing, we must remove the bumps at the nodes. To flatten the nodes, place each one in a metal vise and file it down level with the enamel on the outer surface of the cane. The upper

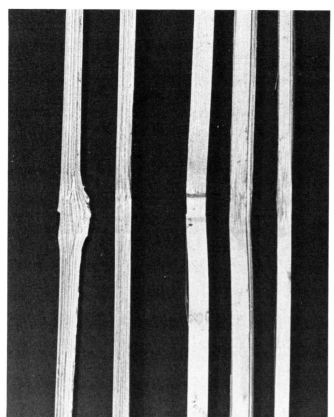

Tonkin cane will split along the grain, producing wavy strips. On the left is the side view of a node as split from the culm. The second piece has been leveled inside and out. To maintain fiber continuity, split the culm (third piece, enamel face), file the nodes level with the surface of the enamel (fourth piece), then heat-bend the strips over an alcohol lamp until they are straight (far right).

Bamboo

Bamboo is technically a grass—and the fastest growing plant in the world. Researchers have clocked some of the Orient's 1250 species at a growth rate of nearly 4 ft. a day. The type used for fly rods *(Arundinaria amabilis)* is cultivated on high, windy bluffs where a less hardy plant would fail. It grows hollow, its ¼-in. walls reinforced by solid plugs every foot or so at the nodes. The 3-in. diameter stems break through the ground and shoot up to 40 ft. tall in just two months. After this initial spurt, the walls toughen over the next 5 or 6 years until they are densely packed with long, resilient fibers. If you break a piece of high quality bamboo, the fibers will stand out in a bundle of 6-in. lances. Poor quality bamboo breaks leaving fibers only half-an-inch long. The growing conditions are part of the difference, and nowhere are they better than in a 25-sq. mile area around Tonkin, China. Tonkin cane is currently available after a 50 year hiatus in trade with China. While synthetics such as fiberglass and graphite fiber may match its lightness, stiffness and strength, they can't match the beauty and traditional appeal of Tonkin cane.

surface is now level (as shown in the photo, left), but the strips are not yet straight. Straightening the nodes is not easy, but it's critical—we want the longest fibers possible in the finished rod. If you leave a little crook or bump in the node area, the plane will rip the fibers there, undercutting the cane, which will weaken the finished fly rod.

We straighten the strips over an alcohol lamp, wearing gloves. At each node, hold the concave underside of the strip over a low flame until it becomes pliable. Then you can bend it straight. Easy does it. Too much pressure or too little heat will crack some of the fibers in the strip. The flame may scorch the underside, but these areas will be planed away.

Preliminary planing and removal of enamel—Each strip must now be planed to a tapered triangle. We use two planing forms. The first, shop-made from hard maple, has a 90° V-notch, oriented 30° to one side, 60° to the other. This V will hold a rectangular strip with its enamel side down, so a 60° angle can be planed on one of the inner sides. Don't plane the enamel face. It is the strongest part of the cane and it must be conserved. When you've planed one side of the strips to 60°, they're ready for another planing form, this one with a 60° V-notch. You can make a 60° wooden form. The easy way to do this is to joint two 1-in. by 2-in. maple boards (5 ft. long, more or less) and then bevel them to

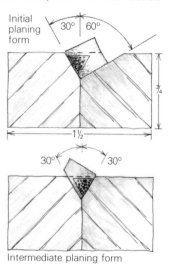

the correct angle on the jointer. Place these beveled edges together to form a V-groove. Then taper the edges of the boards until the groove has the correct size and degree of taper. The width of the faces on each strip should conform to column C in the rod-taper chart (p. 181). Fasten the boards together, and you will have a non-adjustable form—good for a rod or two. This form is so easy to make that you might as well make a few of them in graduated sizes, saving the most precise form for those last few strokes with scraper or plane.

Instead of a series of wooden forms, I now move over to the same adjustable machinist-made form that I use for final planing. I set it wide enough to give the strips good support. Place a strip, enamel face down, snugly in the 60° V-notch and plane a 60° angle on its other inner side. Then turn the strip in the form and lodge it with the enamel surface up. We want to remove as little as possible from the enamel face, but we have to true it so it registers in the form. Using a scraper (since the plane would remove too much material) take two or three passes to remove the thin layer of enamel, making the surface true and flat and bringing out the nice grain beneath. There will be no further scraping or planing on this surface.

Binding and heat-tempering—When you've planed the sides of each of the 18 strips down to approximately 50% larger than the rod designer's specified tapers, they're ready for a heat treatment to dry and toughen the cane's fibers.

The six-strip sets for each of the three rod sections (one butt, two tips) are nestled into shape, then tightly wrapped with cotton twine by a binding machine—this will keep them from warping when they're in the tempering oven. The binding machine operates by means of a stout linen cord wound into a double loop over the hex section, as shown in figure 2. A weight suspended from a pulley provides the proper tension, a couple of pounds. Turning the crank moves the rod section along a cradle. Cotton cord, feeding off its spool through a tension device, wraps around the hex in a spiral for the full length of the section. When you reverse the linen loop you get a snug criss-cross wrap.

After the three sections have been bound, they're heat-treated in an oven to temper the bamboo and increase its resilience. My oven is a length of heavy-gauge aluminum pipe with a perforated propane-fueled gas pipe underneath. The three rod sections are placed inside and rotated by a small rotisserie motor. The sections cook for two hours at about 350°F. Then they're turned end-for-end for another two hours. The once-tight binding is now quite loose, because the cane has shrunk from moisture loss.

Final planing—With the binding removed, the 18 strips are ready for final planing. My final planing form, made of twin steel bars, as shown in the photo on the following page, has screws set every 5 in. One-eighth turn of a screw opens or closes the notch 0.001 in. A 30° angle on the inside edge of each bar forms the required 60° V-notch. The angles are machined on both top and bottom of the form—one for thin tips, the other for hefty butt sections.

I start with the screws of the form adjusted larger than the final taper specifications. I gradually plane the sections, still oversize, to their required taper, alternating the two inner faces. I prefer to begin with a Stanley No. 60 low-angle plane set to take a 0.004 in. or 0.005 in. shaving. Measure the shavings with a micrometer—you want to know how much bamboo you're removing with each pass. Keep the plane level with each sweep to maintain a perfect triangle. Flip the stock between every couple of passes.

You will note that the strips are becoming quite flexible when they are bent in one plane (perpendicular to the enamel face), yet are much stiffer when bent sideways. The hexagonal glue-up will maximize this directional stiffness.

The strips will still be considerably oversize. What we are aiming for is not the final size but the correct taper, so we can take full-length passes. When the taper is right to within 0.010 in., go to a precise plane such as the Stanley No. 9½. This tool, like the low-angle plane, must be razor sharp. Taking off shavings of 0.002 in. with each pass, work each strip down. It's a slow process. Check each strip frequently with a micrometer, as you plane the bamboo down closer and closer

Fig. 2: Rod-wrapping machine

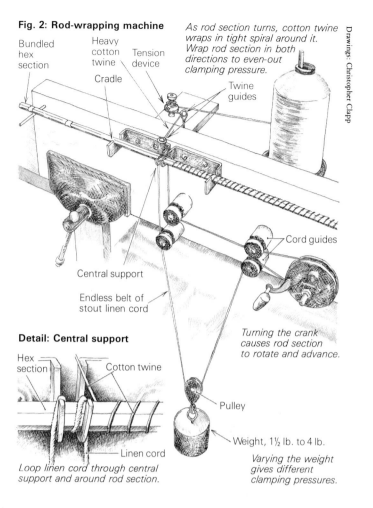

As rod section turns, cotton twine wraps in tight spiral around it. Wrap rod section in both directions to even-out clamping pressure.

Bundled hex section

Heavy cotton twine

Tension device

Cradle

Twine guides

Cord guides

Central support

Endless belt of stout linen cord

Turning the crank causes rod section to rotate and advance.

Pulley

Weight, 1½ lb. to 4 lb.

Varying the weight gives different clamping pressures.

Detail: Central support

Hex section

Cotton twine

Linen cord

Loop linen cord through central support and around rod section.

Drawings: Christopher Clapp

toward the perfect taper. Perfection is when each strip conforms precisely to the design at every 5 in. along its length.

Gluing—Now bundle the thin strips together in proper order, and bind the sections with masking tape every 10 or 12 inches. Using a razor blade, cut each tape so the hex can be opened up and spread apart on the bench. Saturate the exposed edges with strong waterproof and heat-resistant glue, using a wide bristle brush. I use Nelson's Urac 185 or Elmer's resorcinol glue. A 7½-ft. rod with an extra tip will show more than 60 linear ft. of glue line. The Urac formula is honey-colored and thus invisible. The Elmer's will leave a purplish threadline joint.

Tape

With glue applied to all surfaces, fold the strips back into their hex shape (the tape indexes them) and wipe off excess glue. Then re-bind the section with the wrapping machine and wipe off as much squeezed-out glue as you can. Before hanging the section up to dry, hand-twist out any curves to minimize the final straightening procedure later on.

Filing and sanding—After the glued sections have cured for two or three days, cut and pull off the glue-hardened binding

A machine shop made this adjustable steel planing form. The top side is for rod tips, the bottom for butts. Turning the screws adjusts the form to 0.001-in. tolerances at 5-in. intervals along its length.

Heat from an alcohol lamp softens the bamboo fibers and allows rod straightening. Keep the rod moving to avoid scorching it.

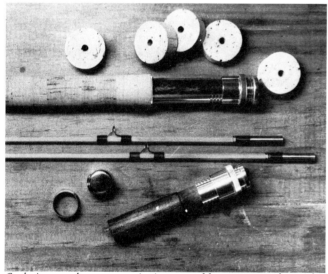

Cork rings, reel seat, mesquite insert, and butt cap, together with a finished rod grip that has been turned to shape.

cord. With a smooth file, clean off the bumps and humps of remaining glue. But remove only glue residue, don't disturb any of the cane surface. Take care to file flat and not to round any edges off the hex. The butt is fairly easy to file, but filing can be mighty tricky on the last 15 in. of each tip, where the diameter goes down to 0.063 in.

Now run a sanding block with 400-grit sandpaper over each surface. Finish up with 600 grit. When I have completed this painstaking business of filing and sanding one of my rods, I usually knock off for a day or two and go fishing.

Final straightening, fitting of hardware and reel seat—
Now sight down each of the flats for any bow, curve or twist. Over the alcohol burner, heat the cane where it requires corrections, moving the section actively to keep from scorching it. When cane and glue become pliable, crooks and curves can be eased straight. This trick also works to straighten older rods that have gone out of shape.

To mount the nickel-silver ferrules that will connect the rod sections, round off the edges at the end of the hex in the lathe. Removing too much bamboo will result in a weak point in the rod, so don't use too small a ferrule size. You want a pretty tight slip-on fit. Glue the ferrule on with a five-minute epoxy, which sets with slight expansion. Handgrips are made from cork rings that can be bought with various sized holes through their centers. Boil the rings to soften them, slide them up the butt section, and glue them together. When they have dried, turn them down on the lathe to shape. Then fit the reel seat and its wooden sleeve insert (I use mesquite).

Wrapping of guides, varnishing—Well, you now have a handcrafted split-bamboo rod blank. All that's needed for completion is to wrap on the line guides, install a tip-top guide on each tip and varnish the cane. Most commercial rods use strong but bulky nylon for wrapping, but a fine split-

This adjustable guide-wrapping tool keeps the thread at the proper tension. Turning the rod produces a silk-smooth wrapping that secures the guide. The wrapping will be varnished for protection.

bamboo rod calls for traditional pure silk. A rod-wrapping tool, which works like a simplified, finger-powered version of the binding machine, keeps the correct tension on the thread by means of a clutch or by the pressure of a spring against the spool. The rod section is turned against this tension until each guide is snugly wrapped in place. For the sake of tradition, I've added decorative intermediate windings between the guides on this rod—they are not necessary for strength.

After you have wrapped the guides along the rod section, at appropriate intervals which you can judge from the full-size photograph, treat the silk with a coat or two of color preserver to prevent its darkening when it's varnished. Then clean the bamboo thoroughly. It is traditional to write the maker's name, the rod length and the weight line for which it was designed on the flats of the shaft near the grip. Use permanent India ink; the rod may last a hundred years.

Varnishing is another meticulous job and must be done in a warm, dust-free room. I use tung-oil varnish and red-sable brushes. While the varnish is drying, I make a ferrule plug to keep the female ferrule free of dust or dirt when the rod is not in use. I use ebony, but any hardwood will do. Turn a 2-in. long, ⅜-in. sq. piece to about ⅟₃₂ in. less than the male ferrule, leaving a larger decorative knob on one end. Then glue on a ½-in. wide cork ring to the part that will fit into the female ferrule. When it's dry, turn the cork to the exact size of the ferrule, and cut off the excess wood.

In between coats of varnish (three or four coats applied over a span of some six or eight dry days) you can sew a cloth sack partitioned to fit the rod sections. An aluminum tube for storage and travel will protect your work. ☐

Les Beitz makes split-bamboo fly rods in Austin, Texas, researching and working from rod specifications that were developed by the craft's most notable designers. He spends about 95 hours working on each $600 rod.

Forms, tapers and materials

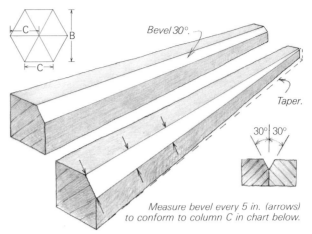

Measure bevel every 5 in. (arrows) to conform to column C in chart below.

To make the tapered planing form, square-up and joint two hardwood pieces. Bevel a corner of each piece to 30° for its full length. Then taper one face of each piece, so the bevel will match column C in the rod-taper chart. Fasten the pieces together to form a tapered V-notch. Several graduated sizes can be made for planing the rough bamboo to final size.

Rod taper specifications:

Below are the measurements for the fly rod that appears full size along the bottom of these pages. It is a medium Garrison pattern, designed for a No. 5 line. The intermediate silk windings between the guides on the L.U. Beitz rod are decorative and optional.
—Column A measures inches from the tip to the butt.
—Column B is diameter of the rod from face to face.
—Column C is the width of the bevel in the form.
—Ferrule size is ¹³⁄₆₄ in., and the guide spacing may be judged from the photograph.

	Tip Section			Butt Section	
A	B	C	A	B	C
0	0.063	0.036	50	0.206	0.119
5	0.078	0.045	55	0.220	0.127
10	0.100	0.058	60	0.233	0.134
15	0.117	0.068	65	0.247	0.143
20	0.131	0.076	70	0.260	0.150
25	0.144	0.083	75	0.275	0.159
30	0.156	0.090	80	0.306	0.177
35	0.168	0.097	83	0.309	0.178
40	0.181	0.104	90	0.317	0.183
45	0.194	0.112	No. 4½ top guide		

Sources:

☐ **Tonkin cane culms:** Charles H. Demarest, Inc., 45 Indian Lane, P.O. Box 67, Towaco, New Jersey 07082.

☐ **Steel planing form and binding apparatus:** Hoagy Carmichael, Cliffield, Indian Hill Rd. Bedford, N.Y. 10506.

☐ **Reel seats, ferrules, aluminum tubes:** Rodon Manufacturing Co., Inc., 123 Sylvan, Newark, New Jersey 07104.

☐ **Guides, tip-tops:** Perfection Tip Company, 4550 Jackson Street, Denver, Colorado 80216.

☐ **Silk thread, cork rings, color preserver:** E. Hille, The Anglers Supply House, Inc., P.O. Box 996, Williamsport, Pennsylvania 17701.

☐ **For further reading** about rodcrafting and Everett Garrison's influence, see Hoagy B. Carmichael's *A Master's Guide to Building a Bamboo Fly Rod*, 1977, from Martha's Glen Publishing Co., Katonah, N.Y. 10536.

For the views of an innovative fisherman/rod-designer with tournament flycasting in the back of his mind, read Charles Ritz's *A Fly Fisher's Life*, 1979, Max Reinhardt, London.

Building a Stripper Canoe
Cedar and fiberglass combine to make a strong, lightweight shell

by Bruce Winterbon

A handsome boat is arguably man's most beautiful artifact, and a canoe with good lines is strikingly handsome. For centuries, canoes were made mostly of wood. American Indians perfected the birchbark canoe, a stressed bark skin over bent wooden ribs. In the 19th century, some makers replaced birchbark with canvas, others developed all-wood and cheaper canvas-covered wood canoes. Today, most canoes are mass-produced or batch-produced of aluminum, fiberglass, ABS composites or a host of molded plastics. But if you want to make a canoe at home, your best bet is wood and fiberglass. I made the stripper, a lightweight ribless canoe of thin strips of cedar reinforced with fiberglass, in my basement. The method of fabricating this light and exceedingly stiff shell is comparatively simple and could be applied, for example, to free-form cabinetry or to moderately large wood sculpture. The stripper canoe looks a lot like other canoes, but can be distinguished from its traditional predecessors by its construction. Birchbark canoes consist of a flexible framework of planking and ribs that has no shape without the stressed skin of the bark, but these canoes need not be small or flimsy. Large birchbark canoes plied the fur-trade routes. Up to 36 ft. long, they held crews of 7 to 15 men, along with all their provisions, gear and payloads of up to $3\frac{1}{2}$ tons. In the 19th century, several companies in Ontario built fine lightweight canoes of wide, thin, carefully fitted cedar planks and ribs, which were made waterproof by coats of shellac or varnish. These companies, however, were driven out of business by the introduction of cheaper, canvas-covered, cedar-strip canoes, which are still popular today. This type of canoe required less skilled handwork to make, and it sold for half the price. Here, unlike the birchbark canoe, the canvas skin covers a rigid assembly of ribs and planks already in the shape of a canoe.

In an age when most canoes are mass-produced, a cedar stripper is a standout.

The stripper's fiberglass skin covers both sides of a wooden shell glued up of thin, narrow cedar strips—hence its name. The fiberglass and wood combination has the same properties as an I-beam: the two layers of fiberglass are the plates and the wood is the web. The structure is exceedingly stiff but brittle, and a stripper may not be flexible enough for white-water canoeing.

Some woodworkers may dislike fiberglass because it's plastic, not wood. If so, they can use it to reinforce only the back or hidden side of a structure, although this surrenders an enormous amount of rigidity. Some may also appease their conscience by considering the fiberglass layer to be just an elaborate, transparent finish. The polyester resin used in fiberglass is about as dark as varnish, and when the resin wets it the fiberglass cloth seems to disappear. In the following I will outline the method I used to construct a stripper hull, and suggest variations appropriate for other projects.

The plans—Designing a canoe is complicated, beyond the inexperienced maker, so I bought plans from the U.S. Canoe Association for their "cruiser" canoe, and consulted their manual, *Construction Techniques for Wood Strip Canoes,* and David Hazen's book, *The Stripper's Guide to Canoe Building.* The USCA book and plans can be ordered from Larry Hempel, USCA Treas., 15 S. 12th St., St. Charles, Ill. 60174. David Hazen's book is published by Tamal Vista Publications, 222 Madrone Ave., Larkspur, Calif. 94939.

These books and the plans tell you how to build the boat's hull, its thwarts, seats, gunwales, decks and accessories. I will concentrate here only on the hull—although the fittings may take longer to make than the hull does. I soon learned that there is no single, right way to proceed, yet the broad outlines are fairly definite. I tried to improve on the manuals' techniques by making tighter, stronger glue joints.

The stripper is built over forms, called stations, attached to a rigid beam, or strongback. The shape of the canoe is determined by the shape and spacing of the stations; the strongback provides rigid support for the stations. The $\frac{1}{4}$-in. thick cedar strips are bent, held tight to the forms with staples (which eventually have to be removed) and glued to each other. The completed shell is smoothed on the outside and fiberglassed over. Then it is removed from the forms and smoothed and glassed on the inside. Last, the resin on the outside is sanded smooth.

Strongback—The strongback is a rigid beam that runs down the center of the length of the canoe, which is built upside down on top of it. My strongback was three 2x4s bolted together, but two 2x6s, or even a U- or box-beam of plywood or particleboard will do. Because the canoe tapers at each end, the last foot or so of the strongback should be narrower than the rest. If you make a lumber strongback, let it sit and stabilize in the workplace for a week or so after assembling it. Mine warped a little during this period, and I had to put another 2x4 on edge under the strongback to flatten it. Fasten it to a pair of sawhorses raised to workbench height and leave room on the sawhorses to fasten a simple planing jig, running parallel to the strongback. Fasten a taut line along, but not touching, one side of the strongback and adjust the sawhorses to level this line. All further measurements should be to this line.

Stations—My stations were made of plywood, fixed at right angles to the strongback, centered on it, and spaced about a foot apart. A canoe has long, gentle curves, so if your project is flatter than a canoe and its planking is thicker than $\frac{1}{4}$ in., you could spread the stations out a bit; for thinner planking and tighter curves, move them closer together. I traced the outlines from the plans, bandsawed the rough shape, and sanded to the pencil line against a rigid sanding disc. If you don't have a stationary disc sander, coarse garnet paper glued to a plywood disc mounted on the radial-arm saw or tablesaw arbor works well. There is no need to bevel the forms.

Lay out the station positions on the strongback. I bolted the plywood to short 2x4s that were screwed to the strongback. Oversized bolt holes in the plywood permit fine adjustment. The station centerlines should be plumb and in line with the centerline of the strongback and each other. Their horizontal cross lines should be the same distance from the stretched reference line, and level. Check and adjust the alignment the next day, and again the following day. Making a canoe is a long job and it's too easy to relax the tolerances along the way. I found that some of the 2x4 blocks had rotated on their screw mounts, so the stations weren't perpendicular to the taut line and the strongback. A temporary strip stapled to the strongback held them square. Put masking tape on the edges of the stations so you don't glue the cedar strips to the plywood.

Stempieces—I made two-part stempieces, an outer part of form-laminated ash and a narrower inner one of solid ash sawkerfed to take the bend. The thin strips butt against the joint between the two. To laminate the stempiece I used resorcinol glue, because it is strong and waterproof and allows a long setup time, though the dark red glue lines might be unacceptable on other projects. The stempiece laminates were cut overlong, glued up on a plywood form, then cut to length. One end was butted and screwed to the top of the first station and to the end of the strongback. These screws must be removed later, after the canoe begins to take shape, but before there are too many cedar strips in the way.

Planking—Making the strips for the canoe's hull is next, and the wood of choice is red cedar. It is lightweight, rot-resistant

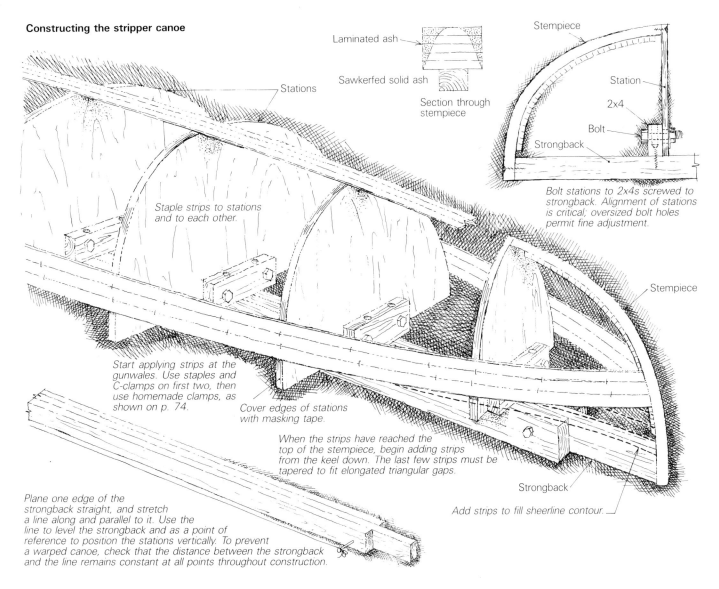

Constructing the stripper canoe

Laminated ash

Sawkerfed solid ash

Section through stempiece

Stempiece

Station

2x4

Bolt

Strongback

Stations

Bolt stations to 2x4s screwed to strongback. Alignment of stations is critical; oversized bolt holes permit fine adjustment.

Staple strips to stations and to each other.

Stempiece

Start applying strips at the gunwales. Use staples and C-clamps on first two, then use homemade clamps, as shown on p. 74.

Cover edges of stations with masking tape.

When the strips have reached the top of the stempiece, begin adding strips from the keel down. The last few strips must be tapered to fit elongated triangular gaps.

Strongback

Plane one edge of the strongback straight, and stretch a line along and parallel to it. Use the line to level the strongback and as a point of reference to position the stations vertically. To prevent a warped canoe, check that the distance between the strongback and the line remains constant at all points throughout construction.

Add strips to fill sheerline contour.

and easy to work, and thin strips of it bend without breaking. Since the surface of the wood will be covered by fiberglass and resin, the wood need not be particularly smooth or hard.

Because the two layers of fiberglass cloth and the wood act like an I-beam, the thicker the strips (the web of the beam), the stiffer the structure. Stiffness increases exponentially as a function of the depth of the web, so you mustn't let thicknesses vary much, or the hull's strength won't be uniform. For my 18½-ft. long canoe, I used ¼-in. thick strips, ripped from 20-ft. boards, nominally 1 in. thick. I anchored an upright to the floor 10 ft. ahead of the saw to help me line each board up with the fence. With a support for the long boards as they come off the saw table, one person can push-feed the stock while another holds it against the fence at the blade.

I checked the strips with a micrometer locked with masking tape at ³⁄₁₆ in. and broke them where they passed through it. If this occurred near the middle of a strip, I scarfed the pieces together after cutting out the thin spot.

Clamps—You need to make special clamps. Cut some hardwood blocks to fit between the stations and groove them down their length wide enough to fit over the edge of the cedar strips. These blocks are held in place by wedges fitted against U-clamps, made of plywood or hardwood, that clamp to the stations. I used wood scraps from the stations for spacers, and shim shingles for wedges.

Planing—The appearance of the job depends on the care with which the strips are fitted, and how well they match for color and figure. You will need a planing jig to help you bevel and taper each piece neatly against its neighbor on the form. In the edge of a 2x4, cut a groove about half as deep as a strip is wide and wide enough to hold a strip on edge. Fasten the 2x4 to the sawhorses, alongside the canoe form, and put a stop at one end. After fitting the strip to its neighbor by trial and error along its whole length, trim one end to fit against the stempiece. The second end is trimmed at the

last moment as you glue up. The strip's exact length depends on its curve and is difficult to get right without going through the entire clamping procedure before gluing.

Glue—Fiberglass will hold everything together, so the manuals suggest white glue. Instead, I used Aerolite, a waterproof, urea-formaldehyde glue that is colorless, doesn't creep and will fill some gaps. It's available from Leavens Bros., Ltd., 2555 Derry Rd. E, Mississauga, Ontario L4T 1A1, Canada, or from Woodcraft Supply.

Assembly—Start attaching the strips at the gunwales and work upward toward the keel. Glue and C-clamp the first two strips on each side to each other and staple them to the stations. You can't use the wedge clamps until these first strips are set unless there is room on the stations to clamp from both sides. I ran the strips fairly straight and didn't attempt to follow the sheerline contour of the gunwales that would rise at each end of the finished canoe. Instead, I added short pieces to the ends later to make up the desired rise.

As the strips rise up the form, position each new one on the form, then tighten the U-clamps over the stations, leaving a bit of space between the clamps and the long blocks placed over the strip. Spread glue along mating surfaces for 2 ft. or 3 ft., then drive wedges between the long blocks and the U-clamps to put pressure on the glue joint. Staple the strips to the stations, one leg in each strip. If the strips don't line up between stations, staple them together there, too. (I used about 1500 staples.) Then move to the next section. Do one strip on each side, then wait for the glue to set. Keep the number of strips on each side about equal, to balance the stresses on the stations. And remember to remove the inside screws holding the stempieces to the end stations before the strips get in the way.

When the strips rise to the ends of the stempieces, it takes more effort to bend the strips into place. Start working from the keel line down. As you approach the previously glued

Clamping the strips

Glue, clamp and staple strips 2 ft. to 3 ft. at a time. Drive wedges between U-clamps and hardwood blocks to apply pressure.

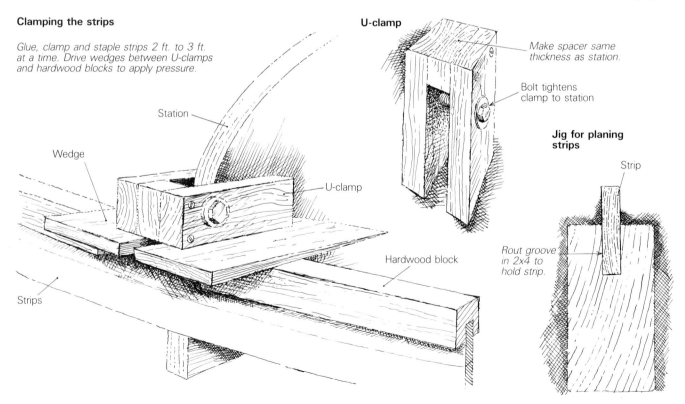

Station

Wedge

U-clamp

Strips

U-clamp

Make spacer same thickness as station.

Bolt tightens clamp to station

Jig for planing strips

Strip

Hardwood block

Rout groove in 2x4 to hold strip.

Strongback, stations and planing jig (left), with groove for holding strips on edge, ready for fitting stempieces and first strips.

strips, put in tapered pieces to fill in the last irregular spaces.

The manuals say that the staple holes won't show in the finished canoe, but this isn't true. However, assembling the hull without putting 3000 staple holes in it would be much trickier. You need to hold the strips tight to the stations and, between stations, flush with each other. You would have to start by nailing on an extra strip along the gunwales and clamping the first strip against it. Then you could use external forms, dogs fitted to the U-clamps, or elastic bands or belts to hold the strips tight against the stations. The clamping force exerted by a belt or band is proportional to the curvature of the band. Hence, on a flat portion you'd need lots of wedging, so you'd have to make a trial run, dry-clamping carefully. Or, you could replace the staples between stations with waxed wooden-faced C-clamps.

Smoothing the hull—When the hull is completed, pull the staples (my sheath knife, blade flat against the wood, worked well here and it took me only about 30 minutes). Next, smooth the surface. I used a plane, spokeshave and paring chisel, and finished with an oscillating sander. Smoothing was the most enjoyable part of the whole project: from the initial mess of roughsawn boards, so rough that even the ultimate shape had been somewhat obscure, the shape and grain gradually appeared.

Fiberglassing—The outside of the canoe is fiberglassed after it has been smoothed but before it is removed from the form. The materials are nasty, toxic and possibly carcinogenic. All the fluids are flammable, and their vapors are explosive. If you don't know something about using fiberglass cloth and resin, get someone who does to help you. (A good book on working with fiber-reinforced plastics is the *Boat Builder's Manual,* by C. Walbridge, published by Wildwater Design Kits, 230 Penllyn Pike, Penllyn, Pa. 19422.)

Six-ounce (per square yard) boat cloth is the usual fiberglass covering for stripper canoes. The cloth should be bought in a width sufficient to cover three-quarters of the canoe's hull circumference. Four pieces, each the length of the canoe, will cover the canoe, with some overlap inside and out. Build up the ends to about four layers, cutting the extra pieces on the bias so they will stretch to conform to the extreme curva-

ture around the ends. Fit all the cloth dry, and get it to lie smoothly before applying the resin.

Red cedar can contain oils that inhibit the setting of polyester resins, so I sealed the hull with two coats of clear, nitrocellulose brushing lacquer. Use a fiberglass resin formulated for boatbuilding; general-purpose resins are too brittle. I used about 2½ gallons on my canoe. Buy a resin without added wax—such resins won't set up hard and will allow the base coats to bond together well. For the final coat, add about as much wax as hardener—paraffin wax dissolved in styrene monomer—to the last resin batch. The dissolved wax will float to the surface, making a protective covering that keeps out oxygen and water vapor so the resin can fully harden. The wax coating is later sanded off.

It takes two to four people to apply the fiberglass and resin. Everyone should have rubber gloves, and you will need a beaker for measuring resin, a dispenser or syringe for measuring out hardener, paintbrushes, rollers and plastic squeegees. Acetone keeps things clean—set out one pot for dirty brushes and such messes, and another for final rinsing. We used Lestoil, a heavy-duty household cleaner containing pine oil, to clean up afterward.

To apply the fiberglass, smooth the first piece of cloth into place dry and work the resin well into it, adding the other piece as soon as the first is well wetted. For a smooth finish, keep painting on more small batches of resin as soon as the last ones become tacky, until you can look obliquely at the surface and no longer see the weave of the cloth. Then apply the last, wax-impregnated batch of resin. Let this sit overnight. The surface will be highly pebbled, but don't sand it yet—you'll just mark it up later when you glass the inside.

Now the canoe can be pulled off the frame. It has little strength with only one side fiberglassed, so gently work it loose from the masking tape on the stations, move it carefully and support it well. Though it's easy to work on the convex outside of the canoe, cleaning up the concave inside is more difficult. I made a little plane with a rounded sole, using a piece of an old file for the iron, to plane the inside. An offset-blade paring chisel would have been useful, too. I used a flexible disc sander chucked in an electric drill in some of the more awkward places, then fiberglassed the inside. The inside surface gets much less resin than the outside because it should be a bit rough, otherwise the least bit of water will make it as slippery as an ice rink.

After the resin on the inside has dried thoroughly, sand down the outside with wet-or-dry paper. In contrast to the inside, the outside should be smooth to cut down on friction as the canoe moves through the water.

Sanding the resin will give a fine satin finish, but try not to sand into the fiberglass cloth, as it will scratch permanently and become opaque. I started with 40-grit and went up to 320-grit. Despite the wet-or-dry paper, there will be plenty of dust. Wear a particle mask, or you risk impairing your health. Keep rinsing the slurry off, keep the paper wet, and change paper frequently to get the maximum cutting action. I used the oscillating sander for most of this job. Add gunwales, thwarts and seats, and your canoe is finished. Mine turned out to be light enough to carry easily: it weighs a little under 65 lb.—wet, of course. □

Bruce Winterbon, of Deep River, Ontario, is a physicist and devoted amateur woodworker. Photos by Lorna Bourns.

Another approach to the stripper

by Richard Swanson

My colleagues Terry Hesse and Boyd Whitt, metalworking and woodworking teachers at the Madison Area Technical College in Wisconsin, built their strippers as school projects. Their "voyager" canoes are a fuller shape than Winterbon's cruiser canoe (see pp. 182-185)—and they weigh only 55 lb., 10 lb. lighter. The men also found the U.S. Canoe Association's manual helpful, though their methods of construction do differ from Winterbon's. For example, they glued up the strips with a casein glue and cured it instantly with the school's high-frequency Wood Welder, so they didn't need clamps. Even so, they put well over 300 hours into each canoe. The result of all that time and attention, Hesse claims, is a canoe that will outperform an aluminum canoe any time. Whitt agrees, "It will take a lot of punishment, but anyone who has made a cedar-strip canoe remembers all the hundreds of hours of knifing, fitting and nudging cedar strips into place. The first time I scraped bottom made me feel like I'd dropped a chisel on a French-polished tabletop."

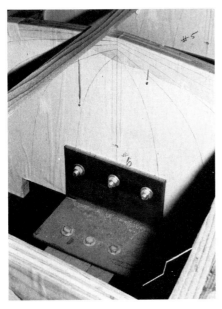

Whitt and Hesse fastened their stations to the strongback with heavy angle-iron. Both men stress the importance of carefully cutting the stations and accurately aligning them on the strongback. A twisted canoe will snake through the water, no matter how expert the canoe-ist may be. They used ¼-in. by ¾-in. cedar strips to form the shell. To make the strips self-aligning, Whitt shaped the edges with standard Rockwell ½-in. flute and bead three-wing shaper cutters on an overarm router. As each individual strip was added to the form, the cutters were also used as hand scrapers to fit the mating edges perfectly. The cedar strips were then nailed to the stations. Curing the glue instantly by using high-frequency radio waves eliminated the need for clamps, and the wait, as each glue joint dried.

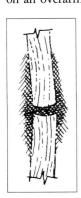

Whitt and Hesse formed the contoured sheerline of the gunwales by bending the first strips to the form, rather than by adding tapered strips later. Then they worked directly up the form until they reached the keel. This creates a different pattern than Winterbon's method does, and some tricky fitting on the bottom of the canoe. After the strips rise to the level of the stempiece, the ends of the remaining strips must be trimmed to fit the taper at bow and stern. To do this accurately, the pieces were roughly shaped, then wriggled into carbon paper placed in the gap. The ink showed high points that needed final trimming, which was done using the round and hollow shaper cutters as scrapers.

The men ran their strips past interior stempieces attached to the strongback and first stations. The laminated ash stempieces are trapezoidal in section and about ½ in. thick. After the outside of the hull was sanded, the ends of the strips were squared with the stempieces, leaving a ¾-in. surface to which was glued an outer, laminated ash stempiece, triangular in section.

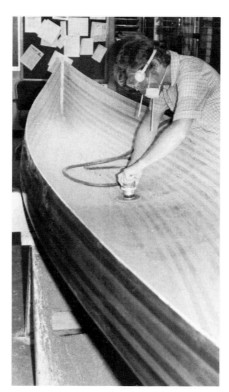

The slots running the length of the gunwales in the finished canoe let water drain when the canoe is turned over to dry, and they cut down on weight. Both men took great care fitting the gunwales, thwarts, seats and decks. Hesse made his of walnut and ash, Whitt of teak. The boats (Whitt's is shown at bottom of page) are fitted with the precision of a piece of fine furniture. ☐

The outsides of the completed hulls were smoothed with rasps and sandpaper. Whitt hand-sanded, starting with 60-grit, finishing with 320-grit. Belt sanders can easily gouge the soft cedar, and orbital sanders create a lot of dust and a terrific racket—the canoe acts as a sounding board. Whitt and Hesse recommend a thin fiberglass cloth, about 4-oz., and a standard resin. To keep weight down, they applied only one coat of fiberglass to the hull, doubling up for strength at the bow and stern. They allowed two days for the resin to cure—if you sand too early, the resin will turn into a gummy mess.

Whitt power-sanded the inside of his stripper—less noise—and both men used the shop's air-powered flexible disc sander. The inside surface of the canoe should be rough: if it's too smooth, a little water in the bottom will have you sliding around. Using only enough resin to cover the fiberglass cloth leaves a suitably pebbly surface.

Photos: Richard Swanson

187

Building a Lapstrake Boat
A traditional design that's ideal for the beginner

by Simon Watts—drawings by Sam Manning

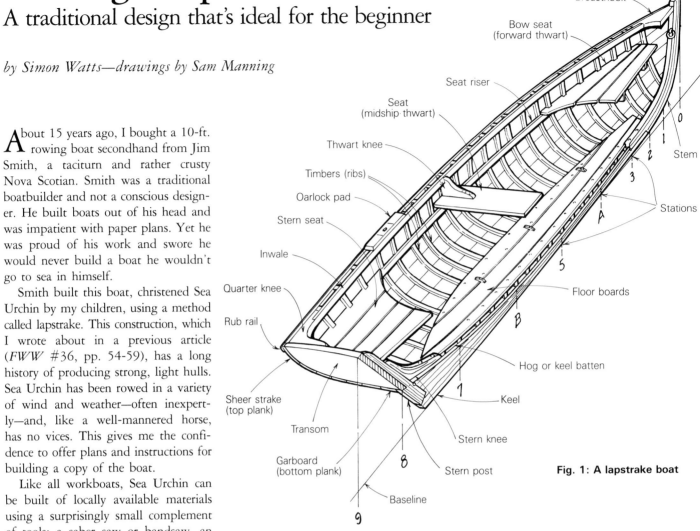

Fig. 1: A lapstrake boat

Labels: Breasthook, Bow seat (forward thwart), Seat riser, Seat (midship thwart), Thwart knee, Timbers (ribs), Oarlock pad, Stern seat, Inwale, Quarter knee, Rub rail, Sheer strake (top plank), Transom, Garboard (bottom plank), Baseline, Stern post, Stern knee, Keel, Hog or keel batten, Floor boards, Stations, Stem

About 15 years ago, I bought a 10-ft. rowing boat secondhand from Jim Smith, a taciturn and rather crusty Nova Scotian. Smith was a traditional boatbuilder and not a conscious designer. He built boats out of his head and was impatient with paper plans. Yet he was proud of his work and swore he would never build a boat he wouldn't go to sea in himself.

Smith built this boat, christened Sea Urchin by my children, using a method called lapstrake. This construction, which I wrote about in a previous article (*FWW* #36, pp. 54-59), has a long history of producing strong, light hulls. Sea Urchin has been rowed in a variety of wind and weather—often inexpertly—and, like a well-mannered horse, has no vices. This gives me the confidence to offer plans and instructions for building a copy of the boat.

Like all workboats, Sea Urchin can be built of locally available materials using a surprisingly small complement of tools: a saber saw or bandsaw, an electric drill and the usual assortment of hand tools. Building this boat is within the reach of even a novice woodworker. In fact, an amateur woodworker friend of mine built one as part of this article's preparation.

Using the traditional lapstrake technique, the boat is constructed right side up, on a hefty frame called a strongback. Two molds, which act as guides in setting the boat's shape, are mounted on the strongback, and the planks or strakes are laid up around them. After the planks have been riveted or nailed together at the overlaps, reinforcing timbers (ribs) are added to stiffen the hull.

Materials—The original Sea Urchin is planked with relatively heavy, ½-in. white pine, to withstand hard use and Nova Scotia's winters. But for recreational use the boat can safely be planked with ⅜-in. white pine, Northern white cedar, red cedar, or cypress. The other parts—transom, thwarts, keel, knees and timbers—are all red oak. In the cold, salt waters of Nova Scotia this combination gives a reasonable lifespan—20 years or more. For warm, freshwater service I suggest the more durable white oak instead of red.

Kiln-dried wood is seldom used for boatbuilding. It is much harder to work than green wood and isn't as amenable to steaming. Once in the water, planks swell to seal any leaks, but kiln-dried stock can swell too much, straining the fastenings. Planking lumber can be barely air-dry, verging on green.

It will continue to dry out on the boat, which helps to "set" the boat's shape. All the oak parts should be air-dry except the timbers, which steam best when green. If you can't buy green oak, soak the pieces in salt water for a week before steaming and installing them—the salt inhibits the formation of fungus.

Butt logs with a natural curve or sweep to the grain make ideal planking—there's less waste and they're stronger since the grain follows the curve of the planks.

Sea Urchin has six knees—wooden brackets that brace the transom, seats and other structures that meet at angles—and they are best cut from natural crooks, wood with curved grain which occurs where tree limbs and roots join the trunk. Sea Urchin has red oak knees, but applewood, tamarack, spruce and locust are often used. You can rough the knees out with a chainsaw right on the tree, well in advance, and coat them with linseed oil so they'll season without checking. Knees and stems can be steam-bent or form-laminated using a waterproof glue (*FWW* #17, p. 57) such as Aerolite. Hardware, fittings and paint can be mail-ordered from Duck Trap Woodworking (PO Box 88, Lincolnville, Maine 04849) or Wooden Boat Shop (1007 N.E. Boat St., Seattle, Wash. 98105), or bought locally from marine suppliers.

You should work in an environment that is cooler and more humid than is usual for a furniture workshop, as dry air will cause fresh-sawn oak to check.

Strongback and molds—Lapstrake boats are best built right side up so each strake, or plank, can be fastened without the need of a helper underneath, and so you can see the evolving shape of the boat without standing on your head. Most boatmakers build these craft on a strongback frame like that shown in the photo at left and in figure 2. If you have a choice, place the strongback at right angles to and about 6 ft. from the workbench so you'll have access to the bench and both sides of the boat.

With the strongback built, construction of the boat begins with the molds, transom and backbone. These parts will form the basic shape of the boat, and the planks will be hung around them. Refer to p. 90 for an explanation of determining the mold and transom dimensions. I usually make full-size patterns on heavy paper folded in half, which assures symmetry when opened up. Make up the molds from ¾-in. dry pine, mark the centerlines and sheer lines, and leave "ears" projecting to attach bracing, as in figure 3.

Make the transom from two pieces of oak joined with cleats fastened with bronze screws. Don't

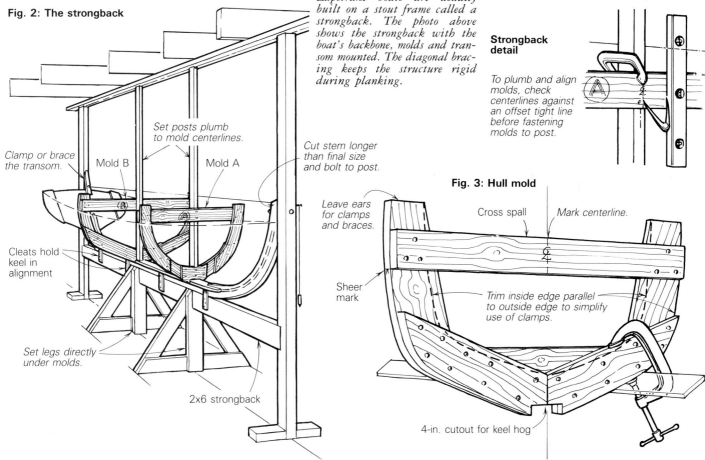

Fig. 2: The strongback

Lapstrake boats are usually built on a stout frame called a strongback. The photo above shows the strongback with the boat's backbone, molds and transom mounted. The diagonal bracing keeps the structure rigid during planking.

Clamp or brace the transom.

Set posts plumb to mold centerlines.

Mold B

Mold A

Cut stem longer than final size and bolt to post.

Cleats hold keel in alignment

Set legs directly under molds.

2x6 strongback

Strongback detail

To plumb and align molds, check centerlines against an offset tight line before fastening molds to post.

Fig. 3: Hull mold

Cross spall

Mark centerline.

Leave ears for clamps and braces.

Sheer mark

Trim inside edge parallel to outside edge to simplify use of clamps.

4-in. cutout for keel hog

leave these cleats off in favor of simply gluing-up the transom, or you'll have only end grain to nail into when fastening the planks at the stern. After you have assembled the transom, set your bandsaw or saber saw to 32° and cut the bevel as shown in figure 4. You'll need to adjust this angle with a spokeshave later, to give the planks a solid landing.

Backbone—Before attaching the molds and transom to the strongback, you must make the boat's backbone. This consists of the keel, the stem, the stern post and its connecting knee, and the keel batten, or hog, to which the first plank will be attached. Refer to figures 5 and 6 for an explanation of these parts, and make a full-size pattern from the drawing and table on p. 196, which you can "loft" into templates to lay out the shapes directly on the stock.

The joints that connect these three pieces, intended to minimize end-grain exposure to water, are critical and must fit well. They can be cut with a bandsaw or handsaw, and then cleaned up with a plane or chisel. The stem joint, called a scarf, is fastened with two bronze carriage bolts and nuts. The stern post is fastened to the keel with a $\frac{5}{16}$-in. bronze carriage bolt (figure 5) countersunk at both ends and bunged outboard. This joint will be further strengthened with bolts when the transom and stern knee are mounted. Before assembling the joints, give them a thick coat of a commercial bedding compound such as Boatlife.

After you've bolted up these joints, drill $\frac{3}{8}$-in. holes through the joint lines. Drive a cylindrical plug of dry pine through the hole (see figures 5 and 6 for exact location), and cut it flush on both sides. This plug, called a stopwater, keeps water from seeping along the joint into the boat.

The next step is to make the hog and attach it to the keel with five through $\frac{5}{16}$-in. bronze carriage bolts, located so they won't interfere with the placement of timbers later. The top surface of the keel must be planed and squared so the hog, when sprung down to it, lies flat.

Now cut and fit the hog, then remove it so that you can lay out the stem rabbet—a V-shaped step in which the plank ends land at the bow (figure 6). Experienced builders cut this out on the bench before planking, but to avoid errors I advise novices to cut a $\frac{1}{4}$-in. deep, 90° groove initially, and then to deepen and enlarge it to fit each plank as it's hung. The rabbet must be stopped at the top edge of the last plank (the sheer strake), so don't take it too far up—leave the last inch to be cut later.

To mark the stem rabbet, draw a pencil line along both sides of the keel, $\frac{3}{8}$ in. (the planking thickness) down from the keel's top edge. This

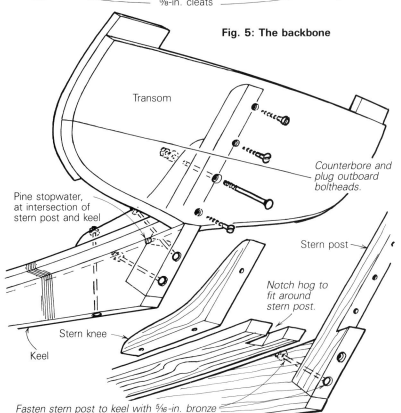

Fig. 4: The transom

Pattern represents outside face. Leave enough stock to accommodate the bevel.

¾-in. oak

Paper pattern

32°

⅝-in. cleats

Fig. 5: The backbone

Transom

Counterbore and plug outboard boltheads.

Pine stopwater, at intersection of stern post and keel

Stern post

Notch hog to fit around stern post.

Stern knee

Keel

Fasten stern post to keel with $\frac{5}{16}$-in. bronze carriage bolt countersunk at both ends.

The stern post is fastened to the keel with a bronze carriage bolt. Then the transom is attached with bronze bolts through the stern post and keel and into the stern knee. The small round plug between the stern post and keel is called a stopwater, but it is misplaced in this boat. It should be higher, just where the keel, hog and stern post intersect. Caulking cotton seals planks where they land on the transom, but bedding compound could be used instead.

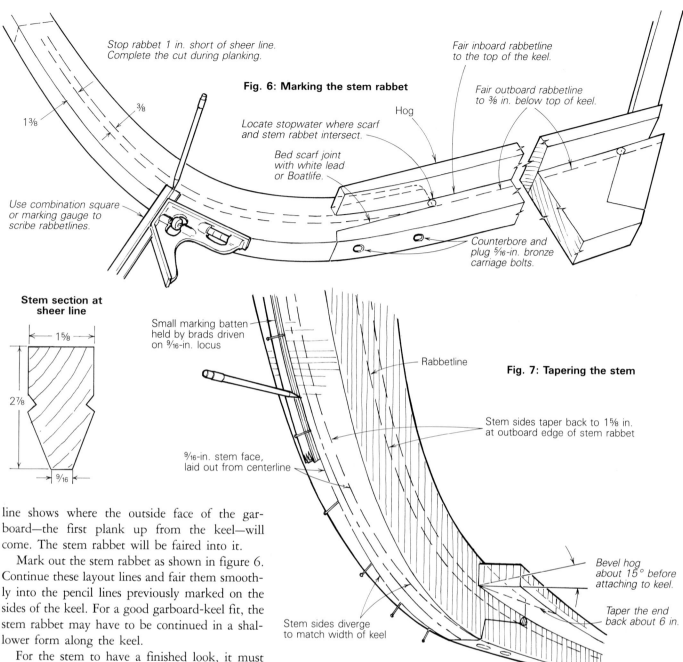

Stop rabbet 1 in. short of sheer line.
Complete the cut during planking.

Fig. 6: Marking the stem rabbet

Fair inboard rabbetline
to the top of the keel.

Fair outboard rabbetline
to ⅜ in. below top of keel.

1⅜

⅜

Hog

Locate stopwater where scarf
and stem rabbet intersect.

Bed scarf joint
with white lead
or Boatlife.

Use combination square
or marking gauge to
scribe rabbetlines.

Counterbore and
plug ⁵⁄₁₆-in. bronze
carriage bolts.

**Stem section at
sheer line**

1⅝

2⅞

⁹⁄₁₆

Small marking batten
held by brads driven
on ⁹⁄₁₆-in. locus

⁹⁄₁₆-in. stem face,
laid out from centerline

Rabbetline

Fig. 7: Tapering the stem

Stem sides taper back to 1⅝ in.
at outboard edge of stem rabbet

Bevel hog
about 15° before
attaching to keel.

Taper the end
back about 6 in.

Stem sides diverge
to match width of keel

line shows where the outside face of the garboard—the first plank up from the keel—will come. The stem rabbet will be faired into it.

Mark out the stem rabbet as shown in figure 6. Continue these layout lines and fair them smoothly into the pencil lines previously marked on the sides of the keel. For a good garboard-keel fit, the stem rabbet may have to be continued in a shallower form along the keel.

For the stem to have a finished look, it must be tapered in cross section from 1⅝ in. in thickness at the outboard stem rabbetline to ⁹⁄₁₆ in. at its leading edge. Mark out the taper, using a thin batten (figure 7) to draw a fair transition as the stem thickness increases toward the scarf and into the keel, then plane the taper.

Before bolting the hog to the keel, saw or plane about a 15° bevel on its lower edges. This angle will be correct only at the center mold, and must increase toward stem and transom to accommodate the changing angle that the garboard makes with the keel. It can be adjusted with a rabbet plane when the garboard is hung.

Now place the completed backbone on the strongback, and secure it temporarily with clamps. Then install the hog and transom. Place the two molds in their proper position and attach them to the hog with diagonal screws. Plumb the stem and the stern post, brace them firmly and then align the mold centerlines, using the method shown in the detail of the strongback on p. 83. Everything must be securely braced so it cannot move during planking.

Planking—A lapstrake boat derives much of its strength from its planks, which are clench-nailed or riveted together lengthwise in overlapping joints. Jim Smith fastened the original Sea Urchin's pine planks with galvanized nails driven in from the outside and bent over (clenched) on the inside. This method is cheap and fast, but the nails can't easily be removed for repairs and they eventually rust. I used an alternative: copper nails with a copper washer called a rove, or burr, slipped over the point and forced down into the wood with a hollow punch. The pointed end of the nail is then clipped off close to the burr and riveted over with a ball-peen hammer. Bronze screws or bronze ring-barb nails fasten the planks at stem and transom.

Begin planking by making a full-size pattern of the garboard. Use a 10-in. to 12-in. wide piece of ¼-in. thick pine or ⅛-in. Masonite (the exact width will be determined later) to cut a rough pattern, and then twist it into place and clamp it lightly, using the method outlined in figure 8 to mark and trim the pattern. Once you've fitted the pattern well into the stem rabbet and along the keel, it's time to determine the widths of the garboard and the rest of the planks. Figure 9 shows a method of determining plank widths, which are then marked on the stem, transom and molds. (For another method,

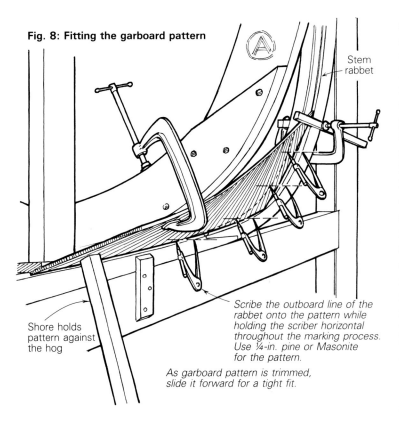

Fig. 8: Fitting the garboard pattern

Stem rabbet

Scribe the outboard line of the rabbet onto the pattern while holding the scriber horizontal throughout the marking process. Use ¼-in. pine or Masonite for the pattern.

Shore holds pattern against the hog

As garboard pattern is trimmed, slide it forward for a tight fit.

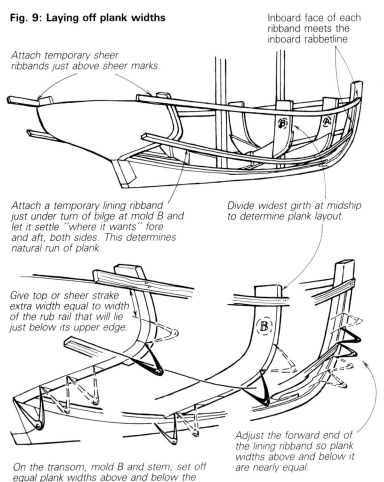

Fig. 9: Laying off plank widths

Attach temporary sheer ribbands just above sheer marks.

Inboard face of each ribband meets the inboard rabbetline

Attach a temporary lining ribband just under turn of bilge at mold B and let it settle "where it wants" fore and aft, both sides. This determines natural run of plank.

Divide widest girth at midship to determine plank layout.

Give top or sheer strake extra width equal to width of the rub rail that will lie just below its upper edge.

Adjust the forward end of the lining ribband so plank widths above and below it are nearly equal.

On the transom, mold B and stem, set off equal plank widths above and below the upper edge of the lining ribband, representing three planks below and four above. Check your marks for fairness with a batten before sawing plank stock.

refer to John Gardiner's *Building Small Classic Craft*—an invaluable book for amateur boatbuilders—which is published by International Marine, Camden, Maine 04843.) Use a straight-grained batten to mark a fair curve between the four width marks on your pattern, then saw and plane down to this line. With the pattern cut and fitted, transfer its shape to your plank (figure 10) so as to avoid dead knots, and try to take advantage of any natural sweep in the board. Any loose knots in the planking should be knocked out, and the hole reamed and plugged with a tapered pine plug dipped in Aerolite or resorcinol glue. The garboard has a considerable amount of twist toward the stem, and it is easier to do the final fitting after this twist has been steamed into it. The easiest way is to wrap it in a towel and pour on boiling water. Clamp it in place and leave it overnight to cool, then cut out the rest of the stem rabbet so the hood (bow) end fits nicely. Take time to fit the garboards properly—they are the most difficult planks to hang, and you can expect to break or otherwise spoil at least one in the process. Don't be discouraged if it doesn't go right the first time.

Before fastening the garboard, sand the inside surface, chamfer the inside corner and run a pencil line along the top outside edge of both garboards to mark the amount the next planks will overlap, ¾ in. Plane a 15° bevel away from this line. This can be done with a bench plane, but a rabbet plane with an adjustable fence is handier. To take the guesswork out of beveling laps, make a lap gauge (figure 12). Use the rabbet plane to cut the gains in the garboard and the other planks, which allow the strakes to lie flush at the stem and stern (figure 11).

Attach the garboard to the stem, hog and transom with 1-in. #10 bronze screws driven on 2-in. centers along the length of the keel and driven through the garboard into the hog. From now on, keep the boat balanced by planking evenly on both sides.

The planks on this boat are limber enough to be simply wrapped around the forms and marked directly from the edge of the plank already in place. Use slightly narrower planks where tight curves on the transom make splitting likely, or plane slight flats on the transom. Before committing planks to the saw, it's a good idea to line off one side of the boat with a batten for each intended plank-edge curve. This playing with battens until a curve "looks right" is a crucial part of lap-

Fig. 10: Marking the garboard template
(drawing is foreshortened for clarity)

Bottom edge is the line marked from stem rabbet and keel

Mark out final template width using marks at stem, molds and transom. Top edge is the fair line run through these marks with a batten.

Mark two identical garboards from template; they will be mirror opposites.

strake construction. An unsightly line cannot be painted out later, whereas flat spots and "quick" turns are apparent at this stage and easily remedied by adjusting mold alignment or shimming flat spots.

Before continuing plank work, mark the centerlines of the timbers—the reinforcing ribs that fall every 6 in.—placing the first one on the centerline of the seat. Use a batten to carry these marks up from the hog to the sheer ribbands. Timbers in the middle two-thirds of the boat run straight up and down, but it is usual to lean them slightly forward as you approach the bow and slightly aft toward the stern.

Wrap the first plank around the boat so its lower edge overlaps the upper edge of the garboard by at least ¾ in. Run a pencil along the top edge of the garboard inside the boat, and also mark the position of the transom, each mold and the stem. If a wide plank must take a severe twist, you may have to cut it roughly to shape and then put it back on the boat for a more accurate line. Use the method in figure 13 to mark the plank's width. Then, using the first strake as a pattern, mark out its mate on the opposite side of the boat. Make an identical pair by planing both edges with the planks clamped or tacked together. Then plane the bevels and the gains, making sure that the beveled surface is flat or even slightly hollow, not rounded.

When the second plank is fitted and clamped to the garboard, fasten it to the stem. Drill pilot holes for the copper lap nails roughly 2 in. apart, laid out from the center of each timber marked on the hog and ribband. Now rove and rivet the nails, leaving the nails out where the timbers will occur.

The remaining planks are marked, cut and fitted in the same way, except that the angle of bevel needed will increase as the curvature of the boat's side increases. Leave the top (sheer) strake about ½ in. wider than the marks indicate. Clamp it temporarily in place and tack a ¾-in. batten up to represent the upper edge of the sheer strake. Stand back and take a look. Starting at the transom, the curve should dip gracefully at the waist and rise jauntily toward the bow. Adjust it until the curve is pleasing, even if it misses the original pencil marks. Few things spoil the look of a boat more than a dead or an exaggerated sheer. A narrow strip called the rub rail will be attached to the outboard top edge of the sheer strake to strengthen and protect it, so this plank must be wider by an amount equal to the width of the rail.

The boat's bottom plank, called the garboard, gets a considerable twist, which can be achieved only by soaking the end in boiling water, or steaming it, and clamping it in place to cool. This bow-on view shows how the stem is tapered back from its leading edge.

Fig. 11: The gains

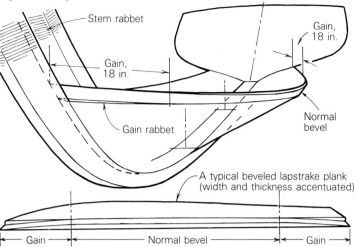

Lapped plank must lie flush in the stem rabbet and at the transom. This is done by cutting the plank bevel inward in the form of a rabbet until it runs out to a knife edge at the plank end. Transition between full lap and flush knife edge is called the gain.

Fig. 12: The lap gauge

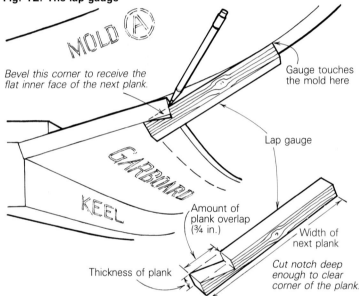

Use gauge to mark bevel angle at molds, transom and stem, and then fair to these marks by eye when planing the bevel.

Fig. 13: Marking and cutting planks

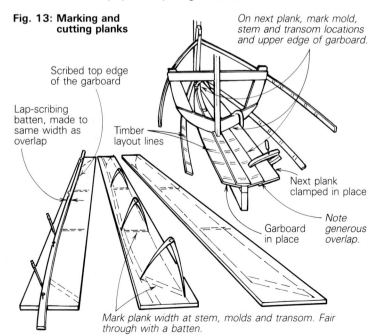

Mark plank width at stem, molds and transom. Fair through with a batten.

193

Fig. 14: Knees, breasthook and inwales

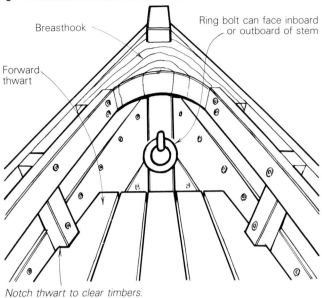

Breasthook

Ring bolt can face inboard or outboard of stem

Forward thwart

Notch thwart to clear timbers.

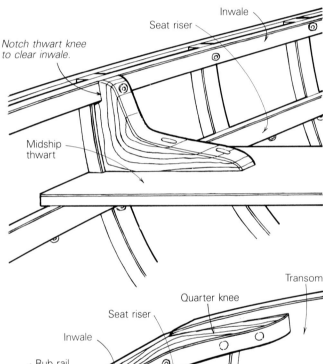

Inwale

Seat riser

Notch thwart knee to clear inwale.

Midship thwart

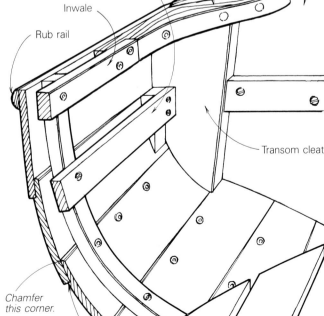

Transom

Quarter knee

Seat riser

Inwale

Rub rail

Transom cleat

Chamfer this corner.

Use bedding compound between laps (optional).

Timbering and knees—It's best to have three people for timbering, two to handle the hot timbers as they come from the steam box and one to drive in the nails from below. (For an article on steam boxes, refer to *FWW* #8, p. 40.) Choose straight-grained oak for timbers; it will be less likely to break, and a coat of raw linseed oil before steaming will make it bend better. Cut the timbers extra long to give you leverage while bending. Leave the molds in place for timbering, but remove the crossbracing. Then start nails in from the outside so they are held firmly but do not stick into the boat through the planking. As each timber comes from the steamer, force it down into the boat and overbend it slightly so it will fit tightly. Then nail it to the hog with a single 1¼-in. bronze nail. Clamp it loosely to the sheer strake and hit the top end smartly with a hammer; this helps to get it lying flush against the planking. Then, working from the keel up, one person holds a backing iron against the timbers inside while another drives the copper nails through from the outside, as in the photo below. Speed is essential. If one timber cracks or begins to split, replace it. Don't be afraid to twist the timbers with an adjustable wrench so they conform to the changing angle of the planking. When all the timbers are nailed in place, let them cool overnight and then rivet them.

Now cut and fit the two quarter-knees and the breasthook, notching them out to receive the two inwales, as shown in figure 14. Inwales, which reinforce and stiffen the top edges of the boat, should be installed slightly proud of the sheer strake so they can be beveled to match the camber of the transom. The inwales are fastened through every other timber and are roved and riveted on the inside. The alternate timbers will be drilled for fastening the rub rail later.

Next install the two seat supports, called risers, which run roughly parallel to the sheer line (figure 14). Nail them to each timber with two small ring-nails or screw them. Install the thwart and the thwart knees, using roved nails through the inwale and thwarts, or screws if the nails are too short.

Rub rails, which mount outboard along the top edge of the sheer strake, should be straight-grained oak shaped to a half-round with a router or molding plane. Nail them through every other timber and set the nail heads far enough

With the planks in place, the reinforcing timbers (ribs) are added. It's a three-person job to bend the hot timbers into place and nail them. In this photo, Simon Watts and Alexis Nason install the aftermost rib. Note that the last two ribs are two pieces so they will clear the transom knee.

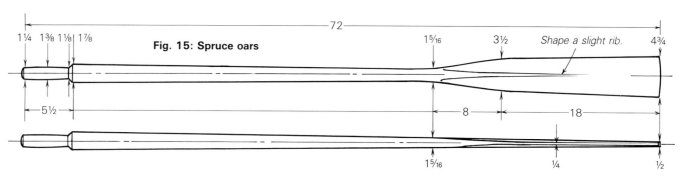

Fig. 15: Spruce oars

72

1¼ 1⅜ 1⅛ 1⅞   1⁵⁄₁₆   3½   Shape a slight rib.   4¾

5½   8   18

1⁵⁄₁₆   ¼   ½

The 10-ft. Nova Scotia lapstrake rowing boat described in this article was built by Jim Smith in 1963. A close copy of it was built by Alexis Nason of Brattleboro, Vt., as part of the preparation of this article. It took Nason about 160 hours to complete the job.

in so they can later be plugged with wooden bungs.

The floorboards are made of five pieces of ⅜-in. pine, as in figure 1. Cut the center floorboard 1 in. wider than the hog and nail it down. So you can bail the boat, make the floorboards to either side removable by fastening them with cross-grain cleats slipped under the center board and by hardwood turnbuttons screwed to the outer floorboards. Nail or screw the outer floorboards to the timbers.

Caulking and painting—This boat has only one seam to fill, the one that runs down the stem and along the keel. The other, running around the transom, has been sealed with bedding compound. Moisture-swollen planks will keep the laps tight. The traditional method of filling seams is to use caulking. This consists of one or more strands of unspun cotton driven into the seams with a wedge-shaped caulking iron. The seam is then filled up flush to the planking with putty or polysulfide. If the boat is going to be in and out of the water a lot, a bead of polysulfide run between the laps during planking will help keep it tight and will stay elastic through seasonal changes. Otherwise you can expect some leaking until the laps have swollen.

Some builders fill in the nail holes with putty. I prefer to sink them just enough to dimple the wood; they are a necessary part of lapstrake construction and nothing to be ashamed of. You can now bung all holes in keel, transom and rubbing strips. Sound knots can be shellacked to keep them from bleeding through the paint, or a shallow hole can be drilled with a centerless bit and bunged.

Before painting, it is a good idea to give the entire boat, inside and out, two applications of warm linseed oil, thinned half and half with turpentine. This helps keep the boat from getting waterlogged and heavy. The outside will need several coats of alkyd primer (give it plenty of time to dry and a thorough sanding between coats) before you put on the finish

coat of marine gloss enamel. If you paint the inside, keep the number of coats to a minimum so you can get by each year with a light sanding instead of the considerable chore of removing the paint with torch or chemicals. If you want the inside finished clear, the oil finish Deks Olje, the marine equivalent of Watco oil, requires less maintenance than varnish, which tends to deteriorate rapidly in sunlight. This material is available from the suppliers mentioned on p. 82. Don't paint or varnish the floorboards—that would make for dangerous, slick footing. If left bare, the floorboards eventually turn an agreeable gray. I varnish the seats and pick out the edges in paint—a tradition in Nova Scotia. Spruce oars, 6 ft. to 6½ ft. long, are right for this boat—they're not difficult to make yourself. Dimensions are shown in figure 15.

I use Davis-type oarlocks because it's impossible to lose them overboard. Mount them on pads nailed to the inwale and sheer strake so the oars won't scrape the rubbing strip. Before launching, attach a ring bolt or pad eye to the stem for securing a mooring and towing line.

When your new boat goes into the water, expect some leaking until the planks swell and the laps close, a process which may take a day or so. Then she should stay tight and dry, and you'll have a craft with a pedigree that represents the accumulated experience of generations of boatbuilders.

Simon Watts is a cabinetmaker, an amateur boatbuilder and a writer. He lives in Putney, Vt. Sam Manning, a boat designer and builder, lives in Camden, Maine. For more on boatbuilding, refer to WoodenBoat *magazine, published by WoodenBoat Publications, PO Box 78, Brooklin, Maine 04616. Plans for wooden boats are available from the above, and also from Maine Maritime Museum's Apprenticeshop, 75 Front St., Bath, Maine 04530; Mystic Seaport, Mystic, Conn. 06355; and Bob Baker, 29 Drift Rd., Westport, Mass. 02790.*

Controlling shape: lofting Sea Urchin

by Sam Manning

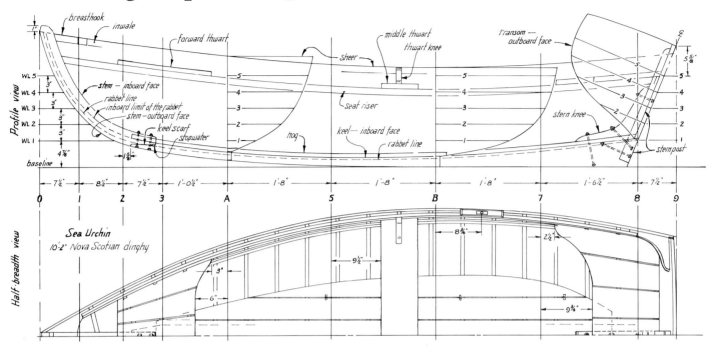

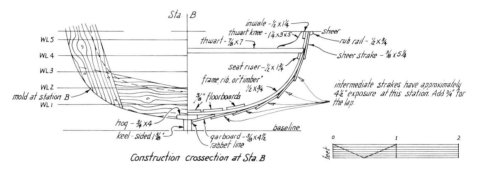

Construction crossection at Sta. B

L ike all round-bottomed boats, Sea Urchin is made up from flat parts sprung and twisted into curves. Her overall shape is governed by two hull molds—A and B—spaced along the keel, and by the slant of the stem and transom. An experienced boatbuilder can set molds and end members by eye and come away with a functional, handsome boat.

I suggest, however, that the first-time builder of Sea Urchin follow the route used by professional boatbuilders who scale up, or loft, full-size the plans of a boat. If the plans of Sea Urchin shown here are lofted to full-size on heavy tracing paper, you will have a template from which to mark critical members directly on the building stock. Included here is a table of offsets (literally, distances set off from a measuring line) with dozens of perimeter dimensions that can be connected with a thin pine batten to form Sea Urchin's graceful curves.

Spread your paper on a large table or the long wall of a corridor. A boat's plan is laid out from station lines ruled perpendicular to a baseline shown in the profile (elevation) view and from the centerline shown in the plan view. Dimensions are shown for the two molds and the transom in half-breadth; the other half is identical. The offsets given are in traditional nautical nomenclature—feet, inches and eighths of inches—so 3 ft. 4¾ in. would appear as 3·4·6.

Reading the table horizontally from the first to last station gives a series of points that are connected to form a particular line of the boat. The first line of the table, for example, describes the points which form the sweeping sheer line—the top edge of the top strake.

Other parts of the table give point dimensions for the molds, transom, stem and keel. The drawings include other dimensions useful in building Sea Urchin. Take the time to be accurate; professionals strive for a tolerance of ⅛ in. over the length of a large hull. □

TABLE OF OFFSETS

STATION:	0	1	2	3	A	5	B	7	8	9
Heights above baseline (profile)										
Sheer line/top of rail	2·1·1	2·0·1	1·10·7	1·9·7	1·8·4	1·6·7	1·6·3	1·7·0	1·8·2	1·9·0
Inboard face of stem and hog		1·2·1	0·7·1	0·5·3&0	0·3·4	0·2·4	0·2·6	0·3·7	0·5·6	
Inboard face of keel				0·4·3	0·2·6	0·1·5	0·1·7	0·3·1	0·5·0	
Rabbet line		0·10·7	0·5·1	0·3·5	0·2·2	0·1·2	0·1·4	0·2·6	0·4·4	
Outboard face of stem and keel	2·1·0	0·10·0	0·4·2	0·2·6	0·1·2	0·0·2	0·0·0	0·0·0		
Distance out from centerline (half-breadth)										
Inside of plank at sheer	0·0·6	0·4·3	0·8·6	1·0·1	1·4·5	1·9·3	1·11·1	1·10·1	1·7·3	1·5·7

WATERLINE:	TOP OF KEEL	1	2	3	4	5	SHEER
Distance aft from station 0							
Stem - outboard face		1·2·3	0·9·5	0·6·6	0·4·4	0·2·7	0·0·0
- rabbet line		1·4·7	0·10·5	0·7·4	0·5·2	0·3·4	0·0·5
- inboard face			1·2·2	0·10·2	0·7·5	0·5·6	0·2·6
Distance aft from station A							
Mold (half-breadth) 'A'	0·0·6	0·5·4	0·10·3	1·0·7	1·2·5	1·3·5	1·4·5
Distance aft from station B							
Mold (half-breadth) 'B'	0·0·6	1·2·1	1·6·5	1·8·7	1·10·1	1·10·7	1·11·1
Distance out from C.L. of transom							
Aft face (half-breadth) of transom	0·0·6	0·0·6	0·9·3	1·3·1	1·5·5	1·6·3	1·5·7

Making louvers

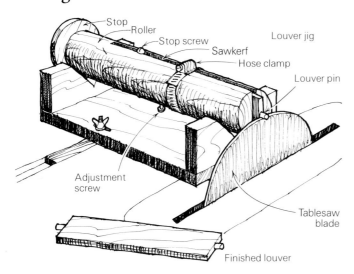

This simple jig cuts the pins on the ends of the individual louvers in homemade louvered doors. It consists of a V-notched base, which slides in the tablesaw's miter-gauge track, and a cylindrical louver holder. A slot in the cylinder holds the louvers in the correct cutting position, using adjustment and stop screws as shown in the sketch. To use the jig, load a louver blank into the cylinder, then tighten a hose clamp around the cylinder to lock the louver in place. Place the cylinder in the base, push the jig into the blade and rotate the cylinder to cut a pin on one end of the louver. Remove the louver, reverse it in the cylinder and repeat to cut the other end's pin. —*R.F. Paakkonen, Stafford Springs, Conn.*

Bending wood without steam

Here's how to bend wood using a solution of hot water and Downey fabric softener. First build a container of black 6-in. ABS pipe by cementing a cap on one end and putting a removable cap on the other. Don't try regular PVC pipe; it won't hold up to high temperatures. The length of the pipe can be whatever fits your need.

Mix one part Downey to twelve parts water, and heat the solution to boiling. Put the wood to be bent in the container and pour in the hot solution. Seal the open end of the container. It is important to keep the container warm. Here in California, I set the pipe out in the sun. On cloudy days I've sat the pipe next to a mirror and heated it with sunlamps. Leave the wood in the hot solution for a minimum of one hour. You'll find that wood softened in this solution will hold its shape better and not snap in the bending process. The solution turns thin wood to spaghetti.

—*David Ferguson, San Clemente, Calif.*

Adjustable curve

To make this adjustable curve, start with a piece of fine, straightgrained hardwood—hickory is best. Cut a ¼-in. thick strip about 36 in. long and 1½ in. wide. Now taper the strip to ¾ in. wide and ³⁄₃₂ in. thick at one end. Glue a reinforcing patch on the thin end and saw a small notch in each end of the piece. To complete the curve tie a series of knots in a string and string up the curve like a bow. Unstring the curve when it's not in use. —*Floyd Lien, Aptos, Calif.*

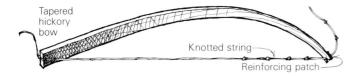

Flush rule joint for oval tables

Simon Watts says (in his article in FWW #18, P. 62) that he does not like "oval-shaped drop-leaf tables because the curve crossing the rule joint makes part of the joint project in an unsightly way." I agree that the projection is unsightly, but there's a simple solution that makes the rule joint flush in both the open and closed positions: bevel the edge of the table top.

Figure 1 shows how the corner of a rule joint projects when the leaf is lowered. The edge of the table continues to curve whereas the top corner of the rule joint swings down in an arc perpendicular to the line of the rule joint. But if the edge of the table is beveled at angle *a* determined from the tangent to the oval at the rule joint, the lower edge of the table top is farther out on a radius than the top corner of the leaf. When the leaf drops (figure 2), the edge and the corner match.

Recently I visited Williamsburg and noticed that many of the oval drop-leaf tables of colonial times also have beveled edges. So, my idea is far from original.

—*James H. Smith, Champaign, Ill.*

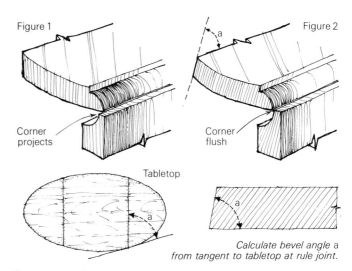

Calculate bevel angle a from tangent to tabletop at rule joint.

Space-saving saw setup

Here's one solution to the problem of squeezing both a tablesaw with long extension rails and a radial-arm saw with long extension tables into a narrow shop. My shop is 10 ft. by 25 ft. and until recently these machines took up most of my floor

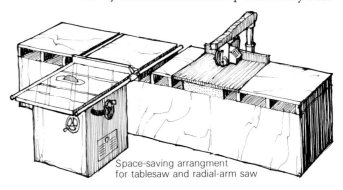

Space-saving arrangment for tablesaw and radial-arm saw

space. But by setting the tablesaw at right angles to the radial-arm saw and combining the extension table space of the two machines I was able to recover much of this lost area.

To combine the machines the two tables must be the same height. I chose to block up my radial-arm saw to the height of my tablesaw. Cut two troughs in the radial-arm table to accomodate the tablesaw's rails. Cut the front trough wide enough for the rip-fence lock. Position the rails so that the rip fence rides just a fraction of an inch above the radial-arm saw's table. —*Andrew A. Ruotsala, Seattle, Wash.*

FINISHING

Period Furniture Hardware

How it's made and where to get it

by Simon Watts

Everyone who makes or restores period furniture is bound to face the problem of choosing the appropriate hardware. The choice is complicated by the wide range of hardware available from many different periods, as well as by several distinct levels of authenticity and quality. This question of authenticity often troubles people most. What is the "correct" hardware for a particular piece of period furniture? All reproduction hardware is copied and there is no such thing as a genuine copy. The copy may be so close to the original that it can be spotted only by an expert, or it may depart to the point of caricature. If your furniture is a faithful copy of an historical original, then you should use only the best hardware. This means accurate copies taken from the right period and, when possible, made in the same way. On the other hand, if your furniture is "in the style of"—similar in appearance but using materials and methods inconsistent with the period—then the choice of hardware is broader. Recognizing this, a number of reputable firms now offer a choice between expensive and historically correct hardware, and a cheaper alternative made at least in part by machine. Modern versions of old hardware are not necessarily inferior, and sometimes the opposite is true. Drawn brass hinges, for example, are stronger and work more smoothly than do the original cast versions.

How hardware was made—To choose period hardware intelligently, you must know the materials and the manufacturing processes in use at the time the furniture was made. This is not as difficult as it seems. Prior to 1750, hardware makers really had limited choices of materials and techniques. They could cast hardware by melting metal and pouring it into molds to cool and harden, or they could forge parts by heating the metal and beating it into the desired shape with hammers. After 1750 the development of the brass rolling mill opened up new design possibilities, and for the first time hardware could be produced on a large scale. Further improvements in technology eventually brought about stamped and die-cast hardware—and with it the excesses of ornament—that enjoyed great popularity in the Victorian era.

Practically all furniture hardware made in America during colonial times was forged by hand by local blacksmiths. Iron was the favored material because it was available and easily worked. Colonial blacksmiths forged a huge variety of hard-

If you make period furniture, chances are you'll be using reproduction hardware. Original brasses like this pull-with-escutcheon from a Newport bureau, c. 1780, are rare.

ware—from the most delicate thumb-latches to massive hinges suitable for the heaviest doors. When heated sufficiently, iron becomes semiplastic. In this state it can be hammered out in thin sections, bent, cut, folded back on itself and even welded. It is this hammering that gives wrought or forged iron its distinctive look. No two forged pieces look exactly alike—there is a pleasing variation and asymmetry. Hand-wrought iron still has many applications on accurate period reproduction furniture and in the restoration of colonial-period architecture. In trying to meet the current demand for this hardware, modern manufacturers often use machines to speed production of forged parts. The basic shape is stamped out by a press and then hammered only to add detail. If you suspect you are looking at hardware made this way, just put two pieces side by side. Although the surface detailing will vary, their profiles will be identical.

Hand-forging is still done with hammer, anvil and coal fire, but its modern version (machine or drop-forging) uses dies and huge power forges. A red-hot bar of metal is placed on a massive iron table on a die in the shape of the hardware to be made. An upper die mounted in a heavy, power-driven hammer is then slammed onto the metal to forge the part. Some metal is squeezed out between the dies, and the eventual trimming of this waste leaves a faint trace that often remains visible after finishing. Machine forgings are identical and lack the surface variations of hand-forged hardware. The forging process toughens materials, so forgings tend to be stronger than castings in the same metal. They also have a distinct "grain" caused by the flowing of the hot metal. This is conspicuous if the surface erodes; an old forged anchor looks like weathered wood.

Historically, casting was used only for brass furniture hardware, particularly that made before 1750. Colonial furniture makers in America did use brass hardware, but by law it had to be imported from England. This fact causes confusion even today. Some good reproductions made in brass are patterned after originals that were made only in wrought iron. The familiar rat-tail hinges and H-L hinges are examples of this; however accurate they may be in form, brass versions cannot be considered authentic.

Brass was commonly used to make a type of hardware known as the pull-and-escutcheon. These "brasses," typically

The basic tools of the blacksmith—fire, hammer and anvil—have remained unchanged for hundreds of years, and the smith's products are similar to those made by his colonial forebears. Wrought thumb-latches and H-hinge by Woodbury Blacksmith and Forge Co., right, show the distinctively varied profiles left by the process—no two are identical, and the marks left by the smith's hammer and anvil are evident.

H-hinges, above, show a mass-production attempt to mimic a wrought look. Profiles of the hinges are identical, but edges have been hammered to add surface detail.

Baldwin Hardware Manufacturing Corp. uses four of these English-made power forges, above. At right is a lower die into which a hot brass rod will be placed. When the upper die slams down, a new piece of hardware is instantly formed, needing only edge-trimming and a shine. Forged parts can be made with fair detail, but each one is identical to the next.

201

Sand-casting is slow, highly skilled work. Above, foundry-man Joe Bossio of Franklin Alloys tamps sand around a pattern which will then be removed to form a cavity shaped like the hardware to be made. At the Horton Brasses foundry, right, co-owner Jim Horton and an assistant pour brass into a gate, an opening in the mold. Too much moisture in the mold can cause the hot brass to geyser back out of the gate, an occupational hazard of foundry work.

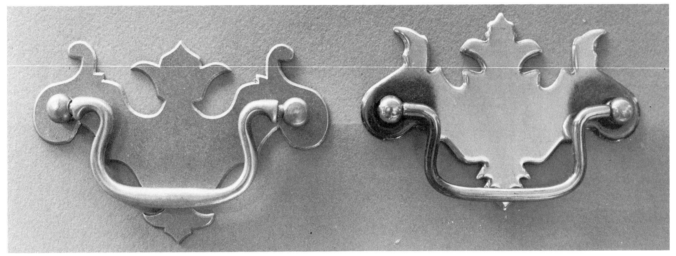

A close look will reveal the difference between cast and stamped parts. The Chippendale pull, above left, is all cast—backplate, bail and loose posts. The pull, above right, is a thin stamping with its edges bent down to create the illusion of thickness. The bail is of bent brass wire, and instead of loose posts the pull is attached to the drawer with studs fastened to the backplate. The assortment of knobs, bails and escutcheons, left, has just come from the sand mold. Even after polishing, you can recognize them as castings by the slight irregularities and traces of the flash lines where the two parts of the mold met. Below, backplate cast in a sand mold is recognizable by the pitting and unevenness on the back side. The front will be polished smooth. This plate has an identification number cast into it at lower right.

consisting of a floral-shaped backplate (escutcheon), and a bail mounted between a couple of posts, were a feature of Chippendale and Queen Anne style furniture. Brass, a copper/zinc alloy, is difficult to forge and weld. But its low melting point makes it ideal for small sections of furniture hardware because it can be poured hot enough to run easily into all the crevices of a mold before it hardens. Thus, brass casting is a good way to make the thin escutcheon, the slender bail, and the threaded posts and nuts that attach the pull to the drawer front. Compacted sand molds (sand-casting) and later metal molds (die-casting) were used in brass hardware manufacture. Sand molds must be made in two halves so they can be separated and the pattern extracted before pouring. This leaves a distinct joint or flash line on the casting that remains visible after finishing. A sure way to tell a sand casting is by the slight pitting in the surface of the metal caused by the sand. Although mostly removed in polishing, pitting can be seen in hard to reach corners of a part. Since a sand mold is destroyed when extracting the casting, no two castings are ever quite the same. They may have slight irregularities or be slightly heavier on one side. Die-castings are smoother and any two in a thousand will be identical.

After the 1750s, the advent of the rolling mill made quantity production of brass sheet possible. Until then, sheet had been used sparingly because it was cast and hand-hammered to thickness. The rolling mill inspired an entirely new design in brass—the Hepplewhite. Instead of being cast, the escutcheon is a thin brass sheet struck between two steel dies often engraved with exquisite designs. Hepplewhite bails were cast but the cast posts were soon replaced by ones machined from newly available brass rod.

Later, the powered blanking press could untiringly stamp out brass sheet to any profile required. This machine could be adapted to cut slots and holes, and to bend and fold the metal. The invention of the screw lathe made possible the replication of accurately machined parts by the thousands.

The unleashing of all this technology did not at first result in any new style of hardware but in the debasement of the old. Copies of earlier hardware continued to be made, but most of the subtle irregularities of sand casting, hand-filing and polishing were lost. It took a while for designers to make the most of the blanking press's potential for new approaches to hardware design. Much of the later, machine-made Victorian hardware has a directness and vigor that is still appealing.

Up to the 19th century, cast iron was little used for hardware. Its melting point is too high to be easily poured in thin sections and it is brittle. But with the new coke furnaces, cast iron came into wide use. Hinges, rim locks, cabinet catches and window hardware were made cheaply and in huge quantity. Cast-iron hardware soon replaced forged for most applications. Later still, a process called extrusion produced hardware that was stronger. Extruded parts are made from metal that is passed through a heated die and then cut into lengths. Extruded stock, also called "drawn," is easily identified by the fine, parallel lines that run along its surface, in the direction of extrusion.

Brass remains a popular metal for period hardware. Polished brass is usually given a coating of clear lacquer to prevent surface discoloration. Some firms lacquer all of their products while others do so only if the customer insists. Brass can be darkened or antiqued, by chemicals that duplicate the effects of time. Cheaper hardware is darkened and then

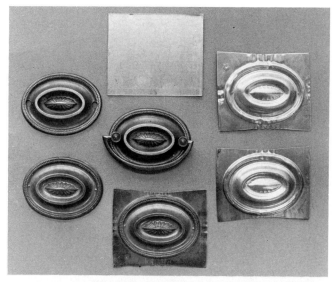

The invention of the rolling mill made possible large quantities of sheet brass and a new style of hardware. At top are the various steps in the making of a Hepplewhite oval pull, starting with a brass blank. The soft metal is struck once, softened by annealing and then struck again for the fine detail. Above is the lower die of the blanking press.

buffed on a satin wheel to create highlights and to simulate wear. Brass can be finished to look like other metals and sometimes other metals are made to look like brass. A small file will uncover the deception. The most frequent substitutes for brass are anodized aluminum and brass-plated steel or zinc alloys. Aluminum is too light to fool anyone; steel will reveal itself to the magnet.

Buying period hardware—The largest period hardware manufacturer is Ball and Ball of Exton, Pa. With a staff of only 42, the firm uses an adroit mixture of skilled handwork and clever machinery to meet the demand for 900 individual items spanning several periods. With its own foundry and blacksmith shops, Ball and Ball makes iron and brass hardware and has recently added Victorian items to its line. Much of the hardware, iron strap hinges for example, is offered handmade or semi-handmade. The former are made in the traditional way, while the latter are cut out of rolled sheet with a nibbling machine—a compromise for sure but a far cry from the manufacturers who stamp their hinges from a coil of pre-textured sheet. "They think they are duplicating a hand-

At Ball and Ball in Exton, Pa., backplates for pulls are made not only by the traditional sand-casting method, but by a metal-cutting pantograph. An overlarge template, top, guides the machine's cutter, center. The pantograph-cut plates are then filed by hand to sharpen the detail of the edge, above

forged finish," says Whitman Ball, "but they are just making modern junk. Unfortunately a lot of people buy it because the price is right."

For some of its brasses, Ball and Ball casts its backplates thick and then sands down the front. The result is practically indistinguishable from an original, thin casting. For those not needing this museum-level authenticity, the firm cuts backplates out of sheet brass on a metal-cutting pantograph. These look like castings until you turn one over and see the diagonal sanding scratches instead of the pitted unevenness of a sand casting. They will also sand-cast posts and even nuts to match, but most are made on automatic screw machines.

The firm even uses cast bails. When asked, Whitman Ball admitted being tempted to substitute a stamping. "But every one of them would be absolutely identical. It just wouldn't look right," he maintains. Ball and Ball sell direct only, from the Exton showroom as well as by mail. If a catalog item can't be filled from stock, there may be a lengthy delay. The firm's 108-page catalog costs $4 and is available by writing them at 463 West Lincoln Highway, Exton, Pa. 19341.

Horton Brasses of Cromwell, Conn., makes fewer items, but the service is speedier than Ball and Ball's. Both firms will copy from a customer's patterns. Horton sells brass and iron hardware and has its own foundry. It's a family-run business and Jim Horton specializes in the decorative "chasing" of brasses, done entirely by hand. A backplate, drilled and finished, is set on a thick iron block and the design is transferred with a single hammer blow to a small, steel stamp. Some dies are elaborate, others are plain circles, dots, crescents or lines. Horton casts its own bails, but they use a blanking press for most of the backplates. Horton's prices are retail and there is a quantity discount. For the 36-page catalog, send $2 to P.O. Box 95, Cromwell, Conn. 06416.

Period Furniture Hardware Co. is a small. merchandise-jammed shop at the foot of historic Beacon Hill in Boston. One wall is small drawers, a sample of their contents screwed to the fronts. This company makes less than half of the brass, iron and other items they sell. Instead, they buy from other manufacturers such as Baldwin Hardware Manufacturing Corp. They too try to offer their customers a choice—but within limits. When I visited the shop recently, the manager was explaining to a customer why three apparently similar door knockers were priced differently. "This is imported from England," he said, pointing to one knocker, "this is a machine forging, and this we make ourselves." The English import, $65, is marred by conspicuous sand pits. The manager snorts. "They think these pock marks make it more authentic, but that's rubbish. The old ones were perfect." We both examine the $45 machine forging. "Notice there are no sand pits, the surface is perfect but there's no detail either." Period Hardware jobs out its casting work—its own version of the knocker at $160 is perfect. The company has a large variety of architectural and household hardware, and I found its selection of weathervanes unique. Period Hardware sells wholesale and retail and its 126-page catalog can be had for $3 by writing to 123 Charles St., Boston, Mass. 02114.

Baldwin Hardware Manufacturing Corp. is best known for door hardware, but the firm also has two lines of colonial brassware that include cabinet knobs, candleholders and a range of household hardware. Baldwin sells no iron hardware nor do they do casting—most of their products are made on four massive forging machines. Adjacent to each is a gas-fired furnace. One man continuously feeds pre-cut brass rod into the furnace at one end while another swiftly places the hot metal between two steel dies that strike the finished part. The process takes less than a minute. Employing 600 people, Baldwin is a factory and there is no attempt to add authenticity by using archaic methods. They choose original patterns carefully and then make close copies in the most efficient way. Baldwin uses forging where another manufacturer might cast the part. Locks need the strength of forging, but other items like candleholders seem a trifle over-engineered. Baldwin hardware is handsome, durable and reasonably priced but it has a uniformity that may not suit everyone. No sales are made from the factory and all of Baldwin's products are sold by retailers and wholesalers throughout the country. Write Baldwin for a catalog at Box 82, Reading, Pa. 19603.

The Renovators Supply was born out of the frustrations a young couple encountered when searching for hardware to restore their old farmhouse. A combination of large volume and foreign labor allows Renovators to sell period hardware very competitively. Renovators buys some of its hardware outright for resale and has some of it manufactured to order—much of it abroad. "We produce handmade components at low labor rates and then do the final assembling and finishing here," says Claude Jeanloz, Renovators' co-owner. They offer a considerable selection of hardware including house fixtures, iron, brass and Victorian reproductions. There are no pretensions to making exact copies, and traditional designs are freely adapted to modern needs. Much of their wrought iron has been stamped out by machine and then hammered by hand for detail. This results not in an inferior product but an excellent value for the money. Renovators sells mail-order only and offers quantity discounts. The firm's 35-page catalog can be had by writing to Millers Falls, Mass. 01349.

Frequently, a search through all the period hardware catalogs won't reveal the hardware needed for a particular job. If iron work is wanted, you might find a local blacksmith who can make it for you. This is not as fanciful as it sounds. Handworking of iron has made a remarkable comeback and the Artist-Blacksmith Association of North America has some 1,500 members. You can contact them by writing ABANA, Upper Gates Road, North Canaan, N.H. 03741.

Tony Millham of Westport, Mass, is a member of the blacksmith association, an accomplished smith and one of a number of craftsmen who publish a catalog featuring handwrought hinges, door hardware, latches and bolts. "I let people order whatever they want. I may tell them it's wrong for their period or a wrong combination of materials, but I'll make it for them anyway," says Millham. He works mostly with the traditional tools of the trade—forge, hammer and anvil. But he also has an electric trip hammer, a bandsaw and welding equipment. To many, blacksmithing has the charm and nostalgic appeal of an earlier era, but as Millham points out, turning out quality reproduction hardware day after day is a struggle. He's firmly committed to his trade yet he sees some irrationality in the quest for authenticity. "People get neurotic about it. They all want it to be 'right,' but right is just what some expert tells you. I wish people would have more fun and simply choose what pleases them. After all, they are the ones who have to live with it." □

Simon Watts is a contributing editor to this magazine. Photos by the author, except where noted.

Jim Horton of Horton Brasses, is an expert in the hand-chasing of brass pulls. A drilled backplate is placed on a steel surface, top, and detail is stamped in the surface with a single hammer blow to a steel die. Horton uses dozens of stamps with various designs, as above. Below is a close-up of a flower-motif stamp.

Hole-cutter for speaker enclosures

I have been involved in making professional sound equipment and speaker enclosures for a number of years. The usual construction routine requires me to cut holes up to 18 in. in diameter for speaker baffles. Here's how I use a modified router table to cut the holes accurately, quickly and safely.

My router table is constructed of ⅝-in. Baltic birch plywood. I've installed an aluminum-channel track and pivot assembly on the centerline of the table as shown in the sketch. The standard 1½-HP Makita router bolted underneath the table is equipped with a stagger-tooth cut-out bit (Wisconsin Knife Works #68802).

To cut a circle on the setup I first slide the pivot assembly

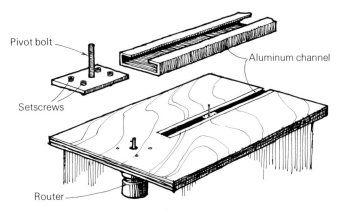

to the right position for the radius I want. Then I lock the assembly in place by tightening the four setscrews. Next I drill a center-hole in the baffle board and slide this over the pivot assembly's threaded rod. I secure the baffle board with a flat washer and a self-locking nut. The baffle board should rotate on the pivot with a mild resistance. Next I turn on the router, bring it up through the wood and rotate the baffle clockwise on its pivot point to cut a perfect circle. Once the device is set, you can quickly reproduce duplicate baffles.

—*James Campbell, Orange, Calif.*

Boss spinner

While visiting a woodworking pattern shop I ran across this tool called a "boss spinner." It is used with a disc sander to make wooden discs of varying diameters and thicknesses. As I found it, the unit was made from wood. Aluminum would perhaps give more accurate adjustment.

The boss spinner consists of three main parts: a slide bar that fits the channel in the sander table, an adjustment plate and a swing arm. A slot in the adjustment plate allows gross circle size adjustment while a screw in the swing arm provides

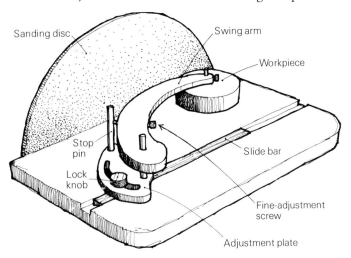

fine adjustment. The sketch shows only one pivot hole and adjustment screw in the swing arm. You can extend the capacity of the spinner by drilling a series of pivot holes and installing a fine-adjustment screw for each position.

To use the boss spinner, first set the rough radius: With the fine-adjustment screw against the stop, rough-adjust the radius of the disc with the adjustment plate and locking knob. Set the rough radius about 1⁄16 in. oversize. Now position the circle blank under the center pin. Feed the workpiece into the sander and rotate by hand until the fine-adjustment screw hits the stock. From there, use the fine adjustment screw to reach the final diameter.

—*Richard M. Williams, Cleveland, Ohio*

Circle guide for the router

This fixture for routing circles has several advantages over commercial circle guides: it's cheaper, it cuts circles smaller than the router base and it allows repeat set-up to precise radii without trial and error.

The guide is easy to make. Screw a piece of ¼-in. plywood to the base of your router, carefully countersinking the screws. The plywood should be as wide as your router base and somewhat longer than the largest radius you intend to cut. Saw or drill a clearance hole for the router bit.

Let's say you need a 4-in. radius circle. Measure from the point edge of the bit out 4-in. and drill a small hole at that point. Insert a brad in the hole, point up, to serve as a pivot. Drill a centerhole in a piece of scrap, place it on the guide, rout a short arc and measure the radius produced. You'll be lucky if it's right the first time. Regardless, label that hole with whatever radius it produces, say, 4⅛ in. Then make another hole closer or farther until you get the radius you want. Remember to mark each hole as you go.

—*Brian J. Bill, Old Bridge, N.J*

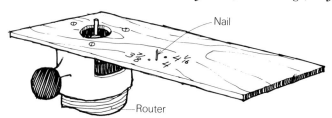

Reducing the diameter of dowels

The sketch below show an old patternmaker's trick to reduce the diameter of a dowel. Simply chuck a router bit in a drill press and clamp down a couple of scrap blocks to guide the dowel and to serve as a length stop. Lower the quill to take a light cut, lock the quill in place and rotate the dowel under the bit. Continue taking light cuts until you're at the desired diameter. —*Wallace C. Auger, Fairfield, Conn.*

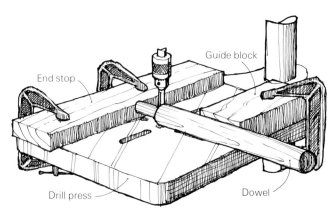

Old Finishes

What put the shine on furniture's Golden Age

by Robert D. Mussey

Finishing is the least studied and most inaccessible aspect of our antique furniture heritage. The proportions and workmanship of a Philadelphia highboy are direct and observable manifestations of the skills of its maker. But what of its finish? Is the mellow patina, much admired today, anything like the finish that left the workshop 200 years ago?

We can't learn much from the pieces themselves. Most museum conservators agree that perhaps only one percent of our antique furniture bears indisputable remnants of its original finish. Scientific tests may inadvertently detect later refinishings or modern materials indistinguishable from the originals: there's no way to tell new beeswax from old.

When we turn to historical documents, much obscure, ambiguous or mysterious material conceals the pearls of hard information. The old craft guilds guarded their trade secrets as closely as the independent finishers who proudly, and loudly, announced the discovery of the "perfect" finishing potion. Formularies, cabinetmakers' and varnishers' account books, bills, histories and dictionaries of the period are difficult to interpret. Account books, for example, so rich in information about woods used and prices charged, say little about finishes. When materials are mentioned, the names vary from region to region: 25 different words may describe just one material. And more than 200 different resins, oils, fillers, waxes and pigments were used in 18th and early-19th-century furniture finishes.

It is equally difficult to say who did the finishing in 18th-century American workshops. I haven't found a single reference to finishers in any of the hundreds of account books I have examined. Finishing was not a specialized trade in the U.S. as it was in Britain, though there were one or two well-known specialists in large cities, like Thomas Johnson in Boston, who did Japanning, graining, marbleizing and gilding. Fancy painting, as on the Baltimore chair, was done by fine-art painters. It seems probable that cabinetmakers, particularly in small shops, did their own finishing, aided by various guide books and formularies.

I have spent the past five years negotiating these obstacles, comparing and analyzing some 5,000 documents, reformulating many of the recipes for stains, dyes and finishes, and applying them using original methods to see how they work and to watch how they age. I have placed more emphasis in my research on books that were frequently reprinted. An often-reprinted book was probably a popular one with working craftsmen. The first furniture-finishing guidebook known to have been printed in America, *The Cabinetmaker's Guide*, (Greenfield, Mass., 1825), was reprinted numerous times, and parts were pirated for other books throughout the 19th century. The *Guide* was pocket-sized, easy to use. I have two copies, from 1827 and 1837, both are dog-eared, paint-splattered and muddied—signs of a well-used book.

I have formed some broad conclusions from my research; several of these have surprised me. I started out wanting to prove that shellac and French polishing were widely used during the 18th century. Instead, I discovered that French polish was not invented until about 1810, and that oil and wax were the predominant finishes of the period, favored even on many high-style pieces. And I found that the finish that left the shop was not mellow and glowing, but probably brilliantly colored, bright and shiny.

Stains, dyes, oils and waxes will be discussed here, limited to the period 1700 to 1830. Before that time, references are too scattered to be of use, and after 1830, mass production, chemical advances and burgeoning world trade profoundly changed furniture finishing. I'll discuss the varnishes of the 18th and 19th centuries in a subsequent article.

Surface preparation—The quality of the piece determined how much surface preparation it received. No elaborate smoothing practices were used on common pieces, and many table tops clearly display the corrugations left by hand planes. Finer furniture required more careful preparation. Andre Jacques Roubo's three-volume treatise, *The Art of the Woodworker* (Paris: 1769-74) suggests this elaborate sequence for veneered and marquetry pieces: smoothing planes followed by a variety of hooked cabinet scrapers, a hard rub with bundles of rushes (shave- or saw-grass), abrasion with solid pumice-stone blocks lubricated with water, further abrasion with sealskin, and finally, burnishing with slightly rounded blocks of hardwood.

The Cabinetmaker's Guide recommends glass-papering the surface after careful scraping. The author complains that glass-paper was being cheapened by adding sand, then gives his own instructions: pulverize broken window glass in an iron mortar, put it through sieves of appropriate fineness, and sift onto the glue-covered surface of heavy cartridge-paper.

Early in the 19th century, many recipes appeared using plaster of Paris, "hartshorn", and other natural clay-like materials to fill open grain before finishing. These could be dyed or stained and were mixed with a binder such as linseed oil or honey. Such fillers were previously used only on Japanned and gilded pieces where intensely pigmented varnish-paints were laid over a thick filler-ground. If clear finishes were applied over plaster-type fillers, the stain would eventually fade, and the filler would appear as unsightly white speckles.

In an earlier grain-filling method, the surface was covered with a thin coating of linseed oil and then abraded with a flat block of solid pumice stone. With enough pressure the resulting paste of oil and fine wood dust would at least partially fill the grain. After dyeing, the excess was wiped or scraped off.

Coloring—Craftsmen of the 18th century experimented with a vast range of materials for coloring wood and wood finishes. Documents of the period complain that colors "flee with the light," and the search for permanent natural pigments and dyes, not only for wood but also for fabrics and paints, spawned an entire industry and vast "scientific" research. The American colonies were a major source of colorants, such as logwood, indigo, oak bark and walnut bark, all of which were exported in quantities of hundreds of tons.

Craftsmen then used the terms "stain" and "dye" as imprecisely as craftsmen today. We define "stain" as a thin layer of colored pigment lightly penetrating the surface of the wood. "Dye" is any substance producing color changes by chemical reaction with the wood fiber or by diffusion of the colored dye-stuff deep into the cellular structure of the wood. Most 18th-century stains and dyes would have colored the wood in several ways at once. Stains with strongly acidic vehicles, like uric acid, or stains containing material like iron filings, would have colored by chemical reaction as well as by pigments contained in the stain. Likewise, many dyes contained pigments, which lodged in the wood fibers.

The Cabinetmaker's Guide distinguishes stain from dye by degrees of penetration: "Staining differs from the process of dyeing, inasmuch as it merely penetrates just below the surface of the wood, instead of coloring its substance throughout, as it does in dyeing; and the one is used for beautifying the face after the work is finished, while the other is employed on the wood before it is manufactured, in the state of veneers, to be cut into strings or bands...for inlaying borders...and which has of late years got much out of use, principally owing to the fault so much complained of, of the colors flying...."

Nearly all the stains and dyes of the period were extremely fugitive by modern standards. Some would not have lasted more than a few years. Often a museum piece displays only the faded glory of the finisher's art. Red and yellow colorants, frequently used, faded quickly. Brown stains, mixed with reds, greens and blacks, soon faded to the faint green tint we see today on some antiques. I have found bright red areas preserved beneath the brasses of mahogany pieces, a far cry from the brown, red-brown or yellow-brown stains used for period reproductions. Some of my reformulations of original mahogany stain recipes come close to this brisk hue.

There is strong documentary evidence that staining of furniture before finishing was much less common in the 18th century than we assume. Thomas Sheraton, in his 1803 *Cabinet Dictionary*, wrote, "The art of staining wood was more in use at the time when inlaying was in fashion;...at present red and black stains are those in general use." It is also possible that staining was more common in America than in England, but the documents I've examined from throughout the colonies infrequently mention staining and staining materials. Rural cabinetmakers may have used stains more often than their city cousins. Rural clients couldn't afford the finely figured woods or expensive mahogany favored in high-style Boston or Philadelphia work. So exotic woods were imitated by graining, mahoganizing and staining, or they emphasized the wild grain of a favorite wood, like tiger maple.

Nearly all colorant formulas were based on water or alcohol. These have great clarity and penetration, and deeply accentuate the structure and figure of wood. The rather muddy oil-based-pigment stains common in today's hardware stores were unknown in the 18th-century finishing shop. Likewise, only a very few period stains resemble the modern class of chemical stains, in which colorants or acids in the wood react with chemical counterparts in the staining solution.

More than one hundred different materials were used in the 18th century in the making of stains and dyes. These range from the exotic to the mundane—like old files or walnut husks in solutions containing vinegar, urine or wine. The *Cabinetmaker's Guide* calls for chipped logwood, a source of a valuable red-black dye, verdigris (copper acetate), copperas (iron sulphate), and barberry root among other ingredients for dyes. Stains might require archil, a Canary Island lichen, or dragon's blood, a resin from the fruit of the East Asian rattan palm. A red stain was made from brazilwood extract soaked in quicklime slaked in urine and painted hot onto the wood. If the customer only knew!

Attempting to give more brilliant lightfast colors, many of the recipes used such strong vehicles as sulphuric, muriatic or uric acids. Unfortunately these acids contributed to the decomposition of varnishes applied over the stains. The resins and oils used in the 18th-century varnishes were very sensitive to acids and alkalies, and may be rapidly degraded in reaction with these. This helps account for the survival of so few original varnish finishes.

Besides staining and dyeing the wood directly, finishers also colored the spirit varnishes they applied to the wood. Used to match the colors of diverse woods or to improve drab wood, they were called "changeing varnish," and were colored with various unusual substances as well as with wood chips and bark of oak, chestnut, walnut or sumac. Similar mixtures applied to tinware, brassware or furniture brasses were called "lackers." Shellac was the dominant resin in these "lackers," its reddish or golden color heightening the golden effect desired from brass. Shellac is a spirit-soluble resin that polymerizes significantly, the process speeded by heat. Shellac-based "lackers" were often baked onto metals, giving a very hard, lustrous surface, resistant to oxidation, discoloration, and the formation of copper acetates. Original furniture brasses were probably bright and "brassy," not at all tarnished like those favored on today's reproductions.

Finishes—Once the wood surfaces were leveled, smoothed, filled and stained, one of several types of coatings was applied. These fall within four broad categories: oil finishes, wax finishes, varnishes, and combinations of these.

Eighteenth-century writers on finishes list a whole array of criteria for the ideal finish: preservation of the wood from decay and insects, preservation of the color of the wood, and exclusion of atmospheric moisture. It should also be hard, shining, transparent and flexible, should not yellow or crack with age or turn white with spills, and it should hold up to hard use. The same qualities are sought by coatings manufacturers today, and no finish, then or now, fills the whole bill. Finishers experimented with an amazing range of materials in the 18th century, and some of their solutions were excellent. Indeed, some are still used today.

Since ancient times, craftsmen have known that various animal, vegetable and seed oils help to preserve wood. A wide selection of these was offered for sale by American merchants and manufacturers in the 18th century. Linseed (flaxseed) oil, the vehicle for most housepaints, was by far the most frequently used furniture-finishing material. Poppyseed and walnut oils were preferred for their light color and transparency, but they were expensive. Since the men who finished furniture were also gilding picture frames, Japanning tea waiters and painting houses and carriages, it is not surprising that, where possible, they used the same materials throughout their work.

Linseed oil finishes were widely used—despite their disadvantages: they were not durable, waterproof or alcoholproof, and they darkened with age, though they were repaired easily with fresh oil and some rubbing. Free from tariffs imposed by the English, both boiled and raw linseed oil were cheap and widely available. In lists of hundreds of furniture types, several influential English and American trade price-books quote prices only for oil finishing and polishing.

Pressed cold, linseed oil has a very light color; pressed hot, it is more plentiful, but considerably darker. To bleach out this color, fresh-drawn linseed oil was placed in shallow pans or bottles in the sunlight. Alternatively, the solid impurities were precipitated by adding fuller's earth (a naturally occurring aluminum silicate) which absorbed the brownish coloring matter. Egg-white was sometimes added as a purifier.

Linseed oil dries very slowly on its own. Coatings of raw oil may remain tacky for years. Over centuries, many methods had been tried to make it more siccative, or fast drying. In the late Middle Ages, the oil was merely boiled. Later, burnt horn and bone, garlic, powdered lead-crystal glass, or alum were added to the boiling oil to try to enhance its drying properties. Most recipes of the 18th century employed lead com-

French polishing with wax

Andre Jacques Roubo's *The Art of the Woodworker* was published in Paris between 1769 and 1774. Although it's out of print this excellent book is available in French at major libraries. Roubo, a master craftsman, set down detailed accounts of carpentry, carriagemaking and furnituremaking, illustrated with hundreds of engravings. This plate shows the methods, materials and tools used in finishing the finest veneered furniture, called *ébénisterie*.

Figures 1 and 2: Preparing the surface. A finely set toothing plane worked diagonally across the grain as indicated by the lines would not disturb the veneer fibers or joints. Planing as in *figure 2* is cautioned against because it will probably break the joint.

Figures 3, 4 and 5: Scrapers, shown here, followed the planes, worked in the same fashion or as indicated in *figures 14 and 15*.

Figure 6: Sharkskin, or "dogfish" skin, was used as an abrasive. For fine veneered work, the fins or "ears of dogfish skin" were recommended, also worked across the grain.

Figure 7: After planing and scraping, abrading with sharkskin or *prêle* (horsetail, a species of rush with corrugated stems) polished away the remaining fine scratches on the veneer.

Figures 8 and 9: The polisher, a bundle of ordinary rush, was bound tightly, dipped in hot wax which rose into the stems, allowed to cool and rubbed over the veneer.

Figures 10, 11 and 12: Polishing sticks, small strips of walnut or other finely grained wood, were shaped to various sizes and used to push wax into areas too small for the polisher or on moldings with delicate arrises.

Figure 13: A finisher forces wax into the grain of a veneered panel with the rush polisher.   —R.D.M.

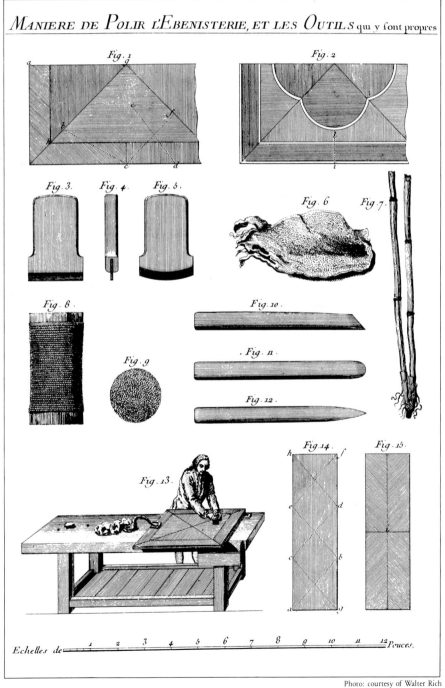

MANIERE DE POLIR L'EBENISTERIE, ET LES OUTILS qui y font propres

Fig. 1   Fig. 2   Fig. 3   Fig. 4   Fig. 5   Fig. 6   Fig. 7   Fig. 8   Fig. 9   Fig. 10   Fig. 11   Fig. 12   Fig. 13   Fig. 14   Fig. 15

Echelles de   1   2   3   4   5   6   7   8   9   10   11   12 Pouces.

Photo: courtesy of Walter Rich

pounds as siccatives: litharge, massicot or minium, all lead oxides long used as artists' pigments. Once boiled, filtered, cooled and bleached, the oil was ready for use. The boiling and purification of linseed oil provided considerable income for many painters and varnishers in New England, but the occupation carried with it the danger of fire. Fire and lead poisoning were the bane of the finisher.

Oil finishing was as simple then as it is today. The oil was applied with a rag or brush, full strength or thinned with turpentine, and allowed to soak into the wood. The excess was wiped off with a coarse rag. After a day's drying time, another coat was applied, and ideally this was repeated until the wood would accept no more oil. In practice, a few superficial coats were probably all that were used. Total oil-finishing time for a desk may have amounted to only two to four hours. Prices for oil polishing formed a small proportion of the total costs recorded for making a piece.

Basic oiling practices varied. Sheraton, in his *Cabinet Dictionary*, outlines a method using brick dust and linseed oil, plain or stained red with alkanet root. Brick dust and oil formed a slightly abrasive paste which was rubbed on the surface until the wood warmed, then cleared off with wheat bran, leaving a bright surface. For off-color mahogany, or better grade mahogany that "wants briskness of color," Sheraton recommends a reddish polishing oil including alkanet root, dragon's blood, and rose pink, a pigment made with brazilwood dye.

I was surprised to find that wax finishes were also among those commonly used by 18th-century cabinetmakers. Wax, like oil, was cheap, available and easy to use. It was frequently listed in account books and mentioned in the literature of the period.

Other natural waxes were known, but beeswax had been favored for centuries as a finish on wood, a medium for paint, a waterproof stopping for boats, an embalming resin, and a flatting agent and final moisture barrier for varnishes. It is probably the natural organic finish most resistant to destructive oxidation. A modern analysis of beeswax used on a Punic warship showed that the wax remained chemically unchanged after 2,000 years. This extreme longevity was noted repeatedly by 18th-century writers on finishes. Beeswax was produced in large quantities in New England, where bee culture was a highly developed art. Samuel Grant, a prominent Boston upholsterer and merchant, bought up to 450 lb. at a time for use in his own shop, for sale to other cabinetmakers and for export to England.

The purification of wax by extraction of the honey impurities with water was cheap and simple, and two forms of purified wax, yellow and white, were known. The yellow still contained some impurities and was less expensive. The white, or clear beeswax, carefully filtered and bleached in the sun, was preferred for the finest work.

Thomas Sheraton describes two methods of wax polishing he says are typical. "Sometimes they polish with bees wax and a cork for inside work. . . . The cork is rubbed hard on the wax to spread it over the wood, and then they take fine brick-dust and sift it through a stocking on the wood, and with a cloth the dust is rubbed till it clears away all the clammings. . . . At other times they polish with soft wax, which is a mixture of turpentine and beeswax, which renders it soft, . . . a cloth of itself, will be sufficient to rub it off with."

For chair polish, Sheraton mixed wax with a small quantity of turpentine, heated this in a varnish pan (a double boiler), added Oxford ochre for color and a little copal varnish. The cooled mixture was worked into a ball and applied with a stiff brush, forced into the grain, and then rubbed off.

Wax finishes were widely used on high-style 18th-century French furniture. The only complete description of this process that I have found is in Roubo's *The Art of the Cabinetmaker*. For veneered cabinetwork, finest quality wax was melted into a polisher, which was a bundle of rags bound tightly with wire, and with which the whole surface was rubbed. The heat generated melted the wax, and the rubbing forced it into the pores. Roubo cautions against using cork polishers, which can get too warm and loosen the veneer.

When the wax was evenly spread, the excess was scraped off. Roubo's wax scraper was similar to a cabinet scraper, but with a slightly rounded edge instead of a burr. Cleaned and polished with a rag, the work was "extremely even, and glossy as a mirror." For porous or reddish woods like rosewood or amaranth, powdered shellac was spread over the wax and rubbed in vigorously with the polisher to fill the open grain and heighten the color. Colophony (rosin) was used to stop up open grain in black woods like ebony.

A high-gloss finish was typical of nearly all high-style furniture finishes of the 18th century. Experimenting with Roubo's wax finish, I found that it gives a much higher gloss than we associate with wax finishes today. Roubo built up a wax finish in the same way as a varnish finish, and the wax became a fairly thick coherent body on top of the wood. And he used only 100% pure beeswax, which has better refracting qualities than today's wax emulsions.

Roubo prescribes a different process for common furniture: the wax was mixed with one-third tallow and rubbed off with a serge cloth. "In order to spread the wax better and drive it deeper into the open pores, one uses sometimes a sheet-metal pan in which glowing coals have been put, and this is held as close as possible to the work in order to warm the wax. In place of the pan one can also use a glowing red-hot piece of iron, which is even better, because it makes the wax liquid which flows into the open pores more easily."

Though it was possible to get a high gloss finish with wax, most finishers probably found the required method too time-consuming. Wax also has many of the same disadvantages as oil finishes. An 18th-century writer summarized the advantages and disadvantages of the common wax finish, noting: "Waxing stands shock; but it does not possess, in the same degree as varnish, the property of giving lustre...and of heightening their tints. The lustre it communicates is dull, but this inconvenience is compensated by the facility with which any accident that may have altered its polish can be repaired, by rubbing it with a piece of fine cork."

Easy to obtain, fast and easy to use and repair, oil and wax finishes were ideally suited for 18th-century finishing needs. Though pure beeswax finishes are rarely used today, the many virtues of oil finishes, particularly their low sheen, are once again appreciated and have made them a finish of choice, as they were 250 years ago. □

Robert Mussey, of Milton, Mass., trained as a cabinetmaker and wood finisher then served an internship in furniture conservation at the Henry Ford Museum. He is head of the furniture conservation workshop at the Society for Preservation of New England Antiquities in Boston, Mass.

Stains and dyes from
The Cabinetmaker's Guide

I reformulate original stain and dye recipes to determine what the original colors were like. But I use alcohol soluble anilines for restoration or conservation work because they dry quickly, don't penetrate as deeply or rapidly as water soluble anilines, and because they are reasonably lightfast—I want my conservation to last more than ten years.

One of the first principles of conservation is to make any repair reversible, so it can be redone if a better technique is discovered. Original colors are dramatic, and not yet completely accepted for conservation, so when I color a piece I put down a barrier coat first, then color the finish that goes over it. The stain has not soaked into the wood so the coloring is reversible. On new work, the choice of color is my own; furniture makers have much more freedom than conservators. I think original colors will become acceptable for furniture conservation, used where appropriate to show people what the maker saw when he had completed the piece.

These recipes are from *The Cabinetmaker's Guide:*

The Cabinetmaker's Guide, *possibly the first finishing guidebook printed in America, was a workshop standby throughout the 19th century. It hasn't been reprinted recently but may be available in major libraries. Note the worker polishing a tabletop by the fire, which is a good way to keep the wax flowing freely.*

Red dye. Take 2 pounds of genuine brazildust, add four gallons of water, put in as many veneers as the liquid will cover, boil them for 3 hours; then add 2 ounces of alum, and 2 ounces of aquafortis, and keep it lukewarm until it has struck through.

Brazildust; dust of brazilwood, *Caesalpinia echinata*, gives a very bright red dye. It was such an important item of commerce that the country was named after the tree. Aquafortis is nitric acid, reagent grade concentration.

Fine blue. Take a pound of oil of vitriol in a clean glass phial into which put four oz. of indigo, and proceed as before directed in dyeing.

This dye, and others for similarly unusual colors, would have been used for marquetry or by musical-instrument makers. Oil of vitriol is sulphuric acid.

To stain beech a mahogany color take 2 ounces of dragon's blood, break it into pieces and put it into a quart of rectified spirits of wine; let the bottle stand in a warm place, shake it frequently, and when dissolved it is fit for use.

Dragon's blood has been used for centuries, it is a dark, red resinous exudation from the fruit of the rattan palm, *Calamus drago*. Spirits of wine is alcohol distilled from wine; rectified means purified. Ethyl alcohol or shellac thinner from a paint store is the same thing. My reformulation of this stain came out a very bright red. Dragon's blood, when compared to other reds, is fairly lightfast. If you stain the wood directly, it is fugitive; but if you dye shellac with it, it is much less so, because the shellac locks the color in.

Another method for black stain. Take one pound of logwood, boil it in two quarts of water, add a double handful of walnut peeling. Boil it up again, take out chips, add a pint of the best vinegar and it will be fit for use; apply it boiling hot. Note—This will be much improved if, after it is dry, we take a solution of green copperas dissolved in water, in the proportion of an ounce to a quart, and apply it hot to the above.

Logwood was an important dyestuff from *Haematoxylum campechianum*, a tree found in Central America and the West Indies. It gives a range of colors from red to purple to black and was used as dust, shavings or chips.

I have obtained materials for these and other recipes from the following firms: H. Behlen and Bros., Rt. 30 N., Amsterdam, N.Y. 12010; Laurence McFadden Co., 7430 State Rd., Philadelphia, Pa. 19136; A.F. Suter and Co. Ltd., Swan Wharf, 60 Dace Road, Bow, London E3, England; James B. Day Co., Day Lane, Carpentersville, Ill. 60110.

For further information: *The Artist's Handbook of Materials and Techniques,* Ralph Mayer, Viking, New York, rev. ed., 1982. *Painting Materials, A short encyclopedia,* Rutherford Gettens and George Stout, Dover, 1966.   —*R.D.M.*

Early Varnishes

The 18th century's search for the perfect film finish

by Robert D. Mussey

The 18th-century finisher looking for a durable, high-gloss surface had only a few choices. He could, and usually did, finish with a wax or an oil (p. 207). Varnish, however, offered greater protection from moisture and wear, and produced a more lustrous shine than all but the most elaborate oil or wax preparations. Today, when we want to use varnish, we can go to any paint store and select from numerous scientifically formulated brands. But in the 18th century, varnishmaking was an imperfect science at best. Achieving a smooth, glossy surface demanded great skill and patience from the finisher.

Varnishes are solvent solutions of resins and gums that dry to form a thin, tough and glossy film on the surface of the wood. In the 18th and early 19th centuries, alcohol and various vegetable oils were the common solvents. Natural gums, which are soft, water-soluble plant fluids, were used only in small quantities as plasticizers. Natural resins, exuded by a vast range of living plants and several kinds of insects, or mined from fossilized vegetable remains, were the most important varnish constituents. They are soluble in oil, alcohol or other organic solvents and vary in hardness. Today most of these natural resins have been replaced in varnishes by chemically synthesized resins or modified natural resins.

Resins, essential to America's growing shipbuilding industry, were readily available to the varnishmaker, more so in urban than in rural areas. When varnishes had a high concentration of hard resin to solvent, they produced a hard, brittle film that could be abraded glass-smooth and polished to a mirror shine. A high proportion of drying oil to certain resins produced an elastic, durable, virtually waterproof film. Each resin had its own advantages. Sandarac was almost perfectly clear and transparent, easy to dissolve. Copal was very tough. Colophony (a type of rosin) gave a high gloss. Tremendous research focused on the varnishmaking industry, hampered by the imperfect understanding of chemical principles and the relatively small number of appropriate resins. During the 150 years prior to 1800, the same 15 or so resins appear in endless combinations in varnish formulas—in the search for a magic elixir that would possess all the advantages, but none of the disadvantages, of the individual resins.

This complex, kitchen-recipe approach to varnishmaking was opposed, however, by a famous Parisian varnishmaker named Watin. He held that, "The real secret of the artist is the simplicity of his procedures. . . . The art should be like Nature when possible, to do the greatest with the least, without complication, without effort." And so, after 40 years of effort, Watin announced in 1776 that he had developed the "perfect" varnish. Of course, he kept its exact formula secret.

These two approaches, the complex and the simple, and a spectrum in between, can be found in the thousands of varnish recipes of the 18th and 19th centuries. It is difficult to form simple conclusions about these recipes. I have looked at

18th-century varnish resins

Here is a list of common alcohol-soluble resins used in 18th- and 19th-century varnishes. It is possible to buy some of these in small quantities, although resins other than shellac can be expensive. H. Behlen and Bros., Rt. 30 N., Amsterdam, N.Y. 12010, carries copal and a range of shellacs. A.F. Suter and Co. Ltd., Swan Wharf, 60 Dace Rd., Bow, London E3, England, stocks most of these resins.

Benzoin: Often called "benjamin," benzoin is derived from the tree *Styrax benzoin,* of Borneo and Sumatra. Used in many 16th- and 17th-century spirit varnishes it was later added as a plasticizer, or for its pleasant smell. Today it is used as a final glaze over French polish to impart gloss.

Turpentine: Called "rosin" in Colonial America, turpentine is the resin obtained from the gum (sap) of fir, balsam, pine, larch, spruce, or other conifers. It was used in inferior spirit varnishes in several forms, including chio turpentine from Mediterranean pines, Strasburgh turpentine from the German fir tree *Abies alba,* venice turpentine from the European larch tree, and rosin (also called colophony), the resin of various species of American pine tree.

Sandarac: From the North African conifer *Tetraclinis articulata,* this brittle resin was often called gum juniper.

Elemi: Also called allemy, any of a large number of resins from the *Burseraceae* family of trees. A softer resin, it was added to varnishes for toughness and flexibility.

Mastic: This soft resin makes a perfectly clear varnish. It is exuded by the Mediterranean tree *Pistacia lentiscus.*

Copal: A tremendous variety of resins, some hard, some soft, are called copal. The hard copals, African, and probably of fossil origin, were highly valued, and insoluble in alcohol. A widely used soft copal, largely soluble in alcohol, was derived from the common American sumac *Rhus copallina.*

Anime: No one seems to know what resin this actually was. Possibly it was a spirit-soluble soft copal and may have come from the Zanzibar tree *Trachylobium mossambicense.*

Shellac: The best known of the three resins exuded by insects, shellac is deposited on branches and twigs by the insect *Coccus lacca,* which feeds on the sap of the tree. The natural grades are reddish, the finer grades are bleached white and used to produce a hard but flexible spirit varnish. —*R.D.M.*

many, in six European languages; each language has its own tangled, inconsistent set of terms and nomenclature. Writers had considerable difficulty differentiating resins. When a recipe called for copal, it could have meant any of 40 different materials, depending on the country of origin, the country of use and the date. Moreover, varnishmaking and finishing practices in Europe and America differed, as did those between urban and rural areas within America. And early varnishmakers may well have deviated from the published recipes. Varnishmakers were competitive and secretive; many of the finest formulas probably never were published. "Almost every varnisher," observed one 18th-century writer, "has at least one or two compositions peculiar to himself, the superior value of which rests chiefly in his own opinion."

Even when the varnishmaker worked his best magic, many obstacles loomed between the finisher and the perfect finish—temperature, dust, moisture, and numerous complicated surface preparations and polishing techniques. The best of the 18th- and 19th-century finishers, driven by necessity and fashion, mastered all these problems. The evidence of their skill remains today in carefully preserved museum pieces.

There are three broad groupings of 18th- and 19th-century varnishes: spirit, essential-oil and fixed-oil. Each is named for the vehicle used to dissolve its resins and gums. Spirit varnishes have alcohol or other volatile vehicles that evaporate, leaving a film of dried resin. Essential-oil varnishes use fluids distilled from one of several natural resins or oils; today we would consider them another type of spirit varnish. Fixed-oil varnishes are solutions of resins and gums in a drying oil, such as linseed, poppyseed or walnut. These varnishes dry by chemical change as well as by solvent evaporation, and they leave a more complex film, a combination of resins and oxidized oils. Resins dissolved partly in a drying oil and partly in alcohol constitute varnishes of a fourth and minor class that was used infrequently and will not be discussed.

Spirit varnishes—The cheapest and easiest varnish to make is the spirit-solvent variety. Because spirit solvents evaporate rapidly, a considerable body of varnish in numerous thin coats could be built up in a short time. And they could have great clarity, or "whiteness," because the dissolution usually did not require heat, and so avoided darkening the resins. On the other hand, spirit varnishes were brittle, cracked easily, were readily spoiled by alcohol or water spills, and were not as easy to polish as drying-oil resin varnishes. They required careful formulation and skillful polishing to get a high gloss.

"Spirits of wine," as alcohol was then called, was the usual solvent for 18th-century spirit varnishes. The production and trading of rum, brandy and other alcohols was an essential part of the New England economy. Cabinetmakers' account books are littered with records of "spririts" purchases, though it is unclear how much of it was used in varnish.

Most 18th-century solvent alcohol was quite impure, as much as half water. It was usually distilled from wine, and frequently from brandy. Some recipes even recommend ex-

tremely strong brandy itself as the solvent. Several methods were used to purify these spirits. Repeated distillation in a glass double-boiler called a *bain-marie* was the usual method. This process, also called rectification, could produce a very pure alcohol. Adding potassium carbonate (salts of tartar) or potash to alcohol, a process called tartarization, also absorbed some of the water and strengthened the solvent.

Several tests to "prove the truth" of the spirits were recommended by various guidebooks. One book suggests half-filling a spoon with gunpowder, covering it with the alcohol, then lighting it afire. Pure alcohol would burn off and the powder would ignite; if the powder had absorbed too much water from the alcohol, it would not. The fanciest, and safest, method was the hydrometer—I've found them advertised in several Philadelphia papers of the late 18th century.

Making spirit varnishes—Only the very lightest, clearest, "whitest" resin lumps, free from dross, sticks and impurities, were recommended. Inferior resin must have been common, and the formularies cite many methods for telling real from false. Of all the resins, sandarac was the most common and most highly regarded. Once the best resin pieces were selected, they were powdered or granulated in a mortar, or pounded in a cloth bag, then submerged in a glass bottle or jar of alcohol. The resins dissolved easily in cold alcohol if the jar was agitated occasionally or placed in sunlight. When the liquid had settled, its top layers were poured off and filtered—this filtrate was the final spirit varnish.

Instead of being filtered, to achieve dissolution the spirit-resin mixture could also be warmed. This was done in a sandbath varnish pan, a sort of tin double-boiler. The sand below the bath's false bottom kept the bottle from direct contact with the fire. It was a dangerous process, and explo-

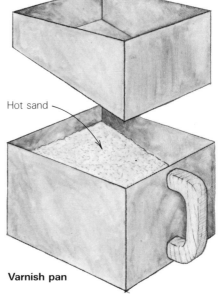

Hot sand

Varnish pan

From the second edition (1851) of *The Painter, Gilder, and Varnisher's Companion* comes this description of a varnish pan (drawing is speculative) used by finishers throughout the 18th and 19th centuries: "The best vessel for holding your varnish while using it, is a varnish pan....It is made of tin, with a false bottom; the interval between the two bottoms is filled with sand, which, being heated over the fire, keeps the varnish fluid, and makes it flow more readily from the brush....a false bottom comes sloping from one end to the other, which causes the varnish to run to one end."

sion and fire were the varnishmaker's greatest enemies. If the resins were heated too much, the varnish darkened. The lightest, most transparent varnishes were the ultimate goal.

Shellac—Restorers and furniture historians have long assumed that shellac was the main resin used in varnishes of 18th-century America. All the evidence from my research directly contradicts this assumption. For centuries shellac had been the primary source of the valuable red coloring matter called lac dye. It was rarely used in 18th-century America. It was relatively expensive, and the resultant dark varnish obscured all but the darkest woods. The reddish dye could be only partially extracted from the resin, and it was not until the late 18th century that chemical bleaches enabled the production of colorless shellac resin. Modern shellac is actually a spirit varnish consisting of shellac resin dissolved in alcohol.

Until about 1820, spirit varnishes were applied only with a brush, and were usually thinned considerably and warmed to make them flow out and dry rapidly. The method of rubbing on spirit varnishes that is called French polishing was first mentioned, as far as I know, in the 1818 London edition of *The Cabinetmaker's Guide,* where it was compared favorably with beeswax. The *Guide* gives seven formulas for spirit varnishes that may be French polished, none of which calls exclusively for shellac resin. One of them, called "The True French Polish," includes one pint of spirits of wine, a quarter-ounce of gum copal, a quarter-ounce of gum arabic, and one ounce of shellac. This influential recipe is repeated exactly in over 30 formularies dating up to the 1920s, and several museum restorers have recently begun to use a French polish based on it. The method the *Guide* describes for applying this French polish is nearly identical to that used today (see *FWW* #20, p. 66). Open-grained woods were sized with glue and lightly sanded. The polisher, a wad of coarse flannel wrapped in a fine, soft linen rag, was dampened with the polish and rubbed onto the work with a circular motion, covering about one square-foot at a time. The whole surface was rubbed until the rag appeared dry, then the process was repeated three or four times, producing, the *Guide* says, "a very beautiful and lasting polish." A final polish of half a pint of best rectified spirits of wine, two drams of shellac and two drams of gum benzoin was recommended.

Fixed-oil varnishes—With the English publication in 1776 of the "Genuine Receipt for Making the Famous Vernis Martin," British and, eventually, American workers finally possessed the recipe for the most famous Continental varnish (see box at left). For 150 years Europeans had sought to imitate the finest examples of Oriental lacquerware. Craftsmen of each country touted their "Chinese" or "Japanese" or "Turkish" varnishes, raving about the brilliant colors, high gloss and durability. Although Europeans could not get the actual resin of Oriental lacquer (which was obtained from the shrub *Rhus verniciflua*), that didn't stop them from trying every available alternative. The Martin family of Paris, eight makers of lacquer and varnish spanning two generations, produced varnishes that were said to achieve unparalleled brilliance, clarity and durability, in addition to being waterproof and crack-free. The Martins had overcome, or so it was claimed, all the disadvantages of oil, wax and spirit-varnish finishes. The Martins' ingredients and laborious procedures represented the peak of the varnishmakers' art, but they became typical of most such hard-resin, fixed-oil varnishes of the 18th century.

Fixed-oil varnishes employed a drying oil (linseed, poppyseed or walnut) in which one or more oil-soluble resins were dissolved. Suitable resins included copal, amber, rosin, dammar and anime. Copal and amber, vegetable resins of both fossil and recent origin, were the hardest resins known, and also the most difficult to dissolve. By liquefying, "running," the resins at high temperatures (300°F to 400°F), they would, on cooling, become soluble in hot oil. This process is described in the recipe for the Martin copal varnish. A second method employed tartarization or a similar process. Here, various strong alkalis (tartar salts, lye, potash or ammonia solutions) broke down the resin chemically, by alkaline hydrolysis, then it was dissolved in hot oil. A third method, involving infusions of water, alcohol or ether, extracted some of the resin constituents that were insoluble in oil.

Ironically, both heating and tartarization probably contributed significantly to the rather rapid deterioration of these hard-resin varnishes. Both the extreme heat needed to run the oil and the chemistry of tartarization accelerated destructive oxidation. The widespread use of both processes makes it unlikely that any of these hard-resin amber-copal varnishes remain on antique woodwork today.

Copal and amber varnishes were valued for four reasons. They were extremely clear and colorless when first applied. They far surpassed the spirit varnishes in hardness and durability. They could be rubbed to a very high polish. And they were waterproof—made with a large proportion of drying oil, they would hold up outdoors better than any other varnish then known. Because of the difficulty and expense of making

---

GENUINE RECEIPT
FOR MAKING THE FAMOUS
VERNIS MARTIN

After the melting pot is warmed, we pour into it four ounces of chio or cyprus turpentine; we let it dissolve till it is fluid, then pour to that eight ounces of amber finely bruised and sifted; mixing it well with the fluid turpentine, and then we set it on the fire for a quarter of an hour. After that time, we take off the pot, and gently pour into it a pound of copal bruised fine, but not to a powder; these we stir well together, and to these we add four ounces more of the chio turpentine just mentioned, and a gill [4 fl. oz.] of warm turpentine oil; set it again on the fire, blowing it rather more briskly.

When it hath stood on the fire about half an hour, we take it off, uncover the pot, and stir the whole well together, adding as we stir, two ounces of the finest and whitest colophony. We then set it again on the fire, blowing more briskly than before, and let it remain till the whole is dissolved and fluid as water. This done we take off the pot, remove it...and let it stand a few minutes....Having now twenty-four ounces of poppy, nut or linseed oil, made drying, ready at hand, we pour it into the dissolved gums, by degrees, boiling hot...and stir the whole well together with a long stick....When we have thoroughly incorporated the fluid gum and oil, we set them over the fire a few minutes till the whole boils once up, then we take it off, carry it to some distance, and pour into it a quart of turpentine made hot over the second fire. All these we stir well together, and give them one boil up, then take it off again, and again pour into it a pint more of turpentine made hot....

If the gums are thoroughly melted, and have incorporated well, the varnish is made.

This recipe, like others of the period, uses the terms gum and resin almost interchangeably. No true gums are used here, and they appear only in small quantities, as plasticizers, in other recipes. It goes almost without saying that the process as described here was extremely dangerous.

such varnishes, even the finest finishers often bought them ready-made. Copal varnish was probably the most common hard-resin, fixed-oil varnish in 18th-century America.

A number of softer resins could be dissolved in drying oils to make a second type of fixed-oil varnish, called "common brown varnish." Boiled linseed oil was the usual vehicle and solvent, and rosin in one of its various forms was the common resin. Colophony, venice turpentine, Strasburgh turpentine or plain turpentine was mixed in the drying oil at a low temperature. Various resins were then combined in the mixture, in an attempt to borrow the best quality of each. It was not durable, did not stand up to water, and had a dark color. But it was cheap, easy to get and simple to make. Despite the widespread use, it is unlikely that many original soft-resin varnish finishes remain.

Essential-oil varnishes—In the 18th century it was believed that oils or fluids derived by distilling resins were the essential volatile oils of those resins. Oil of rosemary and "spirits of turpentine" (derived by distilling conifer sap) were in this category. Today we know that the latter is a complex organic solvent with some resin impurities, and we would classify varnishes made with it as spirit varnishes. These solvents dry strictly by evaporation, not by the complex oxidation reaction of resin and drying oil or by polymerization and cross-linking of resin molecules into molecular networks.

Essential-oil varnishes were soft and not durable, and were recommended only when the varnish had to be periodically removed, as on fine paintings. Inferior furniture might have been finished with these varnishes. I have found a number of references in account books to "turpentining" a table or a wheel. Turpentining probably refers to the application of raw conifer sap as a preservative, but it may also mean a cheap varnish made with spirits of turpentine as the solvent and rosin as the resin. It is unlikely that any of these varnishes remain on surviving furniture.

Varnish polishing—The "Genuine Receipt for Making the Famous Vernis Martin" describes how to apply and polish it. The process is laborious and the explanation takes three full pages. In summary, the procedure starts with the laying on of six coats of varnish, each allowed to dry in a warm room-size chamber heated with stoves. Then the panel is rubbed smooth with a coarse wet rag dipped in pulverized, sifted pumice stone. After the surfaces have been washed, another ten or twelve coats of varnish are laid on, each coat again "stoved." The varnish was probably quite thin, which might explain the many coats required. This built-up finish is then rubbed down with the same pumice-stone process as before. A rubbing with fine emery powder follows, "till our pannel bears a surface smooth and even as glass." The emery is dried and wiped off, and the process continues with fine rottenstone. The final polish is achieved with a rubbing of "sweet oil" (olive oil), the excess oil cleared with fine powder or flour. Last, the panel is burnished to a high shine with fine flannel dipped in flour, giving it "a lustre as though the [panel] were under a glass . . ."

This process is fairly typical, although the most extended I have found. Many abrasive materials were used, including sandleathers (soft, wet leather impregnated with sand or tripoli), shave grass, soft rushes, sealskin and sharkskin.

True "English polishes" (spirit varnishes made with copal

Roubo's spirit varnish

Of all spirit-varnish recipes of the 18th century, those using sandarac (from the North African alerce tree *Tetraclinis articulata*) were the most common and the most highly regarded.

In *The Art of the Woodworker* (Paris: 1769-74), Andre Jacques Roubo offers a recipe for white (clear) varnish to be used on fine woods such as rosewood or holly, to alter their color minimally. The varnish is "composed of a pint or two pounds spirits of wine, five ounces of the palest sandarac possible, two ounces of mastic tears, one ounce of gum elemi, and one ounce oil of aspic [oil of lavender], the whole dissolved in a *bain-marie,* not allowing the alcohol to boil; when the varnish is cooled, one filters it with a width of cotton, so that it is free of any kind of dirt or filth." Roubo recommends building up a surface with up to eight thin coats.

I have reformulated several of the old recipes and found it virtually impossible to get satisfactory results when mixing up only small quantities of the ingredients. Also, making fixed-oil varnishes is dangerous. You can buy ready-made varnishes that use traditional resins from artists' supply stores. Windsor and Newton produce sandarac, elemi, mastic and copal varnishes, and possibly more. These come in small quantities, and are very expensive. —*R.D.M.*

and shellac resins) of about 1815 were rubbed to a high polish, after the varnish had dried, with a cotton cloth wrapped around a wool cloth and saturated with pumice powder and linseed oil. Hartshorn (powdered animal horn) removed the oil residue. This polish was said to give the same beauty as the finest rubbed amber and copal varnishes, even if it wasn't as hard or durable.

Until the first quarter of the 19th century and the advent of French polishing, final polishing with a rag or pad moistened only in alcohol or other spirits was never mentioned in the guidebooks. Nor have I seen any reference to backing up polishing leathers, cloths or pads with any sort of flat rubbing block (cork or wood), as is the common practice today. Perhaps the extraordinarily careful preparation and smoothing of wood grounds made this less necessary than it is today.

Despite the variety of varnish-polishing techniques and materials, writers of the period agreed on one thing: the final polished surface should be "brilliant, delightful and shining and glossy as glass." None of the formulations contains anything that could be considered a flatting agent like the metallic soaps (stearates) used today. Flat, semigloss, or rubbed-effect finishes were simply not wanted in the 18th century. They suit today's taste and they can hide manufacturing defects. But, in an age when people were surrounded by roughhewn, worn surfaces, a perfectly flat, highly lustrous surface was a mark of consummate workmanship, eagerly sought by those patrons who could afford it. □

Robert D. Mussey is head of the furniture conservation workshop at the Society for the Preservation of New England Antiquities in Boston. For more about period varnishes, consult the published Proceedings of the Furniture and Wooden Object Symposium, *which was held in 1980, available from the Canadian Conservation Institute, 1030 Innes Road, Ottawa, Ont.*

Repairing Finishes: Two Ways

1. Burn-in resins hide deep scratches

by Rick Bütz

It's frustrating to discover a deep scratch in a nicely finished piece of furniture. A scratch rarely goes unnoticed and it may be unfairly interpreted as a glaring defect in the furniture itself. With any luck—and light damage—a surface scratch may be easily rubbed out with steel wool, but usually not.

Over the years, furniture makers have developed lots of tricks for touching up damaged finishes. A favorite method for repairing deep scratches is called "burning-in." The repairer fills the scratch with melted shellac resin, matches the color and grain of the surrounding wood with stains and a small brush and, finally, touches-in the appropriate finish. Damage to oil, varnish, shellac and lacquer finishes can be burned-in; polyurethane and other plastic finishes sometimes blister.

For burn-in work, you'll need shellac sticks of various colors, a special knife, a heat source, padding lacquer and powdered blending stains. Burn-in sticks are sold in hundreds of colors, but I keep only a dozen on hand in the colors of woods I usually repair. Clear or translucent sticks are available and they can be color-matched using the blending stains. Burn-in or shellac sticks are made of various pigments and resins and have a consistency similar to the wax used for sealing letters. My burn-in knife is like a palette knife with a curved, flexible blade. A small alcohol lamp is a good heat source. Use the lamp carefully; never leave it burning unattended. Although electrically-heated knives can be used, I prefer the alcohol lamp for its more delicate heat control.

To repair a scratch heat the knife tip with the concave side toward the flame. This keeps any soot that forms from contaminating the resin. Judging the proper temperature takes practice. If the resin bubbles and smokes when it touches the knife, it's too hot. If it forms drops that quickly resolidify, it's too cool. When it's right, it's almost watery. Once you've found the correct temperature, hold the knife like a pencil and carefully flow the hot resin into the scratch. The knife can touch the wood surface, but you must keep it moving to get an even flow. Fill the scratch, clean the knife by heating it and wiping it with a rag, then level the resin by heating the knife once more and moving the convex face quickly over the surface. Keep the knife moving whenever it's hot enough to soften the resin, or you will damage the surrounding finish. Aged shellac and varnishes can be particularly sensitive to heat. If the resin from the burn-in stick bubbles up and sticks like chewing gum instead of flowing smoothly when heated, the stick is probably stale and should be replaced. The sticks have a shelf-life of six months to two years and if cracked and checked are probably stale.

When the scratch is completely filled and the surface is smooth, the final leveling is done with a piece of 600-grit wet/dry sandpaper wrapped around a small felt block. With water as a lubricant, gently remove any excess resin. Be careful not to sand through the finish surrounding your repair.

There's another method using a different burn-in stick—called a Nolift-stick—which was developed several years ago by Mohawk and Behlen. It uses a resin stick that dissolves in a solvent that won't affect the surrounding finish. During sanding the solvent is used as a lubricant and can be applied directly with a felt block. The solvent is called Brasive by Mohawk; Behlen sells it as Abrosol.

Regardless of which stick is used, once the surface of the repair is level with the finish around it, color and grain differences can be matched. The traditional method of applying color over a small area is to use a French polishing technique with padding lacquer and finely powdered blending stains. These dry stains come in many different shades and can be mixed to create an infinite range of colors. You can match the most delicate shades with surprising control. Padding lacquer is compatible with many finishes, but you should experiment with it before trying to repair a valuable piece. If the lacquer's gloss is higher than the surrounding finish, you can rub it out with fine steel wool. An alternative to commercially made padding lacquer is a traditional French polish solution of equal parts of boiled linseed oil, 5-lb. cut shellac and alcohol. Experiment with the proportions to get a quick-drying mixture.

To use the padding lacquer or French polish, make a cloth rubbing pad out of lint-free, absorbent cloth. Fold the cloth upon itself to make a ball about the size of an egg. Apply a small amount of padding lacquer to the cloth and tap the palm of your hand against it to evenly disperse the liquid. Don't saturate the cloth. Then apply the lacquer over the scratch by stroking lightly in the direction of the grain, with the pad barely touching the wood. You want to build up a thin layer of lacquer, to which the stain will adhere.

Next, select the desired color of blending stain and apply a thin layer with your index finger. Again, pad lacquer several times over the filled area and wipe a thin layer of the stain from your fingertip onto the surface. Once the stain has been applied, lightly pad lacquer over it. The powder will dissolve when it comes in contact with the liquid, and create a stained finish. Repeat this process until the desired shade has been gradually built up over the burned-in area. If the color should go too dark or doesn't match, clean away the stain with alcohol or padding lacquer solvent. Let the finish dry for a few minutes before starting over. Padding technique requires a little practice, but in time, you will be able to match the most subtle color variations. The real secret is to apply the padding lacquer with as light a padding stroke as possible. This will prevent the stain from "shifting" or washing away. It's better to apply too little stain than too much, as it is easy to darken an area but impossible to lighten it without starting over. Experimenting on scrap pieces will give you a taste of controlling color. Use as little stain as possible to achieve the desired effect.

With the wood color matched, the grain lines can be touched in. If the original wood finish shows porous grain texture, as in oiled walnut, teak or oak, it's a good idea to duplicate this texture in the repair. Use a needle or razor blade to carefully scratch the grain texture

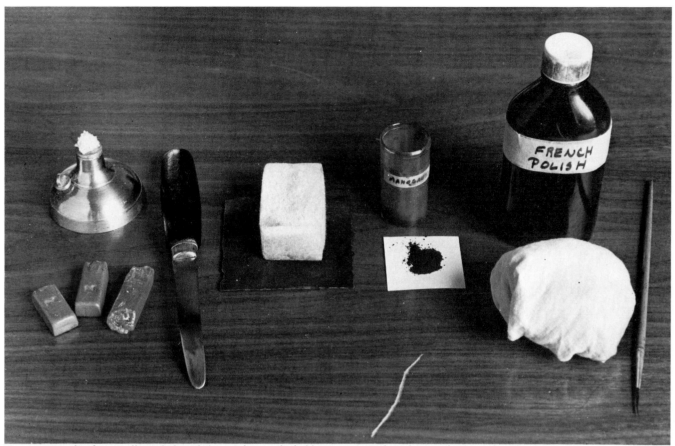

For repairing finishes you'll need (from left to right) an alcohol lamp, resin sticks, a burn-in knife, and a felt sanding block. To match colors, blending stain, French polish or padding lacquer, a cloth pad and a fine brush are used.

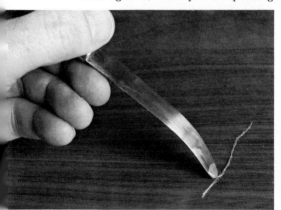  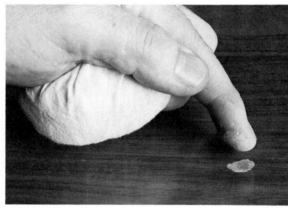

With the heated burn-in knife, concave side down, fill in the scratch by flowing hot resin into it (above, left). Be careful not to get the knife too hot. When the scratch is filled, reheat the knife and wipe it clean with a rag before leveling the built up resin (above, center). Keep the knife just hot enough to make the resin flow as you work it. After the repair has been leveled and sanded with 600-grit wet/dry sandpaper, apply padding lacquer or French polish to act as a base for the powdered blending stain (above, right). The stain evens out color differences. Use a fine sable brush to touch-in grain detail over the repair (left). Then pad over a couple of coats of padding lacquer and when that has dried overnight, gently rub out the repair with steel wool and blend it into the surrounding finish.

into the resin. Then mix a few drops of padding lacquer and dark powder stain on a small piece of glass. Carefully paint in the grain lines over the repair, using a fine sable brush. Blend these lines and carry them into the natural grain on either side of the repair. After letting the repair dry for 30 minutes, lightly pad several layers of padding lacquer over the patch to seal and protect it.

You can let the padding lacquer serve as a final finish but it's better to apply a coat of the finish used on the rest of the piece. Once dry, the entire repair can be rubbed with steel wool or pumice to match the gloss. The result will be an invisible repair permanently bonded to the wood and indetectable under the closest scrutiny. □

Rick Bütz is a professional woodcarver and he repairs furniture in Blue Mountain Lake, N.Y. Photos by Ellen Bütz. Materials for burning-in can be purchased in professional quantities from H. Behlen and Bros. Inc., or from Mohawk Finishing Products, both at Route 30N, Amsterdam, N.Y. 12010, and by mail order from Constantine's, 2050 Eastchester Rd., Bronx, N.Y. 10461, or Garrett Wade Co., 161 Avenue of the Americas, New York, N.Y. 10013.

2. Knife technique makes the difference

by John Revelle

You can fill scratches by burning-in on new furniture and in refinishing, repair or restoration work. In the first two, knife technique isn't important since the repair will be finished over. In repair and restoration work, however, a hot knife in a clumsy hand can damage as much as it can fix.

When burning-in already finished work, I like to run the resin into the scratch and smooth it completely with my knife, skipping padding lacquer and stains and all but a cursory sanding. I prefer the Nu-Glo sticks made by the Star Chemical Co. Inc. These sticks were developed for marble repair and have an indefinite shelf life. They don't crack and go stale as do other types. Mohawk sells an equivalent product called MF or marble-fill stick. There's an assortment

of colors so it's not hard to match whatever wood you happen to be working on. Since I don't use stains, I pick a stick that exactly matches the background color of the wood I'm repairing.

I've found that Star's Opal #750 knife works best for me. The tool has a ¾-in. wide flexible steel blade with a shallow bevel ground on one side of its skewed working end. It's sometimes sold as a cement finisher's knife. I use the electric knife-oven sold for the Opal knife. If you use two knives, one can be heating while you work with the other. It takes about a minute to bring a knife to the right temperature. To make a repair I heat the blade and touch the bevel side of the knife's heel (its obtuse point) to a resin stick so it melts just a small bead. I quickly push the resin-coated heel into the scratch at a point farthest away from me. Rocking the knife gently back and forth flows the resin evenly into the scratch. I repeat the process until there is just enough to fill the scratch level with the surrounding surface. Then I wipe the hot knife clean with a rag or a paper towel and reheat it. To level the patch, I drag the heated knife along the scratch, bevel-side down, in light rapid strokes, lifting the knife off the surface between strokes. Moving the knife continuously is critical. You can light a cigarette with a hot knife, so stopping it even for an instant will char the finish around the repair.

Small repairs can be done with just a bead or two of resin, larger ones take more. Take care not to mound the resin above the level of the surface around it, or the repair will be conspicuous. If you do get too much resin in the repair, hold the knife firmly, bevel down, and with short, chevron-shaped strokes work the excess resin back and down into the scratch. If air bubbles turn up, pierce them with the heel of a hot knife and rework the resin. The temperature of the knife can be varied to help control resin flow. As the knife gets cooler, the material gets harder to spread. With practice, you should be able to smooth the resin without sanding. But if you can't get a perfect surface with the knife alone, complete the smoothing with 400-grit or 600-grit wet/dry paper.

With the scratch filled and leveled, you can grain the wood with a hot knife and a resin stick that matches the color of the grain lines in the wood. Draw a hot knife's sharp edge through the darker stick to coat it from heel to toe,

To fill a scratch, apply a bead of resin to the heel of the hot knife. Then push the resin-coated heel into the scratch and rock it gently to distribute the resin.

Clean and reheat the knife and drag it bevel-side down to smooth the resin to the surrounding surface.

then press the sharp edge straight into the repair in the same direction as the grain you are simulating. Some of the darker color will transfer to the patch. Continue the process until the grain lines match the surrounding wood. You can smooth the patch by dragging it with a hot knife as before. If you're repairing an open-grained wood, skip the smoothing step and sand with 400-grit wet/dry paper using mineral spirits or sanding oil as a lubricant.

Finally, I match the repair to the sheen of the existing finish by rubbing with fine steel wool or a soft cloth and rottenstone. I usually don't put any finish over the repair since I'm never sure what the original is. Overlaying with the wrong finish will often cause more problems than it will cure. □

John Revelle is a professional furniture restorer in Rohnert Park, Calif. Photos by the author. The materials he describes can be purchased from Star Chemical Co., Inc., 360 Shore Drive, Hinsdale, Ill. 60521.

Fine-Tuning Color Finishes
Get lustrous depth with transparent top coats

by Don Newell

Most woodworkers use a clear finish such as varnish or oil, particularly when working with fine, well-figured hardwoods. Many craftsmen probably have never considered using anything other than a clear finish. But there's a time and place for everything. When the wood you're working with is lacking in figure, or you're building a piece from undistinguished pine or mixed woods, or you want the piece to stand out in an otherwise monochromatic room, a color finish may be just the ticket.

A color finish—paint—is merely a clear finish with pigment mixed in. The familiar store-bought antiquing kits work, but they come in unimaginative colors with variations limited to wiping on different shades of toning inks. For your next project, why not select a color that sings, or at least hums a little? Orange or purple might be a bit much, but a small object such as a side table done in viridian green or alizarin crimson can add a dramatic touch to a room decorated mainly with the brown and sienna tones of traditional clear-finished furniture and cabinetry. Modern latex paints—the same ones you'd use on walls and trim—are a good choice and they're available everywhere. But whether you use oil-base or latex paint (semi-gloss or satin) is really not important.

A color finish requires as much surface preparation as a clear finish. Even though the color finish is opaque, imperfections in the surface of the wood will show through when the finish dries and shrinks. A color finish, however, hides sanding scratches somewhat. Where you might final-sand the wood with 240-grit paper for clear finishing, often you can get away with 180-grit under color.

Should you fill the grain under a color finish? Not necessarily, but you can. With close-pored woods such as pine or birch, you wouldn't use a filler anyway, even in clear finishing. On open-pored woods such as oak or mahogany, however, a filler is mandatory if you want to produce a smooth surface. This is a matter of personal preference, however. Since you're using color for its aesthetic value, there's nothing wrong with having the wood structure show. In fact, wood grain often lends interesting texture.

Use a tack rag on the surface and stir the paint thoroughly. Apply a moderately heavy coat as evenly as possible using a clean brush. Brush with the grain, particularly on unfilled, open-pored wood. Let the paint dry overnight.

Now for the step that makes the difference between a fine finish and just a finish. Run your hand over the dry finish and examine the surface in a strong sidelight. You'll see and feel brush marks and specks of dirt or lint. Those, plus the graininess of the suspended particles of flatting agent used to pro-

duce a satin surface, must be removed. Using 320-grit wet-or-dry sandpaper (coarser is too coarse and finer takes too long) and plain water, wet-sand the entire surface to remove irregularities without cutting through to the wood. Wet the surface well with water and, using a light touch, sand the surface in long, overlapping strokes. Use a pad of felt or rubber behind the paper to evenly distribute finger-pressure. And always keep the work area wet. The water acts as a lubricant and keeps the paper from loading up with paint particles.

Frequently dip the square of sandpaper in the water to wash off accumulated sanding residue and keep turning it to present a fresh abrasive surface to the paint. Remember, a light touch does it. Periodically wipe the sanded area dry with paper towels or clean rags and inspect it. If the brush marks and dirt particles have disappeared, you've gone far enough.

If you do cut through to the wood, don't panic. When the surface is completely dry, clean off all sanding dust. It's difficult to repair just one spot, so recoat the entire surface, then resand. The piece should now have a uniform, matte appearance and is ready to be given the final, lustrous touch.

For both protection and beauty, apply a high-quality, durable clear film over the color coat. Since your color coat will be either latex or alkyd (enamel) paint, a clear varnish is the material to use. You could rub in tung oil without damaging the color coat, but its ultimate appearance and film thickness are not nearly as satisfactory. I've tried both gloss and satin varnishes and found that the satin polishes more uniformly. Don't use polyurethane. It will not adhere well to any substrate containing a flatting agent, which most satin or semi-gloss paints contain.

Almost any good brand of standard interior varnish will work well, especially if the information on the label indicates it can be used for furniture, trim or the like. Look for the words "alkyd" or "modified alkyd" on the label. This type provides excellent adhesion, good wear characteristics, and good rubbing or polishing properties.

Wipe down the sanded color coat with a damp cloth to eliminate all traces of sanding dust. One medium-heavy coat of varnish (just as it comes from the can) is preferable to two thin, drier coats simply because a heavier coat will flow better, leaving fewer brush marks to correct when the varnish has dried. Since this coat of varnish is the final coat, let it dry a full 30 hours rather than merely overnight. You want to give the thinners in the varnish time to evaporate so that the film is hard clear through.

To brighten the luster of the clear coating and to polish out any airborne dust or dirt that may have settled onto the surface, fine steel wool works well. But lightly wet-sanding with 400-grit or 500-grit paper is even better. Follow this by hand-rubbing the surface with rottenstone or automotive polishing compound. Finally, polish the clear coating with a sheepskin buff chucked in an electric drill. This will impart a

Don Newell, of Farmington, Mich., is a former paint and varnish chemist, an amateur furnituremaker and a frequent contributor to FWW. *He tackled general finishing in issues #16, #17 and #18.*

beautiful sheen, an appearance impossible to duplicate straight from the can. In fact, the luster will be close to that of a fine rubbed and polished clear lacquer.

Why not simply wet-sand, polish and buff the paint film itself? Two reasons: first, the paint film is much more susceptible to marking and scuffing than the tough clear coat of varnish, so it's less durable; and second, a clear coating over a color coat produces great depth and clarity.

Lacquer—While the paint-and-varnish system is the simplest to use because you can buy the materials at any paint outlet, lacquer produces equally beautiful, functional results. The basic technique—a color coat (over either filled or unfilled wood), followed by a clear protective film—is the same in either case, but the details vary.

Bare wood should be coated with lacquer sanding sealer for optimum adhesion. The sealer, color coat and final clear coat should be from a knowledgeable supplier. H. Behlen & Bros. (Rt. 30N, Amsterdam, N.Y. 12010), for example, sells brushing and spraying lacquers, both colored and clear, as well as sanding sealers, all of which are compatible.

Why not use a spray can? Simply because aerosol materials are heavily thinned to permit spraying under the very low spray-can pressure. The resulting film is extremely thin, so you have to apply many coats to build up a reasonably heavy layer. You can't rush it either: if you apply too many coats too soon, before the previous coats have had a chance to dry hard, the finish will remain soft for days. Stick with brushing lacquer if you don't have a good spray outfit.

Apply a sanding sealer and wet-sand it to a smooth, clean surface. Because lacquer shows coarse sanding scratches, all wet-sanding should be with wet-or-dry sandpaper of 360-grit or finer. Now put on several coats of color lacquer to build up a good film, lightly wet-sanding between coats to remove brush or spray marks. Then apply two coats of clear lacquer, allowing sufficient drying time in between for the thinner to evaporate. After the final coat of clear lacquer, let the finish dry for at least 72 hours before you polish it. Even though lacquer may appear hard on the surface, a substantial amount of solvent still remains in the film, and as this evaporates the film will continue to shrink.

To produce maximum sheen without gloss, rub the surface with fine-textured automobile rubbing/polishing compound, or with fine pumice or rottenstone. Then give the piece a final polishing with a dry sheepskin buff.

The result, whether you use varnish or lacquer, is superb. If you've ever seen a custom-finished car with coat after coat of semi-transparent paint hand-rubbed to a mirror gleam, you'll recognize the difference between merely finishing *with* color and clear-finishing *over* color. □

The aesthetics of clear finishes

Thinking of a finish only as a protective skin misses its aesthetic impact. The finish you apply becomes an inseparable part of the object and visually represents it. The right finish is a matter of function, appearance and historical precedent. All three must be considered if the finish is to complement the construction.

Consider a small rosewood music box inlaid with antique ivory and adorned by an heirloom cameo let into the lid. It will not be harshly handled, so the finish need not be extremely rugged. Moisture resistance in such a small piece is not a major consideration either. In fact, with this box, as with most small, cherishable objects, the meaningful consideration is aesthetic: does the finish help achieve, or amplify, the artisan's intended effect?

In this box, the maker used rosewood and ivory for their rich, nostalgic character. The finish should heighten this effect, and be one with the object. The grain and color of the rosewood should be allowed to show.

A drying oil such as boiled linseed or tung, hand-rubbed, will produce a dull surface. A gloss varnish will glare. And lacquer, rubbed and buffed, will give a high luster without shine.

Water-clear lacquer would be my choice. It can be wet-sanded between coats to eliminate brush or spray marks, and it yields not only a protective film that is completely transparent but also one that brings out color to the maximum. The final film can be rubbed and polished to a high luster.

Why not use varnish or drying oil? You could, but to me a drying oil's comparatively matte finish reduces the visual drama. A good rubbing-type varnish could probably serve as well as lacquer, but the clarity of lacquer is more jewel-like. It is compatible with the rest of the materials in the music box and their actual and subjective functions.

In contrast to the box, consider an oak desk—large, obtrusive and utilitarian. The wood, as beautiful and striking as its grain may be, was chosen to be used, and used hard. So it calls for a working finish. But the finish needn't look as though it was slapped on with a whiskbroom. Even a workhorse desk is entitled to face the world with a smooth coat. I'd use a sturdy satin varnish. Why varnish? Just as rubbed and polished lacquer expresses delicacy and refinement, so varnish projects a shirt-sleeves character. Historically, strong oak and durable varnish go together. A craftsman who makes or buys a desk of oak rather than of metal or laminate-covered particleboard is tying himself to a tradition. And for the same nostalgic reason, a mellow varnish is the logical choice. Gloss varnish would feel wrong. Its glinty, shiny surface begs attention, thereby embarrassing a working-class desk. Satin varnish, on the other hand, is comfortable on the desk and lets the wood come through, because there is no shine to interfere. The subdued luster also implies that the desk has been well used, its finish dulled by time and wear.

In another case of matching perception to function, consider a fine walnut gunstock. Historically, gunstocks have been finished with rubbed-in linseed oil, a material of countless shortcomings and only two possible virtues: it is easy to apply, and it is capable of producing a soft, pleasing luster if rubbed often and long enough. This soft sheen is generally believed to be a clue to a gun's quality, a perception that the gun is better made than one whose stock is not hand-rubbed. Ironically, for durability and moisture resistance, linseed oil is not a good finish for a gunstock. Tung oil, the popular Danish oils and certain penetrating varnishes can be made to look about the same as rubbed oil, and are far more durable. Yet even today, with these other materials available, a "genuine, hand-rubbed linseed oil finish" still sells guns.   —D.N.

Gilding With Metal Leaf
Fit for a frame or a fleur-de-lis

by Erwin O. Deimel

While there is no doubt that genuine burnished gold leaf is the ultimate in gilded finishes for frames, furniture and ornaments, there is a much less costly alternative. Schlagmetal, thinly beaten metal alloy, is the material used on most picture frame moldings and other gold-leafed articles. The result is meant to look like the burnished-gold leafing that was extensively practiced during the Renaissance, but which, due to cost, is seldom done today. Schlagmetal is much easier to handle than real gold, which is beaten so thin that it is transparent when held up to the light—you can touch schlagmetal without having it disintegrate.

As a picture framer who finishes most of his own moldings, I use a process not much different from that used by commercial molding companies, who gild thousands of feet a day. This process, however, can be adapted to small scale, using brushes instead of air guns, and not requiring such elaborations as spray booths; in short, adapted to the home workshop or retail establishment.

In the original process, water gilding, genuine gold leaf is applied to a colored ground of gilding clay mixed with animal glue. The clay has a high iron-oxide content, which gives it a barn-red color. The glue is the binder for the coating, and can be burnished to a high gloss and reactivated with moisture to hold the leaf to the clay. Because leaf is an uninterrupted sheet of reflective metal—not ground-up particles in a dulling binder—it has a luster that paint cannot match. Renaissance frames were probably left very bright, to look like solid gold. But during generations of being dusted and cleaned, the gold wore off the high places, dirt accumulated in the low spots, and the frame acquired a soft patina that pleases us more today. Contemporary gilders simulate this patina by sanding or scratching the leaf to expose the color underneath, applying imitation flyspecks (meant to be the work of generations of flies), and using a thin wash of paint instead of waiting centuries for dust to build up.

I buy unfinished molding instead of milling it myself. A splendid array of shapes and sizes, in a variety of woods (mostly bass, poplar and virola), can be bought wholesale from distributors, or one-frame's-worth at a time from frame shops. Old frames can be salvaged and refinished, too. While you can work on a frame after it has been assembled, it is easier to gild the lengths separately because you won't have to fold the leaf into tight corners. Cut the sides of the frame a little longer than necessary—you will make fresh miters after the leafing and antiquing have been completed.

Whether you are gilding a frame, a box or a piece of furniture, begin by priming the wood with orange shellac (4-lb.-cut, diluted with about five parts alcohol) to seal it and set up the fibers for sanding off with 150-grit paper. Remove the

Erwin Oskar Deimel, a retired aerospace engineer, owns Oskar's Picture Framing in New Hartford, N.Y.

fuzz, then paint on two or more coats of acrylic paint. This base coat softens the molding shape and provides tone, just as clay originally did. Commercial molding companies often use a brilliant crimson under the leaf. A muted red, like burnt sienna, looks more like the real thing. For silver leaf, a blue clay was frequently used. When I gild with aluminum leaf, to simulate old silver, I prefer a black ground.

You can get acrylic paint in tubes from an art supply store. Mix it roughly half-and-half with acrylic medium, thin enough to brush smoothly but with enough body to fill small irregularities. Acrylic paint is a polymer, but if you catch it before it cures, you can clean up with soap and water. Two coats can be applied in an hour or so, and the ground will be ready for sanding after it has dried overnight.

Sand the ground coat smooth, then apply one or two coats of undiluted 4-lb.-cut orange shellac, sanding lightly between coats. This step is important. If the surface isn't completely sealed, the adhesive that holds the leaf will dry too quickly in patches, and the leaf won't stick there.

Since we don't have animal glue in our ground, we must apply a layer of gold size (adhesive) to hold the leaf. The size is an oil-based varnish specially developed for gilding. It comes in two varieties—slow and quick. Quick size dries in about an hour or so, but I've found it too irregular for good results. I use the slow size, which reaches the proper tack in about 12 hours and is workable for 12 hours after that. Whichever you use, the object is to have as thin a coating as possible, with just enough tack to hold the leaf. If size is applied too heavily, or accumulates in low places, it will skin over but remain liquid underneath. This will turn to goo and spoil the job when you rub the leaf down. Gold-leaf size will polymerize if there is any air in the can, so when I open a new liter I immediately put it into 2-oz. medicine bottles and seal them tightly. In my shop, where I leaf 20 ft. to 30 ft. of molding a week, an ounce of size lasts a month or more.

I apply the size using a velveteen pad about 2 in. square. On frames without carving this pad gives me better control than a brush would, and when I'm finished I can just throw the pad away. Slow size comes either clear or with yellow pigment added for visibility. I use the yellow, and apply just enough to be able to see a faint yellow color over the ground. Apply size in the late afternoon. By the following morning it will be ready to gild, and it will keep its tack through most of the day—you don't have to rush. A properly prepared frame will seem to have dried too much—the size will not feel tacky, but smooth and hard, with a squeaky clean kind of feeling. A fingerprint may prevent the leaf's adhesion, so try to do your

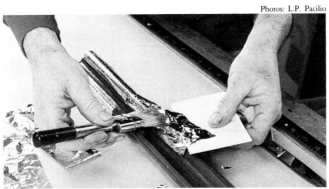

Photos: L.P. Pacilio

To apply the metal leaf, first prepare the wood surface with shellac and acrylic paint. Then apply a special oil-based varnish. When the varnish is tacky, transfer the leaf to the molding using a paintbrush. Cover the high spots first to avoid tearing the leaf, which won't stretch into the valleys.

Buffing the leaf with cotton forces it to conform to the base coat's polished surface. Excess leaf is dusted off.

testing, if you must, on some inconspicuous part of the frame.

Leaf is available in several forms: most commonly in books of 25 sheets, about 5½ in. square, separated by paper sheets, or in bulk packs of 50 sheets stacked together, 10 packs to a box, about 7 in. square. I use bulk leaf, picking it up from the box with a 1½-in. paintbrush, and laying it on a flat surface so it can be cut. With scissors, cut strips of the desired width. Slip one strip of leaf, with the help of the paintbrush, onto a piece of cardboard a little longer than the leaf, and slide it onto the sized surface of the frame. Aim for the right place. Once the leaf touches the size, you will only tear it if you try to move it. But if you have placed it a little crooked, no matter. Lay it down as it lands and overlap the next piece to fill the gap. The leaf will stick only to the size, not to itself, and the extra will be dusted away later.

Leaf doesn't stretch. On many moldings, it will stick to the high spots and tear raggedly when you try to force it into the low spots. The solution is to gild the high sections first with narrow strips of leaf, coming back to coves and valleys later.

After the entire length is covered with leaf, take two or three cotton balls and rub the surface smoothly but firmly to ensure that all the leaf contacts the size. Rub in the direction that will press the overlaps down, not tear them up. Give an extra rub parallel to each joint. If there is a holiday (bare spot) in the job, place a piece of leaf over the spot and press it into place with cotton, then rub the patch smooth. The hairline joints between leaves are called spiderwebbing and will become part of the antiquing.

If your size was too heavy or not dry enough, wrinkles in the leaf will set into the finish when you rub it down. Puddles of undried size can smear over the surface, irreparably dulling

it. In this case, it is best to let the size dry thoroughly, then sand the leaf smooth and gild again. Usually, though, the problem is poor or spotty adhesion. If the problem is extensive, sand and reprime. Small blemishes, however, can be corrected by adhering fresh leaf with shellac. Dab on a thin layer with your fingertip, feathering the edges so a ridge doesn't form. Within a few seconds, the shellac will have the correct tack for the leaf to be applied.

Unlike real gold, schlagmetal is subject to corrosion, so to prevent it from tarnishing, seal the surface with the same dilute alcohol-shellac mixture used to prime the wood. This will reduce the glare of the leaf slightly, but the molding is quite garish at this stage, looking like a chocolate candy wrapped in gold foil. It will need even more antiquing to tone it down.

To obtain a typical finish, first apply the thin sealer coat, then give the molding a coat of undiluted orange shellac to make the gold a little deeper in color, a little redder or warmer. In fact, even aluminum leaf can usually do with some warming up. Next paint the molding with an antiquing coat of acrylic paint, a mixture of burnt umber with a little black added, then wipe it off lightly with a paper towel to leave some color in the low areas and a light, streaky finish in the high spots. When this is dry, use a toothbrush and some dark paint to imitate flyspecks. Point the toothbrush at the frame, then stroke the bristles toward you. Tiny drops of paint will spatter the frame. New flyspecks are raw umber, ancient ones are black. They are put on not so much to immortalize the housefly, but to give depth to the finish. From a few feet away, they will not be noticeable. Remember what we are aiming for: years of considerate care that have nevertheless left their mark, not what looks like half-a-day's vandalism.

To age your molding, scrub off some gold. Sandpaper rubbed with the grain imitates the effect wood movement has on clay. Fine steel wool can rub the gold from the high spots to expose the ground color. You can stipple the wash coat instead of wiping it, and you can increase contrast by wiping the wash coat away from the high spots with a damp paper towel. Instead of the dark wash coat, you can try raw umber and white, which makes a warm gray. After the frame has been mitered and joined, you can touch up the joints with a little antiquing color to cover up any hairline of raw wood. Experimentation will show you a boundless variety of finishes. I once tinted the shellac with aniline dyes to yield a molding of warm brown-gold with a stripe of brilliant green—the colors of a Japanese beetle.

A final coat of clear acrylic medium will yield a remarkably durable, low-luster finish. In ten years, I have never had a job come back because the finish failed. I have scrap pieces that have been kicking around my outdoor kindling shed for years, exposed to heat, humidity and drifting snow. They still look as good as gold. □

EDITOR'S NOTE: Gilding supplies are available in small quantities from Dick Blick Co., Box 1267, Galesburg, Ill. 61401. H. Behlen Bros. sells supplies for both oil and water gilding through a network of distributors; for more information, write to them at Rt. 30 N., Amsterdam, N.Y. 12010, or phone (518) 843-1380. Other sources worth checking out are Art Essentials, Drawer 260, Monsey, N.Y. 10952, and The Durham Co., Box 1548 GMF, Boston, Mass. 02205.

For further reading, get a copy of *Gold Leaf Techniques,* by R.J. LeBlanc, revised by Arthur O. Sarti, 1980, available for $13.95 from Signs of the Times Publishing Co., 407 Gilbert Ave., Cincinnati, Ohio 45202.

Gilding: On the trail of Cennino

by Henry E. Sostman

Clocks tell time, but time also tells on clocks. The clock at right is one of two that were built in Holland in 1722, with hand-cut clockworks by Jonathan Marsh. Clockmakers in the early 18th century made only the movements, and Marsh's were put into twin cases by some unknown woodworking shop. My wife's ancestors bought this one new.

It is only recently that my wife, Theodora, and I have lived in a house whose ceiling can accommodate the clock's 9½-ft. height. We had the works restored, and the movement keeps excellent time now. All the delightful figures—the boy who pulls a fish out of the river once a minute, and the windmill that turns when the hour and half-hour strike—work again. I restored the case myself, because I wanted to have a hand in its future.

Moisture and age had reduced the crowning figures to bare wood. The angels had lost their trumpets and wings. Atlas, in the center, looked like he was losing his battle to hold up the world. A photograph of the twin clock provided a design for the missing parts and confirmed that the figures had been covered with gold. I was anxious to learn about the techniques used by the original maker, but information was scanty. Medieval painters, excellent gilders, kept their methods secret. During the Renaissance, however, one artist broke security. He was Cennino d'Andrea Cennini, and his book tells almost all we know about tempera painting and its integral component, gold. In a translation by Daniel Thompson, *The Craftsman's Handbook,* I found the source for a process that has remained virtually unchanged for at least 500 years. Although I substituted modern materials, I tried to recondition my angels in the spirit in which they had been made.

One chapter of Cennino's book takes the reader through the gilding process. In the 15th century, the first step was to choose a gold coin and deliver it to the local gold beater, who methodically pounded it between sheets of leather until it became flattened into many leaves. Cennino even tells us that the beater "ought not to get more than a hundred leaves out of a ducat."

The wood was prepared with many coats of gesso and clay, smoothed and polished with stones. Cennino used powdered chalk for gesso, and Armenian bole for clay, both mixed with a

An angel restored and gold-leafed.

binder made by boiling animal skins. Fine carving could be incised into the surface before the gold was put on, and the surface burnished to look like solid, polished gold. Cennino used a dog's tooth to burnish the gold. Today, gilders use a tooth-shaped agate.

I used plaster and gelatine for the gesso, and Hastings clay instead of Armenian bole. To adhere the leaf, I substituted slow-drying size for Cennino's boiled parchment glue. I used as much care and time to prepare the surface as Cennino said was necessary. After so much work, it seemed a foolish economy to substitute brass leaf. Brass would have to be sealed with a lacquer or shellac that would deteriorate in a few decades, while pure gold would never tarnish, and its thinness would allow it to follow every detail of the carving without hairline wrinkles. It seemed to have every advantage, so I took Cennino's advice, and for gold I used gold. □

Henry E. Sostman is vice president of the Yellow Springs Instrument Co., Inc., in Yellow Springs, Ohio. He is a registered Professional Engineer whose activities include temperature physics and Federal regulatory law. Photos by the author. Cennino's book, translated by Daniel Thompson and published by Yale University Press in 1933 as The Craftsman's Handbook, *is available from Dover Books, 180 Varick St., New York, N.Y. 10014, for $3.00.*

The stately clock with its golden crown.

Photographing Your Work

Like woodcraft, the more care you take, the better the results

by Gary Zeff

As with most art, things made of wood have to be seen in their three-dimensional form to be fully appreciated. But if you're a professional woodworker, or a generous amateur, you don't keep your best pieces around as samples. So when a prospective client or an exhibition jury wants to see your work, photographs may be all you can show. The formula is simple: the picture of your last piece clinches the commission for your next. At times, then, the quality of your photographs is as important as the quality of your woodworking. For promoting and marketing your work, your camera is possibly the most important career-making tool. And the photos you take can also serve another purpose: they're a visual chronicle of your progress.

As professions and hobbies, photography and woodworking have many parallels. In both pursuits the more care you take, the more satisfying the results. A snapshot can give you a picture of your work but not show its quality. With the right camera, some inexpensive lights and a few accessories, you can take photographs whose quality does equal your woodwork. Once you have established a studio setup, you may want to give it permanent space in your shop so that everything you make is easily recorded before it goes out the door.

Camera—To obtain sufficient quality, you need a camera that uses 35mm or larger film. Some 35mm cameras—rangefinder types—have a viewing lens separate from the taking lens, and some are single-lens reflex. The main advantage of the SLR is that you focus and compose your picture by looking through the lens that will take the picture. You see exactly what the film will see. This feature is almost mandatory when you're taking pictures of small objects. Most 35mm SLRs made today have both manual and automatic modes of operation. To take advantage of the techniques described later, you may need to use your camera in the manual mode.

Lens—Lenses are described by their widest aperture and their focal length, both of which are marked on the front of the lens barrel. A "normal" lens, one that sees objects from the same perspective your eye does, neither enlarged nor reduced, has a focal length of about 50mm, and is suitable for most needs. It has limitations when photographing small objects, details of large objects, and large objects in small surroundings. Most normal lenses, for instance, cannot focus closer than 18 in. from the object, and objects smaller than 8 in. will not fill the frame at that distance.

To photograph small objects or details, you can buy a macro lens, which can focus close to the object and fill the frame. Macro lenses are expensive. A cheaper alternative is a set of close-up lens attachments which screw onto the front of your normal lens. Used individually or in combination, these attachments will allow you to fill the frame when photographing objects as small as 2 in.

Another shortcoming of a normal lens is its tendency to distort the perspective of a subject close to the lens: near parts appear disproportionately larger than parts farther away. The alternative is to use a lens of longer-than-normal focal length, say, 105mm or larger. Such a telephoto lens can fill the frame with a small object or detail, while allowing more room between camera and object in which to maneuver lights. Long lenses, however, distort perspective in the opposite way, flattening the depth of the object. Where space is tight and your subject large, as with installations, you may need a shorter-than-normal (wide-angle) lens, for instance 35mm, to fit the whole subject in your viewfinder. Perspective distortion is the trade-off, although sometimes these distortions can be dramatically effective. For varied needs, you may appreciate the versatility of a zoom lens; 35mm-105mm would be a good choice. But a zoom lens cannot match the optical quality of fixed-focal-length lenses. With all lenses, use a lens shade to exclude stray light.

Camera support—The camera must be held steady during the exposure and while you're arranging the object and lights. An adjustable tripod with a tilting head is a must. A cable release, which allows you to trip the shutter without directly touching the camera, will further reduce the chance of movement and blurry pictures.

Lights—There are basically two types of lighting equipment: photolamps, which are large tungsten light bulbs, and electronic flash. Though cumbersome, photolamps are better because you see their effects while composing your picture. Photos lit with flash are often spoiled by unexpectedly harsh highlights and shadows.

Photolamps balanced for 3200°K color film are EDT (500 watts) and ECA (250 watts). You will need 10-in. to 12-in. reflectors for your photolamps, with sockets that are safe for 500 watts. For many setups, you will want to soften the light, either by bouncing it off some reflective surface or by diffusing it. Umbrellas for bounce-lighting are expensive, but white cardboard can do the same job. You can buy diffusers that clip onto the front of the reflector bell, or you can fashion your own from a sheet of matte acetate. Since photolamps produce light of a different color than daylight, do not allow daylight into the room when shooting color film.

The natural lighting which people are most familiar with is the combination of sunlight and skylight. The sun is the main or "key" light source, which illuminates and casts a shadow. Skylight is a "fill" source, which lightens the shadow without casting a second shadow. Indoors, we can duplicate this dual lighting effect with a main light, high and to one side of the camera, and a fill light near to and on the other side of the camera. The fill light will be of a lower intensity, diffused, reflected, and/or farther away from the object, so that it won't cast a noticeable shadow. An object with two shadows looks unnatural.

Film—Because you will be working with a tripod and lights, you can use slow- to medium-speed films, which have the advantage of being fine-grained. If your photos are for a black-and-white publication (magazine, brochure, etc.), use a medium-speed black-and-white negative film. For color pictures you can use color negative film (for prints) or color slide film balanced for 3200°K. Slides have an increased brightness range, which shows more detail, but exposures are more critical because slide film has less latitude than negative film. In addition, you'll need to carry a viewing system to show your slides. Color prints can be made from color slides, and color slides can be made from color negatives, and black-and-white prints from either, but the quality of the image suffers. Therefore, you should know what you intend to use your photos for before choosing your film.

Filters—A filter is a piece of glass or plastic which is attached to the front of the lens, to change some quality of the light reaching the film. Besides conversion filters, used to modify the color of outdoor light for indoor films, and vice versa, there are filters that can be used in black-and-white photography, but for a different reason. Objects that photograph well in color may lose their tonal separation with black-and-white films: reds, oranges and browns in the wood all may photograph as black. Colored filters can correct this problem. A filter will lighten objects that are the same color as the filter and darken objects that are the complementary (opposite) color of the filter. A general rule would be to try a yellow filter (such as a No. 8) for yellowish woods such as maple or oak, and a red filter (such as a No. 25) for reddish woods such as cherry or padauk. Try a test roll, photographing various woods using various filters, and see what looks best.

Location—The best background is the simplest, because it allows the viewer to concentrate on the work. You can shoot outside, on grass or sand or some such regularly textured background. Pick a day when the sunlight is diffused—you don't want harsh shadows. Or shoot in the open shade. The disadvantage of shooting outdoors is that you have little control: light can change in the middle of your photo session, as can the weather.

A better location is a room or section of a room with light-colored walls, a high ceiling, and no daylight. To keep your photographs free of clutter and to eliminate distracting horizon lines caused by table edges or wall corners, buy a roll of seamless background paper, which comes as wide as 12 ft. You can support the roll above and behind your object with a commercial or a homemade background stand: wire a pipe to eye-bolts in the ceiling. Don't wrinkle the paper, and don't walk on it, except wearing clean socks. Unroll enough paper to form a smooth transition between vertical and horizontal, then place your object far enough forward to keep shadows

This small turned container by Stuart Bicknell was photographed by the author using a 50mm lens with a 2x close-up lens attachment. Two 500-watt photolamps were used, the one on the right of the camera with a diffuser—hence only one shadow. The two rings included in the photo not only indicate a use for the object but also illustrate its relative size. Exposure was ⅛ sec. at f/16 using Kodak Plus-X pan film.

off the vertical area. When you're photographing a small object, it's easier to position the camera and lights if you place the object on a table draped with background paper.

For your first roll of paper, try light gray. But because light-colored woods usually photograph better on darker backgrounds, and vice versa, you may want more than one roll. Wide double-knit cloth can also be a useful background, but avoid bedsheets, which wrinkle into ugly shadows.

Composition—To compose your photo decide first which view best shows your object. Some things will require more than one shot—an overall view and a detail, for instance, or one photo of the piece closed and one open. For a group of objects, you might combine a detail with a full view in one picture. Usually, the camera is positioned above the object and tilted downward, from a little less than standing height, but experiment with different camera angles and positions. Try to fill the viewfinder with the object, without having it touch the frame. A comfortable margin makes for a more attractive—and publishable—print.

As you fine-tune the camera's position, watch for awkward contact points between parts of your object—a chair leg, for instance, that sweeps down and seems to touch the side of another leg, instead of cleanly meeting the floor. The visual rhythm among parts of an object and the spaces between them can appear odd or harmonious, depending on the angle of view.

Keep in mind all of the characteristics of the object you want to show: shape, color, texture, detail, size. The best pictures focus on the object's best characteristic—decide what it is and from where to see it. For some objects, size will be indefinite, unless you provide some familiar context or a prop for comparison. You could, for example, place aspirin next to a pill box, an orange near a bowl, or a magazine on a coffee table. Furniture such as chairs or dining tables is of common

225

enough size to require no context or prop, and may show better without one.

Camera settings—With the object and camera placed, you can focus the lens. For objects that are large from front to back and for small objects close to the lens, you need maximum depth of field. Depth of field is the area in focus, and it varies with the size of the lens aperture. For large lens apertures (low numbers like $f/2.8$), depth of field is shallow. To get maximum depth of field, shoot at small apertures ($f/11$ to $f/16$) and focus about one-third the way back from the object's forward-most point. The catch is that for a given amount of light, small apertures require slow shutter speeds. Inanimate subjects shot from a tripod pose no problem.

With the camera focused and the lights set, take an exposure reading to figure combinations of lens aperture and shutter speed. Because a camera's built-in exposure meter can be fooled by light woods on dark backgrounds and vice versa, use a neutral test card. This is a piece of gray cardboard, standard in photography, that you place where it will receive the same lighting as the object. Take the camera off the tripod and point it at the card, moving in until the card fills the frame. The meter will show the proper exposure. Be sure, however, that the meter does not read glare. Put the camera back on the tripod and look through the viewfinder, using your camera's depth-of-field preview button at the various f/stops your exposure will allow while focusing. This will show you various depths of field, and you can see when all of your object is in focus. If the image is too dark, tape pieces of newspaper on the nearest and farthest parts of your object to aid in focusing.

To ensure getting a good photo, even if your reading is wrong, bracket your exposures. Make one exposure at the combination of lens aperture and shutter speed that you determined with the meter and test card. Then take another picture at settings that allow more light to reach the film, and another that allows less light to reach the film. If your calculated exposure is $\frac{1}{15}$ sec. at $f/16$, for example, your bracketed series would be $\frac{1}{8}$ at $f/16$, $\frac{1}{15}$ at $f/16$, and $\frac{1}{30}$ at $f/16$. You can also bracket by keeping shutter speed constant and changing lens aperture. Bracketing is especially important with color slide films, which have less latitude than negative films. Keep a record of the exposures so you can analyze your prints or slides and decide what to try next.

Once you've had them processed, keep your photos and negatives organized. Attach a contact sheet to each set of negatives, so you can identify the shots without handling the negatives themselves. Store slides in trays for projection viewing or in clear plastic pocket sheets for viewing on a light table. Write your name, address and information about the piece on the cardboard slide mount. But stick a label on the back of prints, since the pressure of writing can damage the image.

In photography, as in woodworking, the more you do, the more proficient you will become. Although there may be times when you will need the services of a professional photographer, your best teacher will be the results of your own photo sessions. Once you find a setup that works well for the woods you use and the things you make, picture-taking will be the final step of your creative process. □

Gary Zeff, of San Diego, Calif., is an avid woodworker and a technical representative for Eastman Kodak Co.

Lighting Wood
How to improve your image

by Ross Lowell

With enough practice, woodworkers often become good photographers, since considerations such as line, shape, proportion, balance, and texture are important to both. As a bonus, careful scrutiny of your work through the unforgiving camera lens can help refine your designs.

You may already have some proficiency in photography but may still be plagued by lighting that is too flat or too hard, by shadows or backgrounds that distract, or by any number of difficulties that prevent your two-dimensional images from doing justice to your three-dimensional originals. Here are some basic suggestions for photographing your woodwork, with special regard to lighting against seamless background paper.

Don't light by formula: Place the key (main source) where it provides the best revelation of form, character and texture, the best definition of subject surfaces, the best separation of subject from background, and the best shadows. Look at the results critically and try various key positions. Experiment, no matter how much you like one lighting scheme. Hone your tastes by looking more carefully and analytically at photographs and paintings, and learn to trust your eye.

Each plane should have a different brightness: Cabinets, tables, boxes will be more attractive and seem to have a third dimension if the top, front and side are not equally bright. Try lighting from above and slightly behind the object, so the top surface and/or side plane is brighter than the front.

When in doubt, use soft light: Hard light (spotlights or small sources) can be dramatic, but the resulting dark shadows interfere with the recognition of shape and detail. A professional, soft light source or light bounced off white surfaces or aluminized umbrellas can provide soft, "round" highlights and shadows, ideal for wood surfaces and complex shapes.

Soft light does not have to be flat light: A light source, whether hard or soft, placed close to the lens will result in flat, characterless lighting. A soft source positioned 45° or more off the lens axis (to the side or above) will provide a soft-light look that is not flat.

Keep the lighting simple: Don't use more lights than you really need. Each new light may introduce new problems, such as more shadows. Often a large white card placed near your subject can provide enough fill to lighten dark areas without creating new shadows.

Use glare: Glare results from light that strikes a surface at the equal-but-opposite angle from the camera. A little glare helps delineate surface curvature, texture and carving relief. Too much will hide grain and figure and detract from form. To control glare, change the angle of the light or subject, use dulling spray on the object (ask your photo dealer), or attach a polarizing filter to the lens.

Use an assistant: It's difficult and time-consuming to keep moving from lights to camera to check the effects of light changes. A helper who can adjust things while you look through the lens can actually improve your photographs. If you have to work alone, position a large mirror behind the camera, to see how the subject looks from there.

Contrast should suit the end use: More contrast (less fill) may enhance slides that are meant for viewing or projection only. However, if the shots (color or black-and-white) are intended for prints or publication, less contrast is necessary because reproduction tends to increase contrast.

Judging contrast: It is difficult to anticipate contrast in the final shot because film does not "see" as great a range of light as the human eye. It helps to keep notes on what you did. Try squinting, or analyze the lighting with the lens stopped down (use the preview button). You can use a spot meter or move in close with your camera to take a reading from the lightest significant area and from the darkest significant area in your scene. Generally speaking, a difference of one or two f/stops can be judged low-contrast; more than three or four f/stops is high-contrast.

Light the background separately: Place your subject well away from the vertical part of the seamless, so that if you want the background bright, you can light it with a separate source, from the side or overhead, being careful to keep this light off the subject. This will solve a lot of common prob-lems, such as peculiar shadows that run up the curve of the seamless background paper.

You can make some useful photographic devices: Why not make a set of wooden brackets to support pipes or poles to hold one or two rolls of seamless paper high up on a wall? Or how about panels of lightweight composition board painted flat white on one side, black on the other? They should be mounted on braced 2x6 crosspieces with casters so they can be wheeled into position to provide large, soft fill light (white side) or to block reflections (black side). Ideally, they can also be dismantled quickly and stored compactly.

Lighting booms can also be made in the shop. Although most are made out of metal, a reasonably useful boom (drawing, below left) can be constructed with 1x3 lumber mounted on a substantial stand or wooden base with wheels. Such a boom could hold an umbrella light to reach out over or behind the subject, to provide soft top or back light.

Useful stuff to keep handy: Plenty of wooden clothespins, spring clamps, various kinds of tape, small wedges, malleable wax, aluminum foil, large white cards, dulling spray, small mirrors or reflectors, non-flammable frost gel, spare stands on which to attach white cards or reflectors, black cards to shade the lens from direct light that can cause flare.

Outdoors, keep background simple: Maximum depth of field isn't always beneficial. You want your object in focus, but in outdoor scenes it distracts from the subject to see every leaf on every tree in the background. To keep your background focus soft, use a telephoto lens, and/or open the lens diaphragm fairly wide, and/or put considerable distance between subject and background. The preview button will help you judge the degree of sharpness of the various planes.

Sculpture may need special treatment: Lighting and composing sculpture, free-form wooden objects or musical instruments with curved surfaces and openings offer creative challenges. It's difficult to choose the most representative angle, but a well-placed shadow or reflection of the piece will reveal another facet of the same object. Sculpture often looks more appropriate outdoors than furniture does.

Safety: Photography has its potential dangers. The small, tungsten-halogen bulbs used in up-to-date, efficient light fixtures get extremely hot, almost instantly. Always unplug the lights before inserting bulbs. Handle the fixtures only by their plastic knobs or with gloves. Considerable heat can be concentrated on the subject at close distances—enough to ruin finishes, scorch wood, conceivably start a fire. If you can hold your hand on the object, the lights are not too hot. Do not place lights extremely close to people; prolonged exposure to the small amounts of the ultra-violet light these lamps emit can cause eye damage.

All of the usual considerations and cautions should be exercised in relation to electricity. Lights that are extended too high on unstable stands or that are improperly mounted can damage your subject—be it animated or wooden. □

A shopmade lighting boom

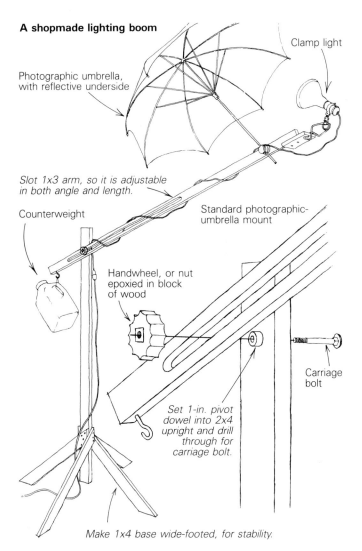

Photographic umbrella, with reflective underside

Clamp light

Slot 1x3 arm, so it is adjustable in both angle and length.

Counterweight

Standard photographic-umbrella mount

Handwheel, or nut epoxied in block of wood

Carriage bolt

Set 1-in. pivot dowel into 2x4 upright and drill through for carriage bolt.

Make 1x4 base wide-footed, for stability.

Ross Lowell is a director, cameraman, and inventor and manufacturer of on-location lighting systems, for which he has won an Academy Award. A catalog of products is available from Lowel-Light, 475 Tenth Ave., New York, N.Y. 10018. Lowell is also an amateur woodworker.

Watching a professional shoot a chair

The usual way to work with professional photographers is to tell them what's wanted, then leave them alone. It takes them forever to set up. Then they fiddle inscrutably and interminably with their lights, their camera and the position of their subject. Or so it seems, when you don't know all they're up to.

To take some of the mystery out of the photographer's craft, we decided instead to watch closely, and to ask the photographer to explain what he was doing while he was doing it. We hired New York freelancer Doug Long to shoot a strikingly well-poised armchair that was being shown last spring at Workbench Gallery, in an exhibit by Rochester Institute of Technology students and alumni. The chair, in Honduras mahogany upholstered with burgundy velvet, was made by second-year furniture student Robert Harper, and was priced at $2,200. So that we could show what a difference Long's techniques would make, we first spent an hour flubbing a few shots ourselves. Those results appear below.

When Long arrived, the first thing he did was look, for several minutes, at the chair. We'd already gotten it onto white seamless background paper, which he appreciated. Then he began digging into his on-location kit, which consisted only of a camera bag and a cavernous duffel.

He pulled out a venerable 35mm Nikon F camera, which he placed on a tripod, about 15 ft. from the chair. He loaded with slow film, Kodak Panatomic-X at ASA 25, because of its finer grain and inherent high contrast. This, he said, would help distinguish the relatively consistent hues of the wood and fabric. A subject with more contrast—say, light and dark woods in the same piece—would be best shot with the faster Plus-X (ASA 125), which can better handle tonal extremes with its wider contrast range.

Long didn't fuss with the position of the chair yet. He just planted it a few feet out from the cove of the seamless, and turned it for a three-quarter frontal view from the camera. This view, he said, could be depended upon for a classic, informative, aesthetically pleasing picture. For the next hour, Long methodically unpacked and set up his lights—four 500-watt photolamps (each bulb packed in a heavy woolen sock) with bell reflectors and standard adjustable stands. The duffel bag also produced some wrinkled aluminum foil, tracing paper, construction paper, gaffer's tape and numerous spring clamps.

He set the first two lights behind the chair on either side, one 4 ft. high and the other 5 ft., but pointed at the background. Their purpose was to light the

seamless paper, so the chair would stand out from it. To keep light off the chair, and thus avoid producing shadows, he taped a sheet of black construction paper, shaped like a hood, onto each reflector. By modeling the mouth of the hood, he could adjust the gradation of light against the background.

Long then began to light the chair itself. He put a light on either side, but a few feet in front, the left one about 3 ft. high and the right about 6 ft. The principal concern here, Long said, was to light all four corners of the piece, for a balance of light overall. Next he taped a piece of tracing paper to the front of each reflector to diffuse the light and soften the shadows. The paper was taped only at the top, so it hung free of the reflector, allowing strong, undiffused light to flood the scene's foreground.

Long looked and wanted one more thing: a highlight. So he borrowed one of our lights and set it up off to the left side, with a long snout of foil aimed at the top rail of the chair. Placing this light off to the side, he said, would throw the hard shadow out of the scene.

At last, Long went to the camera. He attached an 85mm lens, to give a flatter field, a truer perspective than a 50mm lens would yield. To fill the frame with the chair using a 50mm lens, he explained, would have necessitated bring-

A  B  C  D

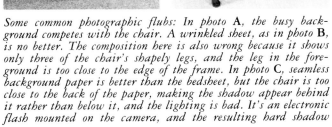

*Some common photographic flubs: In photo **A**, the busy background competes with the chair. A wrinkled sheet, as in photo **B**, is no better. The composition here is also wrong because it shows only three of the chair's shapely legs, and the leg in the foreground is too close to the edge of the frame. In photo **C**, seamless background paper is better than the bedsheet, but the chair is too close to the back of the paper, making the shadow appear behind it rather than below it, and the lighting is bad. It's an electronic flash mounted on the camera, and the resulting hard shadow makes another shape haunting the chair's. Single-flash lighting also causes the harsh glare, the flattened third dimension, and the shallow focal plane. In photo **D**, the chair has been pulled forward a bit and the lighting is softer, but the crisscrossing shadow comes from two equally strong, equivalently positioned lights, instead of a more natural main/fill arrangement. The light meter was used wrong too—held too far from the chair, it measured the light background and indicated an exposure that would yield medium gray there, leaving the chair underexposed.*

ing the camera in too close, distorting the chair and making it look gawky.

"Now the composition," said Long, as he began about a half hour of fine-tuning. "Since I'm shooting only one view, I'm not going to shoot straight on from the front, side or back," he told us, "so I know it's somewhere in between." As he shifted the camera—not the chair, for that would have changed the lighting—he reported what he was seeing: "I know I don't want too high an angle, because I want to show space under both arms. But I don't want it too low, because I get too much negative space." The ideal spot, he decided, was a little lower than eye level, from a shallow three-quarter frontal view.

With the composition thus subtly adjusted, Long then zeroed in on the chair's edges, looking for glare that would melt into the white of the background. "You want some glare," he said, "but you have to make sure the edges separate from the background. And that means making an inch-by-inch survey of the chair . . . it's the only way I know to anticipate what will be obvious on the print in the darkroom." When he spotted a troublesome reflection, he'd identify the offending light and slightly shift it, or the chair, or the camera.

Long put the finishing touches on the lighting with a large piece of white paper taped to the lower half of the front left stand, to boost the light on the front of the chair. It filled in, without casting shadows or introducing new glares. In his studio Long keeps free-standing white partitions that he can park all around an object, to provide soft, even light.

The scene was now fairly incongruous. Within a tight rectangle, the chair glowed perfectly. Everywhere else was a craziness of stands, wires, paper, foil and tape. Almost 2½ hours into the shoot, it was time to take an exposure reading. Long used an incident-light meter, not the reflected-light meter that 35mm cameras contain—because reflected-light meters get thrown off by very light or dark backgrounds. He held his meter near the seat of the chair and read f/22 at 1 second. Finally, Long took a picture. Then he bracketed this exposure, varying the shutter speed from 2 seconds to ½ second, while keeping the aperture stopped down for maximum depth of field. He took two frames at each setting—this was his insurance against the possibility of a scratched or water-marked negative.

The actual snappings of the shutter took only a few minutes. The hours of preparation had been like the making and setting up of a jig. The shoot went like a clean cut.

—*Rick Mastelli, Deborah Fillion*

A professional's touch: Photographer Doug Long's shot was f/22 for 1 second, using an 85mm lens and Panatomic-X film. Chair of Honduras mahogany was made by Robert Harper. Long's setup (below) included two lights for the background (with black construction-paper hoods), two lights for the chair (one high, one low, with tracing paper diffusers), and one for highlighting the top rail (with aluminum foil snout). Most of his accessories are not sophisticated, but cobbled up from whatever's handy.

INDEX